Struggle for the
Round Tops

*Law's Alabama Brigade at the Battle of
Gettysburg, July 2–3, 1863*

By

Morris M. Penny and J. Gary Laine

BURD STREET PRESS

Maps drawn by Larry Erickson.

This Burd Street Press publication
was printed by
Beidel Printing House, Inc.
63 West Burd Street
Shippensburg, PA 17257-0152 USA

In respect for the scholarship contained herein, the acid-free paper used in
this book meets the guidelines for permanence and durability of the Committee
on Production Guidelines for Book Longevity of the Council on Library Resources.

For a complete list of available publications
please write
Burd Street Press
Division of White Mane Publishing Company, Inc.
P.O. Box 152
Shippensburg, PA 17257-0152 USA

Library of Congress Cataloging-in-Publication Data

Penny, Morris, 1942-
    Struggle for the Round Tops : Law's Alabama Brigade at the Battle
of Gettysburg, July 2-3, 1863 / by Morris M. Penny and J. Gary
Laine.
        p.   cm.
    Includes bibliographical references and index.
    ISBN 1-57249-063-2 (alk. paper)
    1. Gettysburg (Pa.), Battle of, 1863. 2. Confederate States of
America. Army. Law's Alabama Brigade. 3. Alabama--History--Civil
War, 1861-1865--Regimental histories. 4. United States--History-
-Civil War, 1861-1865--Regimental histories. 5. Law, Evander
McIver, 1836-1920. I. Laine, J. Gary. II. Title.
E475.53.P473   1999
973.7'349--dc21   99-18426
                                                                      CIP

Dedication

This book is dedicated to the memory of the officers and men of Law's Alabama Brigade.

Alabama Monument—Warfield Ridge, Confederate Avenue

A tribute to the valiant effort by the soldiers of Alabama, located just east of where Law formed his line of battle July 2, 1863

Contents

Illustrations

Maps

For clarity, only the Confederate and Federal Units essential to the understanding of the tactical situation with Law's Brigade are shown on the maps.

Acknowledgements

Many individuals contributed to the preparation of this history. Dozens of others, in libraries, archives and historical and genealogical societies listed in the bibliography whose names we do not know and who are not mentioned, also assisted in the successful completion of this endeavor.

Above all, special acknowledgement is given to Lynda Lasswell Crist and Mary Seaton Dix, editors of the Papers of Jefferson Davis. They furnished valuable research citations, read parts of the manuscript and offered criticisms regarding it. Most of all, they offered wise counsel and friendship. Equal thanks go to Mr. William Hubbard and his staff at the Houston Cole Library, Jacksonville State University, Jacksonville, Alabama, particularly to Debbie Thompson for her tireless hours spent searching for rare material and to Patsy Frost for her encouragement and assistance. The staff the Alabama Department of Archives and History, Montgomery, Alabama are due special thanks for their efforts to locate material and to render valuable assistance in identifying material to search. Peggy Fox of the Confederate Research Center, Hill College, Hillsboro, Texas made it possible to fill in several details that add to a better understanding of the events. Special thanks go to the library staff at the Gettysburg National Military Park, Gettysburg, Pennsylvania and to Richard J. Sommers and his staff, the U.S. Army Military History Institute, Carlisle Barracks, Pennsylvania for making their files available.

Geographer Lawrence W. Erickson, Huntsville, Alabama, researched and prepared the maps, most of which are to scale. He converted several very rough drafts into excellent maps.

Several historians volunteered valuable advice, and we are grateful for their assistance. John Michael Priest, Boonsboro, Maryland made critical suggestions on our manuscript. Sandy Martin contributed valuable suggestions and shared information on the movements of the 47th Alabama. Charles Thorton shared his extensive research of the 47th and located the photograph of the regiment's colonel in the state archives. Equal thanks is extended to Paul Nowlen for his contribution to understanding the lives of James Jackson and William Henry Keller.

Acknowledgements

This study could not have been accomplished without the extensive assistance of the scholars and students of history that follow: the late Sarah Jackson and Michael P. Musick of the National Archives; the late Harold B. Simpson, Confederate Research Center; Robert E. L. Krick, Richmond National Battlefield Park, Richmond, Virginia; W. Stanley Hoole Special Collections Library, University of Alabama; Richard A. Shrader and John White, Southern Historical Collection, University of North Carolina, Chapel Hill, North Carolina; the late Alice Rains Trulock, Indianapolis, Indiana; William E. Simpson, Wallace State Community College, Hanceville, Alabama; Jan Earnest, Anniston Public Library, Anniston, Alabama; Jane Yates and Major Rick Mill, The Citadel, Charleston, South Carolina; Ellen Nemhauser, Emory University; Annewhite T. Fuller and Ranée Pruitt, Huntsville-Madison County Public Library, Huntsville, Alabama.

Grateful acknowledgement is also given to the following individuals for their varied contributions of time and source material: Gordon T. Carter, Montgomery, Alabama; Jack Thompson, Overlook Publishing, Albertville, Alabama; Larry Joe Smith, Jacksonville State University, Jacksonville, Alabama; Judge Bobby Junkins, Gadsden, Alabama; Ann Marie F. Price, and H. W. Cole, Virginia Historical Society; Paul Nowlen, Jenkinsville, South Carolina; and Charles Thorton, Montgomery, Alabama.

We must also mention the valuable contributions of the staffs at the Anniston Public Library, Anniston, Alabama; Department of Archives and History, Ralph B. Draughn Library, Auburn University, Auburn, Alabama; Birmingham Public Library, Birmingham, Alabama; John Hay Library, Brown University; William C. Clements Library, University of Michigan; Rutgers University Library; Bowdoin College Library; New Hampshire Historical Society; Michigan State Archives; Houston Public Library, Houston, Texas; and the Library of Congress, Manuscripts Division, Washington, D.C.

Appreciation is also due to the photograph archivists and photo collectors who helped so much with this volume: Michael J. Winey, the U.S. Army Military History Institute, Carlisle Barracks, Pennsylvania; Gregg D. Gibbs, Austin, Texas; the staff of the Gettysburg National Military Park Library; the Alabama Department of Archives and History; and the Maine State Archives.

Introduction

Today the only disturbance to peace and tranquillity on the battlefield at Gettysburg are visitors who roam the grounds, read markers dotting the terrain, or survey the scenery and wonder about the battle that raged there the first three days of July 1863. During the fighting of July 2 Alabamians, Georgians and Texans grappled with Federal opponents for possession of the boulders and rocks around Devil's Den and the prize of Little Round Top. The soldiers of Law's Alabama Brigade came onto the field believing themselves part of an invincible army. Morale was high and travel en route to Pennsylvania was notably marked by a carefree and joyous attitude. But then four grueling hours before the "Den" and the Round Tops and the heart-wrenching retreat from Gettysburg brought an abrupt end to the sense of euphoria. By the time they were back in Virginia most of the Alabamians knew that Vicksburg had also fallen into Federal hands and deep in his heart each knew the Confederacy's days were numbered.

In July 1863 Brigadier General Evander McIver Law was one of Robert E. Lee's most promising young generals and in command of a brigade in the storied division led by John Bell Hood. He was slightly built and wore a goatee to cover his youthful countenance. His men proudly referred to themselves as Law's Brigade, a testimonial to his charisma and leadership on the battlefield.

Law was an ambitious young man and actively sought higher command. At the Battle of Gettysburg he had already set his sights on acquiring a major general's commission. When Hood was wounded very early in the fighting of July 2, Law, as senior brigadier, was suddenly thrust into the role he sought, commander of a division in battle. However, fate did not smile favorably on the young general and historians have been less than kind in their assessment of his handling of the brigades. Unfortunately, neither Law nor Hood prepared a report of their part in the Battle of Gettysburg, though Hood wrote a lengthy letter in 1873 which sheds some light on his actions. Law noted there was no report on Gettysburg because he received individual reports from the brigade commanders just prior to his command's detachment to Georgia and the Battle of Chickamauga. After that battle he admitted the report was simply not written.[1] In his postwar writings

Law did little to tell us where he was that afternoon and what he did during this very crucial part of the battle. It would be useful to read his account of the discussions regarding a move around the Federal left at Gettysburg, for example. From the reports written by the division's brigade commanders it is fairly easy to conclude Law might not have had a grasp of the situation and exercised little control because there is little mention of direct contact with him. However, on piecing together information gleamed from available eyewitness accounts a picture emerges that shows him organizing charges and sending messages via his couriers. Unfortunately Law appears to have committed his units piecemeal, spent most of his time around Devil's Den and left the conduct of the critical fight on Little Round Top to officers untried at command in battle. The results were predictable. July 3 proved a different story. Through skillful handling of his battered regiments Law easily defeated Hugh Judson Kilpatrick's attempt to disrupt the Confederate operations on Lee's right.

In the postwar era much eyewitness material was written about the Battle of Gettysburg. Most notable of the accounts about the fighting for Little Round Top are by Joshua Lawrence Chamberlain, colonel of the 20th Maine, and William Calvin Oates, colonel of the 15th Alabama. Early accounts by Chamberlain and Oates appear to be fairly reliable, but in their later years the former combatants became entangled in a dispute over a proposal by Oates to place a monument on Little Round Top to honor the memory of Alabamians who fought and died there. As they aged their recollections of the fighting changed. However, Chamberlain and Oates are good eyewitness sources.

William C. Jordan also compiled a history which provides valuable eyewitness accounts of the part taken by the 15th Alabama. Robert Thompson Coles compiled a history of the 4th Alabama at the turn of the century which proved useful in developing the movements of the regiments. Though not as comprehensive, writings by Theophilus F. Botsford and Henry C. Lindsay of the 47th Alabama offer interesting insights into movements at the company level.

William Flake Perry of the 44th Alabama and Elijah Walker of the 4th Maine offer the best eyewitness accounts of the fighting for the east side of Devil's Den. Perry possessed the unique ability to remember minute details of the events and surroundings. His account corresponds closely to those written by opposing Federals. For accounts of the action on the South Cavalry Battlefield we have relied heavily on articles by Henry C. Parsons, Stephen A. Clark and John W. Bennett of the 1st Vermont. Confederate accounts by Law, John Logan Black, 1st South Carolina Cavalry and several members of the 1st Texas give critical insights into the Southern defense of Lee's right flank.

These accounts are augmented by letters and diaries of members from Hood's Division which portray the battle as seen through the eyes of the private. Contemporary newspapers provide additional material, by most notably casualty reports from members of the brigade in the form of letters to hometown editors. Postwar publications, such as the *National Tribune*, the Philadelphia *Weekly Press*, various Alabama newspapers, the *Confederate Veteran*, the papers of the

Southern Historical Society and regimental histories furnish a rich collection of eyewitness accounts of brigade experiences. For any volume on the war between the Union and the Confederacy, the *War of the Rebellion: A Compilation of the Official Records of the Union and Confederate Armies*, generally known as the *Official Records*, is an indispensable source. This book relies heavily on these records. In addition to muster rolls in the National Archives, many Alabama regiments had historical muster rolls compiled during the last winter of the war by a representative of the state of Alabama. William Henry Fowler took blank rolls to Law's Brigade, headquartered at the McKenzie farm near Richmond to record for posterity the names of all Alabamians who served in the brigade. Fowler gave us the most contemporary total of killed, wounded and deserters.

Units of both armies are designated by contemporary terminology. Northern corps were known by roman numerals but Confederate corps of the Army of Northern Virginia were usually designated by the words first, second and third. Federal divisions and brigades were numbered (thus, First Brigade, First Division, IX Corps). Confederate divisions and brigades were normally named for their official commander, as in Law's Brigade, Hood's Division, First Corps. As the war wore on and the Confederacy lost more and more of its capable officers, many brigades were under command of someone other than the commander for whom it was named. In such cases, brigade is not capitalized. An example of this is Bowles's brigade or Law's Brigade, Colonel Bowles commanding. If a brigade or battery is referred to by an unofficial name, neither brigade nor battery is capitalized. The correct capitalization is Smith's battery when referring to the 4th Battery, New York Light Artillery, under the command of Captain James E. Smith, or Vincent's brigade when referring to the Third Brigade, First Division, III Corps commanded by Colonel Strong Vincent, or Reilly's battery when referring to the Rowan (North Carolina) Artillery commanded by Captain James Reilly.[2]

Chapter One introduces General Law and the five Alabama regiments that comprise his brigade. The remaining chapters describes the Alabamians' march into Pennsylvania, their participation in the fight for Devil's Den and the Round Tops the afternoon of July 2 and finally the skirmish with cavalry on July 3. The account of July 3 concentrates on Law and his handling of Hood's Division when Judson Kilpatrick demonstrated against the Confederate right with two brigades of cavalry.

Abbreviations

A	Acting
AA	Absent arrest
ACS	Assistant Commissary
ADAH	Alabama Department of Archives and History
ADC	Aide-de-Camp
Adj	Adjutant
A&IG	Adjutant and Inspector General
AK	Arkansas
AL	Alabama
ANV	Army of Northern Virginia
APJSU	The Correspondence of John M. Anderson, Private, CSA, Jacksonville State University
AQM	Assistant Quartermaster
Ass't	Assistant
Brig. Gen., BG	Brigadier General
B&L	*Battles and Leaders of the Civil War*
Bn	Born
BP	*Bachelder Papers*
Brgd	Brigade
BS	Brigade Staff
BSF	Bulger, Surname File, Alabama Department of Archives and History
BUL	Brown University Library
C	Captured
CAH	Center for American History, University of Texas, Austin, Texas
Capt	Captain
Cav	Cavalry
CGSO	Compiled Service Records, Confederate Generals and Staff Officers, and Nonregimental Enlisted Men, National Archives

CMH	*Confederate Military History*
Co	Company
Col	Colonel
Com	Commissary
CSR	Compiled Service Records
CT	Connecticut
CV	*Confederate Veteran*
DC	Dartmouth College; District of Columbia
DCSU	Letters of James B. Daniel, Samford University
DU	Duke University
EG	England
EU	Emory University
FC	Figures Collection, Huntsville Madison County Public Library
FS	Field and Staff
GA	Georgia
GNMP	Gettysburg National Military Park
HC	Confederate Research Center, Hillsboro College
HMCPL	Huntsville-Madison County, Alabama Public Library
HM	Historical Memoranda
HMR	Historical Muster Rolls
HQ	Headquarters
IN	Indiana
Inf	Infantry
JSU	Jacksonville State University
KIA	Killed in Action
KY	Kentucky
LC	Library of Congress
LCRAI	Letters Received by the Confederate Adjutant and Inspector General
Lt	Lieutenant
LTCAIG	Letters/ Telegrams sent by the Confederate Adjutant and Inspector General
Lt Col	Lieutenant Colonel
M	Microfilm
MA	Massachusetts
Maj	Major
MC	Massachusetts Commandery
MD	Maryland
ME	Maine
MI	Michigan
MOLLUS	Military Order of the Loyal Legion of the United States
ML	John V. McKee Letters
MN	Minnesota
MS	Mississippi

MSA	Maine State Archives
MW	Mortally wounded
MWC	Mortally wounded and captured
n	Number
NA	National Archives
NC	North Carolina
NDP	N. Dawson Papers, Southern Historical Collection
NHHS	New Hampshire Historical Society
NJ	New Jersey
NY	New York
OC	Oates Correspondence, Gettysburg National Military Park
OR	*Official Records*
Ord	Ordnance
QM	Quartermaster
P	Present in battle and unhurt
PA	Pennsylvania
PACS	Provisional Army of the Confederate States
Pt	Part
RBC	Robert Brake Collection
RC	Regimental Command
REC	Record of Event Cards
Regt	Regiment
RG	Record Group
RPSHC	Robbins Papers, Southern Historical Collection
RS	Regimental Staff
RU	Rutgers University
S	Status
SC	South Carolina
Sec	Second
Sgt	Sergeant
SHC	Southern Historical Collection
SHSP	*Southern Historical Society Papers*
SU	Samford University
TLW	Thomas Lewis Ware Papers, Southern Historical Collection
TN	Tennessee
TX	Texas
US	United States
USAMHI	U.S. Army Military History Institute, Carlisle Barracks, Pennsylvania
v, Vol	Volume
VA	Virginia
VT	Vermont
WCL	William L. Clements Library, University of Michigan

WFPP	William F. Perry Papers, War Department Collection of Confederate Records, General and Staff Officers, Box 227, National Archives
WC	Wounded and captured
Wd	Wounded
WV	West Virginia

Chapter 1

Prelude to Battle

The Battle of Chancellorsville is generally recognized as Robert E. Lee's greatest victory. But the triumph was bittersweet. Lee lost "Stonewall" Jackson to a mortal wound. After Jackson's death the Army of Northern Virginia underwent a major reorganization. Lieutenant General James Longstreet retained the First Corps. Richard S. Ewell ascended to command of the Second Corps. Lieutenant General A. P. Hill took command of the new Third Corps. The cavalry remained under command of Major General James Ewell Brown ("Jeb") Stuart. Longstreet's First Corps consisted of three divisions under Hood, George E. Pickett, and Lafayette McLaws. Hood's Division was four brigades strong. Two were from Georgia, and commanded by Brigadier Generals Henry Lewis Benning and George Thomas "Tige" Anderson. Hood's old brigade, consisting of the 3rd Arkansas, 1st, 4th and 5th Texas, was under the able leadership of Jerome Bonaparte "Aunt Pollie" Robertson. The fourth was Law's Alabama brigade of five regiments commanded by McIver Law.[1]

Evander McIver Law

Educated at the prestigious Citadel Academy, McIver[2] Law chose military education as his profession.[3] After a stint as instructor at Yorkville, South Carolina, he started his own military school at Tuskegee, Alabama.[4] When war became imminent he turned his energies to recruiting and training young volunteers. At its organization the 4th Alabama Infantry elected him its first lieutenant colonel. Law's baptism of fire came at First Manassas where he received his first wound.[5] His charismatic leadership and handling of the regiment solidified his popularity within the regiment. At the first opportunity, the men demonstrated their confidence by unanimously electing the South Carolinian to the post of colonel.[6] More important, Law's leadership abilities and coolness under fire were clearly visible to his superiors.

Law was an ambitious young man. He wanted higher command and as quickly as possible. During the winter and spring of 1862, he developed close personal relationships with Brigadier Generals Louis T. Wigfall and Hood. Wigfall was a politician turned general and, for a time, commanded the Texas Brigade. In February 1862 he resigned his commission to take a seat in the senate. Wigfall became Law's political ally. Hood succeeded the politician as commander of the Texans. The good relationship between Hood and Law is not surprising because they shared similar traits. Both were fearless in battle, and their basic battlefield philosophy was to charge the enemy. Each quickly gained the confidence of their men. In 1862 few within the army enjoyed the prestige that Hood had acquired. He became Law's champion within the military. As a result of lobbying by supporters President Jefferson Davis endorsed Law's promotion.[7]

While yet a colonel, Law assumed command of Chase Whiting's brigade, an opportunity he made the most of.[8] Davis had already pressed Lee to promote the promising young colonel, and Law more than vindicated Davis's con-

Brig. Gen. E. McIver Law, Commanding Brigade

MC MOLLUS USAMHI

fidence with superb handling of the brigade during the summer and fall of 1862. The Battle of Gaines's Mill, June 27, 1862, may have been his finest hour when he and Hood pierced the Federal center and then succeeded in breaking a cavalry charge.[9] Second Manassas added to his laurels and his handling of the brigade at the Battle of Antietam on September 17, 1862 cemented his reputation as an excellent brigade commander.[10]

In the meantime Law's supporters continued their efforts to secure him a brigadier's commission. From Tuskegee, Alabama, Congressmen David Clopton and Edmund S. Dargan sent endorsements to President Davis.[11] Thomas H. Watts, attorney general in Davis's cabinet, followed up with a recommendation to Secretary of War George W. Randolph.[12] Hood offered his support in a letter to the secretary, stating in part:

I have the honor to recommend for promotion Col. E. M. Law of the 4th Ala. I have served with him since Nov. last and have had the best of opportunities to judge of his qualifications as an officer, both in the camp and on the battlefield. And I take great pleasure in stating I know of no other officer more worthy of promotion than Col. Law.[13]

About September 1, officers of Law's brigade petitioned Randolph to promote their commander.[14] A follow-up petition, also to Randolph, arrived at the

War Department on September 20. The officers stated he "has led us victoriously through all engagements up to the 20th of September."[15] Efforts on his behalf finally bore fruit in the fall. Congress confirmed Law as a brigadier general, his commission dated from October 3, 1862.[16] In November of that year Law commanded a brigade of two Alabama regiments, 4th and 44th, and three from North Carolina.[17]

On January 19, 1863, Lee, in Special Order 19, ordered the North Carolina regiments transferred from Law's Brigade.[18] These were replaced by the 15th, 47th, and 48th Alabama regiments from Jackson's Second Corps, creating Law's Alabama Brigade. They remained together until the surrender at Appomattox Court House, Virginia on April 9, 1865.

4th Alabama Infantry

Organized at that stage of the war when patriotic young men rushed to volunteer and seek glory on the field of battle, many of the early 4th Alabama recruits listed their occupation as "soldier." Actually most came from plantations and large farms. Its officers were prominent men from the community, lawyers and leading business men. Geographically, four of the companies came from the rich bottom lands of the Tennessee Valley, one was from the southern coastal plain and the remainder were from the fertile "black belt" region of central Alabama.[19] The early volunteers thought the war would offer an opportunity for quick glory and would be over in a few weeks. First Manassas dispelled that illusion. The Alabamians fought alone much of the late morning of July 21, 1861. In the end they fell back before the foe, but not before beating off four charges against their position. Governor Frank B. Moore praised their gallantry in the halls of the state legislature. In its formative stage the regiment was fortunate to have commanders who understood and appreciated the volunteer and molded the regiment into a superb fighting unit.[20] "It was the only regiment I ever saw," wrote William Calvin Oates, "that would fight about as well without officers as with them."[21] The 4th Alabama idolized its colonel. When called upon by "the little gamecock," the men delivered bloody charges at Gaines's Mill, Second Manassas and Antietam.[22]

15th Alabama Infantry

One hundred and twenty-one young men, in the care of the combative Captain Oates, left Abbeville, Alabama, on July 27, 1861. Each had their captain's assurance the company would be home for the fall harvesting. The group sported new homemade gray uniforms with red trim. Their orders were to join nine other companies at Fort Mitchell, Alabama, to organize the 15th Alabama Regiment. Composed of men from the southeast coastal plain of the state, most were young farmers and sons of farmers. Arriving in Virginia too late to fight in the First Battle of Manassas, the regiment did not experience combat in 1861 and subsequently spent a miserable winter in the Old Dominion. In the spring of 1862 the 15th was part of Brigadier General Isaac R. Trimble's Seventh Brigade, Major

General Richard S. Ewell's Division, and proudly counted themselves part of Stonewall Jackson's "foot cavalry." Their first taste of fighting came in Stonewall's Shenandoah Valley exploits. The regiment then followed Jackson to Richmond and the Seven Days' Battle before the Confederate capital. By August of 1862 they were veteran campaigners and in northern Virginia fighting John Pope at Cedar Mountain and Second Manassas. From there the regiment followed Lee into Maryland for the investment of Harpers Ferry and the bloody conflict at Antietam.

In the spring of 1863 Law faced a dilemma with the staff of the 15th Alabama. Its colonel secured a brigadier's commission and departed. The lieutenant colonel resigned. The major was in Alabama, having reported sick the previous four months. Though he was not the senior captain present when the 15th transferred to Law's Brigade, Oates commanded the regiment. A warm friendship developed between he and Law. Oates impressed the brigade commander with his handling of the regiment and the discipline he had instilled in an already good fighting unit. Like Law and Hood, Oates was fearless under fire and was never one to ask his men to go where he would not. In the meantime Major Alexander A. Lowther repeatedly submitted applications for leave extensions. Lowther's absence denied Law a field officer to lead the regiment, a situation he found unacceptable. The solution lay in removing the major. Using a new regulation concerning absent officers, Law unilaterally dropped Lowther from the rolls. Isaac Ball Feagin was next senior in rank, but elected to defer in favor of Oates.[23] Applications for Oates as colonel and Feagin as lieutenant colonel of the 15th Alabama went forward. Unfortunately, the Confederate Congress failed to consider the commissions and though duly appointed, neither were confirmed. While the paperwork languished in Congress, Oates and Feagin received the honor and respect due their respective offices.

Born into a poor family in that part of Pike County from which Bullock was created, William C. Oates came from Welch, French and Irish ancestry. Denied the opportunity to receive the early benefits of formal education, he labored on the family farm until the age of 17. From an early age the youngster easily exhibited the combative side of his character and a nasty altercation led to the need for Oates to leave the state. Oates spent the next two or three years leading a roving life in the southwest, and at various times in his travels

**Col. William C. Oates,
15th Alabama**

Reproduced from William C. Oates, *The War*

worked as a carpenter and house painter. On returning to Alabama he taught school in Henry County and attended nearby Lawrenceville Academy. After reading law in Eufaula, Oates was admitted to the bar and, just before the war, he opened a practice in Abbeville. At the same time he served as editor and publisher of a local newspaper that espoused strong Democratic views.[24] In the spring of 1863 Oates became the junior colonel in the brigade, and was thrust into command of the largest regiment in the division. However, he was ready for the challenge of leading men in action. To meet that challenge he would draw heavily on his combative nature and trust his ability to command a large body of men under fire.

44th Alabama Infantry

Southerners volunteered in great numbers in 1861, but volunteerism slowed after the initial period of excitement. As the twelve-month enlistments expired in the spring of 1862, the Confederacy faced the prospect that much of its armies would go home. To hold it together the Confederate Congress in April 1862 passed the first conscript act in American history. A short waiting period was granted to allow men to volunteer and avoid the stigma attached to conscription. Each recruit was exempt from conscript status and given a bounty. The 44th, 47th and 48th Alabama regiments were organized during this grace period, all in May 1862.

The 44th Alabama came into existence at Selma, Alabama. Farmers from the "black belt," upper coastal plain and the Piedmont plateau regions filled its ranks. The men received minimum instruction in military tactics before leaving for the seat of war. It did not receive arms until after the Seven Days' Battle around Richmond. The regiment was subsequently assigned to Brigadier General Ambrose "Rans" Wright's Second Brigade, Major General Richard H. Anderson's Division of Longstreet's command. It was under fire the first time at Second Manassas, but suffered little loss. Their real baptism into the reality of battle came at the "Bloody Lane," during the fighting at Antietam. Though it fought only a short time before falling back, casualties were almost 47 percent and two field officers lay dead on the field.[25] There was no longer any question about its fighting ability. Sometime prior to the start of the Pennsylvania campaign, William Flake Perry, colonel of the 44th Alabama, appointed George Walton Cary, a dapper young teacher and natural leader of men, major of the regiment.

47th and 48th Alabama—the Twin Regiments

The 47th and 48th Alabama joined the Confederate service at rail stops roughly seven miles apart on the Montgomery and West Point Railroad. They became known as the twin regiments, having been organized the same day in May 1862. The former came into existence at Loachapoka, Alabama, and the latter at Auburn. Both were always in the same brigade and fought side by side. The history of one, it was said, became the history of the other. Upon arriving in Virginia they were placed in Brigadier General William B. Taliaferro's Third

Brigade, Brigadier General Charles S. Winder's Division. Both regiments lost heavily at Cedar Mountain, Virginia. Though driven unceremoniously from the field, both reformed and rejoined the fight. A few days later, the twin regiments fought at Second Manassas, exhibiting the discipline usually shown only by seasoned veterans. Following Lee into Maryland, they were at the investment of Harpers Ferry. Rigors of the Maryland Campaign seriously thinned ranks of the Alabamians. On September 17, 1862 they fought the Iron Brigade near the Hagerstown Pike at the Battle of Antietam. At roll call the following morning, the 47th mustered 15 men under a sergeant.[26]

The Brigade Leadership—Prior to Gettysburg

The only question about the fighting ability of Law's Brigade was the quality of the field leadership. This question deserves examination. A full contingent of field officers was present in the 4th Alabama. All were seasoned veterans of the previous two years' fighting. Veteran campaigners Colonel Perry and Lieutenant Colonel John Archibald Jones, of the 44th Alabama, were both solid officers. Much could be expected of the 4th and 44th Alabama in the coming campaign. Two field officers, each with commissions of less than two months, were present in the 15th Alabama. However, with the combative Oates in command, the 15th Alabama would fight as long and hard as any regiment in Hood's Division. All three field officers were present in the 47th Alabama. Two officers with limited experience at field command led the 48th Alabama.

Law had reason to be somewhat concerned with the situation at the 47th Alabama headquarters. Though always present when the regiment entered a fight, Colonel James Washington Jackson suffered from serious health problems. He had never been a well man and illness continually plagued his military career. This had caused frequent absences from the regiment. But, the 47th Alabama had, under his leadership, matured into a good fighting unit. Michael Jefferson Bulger, lieutenant colonel of the regiment, was untested in field command. He had been in only one engagement and only recently returned from extended convalescent leave. Though he had little formal training in military tactics, Bulger led by example and exhibited considerable courage under fire. If Jackson and Bulger remained in the top field positions during the forthcoming campaign Law could expect to see the 47th charging into the fray.

The 48th Alabama was the real unknown. The mountaineers from northeast Alabama had more than proved their mettle at Second Manassas and Antietam. But Colonel James Lawrence Sheffield had led the regiment in only one battle, Cedar Mountain, and only briefly then. Consequently he had yet to prove himself a disciplinarian and able field commander. William McTyiere Hardwick, acting lieutenant colonel, pending confirmation by Congress, was untried at field command. The office of major was vacant, which Sheffield temporarily filled by elevating Lieutenant Columbus B. St. John of Company F to acting major.

In spite of apparent weaknesses in the command structure, Law's Brigade, in the spring of 1863, was a solid fighting unit. At age twenty-six, Law was one of

Lee's youngest brigadiers. He was also recognized as one of Lee's most promising young generals, and if all went well in the campaigns of 1863 Law could reasonably expect to earn his major general's commission.

Lee Decides to Take the Army North

The dwindling size of his army and the need for provisions concerned Lee. A shortage of manpower made it difficult to replace losses and supplies were increasingly hard to obtain.[27] Lee's instincts told him there was little to gain by remaining on the defensive. He believed the Confederacy's best chance to survive was to draw Major General Joseph Hooker's army from its secure positions around Fredericksburg and strike it a decisive blow.[28] Lee reasoned a decisive victory on northern soil would reinforce a growing peace movement in the North, and perhaps obtain foreign recognition of the Confederacy.

On June 3 Longstreet put Hood's and Pickett's divisions in motion for Culpeper County, arriving there June 5. McLaws's Division marched from Chancellorsville. As the First Corps divisions converged on Culpeper, Hooker crossed the Rappahannock River with a small force. Hood led his division to Ellis Ford (today's Barnetts' Ford) on June 6 to check Hooker. But the Federal commander quietly withdrew before shots were fired.[29] Except for that brief excursion, Law's Brigade remained in camps around Culpeper from June 5–15.

Lee's Plan for the March North

While the Confederate hierarchy considered its options, the army grapevine was active. About the first of June rumors throughout the camps had it that the army was about to move north. Coincidentally there was much correspondence and discussion between Lee and the seat of government on that very subject. They decided to do just that.

Lee's plan called for the First and Second Corps to concentrate around Culpeper before departing. The Third Corps would remain in position near Chancellorsville to watch Hooker's army in its defenses around Fredericksburg. Ewell's Second Corps drew the assignment to initiate the move toward northern soil. The plan called for him to march through the Shenandoah Valley, drive off or capture Federal forces located there, and then continue into Pennsylvania to gather supplies. The First Corps would march near the eastern base of the Blue Ridge Mountains to threaten the rear of Hooker's army and occupy strategic gaps. Lee ordered Stuart to keep the cavalry between Hooker's army and the First Corps.[30] Simultaneous with Longstreet's movement, the army's trains and the Third Corps were to travel north on the western side of the Blue Ridge.

Chapter 2

Route to Gettysburg

Marching to Pennsylvania

About 5 a.m. on June 15 Longstreet's corps took up the line of march for the Shenandoah Valley.[1] The column marched an hour and rested ten minutes. There was an hour's rest at noon.[2] Law's Brigade made an extended march the first day, crossing the Hazel River about 3 p.m., and then on to Woodville and Sperryville. Thornton's River was forded at 5 p.m. Camp was in the vicinity of Washington, Virginia.[3] June 16 found the line of march along the road to Salem. The brigade crossed the Rappahannock at Rock Ford and moved on to Piedmont before going into bivouac June 16 near Markham Station on the Manassas Gap Railroad. As they passed the station, twenty-four-year-old-Paul Turner Vaughan, Company C, 4th Alabama, paused before the familiar structure. His mind drifted back in time to a day 23 months earlier. The 4th had been little more than raw recruits when they boarded the cars en route to the Battle of First Manassas.[4]

Early on the morning of June 17, Hood marched to Upperville, turned onto the road to Paris, and crossed the Blue Ridge Mountains through Ashby's Gap. As the sun rose higher in the morning sky, the air became oppressively hot, and passage through the gap was made worse by narrow winding roads.[5] Stragglers appeared and men began falling out from heat exhaustion. But Law pressed on and led his men through Paris about 11 a.m., and about 2 p.m. the brigade forded the Shenandoah River at Berry's Ferry. To keep the column moving, the men were ordered into the river as they arrived at the water's edge. Private John M. Anderson of Company K, 48th Alabama, in a letter to his wife, dated July 13, 1863, wrote, "We crossed the creeks and rivers as we come to them, just like horses, without stripping anything a-tall we waded in. Our clothes had to dry on our bodies when they did a-tall."[6]

Despite the extreme heat, there were those who objected. One of these was William Youngblood, a private from Company I, 15th Alabama. On seeing Hood observing the division splash into the water, he boldly sought permission to remove his clothes. Hood denied the request. Although the day had turned quite

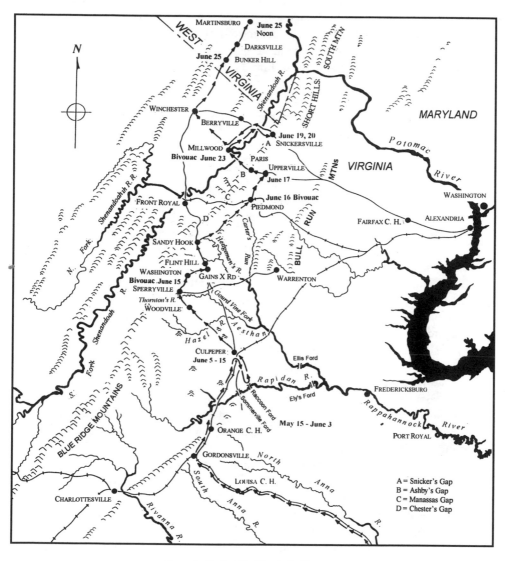

Law's Brigade Travels North
May–June 1863

warm Youngblood recalled the Shenandoah's "water was biting cold." About half way across he decided to climb upon a rock and seek the warmth it surely provided. Unfortunately his time in the sun was all too short. An officer soon rode by and ordered the private back in line.[7]

From Berry's Ferry the column moved downriver to Castleman's Ferry. Most of the journey occurred in a rainstorm, one of several over the next couple of days. Law bivouacked the night of June 17 on the west side of the Shenandoah River.[8]

Longstreet's column resumed its march June 18 and halted for a midday rest. While the men rested, scouts brought reports to First Corps headquarters that a Federal force was approaching Snicker's Gap in force. Hood received orders to recross the river and occupy the gap about 12 miles downstream. Rations were half cooked when Law left with his own and Anderson's Brigade and a small body of cavalry. The South Carolinian set a fast pace over narrow, winding, and often hilly, roads. The afternoon had turned intensely hot and the physical exertion caused men to fall out by the score. Fortunately a heavy afternoon thunderstorm cooled the air and brought welcomed relief to the struggling column.

The command bivouacked in a cold drizzle that fell most of the night. A camp rumor had it that a captured dispatch indicated the Federal cavalry rode under orders to seize and hold Snicker's Gap at all hazards. But, at the moment the elements were more of a problem than the supposed Federal threat. Due to a lack of rails, there were few fires and the cold drizzle chilled to the bone. Under the circumstances men settled in and sought whatever comfort they could. Dampness still hung in the air when Law put his command in motion shortly after daybreak. Fortunately the morning remained cloudy giving needed respite from the sweltering heat of the previous afternoon.

Both brigades recrossed the river in the early afternoon, moved up the mountain and deployed across the gap with the remainder of the division.[9] Just before darkness settled another late afternoon thunderstorm drenched the column. To protect against a surprise advance the men slept with their weapons at the ready. But the only thing that descended on Snicker's Gap that night was a mixture of dense fog and heavy mist. Weary soldiers slept in damp blankets and clothing. Next morning the line of battle literally lay in the clouds, although there was sunshine at the foot of the mountain.[10]

The Federal threat failed to materialize, and in the afternoon the brigade retraced its steps to the Shenandoah and waded the river for the third time. Heavy rains from the past few days had caused the river to rise, producing a strong current. Waist deep water and poor footing presented some peril to the men during the crossing. To catch anyone swept downstream, a line of cavalry formed a safety net below the ford. Law divided his command into several columns. All splashed into the Shenandoah at the same time. Privates attached cartridge boxes to their bayonets to keep the ammunition dry. Others yelled encouragement to companions encountering difficulty. Horseman loudly cursed their fidgety mounts. Some found the soldiers' plight amusing, and laughter intermingled with cursing and encouragement.[11]

Adjutant Robert Thompson Coles of the 4th Alabama followed his regiment on a small mare and thought he might get across in a relatively dry condition. Several men even handed him their valuables for safe transport. But just before reaching the west bank the little mare stepped into a hole. Only her head remained above water and much to his dismay, thoroughly soaked Coles. He and the mare left the water to the hoots and laughter of those near enough to see the incident.[12]

Because Law's Brigade did not complete the crossing until late in the afternoon, it bivouacked the night of

**Adj. Robert T. Coles,
4th Alabama**

ADAH

June 20 a short distance from the river. It spent most of the next two days marching and countermarching along the river's west bank. Law and his men made camp the night of June 22 a mile beyond Millwood, only ten miles on a straight line from the camp site of June 20.[13]

June 23 began on a pleasant note. Rain from the previous day had cleared out and wagons were already on the road. Most men were up early, expecting to resume the march. At midmorning the column had not departed. Then orders came down to wash and rest.[14]

Law's Brigade lay in a quiet little valley on the estate of a wealthy gentleman. Coles observed that the owner maintained a large reserve for a herd of English fallow deer. However, there is no report that any deer found themselves in Confederate kettles.[15] William Youngblood took advantage of the rest to approach Longstreet and request assignment as a courier. Interestingly enough, the corps commander granted the request. The enterprising private departed on a leave of absence to obtain a mount. He rejoined Longstreet at Chambersburg.[16]

The Confederates sought relief from boredom by indulging in a variety

**Pvt. Mitchell B. Houghton, Co. H,
15th Alabama**

Two Boys

of games. When the column stopped for rest or bivouac gamblers sat up for roulette, chuck-a-luck and faro spreads. Private Mitchell B. Houghton, Company H, 15th Alabama, recalled "crowds surrounded the layout, eagerly reaching over the shoulders of the nearest person to lay a bet on their color or number of card."[17]

The camp rumor mill remained active. One story going around was that Hooker had left Fredericksburg with the Federal army and was moving in great haste for Washington to guard that city. Henry Stokes Figures, adjutant of the 48th Alabama, got his information directly from the brigade surgeon. The Army of Northern Virginia would definitely be moving into Maryland and Pennsylvania. Lee intended to subsist his army in greener pastures, at least during the summer months.

Once again camp rumor proved to be correct. That night instructions came down from division headquarters to march on June 24. They were going into Maryland. The orders forbid taking of private property. Furthermore, each man would keep his place in line. At daylight the brigade resumed its march.[18] The destination of the Army of Northern Virginia was Pennsylvania.

By 7:00 a.m. the Alabamians were in Berryville. After a steady march they bivouacked that night two miles beyond the hamlet of Midway beneath a beautiful starlit sky.[19] Ewell's Second Corps had been leading the army, but A. P. Hill's Third Corps overtook Longstreet at the Shenandoah River. Daylight of the 25th found the brigade marching toward Bunker Hill and passing through Martinsburg about noon. Law went into camp near the Potomac, not far from Falling Waters.[20] They had covered twenty-one miles that day, much of it over rocky roads. Though the men were very tired, orders came down to cook a day's rations of beef. To make matters worse a light rain brought on an unwelcome chill to the night.

Later, a heavy rainstorm moved in and thoroughly drenched the camps. In the morning wet and weary men marched over a very sloppy road to the Potomac.[21] This time there was no need to worry about soaked clothing. Because neither bridge nor ferry was available, a Texan quipped "we had to resort to the rather primitive method of wading, so we all got a bath."[22] The Potomac, like the Shenandoah, was more than waist deep. Not only was the water chilly, but the bottom was rough and rocky. Because of the depth of the water, extra precaution was necessary to maintain proper balance and remain upright.[23]

Private Houghton served in a provost guard detail and witnessed the crossing that he described as the "grandest military display I ever witnessed." Headquarters escorts, riding horses that were in good trim, trotted by in columns of fours. Then battery after battery went by, followed by the "gray hosts of infantry." Men marched in close order and exhibited an air of conscious power and superiority. According to Houghton: "I had seen many bodies of fine soldiers, but this army of invasion impressed me at the time as being the most superb fighting machine the world ever saw."[24] William C. Jordan, Company B, 15th Alabama attributed this to a "hardening process" from previous campaigns, recalling, the men were "well disciplined, in good spirits and in the main well officered."[25]

A short distance from Williamsport the rain subsided and eventually stopped. Hood then halted to let the men rest and dry out a bit. Someone discovered a large store of liquor and Longstreet directed the confiscated prize be served to the weary troops.[26] Private Henry H. Sturgis, Company G, 44th Alabama, recalled "boys help yourself was the order of the day." Hood's men received their portions by passing before barrels from which the tops had been removed.[27] Each soldier dipped his own serving with whatever was available. Some portions were larger than others and when quickly consumed, caused more than one Confederate to become quite intoxicated. Some most likely gulped their allotment down and went out in search of more. Colonel Robert M. Powell, 5th Texas, described the delicious liquid as better "than Virginia apple jack."[28]

Major General Lafayette McLaws was sitting on his horse near a large brick building when an aide rode up and pointed out a group of young people on an upper balcony waving a United States flag. Fearing the worst, given the current state of his soldiers, McLaws directed the aide request the flag be removed, lest the men take on the task themselves. The lady of the house "turned very pale, and clasping her hands, assured the Confederate visitor the flag was being displayed without her knowledge."[29] Fortunately for all involved, the flag disappeared before any harm came to the residence.

Wet clothes were hung by roaring campfires while Hood's men warmed their insides with Longstreet's "medicine." Sergeant William C. Ward, Company G, 4th Alabama, considered his share too precious a delicacy to down in one setting and filled his canteen with the whiskey. His resolve was to make it last as long as possible and if necessary use the whiskey for future medicinal purposes. An hour later the column stopped to rest and most of the men, including Ward, lay down on the wet ground to rest. When he rose to resume marching Ward sadly found the canteen's contents had been spilled. He later remembered that all the good things that came his way never compensated for the loss of that portion of whiskey.[30]

Many years later Corporal Joseph B. Polley of the Texas brigade recalled the "road's width that afternoon was more of a problem than its length."[31] Most of the regimental commanders from the Texas brigade were tolerant of the situation. The lone exception was Colonel Van Manning of the 3rd Arkansas. He posted sentries at a cold stream. Their instructions were simple. Heave anyone into the chilly water that was unsteady on his feet.[32] A private in the 15th Georgia reported the boys had a jolly time and several became quite drunk.[33] Private Sturgis was less diplomatic, remembering that men were scattered from the Potomac to the night's bivouac, and many were "lying along the roadside dead drunk." The night was well along before most of the more intoxicated "came staggering in."[34]

Thirty miles to the southeast Private Elijah Woodward, Company K, 15th Alabama, fell into Federal hands. Since enlisting June 15, 1861, the twenty-eight-year-old soldier was frequently sick and absent, and saw little active service during the previous year. On the march toward Pennsylvania, Woodward had trouble keeping up with the regiment and as the column approached Pennsylvania became an outright straggler. His last known presence in the regiment was June 21. He eventually made his way to Frederick, Maryland, and surrendered to Federal authorities on June 26. After being sent north Woodward made it known he was willing to take the oath to the United States. His captors did not consider the Alabamian's proposal credible. He did not secure his release until May 10, 1865.[35]

Fear of the rebels spread quickly. Local citizens expected the worst from the Southern invaders. Correspondents traveling with the Army of the Potomac did much to contribute to the growing fear. A note appearing in the June 25 issue of Philadelphia *Daily Evening Bulletin* reported a typical rumor that read:

> *The rebels are seizing all horses and cattle they can lay their hands upon and sending them to the rear. Orders have been issued by the rebel commanders to spare the property of Marylanders, but when they arrive in Pennsylvania they shall have unbridled license to plunder and devastate.*

Law's Brigade crossed the border into Pennsylvania the evening of June 26.[36] The Alabamians boasted they breakfasted in Virginia, dined and wined in Maryland, and ate supper in Pennsylvania. Coles jokingly recalled they "marched in four states that day, the fourth in a state of intoxication."[37] Law and his men spent the night a short distance south of Greencastle.[38]

While the brigade rested, Lee issued orders that prohibited disturbing personal property and burning rails, even for the purpose of cooking.[39] More than one soldier ignored the order and left camp in search of fresh meat, butter, eggs, and chickens.

Most of Jerome Robertson's Texans seemed to consider the private acquisition of supplies "an imperative duty." According to one veteran writing in 1901, "It was incumbent upon us to retaliate for the marauding of the Yankees while they were in our country." Consequently, considerable time was spent in "testing the qualities of Pennsylvania poultry, which proved to be very palatable."[40]

Soldiers of Law's Brigade confiscated anything they considered edible and each night burned fence rails in their campfires. They had, according to Lieutenant Reuben Kidd of Company A, 4th Alabama, "killed, captured or destroyed everything that came in our way."[41] Men of the 47th Alabama foraged

**1st Lt. Reuben V. Kidd,
Co. A, 4th Alabama**

ADAH

among the local farms, boldly going to houses and demanding what they wanted. Few residents resisted. They were terribly afraid of the rebel hordes and gave with the fervent hope the unwelcomed visitors would go away.[42] Willful acts of thievery disturbed the youthful Henry Figures. He sadly recalled the Federal occupation of Huntsville, Alabama in 1862 and the letters from his mother describing the behavior of the occupying force. Figures wrote home that he did not kill the local farm animals, but, indicated there was much to eat. He assured his mother that he purchased everything he ate. His mess enjoyed short mutton, light bread, butter, and fresh apples, milk and plenty of vegetables.[43] Colonel Powell, 5th Texas, described the "delirious fumes of coffee and frying bacon" as an example of the good things in this land of plenty.[44]

A large spring near camp became the brigade's source of fresh water. The night of June 26 a private from Company K, 48th Alabama, went to the spring, carrying a large kettle. After dipping the vessel in the pool, he attempted to lift it, but a weakened condition caused by a meager diet in Virginia and the weight of the kettle caused him to lose his balance. He staggered about the spring's perimeter while trying to lift the kettle to his shoulder. In the process his lost the hat from his head. That loss was a serious matter and the Alabamian searched unsuccessfully for it. But the hat's resting place was somewhere in the spring. Because dirt, oil, and perspiration from long service on the road had saturated the hat, it had quickly disappeared beneath the surface of the water. Sometime later Sergeant John ("Jack") Stewart, Company G, 4th Alabama, appeared out of the darkness with his kettle. He quickly dipped it in the pool and returned to camp. Stewart then cut up a ration of beef, threw it in the pot and set it over a low fire to cook. When the mess rose early the next morning the broth that had simmered all night was dingy. Traces of oil floated on the surface and surrounded chunks of beef. Someone stirred the dirty looking liquid and discovered the cause was a very soiled hat. The thought of going without rations thoroughly disgusted his messmates and each hurled loud expressions of displeasure at the unlucky cook.[45]

Law's Brigade entered Greencastle the morning of June 27. The march through town became a festive occasion.[46] Sheffield ordered the regiment's drum and fifers to the front and the 48th Alabama's musicians played their rendition of "Bonnie Blue Flag." Sergeant Ward passed by an open window and saw in the shadows a young woman singing along. Many years later Ward remembered she sang with much gusto and kept time with music by a swaying motion of her hips. Local citizens lined the streets for a look at the Confederate visitors. Somewhere on the line of march a well-dressed man leaned over a picket fence for a better view. He and two lady companions were completely absorbed in watching the ragged gray line when a tall, rangy Alabamian drifted toward the trio. His head was hatless, leaving bare a shock of thick hair. The Alabamian carefully timed his gait so that when he drew abreast the Greencastle citizen he was just at arm's length. In the blink of an eye he cleanly picked the man's hat from his head and disappeared into the marching column. A bewildered man, less one hat, and two very amused women were soon left behind.[47]

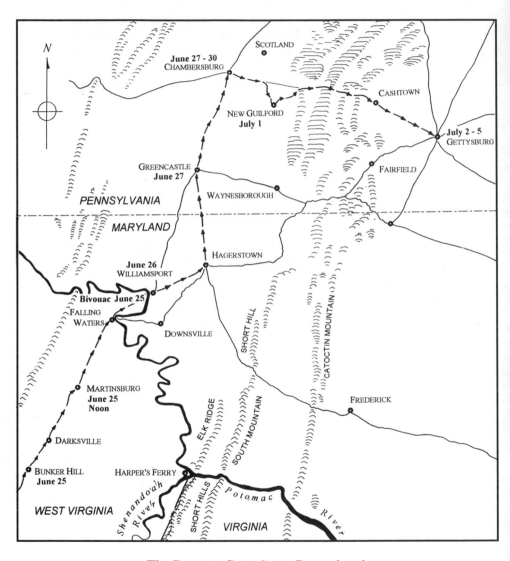

The Route to Gettysburg, Pennsylvania
June–July 1863

A Texas veteran remembered "the inhabitants crowded themselves upon the side walks with as much apparent curiosity as if we had been orangutans or baboons." Like the Alabamians, the boys from Texas presented a sight that was anything but military in appearance. According to one Texas veteran, "We were clad in garments very much damaged by hard usage." When some remark was heard about their personal appearance, a Texas private snapped back, "We don't put on our best clothes when we go out to kill hogs."[48]

As John W. Young, a private in Company I, 4th Alabama, passed through the village he also remembered the Federal occupation of Huntsville, Alabama, the year before. His folks had endured pillage and humiliation. Unlike Henry Figures he decided to pursue his version of retribution. He walked up to an elderly gentleman standing in a doorway, removed the man's beautiful felt hat and placed it on his head. It was not much in the way of revenge, but Young apparently gained some satisfaction and quickly continued on his way.[49]

The brigade left Greencastle by the northeast pike, and a short distance outside town passed a beautiful house that stood on a hill overlooking the turnpike. Several well-dressed women stood in the front yard, defiantly waving Federal flags at the passing Confederates. A rather buxom young lady made herself somewhat more conspicuous than her friends. She vigorously waved a Union flag while shouting taunts at the passing troops. Not to be outdone, a Texan left the line of march, ambled up to the trio and in his best Texas drawl, addressed the young lady: "Madam, you are doing a dangerous thing waving that flag at Confederate soldiers." "How sir?" came the tart reply. The Texan blandly retorted, "We rebels never see that flag flying over breastworks without charging them." The young lady was speechless, and her companions enjoyed a good laugh at her expense. Satisfied that he had scored another victory for the cause, the Texan shouldered his Springfield and went on his way.[50] Law's Brigade reached Chambersburg in the evening, and bivouacked two miles beyond town.[51]

Two days of rest followed while foragers made a sizable dent in the local supply of apple butter and light bread.[52] In camp some of the men engaged in card games. Others passed away the time in idle conversation or explored the surrounding countryside. Still others wrote letters home.

A slave named Ned accompanied a soldier from the 4th Alabama. Someone came up with the idea to send Ned out to mingle with the locals. Maybe some unsuspecting farmer might take pity on him, a humble servant, and decide to do something for him. So Ned, loaded down with empty canteens, trudged off in search of pity. He returned with every canteen filled with milk.[53]

Two privates from the 15th Alabama slipped away in the late afternoon and approached a farmhouse. The only desirable forage turned out to be a few beehives. They were reluctant to visit the hives in daylight and found a suitable hiding place until dark. A fierce dog guarded the prize. Somehow they made friends with the animal and returned to camp with two hives filled with honey. A rather distraught farmer appeared the next morning, complaining about the theft.

Someone inquired why the animal had not done its duty. Because, "the scoundrels stole the dog too," came the retort. All enjoyed a good laugh.[54] The lone exception was probably the farmer who was short a watch dog and two hives of honey.

Private Henry B. Love, Company F, 4th Alabama, noticed a number of fine looking large barns that were not unlike the one his grandfather once owned in Madison County, Alabama. His grandfather had the misfortune of living near the place where an ambush of Federal troops took place the previous year. Because the Federals thought the ambush had been carried out by bushwhackers, the incident led to punitive action against the local populace. The house and surrounding buildings were burned. As he sat in camp Love thought about the events in Madison County and decided the time had come for justice on Yankee soil. After selecting a barn, he could not deliberately set fire to the structure. After some thought about the matter, he realized he would have to be very angry to carry out his intentions. With the aim of provoking the owner into an action that would warrant retaliation, Love proceeded to shower the poor fellow with stories of Yankee atrocities. He carefully recounted the callous burning of his grandfather's property, the insulting behavior of Federal soldiers and emphasized the wanton destruction of private property. The only problem was that the Pennsylvania farmer was totally sympathetic, going so far as to say the Yankee soldiers were certainly a sorry lot. In the end Love did not have the heart to fire the farmer's barn. He killed a chicken instead and returned to camp.[55]

Sergeant James B. Daniel, Company H, 47th Alabama, looked over the countryside and noted its vast difference from Virginia and Alabama. Wheat grew as high as his head, corn was plentiful and the pasture land plush. Writing to his wife from Chambersburg, Daniel noted that the buildings, which were generally constructed of brick and stone, were the finest he had ever seen. He astutely observed that the people of southern Pennsylvania had never felt the sting of war, but that would change if the Confederate army continued foraging.[56]

Similar thoughts were expressed by Private John Anderson, 48th Alabama. "It was a beautiful place," he wrote to his wife, Elizabeth, and the "richest country and the most plentiful that I ever looked at."[57] Colonel Robert Powell, 5th Texas, recalled, "We saw on every side of the road white cottages embowered in groves of trees laden with

**Sgt. James B. Daniel,
Co. H, 47th Alabama**

Gordon Carter, Montgomery, Alabama

fruit around which spread out fields of wheat like restless seas of emerald." In his words "the evidences of prosperity, happiness and comfort were in striking contrast to the dismal mourning, half peopled land we had just left over the river."[58]

The stark differences between war-torn Virginia and lush Pennsylvania were not lost on Federal troops either. Two days later Captain Henry C. Parsons, Company L, 1st Vermont Cavalry, noted "there was no more fruitful or comfortable region in the north, nor in the world." He rejoiced when they entered Pennsylvania and concluded they "were once more in God's country, and the hard plains of the south were far behind." Parsons described the countryside as covered with lush green fields; ripening fields of wheat had turned hillsides yellow; and bountiful orchards were laden with ripening fruits. Comfortable barns and granaries dotted the terrain. There were frequent peaceful hamlets and picturesque church spires. It was harvest time in Pennsylvania.[59]

During the night of June 28–29, one of Longstreet's couriers galloped into the First Corps headquarters and reported the Federal army across the Potomac and in pursuit. He also brought news that reported the head of the Federal column at South Mountain and thus it threatened communications through Hagerstown and Williamsport. Another bit of surprising news was that Major General George G. Meade was the new commander of the Federal army.[60]

While Law's Brigade camped at Chambersburg, the 4th and 48th Alabama guarded commissary stores near Scotland, a hamlet about two miles from the brigade camp.[61] Camp was opposite a large dwelling occupied by a family with two young daughters. The gentleman of the house proved friendly to the Confederates, and spent considerable time with the Alabamians. In short time a warm relationship developed, though the young ladies of the house drew most of the attention. They were frequent visitors, charming, and a delight to the young Alabamians. Henry Figures became captivated by their charms, and in a letter to his sister, claimed they were almost as pretty as the women in Huntsville, Alabama.[62]

While at Scotland, Sheffield ordered the 48th Alabama rolls for May–June 1863 prepared and its fighting condition assessed. At inspection clothes and military appearance were found to be "bad." However, on the plus side discipline, instruction, arms and accouterments were recorded as "good."[63] The Alabamians did not exhibit a good military appearance, clothes appearing shabby at best, but in June 1863 their esprit de corps was high. They were part of an army that felt itself invincible.

Born December 5, 1819, in Huntsville, the same year Alabama became a state, James Lawrence Sheffield attended the local schools. At age eighteen Sheffield moved to Claysville in Marshall County, Alabama where he clerked in a store and served as deputy sheriff from 1844–1847. He then pursued the life of a planter and through hard work and good fortune accumulated considerable wealth. In the 1860 census enumeration of Marshall County, forty-one-year-old Jim Sheffield listed his occupation as retired farmer. He was active in Marshall County politics and served in the state legislature from 1852–1855.[64]

Sheffield described himself as a Union man and proponent of constitutional principles, but believed in secession if Alabama's rights were denied in the Union.

Nonetheless, in an impassioned speech to the Alabama Secession Convention, he warned of the consequences of secession. "In my judgment, its [Union] dissolution is a calamity, and upon its preservation, perhaps not only depended our own happiness, but that of countless generations yet to come."[65] Joining others who saw passage of the secession ordinance as inevitable, he finally voted in favor of the ordinance, promising the other delegates to defend his state if she were threatened.

After Alabama seceded, Sheffield made good on his promise, raising a company of volunteers that became Company K of the 9th Alabama. At the election of officers he became first lieutenant of the company and later its captain. In the early spring of 1862, Sheffield began the task of raising a

**Col. James L. Sheffield,
48th Alabama**

Katherine M. Duncan and Larry Smith
Duncan, *Marshall County*, 51

regiment, drawing recruits from Marshall, Blount and DeKalb counties. In the process he used nearly $60,000 of his money to outfit the regiment that became the 48th Alabama. At the regiment's organization, the rank and file elected him the first colonel, an obvious reward for his efforts and contribution.[66]

Sheffield and his company commanders took the opportunity to tidy up a few administrative loose ends. Captain Thomas James P. Eubanks, Company D, reduced First Sergeant Jonathan Gross to the ranks. No one immediately replaced him. A. J. Turner would assume the duties of first sergeant in the coming fight. By order of General Lee, Private Henry Fortenberry, Company H, returned to the regiment from arrest for desertion. Twice wounded and a proven veteran, he had deserted in May 1863, but was quickly captured. In the terminology of the time, Fortenberry "did his duty" afterwards. He surrendered his arms with the 48th Alabama at Appomattox Court House, Virginia.[67] There were two promotions confirmed in Company F, 48th Alabama. John B. Eubanks became the company's second lieutenant and James F. Adrain replaced him as the third lieutenant.[68]

Commissions for William Hardwick and George Cary, with date of rank from June 17, were received. The former officially became the lieutenant colonel of the 48th Alabama. The latter became major of the 44th.[69]

Eubanks, co-owner and co-editor of the *Marshall News* before the war, enlisted with Sheffield in the 9th Alabama and was given the honor to receive his company's flag from the local ladies. He became the 48th Alabama's second adjutant and was serving in that capacity when promoted to captain.[70]

Private William Lee transferred from the 13th Alabama to Company I of the 44th Alabama. In exchange the 13th Alabama received Private William Lovorn, also of Company I. Frederick Nance transferred from Company A of the 4th Alabama to Company D, 44th Alabama and was promoted to the rank of first sergeant. Both careers with the new regiments would prove short lived. Each died in action September 19, 1863 at the Battle of Chickamauga.[71]

When orders arrived to rejoin the brigade, the departure brought a sense of sadness to the soldiers of the 4th and 48th Alabama. The return route on the morning of June 30 took the 4th Alabama through Chambersburg under a cloudy and rainy sky. But this time the locals' mood matched the atmosphere and none were amused by the march through town. Women stood on porches or looked out from open windows and shouted insults. The situation could very easily have gotten out of hand because the Alabamians themselves were not in the same festive spirit as the first time through town. Fortunately the 4th chose only to exchange insults. Henry Figures recounted the incident to his mother, assuring her he never said a word.[72]

After the 4th Alabama returned to camp, Law's Brigade and Captain William K. Bachman's South Carolina battery (German Artillery) pulled outpost duty on July 1 at New Guilford, traveling by way of Fayetteville.[73] Turner Vaughan described the small hamlet about three miles south of Fayetteville as an insignificant place. Camp was in a large oak grove located in a picturesque little valley. Fortunately there was an ample supply of apple butter, pigs and light bread, and the men continued to eat well.[74]

A large herd of pigs browsing near the 15th Alabama camp caused many mouths to water in anticipation of fresh pork. Near the end of the day word came that the 15th Alabama would be without a supply of meat. Colonel Oates gave his permission to butcher a hog for the evening mess. Captain William A. Edwards sent a squad out with instructions to kill the largest hog they could find.[75] The men slaughtered three before Edwards discovered the extent of their foraging, and a fourth was so near death that he let the men finish the job. Two soldiers from Company E in the detail were Silas B. Peters and Sergeant Samuel Hogg. Peters, a small one-eyed man with a dry sense of humor, loved to play jokes on his fellow soldiers.[76] During the episode Hogg, a large man, became the object of his sport. Peters threw rocks at the hogs instead of using his musket and accidentally struck Hogg a sharp blow on the leg. Hogg was furious and though in considerable pain went after his antagonist. Peters ran for his life with Hogg in hot pursuit. Hogg was fast for a large man, and was about to catch Peters when Edwards saw the two. Peters pleaded for Edwards to save him. Questioned on the circumstances leading to the chase, he blandly replied that the detail went out to find the largest hog, and Hogg was the largest one he saw. Hogg suddenly realized how ludicrous the whole thing was and burst into laughter. With a noticeable limp he turned and made his way back to quarters. Boiled hog's head, spare ribs and baked bread were the day's fare.[77]

Mitchell Houghton, Company H, 15th Alabama, and two companions secured permission to venture out on a foraging expedition. The real purpose, in Houghton's words, was to "buy something better to eat than our army rations." Expectations of ample supplies were high when they discovered a farmhouse.

Much to their dismay another detail was already hard at work when the trio arrived. According to Houghton, "The sight of a half dozen birds of the same feather as ourselves blighted our hopes."[78]

Moving on, they discovered an abandoned house. Beyond it, a recently traveled trail led to a dense thicket in the foothills of South Mountain. Some distance inside the woods they found a horse tied to a sapling near the entrance to a cave. Houghton ventured inside and found a boy and girl of Pennsylvania Dutch origin hidden in a chamber. The boy carried a weapon, but the Confederate managed to surprise the pair and get the drop on the fellow. Terribly frightened at the sudden appearance of a rebel, the girl began screaming. Her companion cried, "Mine Got! We will be kilt already! Mine Got!" The boy was firmly instructed to "stuff his hat in his mouth and stop that noise, for I would not hurt him." Houghton's tone produced the desired effect, but the boy and girl trembled perceptibly. A few minutes later the captives revealed they had been on the east side of South Mountain when the rebel cavalry passed through. "Filled with fear of the horrid rebels," they had sought refuge in the cave. After being led to their wagon and sent on their way, Houghton and his companions last saw the pair "rejoicing and heaping blessings on the 'repols' generally."[79]

We Must Go Quickly because General Lee Needs Us

The first day of July turned into a warm cloudy day and became quite humid. Occasional showers made the roads muddy and very slippery. In the afternoon the distant boom of cannon rolled in from the east, and after dark a courier rode into camp and asked for the brigade commander.[80] Longstreet sent orders to join the First Corps at Gettysburg. Regimental commanders prepared to move at a moment's notice. Law brought his pickets in and ordered three days' rations cooked.

Private Joseph Harper, Company G, 44th Alabama, decided to skip the next fight. This was not his first venture from the ranks without permission. He had deserted when the regiment reached Richmond the previous summer. Authorities cut short his quest for freedom and he returned to camp under guard. On October 8, 1862 then Lieutenant Colonel Perry signed an order returning him to duty. Harper remained with the 44th until the thunder of the guns rolled across South Mountain. This time he disappeared into the Pennsylvania countryside.[81] Private John A. Green of Company D had been under arrest a month before for desertion. But on this day he found his place in the ranks when the regiment began its march to the Gettysburg battlefield. He maintained his resolve and courage to do his duty and commanding officers afterwards twice cited Green for gallantry. A wound at Spotsylvania ended his military career.[82]

They had barely packed the haversacks when a second courier arrived with urgent instructions to join Hood's Division. Law set the departure for 3 a.m. but was unable to get the brigade in motion until almost 4:00 a.m.[83] Eighteen miles separated the Alabamians from Gettysburg. In between lay South Mountain and rolling Pennsylvania countryside.

At this critical moment Colonel Pinckney Downey Bowles of the 4th Alabama was under arrest, though the specific charges are unknown. The records do show that Law had him court-martialed and a four-month sentence imposed. Bowles petitioned Longstreet to investigate the matter, but he either declined or ignored the request.[84] Facts of the case are obscure, and Bowles was angry over his arrest for many years. But by 1909 his anger had subsided sufficiently for him to serve as a witness when Law applied for a pension.[85]

Lieutenant Colonel Lawrence Houston Scruggs, a twenty-eight-year-old merchant from Huntsville, Alabama, commanded the 309 men of the 4th Alabama as it marched for Gettysburg.[86] Oates led the 15th Alabama, the largest

Lt. Col. Lawrence H. Scruggs, 4th Alabama

ADAH

regiment in the brigade with 543 men. The 44th, 47th and 48th numbered 372, 418 and 394 men, respectively. Brigade strength, including men assigned to various regimental and brigade details, was estimated at about 2,042 officers and men. Not only did the 15th Alabama field the largest regiment in terms of fighting power, but it also boasted one of the larger musician corps, carrying eight in Pennsylvania.[87]

By daylight of July 2, Law's men were descending into the valley at Cashtown. Behind them lay the summit of South Mountain and the fertile land that provided such marvelous food the past few days. Four miles west of Cashtown, the column passed the smoking ruins of Thaddeus Stevens's Caledonia Furnace.[88] As the Alabamians passed through Cashtown the company commander detailed two members from Company G, 15th Alabama to find water. Privates James W. Gallaway and Allen W. Sholas disappeared into the countryside and were not heard from again. Records show the pair as deserters, but Oates chose to believe the pair died at the hands of the local populace.[89]

By the time the brigade reached the battlefield John J. Carter, a fourth corporal from Company K, became the third member of the 15th Alabama to leave the ranks. He chose to remain within the Confederate lines, but his luck ran out on July 19. However, Carter proved a hard man to keep confined, and he escaped on August 5, only to be re-captured and sent to prison at Castle Thunder in Richmond. He returned to the 15th Alabama May 1, 1864 and deserted again. This time he chose to go over to the Federals. At Carter's request the authorities sent him to Chicago on November 14, 1864.[90]

The morning of July 2 brought a boiling sun, but, because of the urgency Law set a blistering pace. There were few rest stops.[91] As the morning wore on, canteens began to run dry. The heat and exhaustion caused stragglers to appear behind the column. Two or three miles from town, field hospitals provided the first evidence of the previous day's fighting.[92]

Eight hours after he led his brigade from its bivouac, Law joined the Texas brigade on Hood's right near Herr's Tavern on the Chambersburg Road. Longstreet would write many years later that no other brigade in either army did as good a day's marching to reach the battlefield.[93] Accounts as to the time and miles covered differed, but most of the eyewitnesses appear to include the distance from Herr's Tavern to their position in front of Round Top in the count of total miles covered.[94] Law's march from New Guilford to Herr's Tavern covered approximately 20 miles, much of it nonstop. Because they made a significant detour on the march to Round Top that portion of the march covered about five miles. When the brigade went into position before Round Top, it had covered about 25 miles.[95] They still had another mile to charge before engaging the Federal infantry.

By any measure this was an incredible feat in the heat of July and with little water.

Chapter 3

Before the Round Tops

The Battlefield—Afternoon of July 2

Gettysburg, Pennsylvania is nestled in a shallow valley. In July 1863 the thriving town was surrounded by rich farmland. The most prominent nearby landmarks were two ridge lines. Seminary Ridge ran north and south about one-half mile west of town. Cemetery Ridge lay to the south. Its north end curved like the eye of a fish hook and was capped by an elevation known as Culp's Hill. Two steep hills firmly anchored the south end. One would forever be known as Little Round Top. The larger, more southerly hill took on the name Big Round Top.

Two other ridges, known as McPherson's and Herr's, lay west of Seminary Ridge. Willoughby Run, which flowed south between the two, emptied into Marsh Creek south of the battlefield. Seminary Ridge terminated near the Snyder and Warfield houses and rose again south of the Warfield house. The new elevation is known as the Warfield Ridge and crossed the Emmitsburg Road west of Big Round Top.

Ground to the east of Warfield Ridge fell off to a valley bounded on the opposite side by Big Round Top. Devil's Den lay several hundred yards to the west of Round Top's northern base. Its huge boulders ranged from six to fifteen feet in height.[1] Spaces between the boulders were just wide enough to pass through and provided winding passage ways carpeted with moss.[2] Many years after the battle Colonel Perry doubted that the light of day had ever made its way to some of the passages. Devil's Den was at the terminus of a low ridge known as Houck's Ridge, named for John Houck who owned 47 acres on the ridge's eastern slope.[3] The ridge, its crest rising approximately 60 feet above the valley, sloped gradually downward to the north.

Big Round Top rises 300 feet above the valley floor south of Devil's Den. In July 1863 a dense stand of timber that hid huge boulders covered its western face and crest. The crest of Little Round Top is 200 feet above the valley floor. Large boulders and rocks covered the western slope, which about three-quarters up the slope formed natural fortifications. Plum Run meandered through marshy land east of Houck's Ridge, entered a rocky wooded ravine known as Plum Run Gorge, and finally emptied into a shallow valley below Devil's Den. A tributary, known as Rose Run, flowed into Plum Run south of Devil's Den, creating a "Y." Plum Run Valley encompasses the area from its source to the south end of Big Round Top.

Numerous fields dotted the landscape between Warfield Ridge and Big Round Top. Some contained grassy hayfields and meadows. Crops of various varieties grew in others and at least two had been recently plowed. Wooden worm fences or low stone fences enclosed several. The Alabamians would long remember two farmhouses and associated dwellings situated south of Devil's Den. The Bushman farm buildings stood a short distance east of the Emmitsburg Road. The Slyder dwellings were just west of Plum Run.

A Brief Rest and Then We're Off

After joining Hood's Division Law's Brigade rested on Herr's Ridge. Tired and weary bodies quickly sought relief from the noonday sun under nearby shade trees. In the distance the rattle of musketry gave evidence of skirmishing along the lines and the occasional thunder of artillery rolled across the countryside from their front and right. The 4th Alabama sent out a water detail with each man carrying a dozen canteens. A quick search of the immediate area revealed the only source was a small pond filled with greenish water.[4] The brigade took up the line of march before the men returned and catching up required considerable effort.[5]

Henry Figures conducted his own search for water and approached a house about one hundred yards from the road that he found occupied by women with small children. The youthful Confederate's presence visibly upset the occupants. A shell burst overhead caused a spell of wailing; then the women went into hysteria and ran about. An elderly woman thought the shells were meant for Figures and cried out in anguish for the young soldier to move on. Her plea touched the lad's heart. It was obvious he had found an absolutely terrible situation and decided the brigade was a better place to be.[6]

Lee's Plan of Attack

On the morning of July 2 Lee intended to maintain the initiative he had seized July 1. It was acertained very early in the morning that Meade had taken position on the north end of Cemetery Ridge. But Meade's left, which extended southeast of and at an oblique to the Emmitsburg Road as far as the terminus

Adj. Henry S. Figures,
48th Alabama

of the ridge, was in the air. Sometime around midmorning the commanding general decided that an attack against the Federal left offered the greatest opportunity for success.[7] Lee devised a plan that called for two divisions of the First Corps to deploy astride the Emmitsburg Road, sweep forward and seize the Peach Orchard and the high ground west of Little Round Top.[8] Colonel E. Porter Alexander, commanding the First Corps artillery, would then use the elevated ground to give artillery support for an oblique assault by the infantry against Cemetery Ridge.[9] Ewell would attack the Federal right while A. P. Hill threatened the center to prevent Meade from sending reinforcements to either wing.[10] As Lee completed the plan, Hood and McLaws were near army headquarters. Lee called

Robert E. Lee, Commanding Army of Northern Virginia

MC MOLLUS USAMHI

McLaws to his side and pointed to the exact location on a map of the area where the Georgian was to place his division. His instructions were to get there without being discovered, place his line across the Emmitsburg Road, and lead the assault.[11] It is not known if Lee gave personal instructions to Hood, but he wanted his division to follow en echelon on the right of McLaws.

Longstreet opposed Lee's plan, preferring instead, to turn the enemy's left and place the Army of Northern Virginia between Meade and Washington. But Lee believed a turning movement impractical. Withdrawing through the mountains with his long train would be very difficult. In addition, the commanding general knew supplying his army would be nearly impossible if he held his position for any length of time. The Army of Northern Virginia would attack Meade where he lay.[12] Lee later explained to President Davis that a battle on July 2 was unavoidable.[13]

The plan called for the First Corps to open the attack at 11 a.m. but at Longstreet's request, Lee agreed to a delay until Law arrived with his brigade.[14] In the meantime, Alexander, after being cautioned to remain concealed from the signal station on Little Round Top, prepared to move to the Confederate right with the First Corps's artillery. After a careful reconnaissance, which consumed the better part of three hours, he sufficiently understood the ground to move southward. By traveling through fields and hollows, three battalions of artillery managed to navigate the route undetected.[15] In the meantime, McLaws returned to his division near Herr's Tavern and at the head of his column, sat on his horse after having observed the Federal infantry filing onto the battlefield.[16] The Confederates' opportunity to deliver a decisive blow to the Federal left was slipping away.

A Circuitous March to Battle

Longstreet finally put the column in motion about 1 p.m. For tired and weary soldiers the rest afforded Law's Brigade was all too brief. In the initial part of the march south, Hood's Division followed a road that ran along the west side of Herr's Ridge. Longstreet rode in the center of the column. McLaws rode at the head with an officer from Lee's staff who was acting as a guide.

From the start, the march was slow, and frequent halts impeded progress.[17] Colonel William Wilkerson White, commanding the 7th Georgia of Tige Anderson's Brigade, reported relentless heat from a boiling sun only served to make the lack of water more acute.[18] As the head of the column topped a rise, the signal station on Little Round Top was visible. After conferring with Lee's staff officer, McLaws thought the only way to avoid detection was to countermarch.[19] When Longstreet became aware of the situation he too agreed. The First Corps subsequently took a circuitous route south. No one ever explained why it did not follow the path followed by the corps's artillery. Certainly the tracks were visible.

The head of the column was some distance southeast of the Black Horse Tavern when it halted and retraced its route almost to the starting point. From there it marched east to Willoughby Run, turned south again, and then marched toward the Emmitsburg Road.[20] In spite of all the efforts to remain undetected, the Federals did discover Longstreet's column and batteries played on the Confederates.[21] The First Corps approached the Emmitsburg Road when Longstreet began issuing orders for the impending attack. He reminded McLaws his division would deploy on the enemy's flank.[22] Brigadier General Joseph Brevard Kershaw,

leading McLaws's Division, was just opposite the Peach Orchard when he became aware of his role in the attack. His brigade would have the honor of attacking the Federal left flank. The left of the South Carolinians' line of battle would rest on the Emmitsburg Road and extend along the road next to the orchard.[23] Hood's Division approached Pitzer School when Longstreet ordered Hood to push ahead of McLaws.[24]

Kershaw emerged from the woods along Warfield Ridge expecting to see the Federal flank to his left. But, much to the Confederate's surprise Federal infantry, supported by artillery, lay in strength on his front. The blue-clad line stretched southeast, extending almost to Little Round Top. The South Carolinian quickly surmised that carrying out his orders would present his right and

**Lt. Gen. James Longstreet,
Commanding First Corps**

MC MOLLUS USAMHI

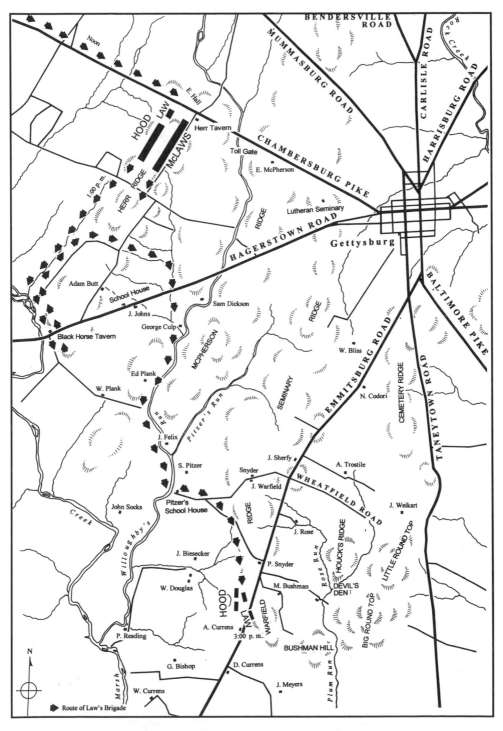

Route from Herr's Tavern to the Battlefield
July 2, 1863

rear to a destructive fire. The strength of the Federals massed on the division's front also astonished McLaws.[25] The plan of battle, as formulated in the morning, was unworkable in the afternoon.

Lee's battle plan underwent an eleventh hour change. The situation dictated that the new plan evolve as the Confederates evaluated the Federal position. Kershaw reported he received his directions in various messages from McLaws and Longstreet as well. There were also personal communications with both.[26] Lee's objective remained the high ground on the lower end of Cemetery Ridge and to achieve that goal his right would attack up the Emmitsburg Road. Lee ordered Longstreet to open the attack with his right division, Hood, instead of McLaws as originally planned. Hood would attack up the Emmitsburg Road, holding his left as close as possible to that road. McLaws would follow en echelon.[27] Hood was still filing past the South Carolinians when a courier brought Kershaw a note directing him to assault when Hood became engaged. Kershaw reported the plan of attack specified that the artillery should open along the front for ten minutes and then pause. The designated signal for the attack to begin was three guns fired in rapid succession by the right battery. Directions contained in the order were "to dress to the right and wheel to the left." This was understood to mean his line was "to swing as we could towards the left, probably with the view of gaining a line resting upon Little Round Top on the right and the Peach Orchard on the left." At the same time Kershaw's right would establish a connection with Hood's left. Each of the South Carolina regimental commanders were so instructed.[28] It was also his understanding that Hood "was to sweep down on the enemy's line in a direction perpendicular to our then line of battle."[29]

Before the Round Tops

A quick look at the terrain caused Hood to realize his men were in for a rough afternoon. The enemy, the left of Major General Daniel E. Sickles's III Corps, deployed along a generally concave line and extended from the base of Big Round Top to the Peach Orchard and then north along the Emmitsburg Road as far as the Rogers house. As a result the Confederate line would come under fire from the flank, rear and front. To make matters worse, the rocks around Devil's Den would break up the alignment. If he did carry the heights, Hood concluded it would be at a fearful sacrifice of his brave and gallant men.[30]

Long before he arrived at the Emmitsburg Road Hood sent out scouts from Robertson's Texas brigade to locate the Federal left. His division was filing into line when the scouts returned. Lieutenant Colonel Phillip A. Work, 1st Texas, listened as they talked to Hood. There was not a gun or man on Big Round Top. A two and a half mile long ridge stretched to the north, and behind it lay a line of Federal infantry, and battery after battery of artillery.[31] Hood knew they had found the Federal left in the air and that it would be vulnerable from artillery placed on the Round Tops. He concluded his veteran division could easily get in the Federal rear through open woods and pasture land about Big Round Top.[32] Pointing to the rocks around Devil's Den and the terminus of Houck's Ridge, Hood turned to Major William H. Sellers, one of his staff officers, and gave him urgent instructions, "go as fast as your horse will carry you and explain all this to General Longstreet and ask him to permit me to move by the right flank and envelope that knoll."[33] The quick reply was: "General Lee's orders are to attack up the Emmitsburg Road. You will execute the orders you have already received."[34] Hood did not lack courage on the battlefield, which he had amply demonstrated at Gaines's Mill, Manassas, and Antietam. But the intended attack, as he saw it, would bear little fruit and result in the destruction of his division. He sent a second request to First Corps headquarters. Again the reply came back: "General Lee's orders are to attack up the Emmitsburg Road." Work later recalled that Hood remarked, probably out of frustration and to no one specifically, "Very well, when we get

Maj. Gen. John B. Hood, Commanding Division

MC MOLLUS USAMHI

under fire I will have a discretion."[35] The literal interpretation of his comment is when the attack got under way Hood felt he would have the latitude to envelope the Federal left.

Hood was very busy during the short time he had to prepare for the attack. Messengers scurried back and forth between division and corps headquarters. Brigade commanders were briefed on the assault. But Hood remained highly disturbed over the intended role assigned his division. Preparations for the attack were barely under way when he concluded the Federal position was, as he termed it, "...impregnable and that independently of their flank fire, they could easily repel our attack by merely throwing and rolling stones down the mountain side, as we approached." In a desperate move he sought out Moxley Sorrel, chief of staff for Longstreet, and beseeched him to examine the situation. Hood was sure the staff officer would see the folly of the order and persuade the First Corps commander to modify the plans. Sorrel did go to Longstreet on his behalf, but the answer came back the same as before.[36] In the meantime Hood superintended the placement of his brigades.

It is not known if Longstreet gave his division commander the specifics of his formation and the order of attack by brigade, or if he permitted Hood the latitude to arrange the brigades. In any event, Hood formed in two lines. Law's Alabamians and Robertson's Texans were on the front. Law's Brigade became the extreme right of the Confederate line, deploying in a wooded area under cover of Warfield Ridge. The brigade was east of the Emmitsburg Road. Hood designated Law's the brigade of direction. It would lead the assault with succeeding brigades taking up the attack en echelon from the left.[37]

Law's objective was the Federal left flank. Hood believed it either rested on the terminus of Houck's Ridge above Devil's Den or extended to the base of Big Round Top.[38] Robertson reported his orders were to keep well closed on Law's left while his left hugged the Emmitsburg Road. In Robertson's words "in no event to leave it unless the exegency [*sic*] of the battle made it necessary or proper, in which case I was to use my judgment."[39] The Texas brigade of four regiments crossed the Emmitsburg Road at an angle. The 3rd Arkansas, on the extreme left, lay about 200 yards west of the road. On its right were the 1st, 4th, and 5th Texas in the order indicated. Because of the wooded terrain, the road was not visible to those regiments on the left of the Texas brigade.[40]

Benning's and Tige Anderson's Georgia brigades occupied positions about two hundred yards in rear of the Alabama and Texas brigades.[41] Benning went into battle with little knowledge of the plan of battle. He only knew that the division would attack the Federal left and that he would follow Law's Brigade at a distance of about 400 yards.[42]

Benning brought on the field the 2nd, 15th, 17th, and 20th Georgia. Anderson's five regiments were the 7th, 8th, 9th, 11th, and 59th Georgia. A veteran of the war with Mexico and a Georgia native, Tige Anderson was before the war a lawyer, state legislator and a man of considerable wealth.[43]

Hood took the precaution to cover the right flank and watch for cavalry. Colonel White and the 7th Georgia went beyond the division's artillery and deployed on a line perpendicular to the Emmitsburg Road.[44]

Hood's division artillery lay to the front of his infantry. Captain James Reilly's North Carolina (Rowan Artillery) battery rested on Law's right. Captain Alexander C. Latham's battery, known as the North Carolina Branch Artillery, occupied a position on Robertson's right and slightly forward of the 5th Texas.[45]

The artillery had been in place for some time when Hood's infantry began filing into position about 3:00 p.m.[46] Though the shelling had ceased, results of the previous action were clearly evident to Law's men. A three-inch gun had burst and lay by a gun carriage. Reilly's gunners welcomed Law's men with "suppressed cheers."[47] Coles implied the cheers were expressions of joy at having infantry support. More likely, they were a good-natured rebuke directed at the infantry for taking so long to march south.

The grueling march from New Guilford extracted a heavy toll. By the time that Law's Brigade went into line

Brig. Gen. George T. "Tige" Anderson, Commanding Brigade

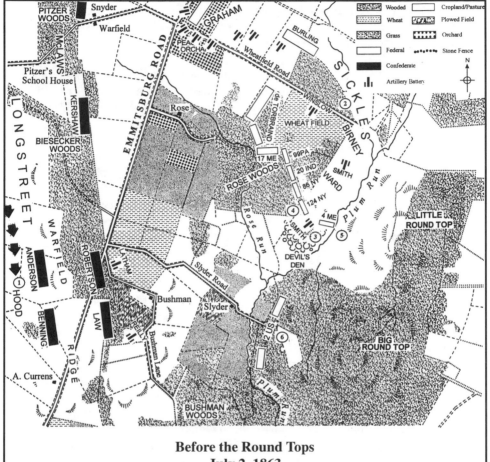

Before the Round Tops
July 2, 1863

1. Hood arrives on the Federal right around 3:00 p.m. expecting to find the Federal right flank resting on the southern end of Cemetery Ridge.
2. Sickles has thrown the Federal III Corps forward. His right and center rests on the Emmitsburg Road. His left extends along a line from the Peach Orchard to the southern terminus of Houck's Ridge.
3. Smith's battery is stationed above Devil's Den.
4. The 124th New York supports Smith's right.
5. The 4th Maine covers Smith's left rear.
6. Stoughton's 2nd U.S. Sharpshooters are deployed as skirmishers east of the Slyder house.

it is estimated available manpower decreased from about 2,042 to 1,645, or a little over 19 percent. Straggling in some of Law's regiments exceeded 30 percent. The 4th, 47th and 48th bought on the field 274, 290 and 275 officers and men respectively. Perry went into line with approximately 319. Oates could still boast of commanding the largest regiment in the division, numbering an aggregate of about 487.[48]

From left to right Law's order of battle was the 4th, 47th, 15th, 44th and 48th Alabama Regiments.[49] The 47th Alabama led Law's Brigade across the Emmitsburg Road, but was not on the extreme right when his line formed.[50] Law placed his senior ranking colonel, Jim Sheffield, in that position. His right rested nearly opposite the center of Big Round Top.[51] The 48th Alabama had just completed forming line of battle when Law sent orders to throw out skirmishers on the brigade's right flank. Companies A and H drew the assignment.[52] There is no indication the officer commanding the detachment received instructions to cooperate with the 7th Georgia.[53] Law placed the brigade's junior regimental commander, Oates, in the center. According to Adjutant Coles, the 4th Alabama's left was practically touching elbows with the 5th Texas.[54] Law completed deploying his brigade between 3 and 3:30 p.m.[55]

The Federal Left

Major General David B. Birney's First Division, III Corps, lay along the terminus of Houck's Ridge. A battery and its infantry support anchored Birney's left. The only Federal presence on the Round Tops at the time was the signal station on Little Round Top and a picket line on the lower slopes of Big Round Top. Longstreet's divisions were deploying when Meade sent his chief engineer, Brigadier General Gouverneur K. Warren, to observe the situation on the Federal left. Lieutenant Washington A. Roebling, brother-in-law and aide-de-camp to Warren, was at Meade's headquarters when Warren was dispatched to the vicinity of Little Round Top. Roebling had ridden with the V Corps part of the morning and arrived on the field about an hour in advance of the corps. He found Warren at Meade's headquarters. After familiarizing himself with the situation, Roebling was observing the field when, as he later described it, "Meade suddenly spoke up, and said, 'Warren! I hear a little peppering going on in the direction of that little hill over yonder. I wish you would ride over and see if anything serious is going on, and attend to it.'"[56] Warren, accompanied by Roebling, Lieutenant Ranald S. Mackenzie and Captain Chauncey B. Reese and several aides, reached Little Round Top about 3:30 p.m.[57]

When Warren reached the crest of Little Round Top, Hood's men rested in the woods along the Emmitsburg Road.[58] Federals around the Devil's Den area certainly knew there were Confederates on the left. However, Warren at the time was likely unaware that a corps confronted the Federal left. In 1872 he wrote that he immediately determined that Little Round Top was the key to holding the Federal left.[59] A signalman thought he had seen Confederate troops between Plum Run and the Emmitsburg Road. Warren decided to identify their position and requested a battery on the south end of Houck's Ridge throw a shell in the direction of Warfield Ridge. A short time later a round whistled over Hood's men. Its ominous sound caused the hidden troops to instinctively move. Warren claimed the glint of sunlight from the musket barrels revealed the Confederate presence in force, and in position to overlap the Federal left. He knew an attack would likely turn the Federal left, and immediately sent Reese to Meade requesting a division. Mackenzie rode to find Sickles and request a brigade.[60]

The shell came from Captain James E. Smith's 4th Battery, New York Light Artillery, of the III Corps Artillery Brigade. Smith arrived on the field at 9:30 a.m. and parked in the Wheatfield until 1 p.m., at which time Captain George E. Randolph, III Corps chief of artillery, personally led the battery south to the terminus of Houck's Ridge. Four of the 10-pounder Parrotts became the anchor of the Federal left. Because there was only room for two sections on the crest and none for the limbers, these were placed at its base. Once on the ridge Smith found his gun elevation could not be lowered to cover an advance through Plum Run Gorge. The remaining section was then placed three hundred yards to the rear in Plum Run Valley, and facing south to cover Plum Run Gorge.[61]

Earlier in the afternoon, Brigadier General Henry J. Hunt, chief of the artillery, Army of the Potomac, visited Smith's position and at first, thought the position a favorable one because it gave the guns an oblique fire. But when Confederate infantry began filing into position, he concluded the guns were vulnerable. Telling Smith he would probably lose his battery, Hunt left to seek infantry supports.[62]

Brigadier General John Henry Hobart Ward's Second Brigade, First Division, III Corps, deployed in a "L" shape along Houck's Ridge, and provided Smith's support. The 4th Maine, commanded by Colonel Elijah Walker, lay to the rear and left of Smith's guns and formed the base of the "L".

Organized in early June 1861, the 4th Maine left the state of its origin June 17. An inscription on its regimental banner read "From the Home of Knox," indicating that portion of the state from which it had been recruited. The men from Knox arrived on the field south of Gettysburg at 7:00 p.m. the evening July 1. About 9:00 p.m. Colonel Walker established a picket line, remaining there until mid-afternoon of July 2. When his men moved into line behind Smith's battery, hunger pains were foremost on their minds because water constituted the sole item in their diet the last three meals. "Fires were kindled," recalled Walker, "a heifer was found near by and slaughtered, coffee was steeped and beef impaled on sticks was warmed over the blaze. We drank our coffee and ate the very rare and thoroughly smoked meat, sprinkling it with salt, of which condiment every soldier carried a little in his pocket."[63]

Walker's objective was to cover Plum Run Gorge and the approach to Devil's Den. The 124th New York lay to the right of Smith's guns, its right extending into Rose's woods immediately north of Devil's Den. Eight companies of the 2nd U.S. Sharpshooters, under command of Major Homer R. Stoughton, a former railroad employee from Vermont, covered Walker's front.[64] Smith's supporting infantry went into line around noon and spent the early part of the July afternoon in relative leisure.

Known as the "Orange Blossoms," the 124th New York was a relatively new regiment. Its first serious fighting occurred at the Battle of Chancellorsville, Virginia, May 2–3, 1863. Writing of their inexperience the regimental historian recorded:

> *We had not yet learned the inestimable value of breastworks, and instead of spending our time rolling the loose stones into a bullet proof line, we lounged about on the grass and rocks, quietly awaiting the coming shock, which many declared themselves ready and anxious to receive. But there were undoubtedly those among us who ardently wished and perhaps secretly prayed that when the battle opened, it might rage the most furiously along some other portion of the line.*[65]

Their wish was not to be granted. Hood was about to unleash the full fury of his assault over the ground they now occupied.

The U.S. Sharpshooters were an elite unit. In 1861 the War Department had authorized Colonel Hiram Berdan to organize the 1st Regiment U.S. Sharpshooters. Its ranks were filled from companies recruited from a number of states. Selection was by an exacting test of shooting ability. Each recruit was required to place ten consecutive shots within five inches of the center of a circle two hundred yards distant.[66] Berdan's recruiting effort was so successful that two regiments were ultimately formed. Members wore deep green uniforms instead of the regulation blue, and each man wore leather leggings, and a cap with a black plume.[67]

Stoughton, described by Private Wyman S. White, Company F, as a drunkard who "was never known to go into a fight without an edge on," spent the morning of July 2 picketing the north end of Plum Run Valley.[68] One company was posted on Houck's Ridge, four lay in line perpendicular to Emmitsburg Road, and three were held in reserve. About 3 p.m. Stoughton was sent forward to cover the terrain south of the Devil's Den area. His men deployed behind stone fences on the Slyder and neighboring farms and in the edge of woods along Plum Run. Company D lay on the regiment's right. Stoughton spent a considerable period of time personally adjusting his companies.[69] In the meantime, Ward threw forward

**Maj. Homer R. Stoughton,
2nd U.S. Sharpshooters**

skirmishers from the 20th Indiana and 99th Pennsylvania, though they did not move out as far as the sharpshooters.[70]

Law Evaluates the Right

The Federal line was clearly visible in the Peach Orchard and around Devil's Den. Law concluded that if the Federals occupied the Round Tops the task confronting his brigade was formidable, if not impossible.[71] The absence of cavalry on his right and no visible evidence of infantry, either in the form of skirmishers or a line of battle, led Law to believe the Round Tops were not defended. However, Smith's guns and his supporting infantry caused him much concern. Law therefore decided on a reconnaissance of Big Round Top. Law personally selected six scouts to reconnoiter as far as the summit of Big Round Top. From this vantage point they were to look for the Federal left and send back a runner to report their findings.

A few minutes after the scouts left, several men were seen crossing the fields south of Big Round Top, moving in the general direction of the Emmitsburg Road. The unlucky fellows were quickly captured and proved to be Federals with surgeons' certificates headed for what they hoped to be the Federal rear at Emmitsburg, Maryland. These captives reported the Federal ordnance and medical trains were parked on the other side of Little Round Top, both lightly guarded. A good farm road around the mountain offered easy access to the trains, confirming what Hood's scouts had reported earlier. There was even better news. The captives did not think the Federals expected an attack to come from the left. Law was convinced that Big Round Top was the key to victory. He believed it should be secured and the Confederate line extended toward the Taneytown and Baltimore Roads to envelope the Federal left and rear.[72]

Law wanted to change the plan of attack outlined by Longstreet, and set out to find Hood. Along the way one of his scouts arrived from Big Round Top with the report that indeed there were no Federal troops on Big Round Top. Law found his division commander near the left of the Texas brigade, and quickly explained his findings and outlined a proposed modification of orders. Hood agreed with Law but reminded his subordinate that the orders were explicit. Longstreet's Corps was to attack en echelon up the Emmitsburg Road. Law persisted, lodged a formal protest, and outlined four reasons why the Round Tops should be occupied and the Confederate line extended around the Federal left. The points of his protest are repeated in his own words:

> 1. *That the great natural strength of the enemy's position in our front rendered the result of a direct assault extremely uncertain.*
> 2. *That, even if successful, the victory would be purchased at too great a sacrifice of life, and our troops would be in no condition to improve it.*
> 3. *That a front attack was unnecessary—the occupation of [Big] Round Top during the night by moving upon it from the south, and the extension of our right wing from that point across the enemy's left and rear, being not only practicable, but easy.*

4. That such a movement would compel a change of front on the part of the enemy, the abandonment of his strong position on the heights, and force him to attack us in position.[73]

Though he had previously made three unsuccessful attempts to change Lee's plan, Hood decided on one more request, his fourth direct appeal to the First Corps commander.[74] Law was asked to repeat his protest and plan in the presence of Captain James Hamilton, one of the division's staff officers, also went to Longstreet's headquarters with Hood's endorsement of the protest.[75] Ten minutes later Hamilton returned with Longstreet's adjutant, Colonel John Walter Fairfax, who repeated Longstreet's orders in Law's presence.[76]

Off to the right of the group, Law's Alabamians saw the colonel gesturing and pointing in what appeared to be the direction of the Round Tops. The men easily recognized the tall colonel who invariably wore his dress uniform in battle and had gained the reputation of appearing where the fighting was expected to be the severest.[77] Hood inquired if his brigadier understood the order. There was no need to reply.[78] A few minutes later Law put his brigade in motion.

Chapter 4

Plum Run Valley

Send the Troops Forward

Before the infantry moved out a duel erupted between Smith and the First Corps artillery. A round landed east of the line, bounded harmlessly through the timber, and over the heads of the Texans. Another plowed into the earth west of the line. When Smith found the range, shells crashed into Robertson's and Law's brigades. A direct hit killed two men in the 4th Texas. John C. West of Company E believed solid shot rained on the Confederates. Private James O. Bradfield recalled the worst part was remaining in place and enduring the shelling.[1] Farther to the right, Michael Bulger described the cannonade as a constant menace until the order came to advance.[2] Several men from the 47th Alabama also became victims of the Federal guns.

Fifteen minutes later the general attack began on the Federal left.[3] Hood rode his roan horse that afternoon and placed himself a few paces in front of the 1st Texas. Rising in his stirrups to a full upright position, the man who had adopted Texas as his home extolled his beloved men: "Forward my Texans and win the battle or die in the effort." "His thrilling words," recalled Philip Work, "like an electric shock, passed along the Texas regiments arrayed in line of battle impatiently waiting the shrill notes of the bugle for advance."[4]

Somewhere in the ranks of the 4th Alabama Private William C. Ward, Company G, silently prayed for just thirty more minutes rest.[5] Musician Henry M. Schaad, Company E of the 44th Alabama took his place in line, having replaced his drum with a musket. Sometime in the next couple of hours he would receive a nasty wound and be left on the battlefield.[6]

Adjutant Leigh Richmond Terrell rode to the front of the 4th Alabama and gave the order that put the Alabama brigade in motion. Commands raced along the line: "Shoulder arms! Right shoulder! Shift arms! Forward, guide center!" Colonel Jackson struggled to his feet in the rear of the 47th Alabama. Though his legs were weak and he was unsteady, the former doctor found sufficient strength to call his regiment to arms.[7] Company commanders hastened to dress the ranks. Tired bodies found new energy: Jackson recalled the "brave fellows answered the order with a shout and clash of bayonets." A few monents later he put the regiment in motion with: "Trail arms, at the quick time, march![8] Similar commands sent the other regiments forward. According to Ward "...the men sprang forward as if at a game of ball."[9] It was a little after 4:00 p.m. when Law's Alabama brigade advanced at the quick step.[10] Reilly's gunners temporarily paused from their work to permit the brigade safe passage into Plum Run Valley.[11]

Col. James W. Jackson, 47th Alabama

ADAH

Jackson, a Georgia native, attended a military academy in Greenville and studied medicine in New York City. Before the war he opened a practice at Lafayette, Alabama and was instrumental in organizing and drilling a volunteer company known as the "Lafayette Guards." Jackson was a strong secessionist and among the first volunteers when Alabama seceded from the Union. Unfortunately failing health caused him to resign his commission as captain of Company A, 7th Alabama. He was sufficiently recovered by the spring of 1862 to raise a another company of volunteers that was assigned to the 47th Alabama. Though ill health plagued him at the regiment's organization, he waged a successful campaign for lieutenant colonel. Disgruntled privates and officers openly expressed their opinion the regiment had elected a dead man. However, friends vigorously defended the choice, declaring Jackson their man dead or alive.[12]

Hood Goes Down

Longstreet joined Hood as the division started forward. The latter still complained about the plan of battle and expressed his regret that he could not turn the Federal left. The corps commander responded, in effect with, "We must obey the orders of General Lee."[13]

Hood rode ahead of the Texans and started down the slope toward the wheatfield west of the Slyder house. Jerome Robertson and his staff rode in rear of the 3rd Arkansas and 1st Texas and at first followed Hood. As they crossed the stone fences on either side of the lane in front, Robertson became separated from his division commander.[14] A few minutes later a shell fragment ripped into Hood's left arm.[15] Colonel Work recalled: "I saw a spiracle [*sic*] case shot explode twenty feet over Hood's head, saw him sway to and fro in the saddle and then start to fall from his horse, when he was caught by one of his aides."[16] He resolved to take Smith's battery and described his next action: "I directed my command to charge

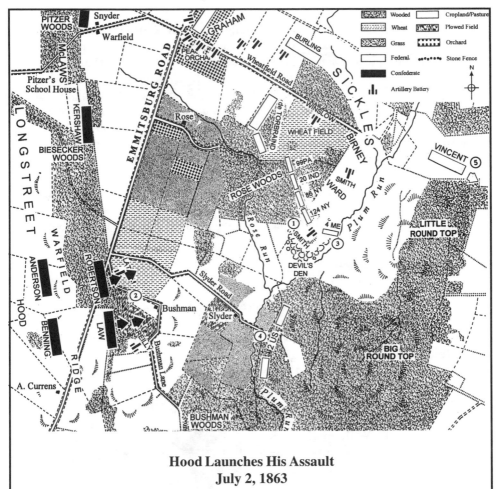

Hood Launches His Assault
July 2, 1863

1. Smith's battery, stationed above Devil's Den, fires into Hood's Division before it moves forward and continues to play on Hood's men with telling effect as they move into Plum Run Valley.
2. Hood's Division begins its assault at approximately 4:00 p.m. Robertson's and Law's men race forward. Benning and Anderson move forward after the front brigades are in the valley.
3. Smith has requested that Walker move the 4th Maine forward and to the left into the ravine through which Plum Run flowed.
4. Stoughton's 2nd U.S. Sharpshooters open, at long range, on Law and Robertson.
5. Vincent's brigade is moving to occupy Little Round Top.

it, as it was always my rule when under fire in battle not to halt until I took the battery in front of me."[17]

A lawyer, and volunteer soldier, Philip Work was born at Cloverport, Kentucky and removed to Velasco, Texas at an early age. The elder Work later settled the family on a plantation near Town Bluff. Philip joined the bar in 1853 and also served as a volunteer in the Regular Army on the Texas frontier. In his elder years the United States granted a modest pension for this service. Answering the call for Confederate volunteers in 1861, he raised a company of Texas militia that became Company F of the 1st Texas. At the regiment's re-organization its members elected him lieutenant colonel, and he became commander when the colonel fell severely wounded in the fighting around Richmond, Virginia.[18]

With Hood wounded, Law, as senior brigadier, ascended to division command. However, he was to the right with the Alabama brigade, and it is uncertain when he became aware that three additional brigades were now his responsibility. More importantly, Hood's Division was, for all intents and purposes, without a commander during this time.

Confusion in the Attack

The charge was barely under way when the plan of attack started falling apart. Men clamored over numerous fences as best they could. The 47th emerged from the woods about 50 yards ahead of the other four regiments. Fatigue caused it to pause for rest at a fence. Jackson worked hard to get the men back on their feet. A few moments later the regiment tumbled over the obstruction and moved forward.[19] But Jackson had collapsed and could not keep up with his command. From his post on the regiment's extreme right, Adjutant William H. Keller, Jackson's brother-in-law, saw the colonel fall and went to his aid.[20] Lieutenant Colonel Bulger was on the regiment's right and unaware of Jackson's plight. The 47th Alabama descended into Plum Run Valley before he assumed command.

Very few participants described the obstacles in their path, but some probably paused to tear down sections of worm fences. On the right of the line Sheffield marched through the rocks and trees on the north end of the Bushman Woods. Because he pressed on there was no time to redress the lines and Law experienced considerable difficulty maintaining formation.

Adj. William H. Keller,
47th Alabama

Mrs. Ben F. Keller, Jr., Greenville, Ga.

Marksmen from Company F, 2nd U.S. Sharpshooters were afforded a good look at Law's and Robertson's line. Wyman White described the Confederates bearing down on him as a "solid mass of rebels" that came "yelling, firing and struggling over fences and through the timber." Dressed in butternut clothes and massed in line of battle, Law's line took on the color of a freshly plowed field. [21]

During the descent into Plum Run Valley, officers from the 4th Alabama sprinted past the front ranks urging the men to move faster. Private Rufus B. Franks, Company I, sporting a new uniform recently brought from home, yelled that the Texans would be there before the 4th Alabama. A moment later they were at the double-quick step.[22] Little time passed before the left of the brigade, with the indescribable Rebel Yell filling the air, broke into a sprint.[23]

The euphoria of the moment swept into the ranks of the 47th Alabama. It too began to run, as did the 44th Alabama. Law's sudden surge surprised Robertson. The Texans lost contact with the 4th Alabama. To close the gap he broke out of the quick step. Lieutenant Colonel King Bryan, 5th Texas, reported the Texans crossed the valley at "a double quick and a run."[24] Nineteen years later Robertson complained to John B. Bachelder: "A charge was started by Law's Brigade on my right as I thought prematurely a full mile from the enemy's line of battle."[25]

A Kentucky native and orphan at age 12, Robertson enjoyed only three months formal education before his eighteenth birthday. Hard work enabled him to complete a course in the study of medicine and move to Texas. After participating in the war with Mexico, he settled in Washington County and engaged in the practice of medicine until the Civil War. Robertson was elected captain in the 5th Texas, commissioned colonel in June 1862 and brigadier in November 1862.[26]

Terrell rode through the line of the 4th and attempted to restrain the men. By now they were in open ground, crossing a plowed field south of the Bushman farmhouse, and in full view of Smith's guns posted above Devil's Den.[27] Shells exploded within the ranks while Stoughton's sharpshooters fired on the line from long range. Law's Brigade ran for the wooded slopes of Big Round Top.

On Law's left Robertson discovered the Emmitsburg Road fell away to the west more rapidly than he and Hood originally believed. To make matters worse, Law was moving too far right. With the two events working against him, a gap developed when the 3rd Arkansas and 1st Texas attempted

**Brig. Gen. Jerome B. Robertson,
Commanding Brigade**

to follow the Emmitsburg Road while the 4th and 5th Texas closed on Law. Robertson quickly concluded that Smith and his infantry support held the key to over-running the Federal left. As a result, he decided "to abandon the pike and close on General Law's left," and so ordered the 3rd Arkansas and 1st Texas, now under the command of Work. However, Work had already set a course for Smith and the two regiments did not re-establish contact before arriving at the Federal defenses around Devil's Den.[28] The 44th and 48th Alabama would partially fill the gap.

Smith's Guns—above Devil's Den

From his position in rear and to the right of Smith's artillery, Captain Silliman, commanding the 124th New York color company, enjoyed the splendor unfolding before him. He had an unobstructed view of Hood's advance and at the same time witnessed Smith directing fire on the Confederate line. The charging column seemed larger in strength than it really was. The gap between the 1st and 4th Texas was already evident. Silliman counted four distinct lines of battle. As the Confederates moved forward he saw Law's brigade with the 4th and 5th Texas connected to its left and incorrectly assumed the 3rd Arkansas and 1st Texas made up a separate line. The third and fourth lines would have been Benning's and Anderson's Georgians when these emerged from the woods. Silliman would later write: "We held the position by a single line of battle, unsupported, the enemy's superiority in numbers, as seen at a glance, seemed over whelming."[29]

Once Law and Robertson were in the open fields below Devil's Den, Smith made the most of his opportunity, pounding the gray line unmercifully. Though he maintained a calm demeanor, he surely experienced considerable anxiety for the safety of his guns. Those around him never forgot the authority in his voice and skillful handling of the pieces.[30] To maintain an adequate supply of ammunition, officers and available men from the 124th New York were impressed into service to carry shells up the ridge from the limbers below.

Confederate Line—Plum Run Valley

Smith used case shot on the Texans and Alabamians when they were in the fields.[31] Charge after charge exploded over their heads or fell into the ranks. Colonel Robert M. Powell remembered "we were greeted with a volley of...[canister]," but thought it did little damage.[32] Others retained more vivid memories of Smith's handiwork. Sergeant Ward said he "...could hear the shot passing over us with the noise of partridges in flight."[33] J. Mark Smither, 5th Texas, informed his mother that canister "mowed down the grass all around our feet."[34] Another Texas veteran likened the situation to one where "all demons had forsaken the internal regions and congregated in that field and with sulfur breath were shrieking their diabolical precautions in our ears."[35] Colonel Jackson recalled the "enemy threw canister and shell thick as you ever saw hail stones."[36] Private John Anderson, Company K, 48th Alabama, suffered from shrapnel wounds to a leg, arm and his forehead. Writing to his spouse in Alabama, he related how "the shot and shell fell like hail while the miney [*sic*] balls were whistling around on every side."[37] Second Lieutenant John M. Turnbow, Company G, 4th Alabama, fell dead near the Slyder dwellings.[38]

In the meantime Law's line also felt the sting of Stoughton's Sharpshooters who inflicted a number of casualties.[39] Though he was down, James Jackson witnessed the handiwork of the marksmen, recalling the "slaughter commenced in earnest."[40] Members of the 2nd Sharpshooters saw a number of men throw up their arms and fall. Undeterred by the fire playing on the line, the Alabamians and Texans pressed on, yelling and running. A spent bullet struck Sergeant Ward's left thigh

Capt. James E. Smith, New York Light Artillery, 4th Battery

MC MOLLUS USAMHI

a painful blow, but he managed to keep pace with his charging comrades.[41] His friend Sergeant John Taylor Darwin, Company I, 4th Alabama, was not so lucky. The youthful soldier suddenly stopped, quivered in agony, then sank to the ground with a bullet lodged in his brain.

William O. "Billy" Marshall, Company G, 4th Alabama, challenged Ward

Lt. Col. Isaac B. Feagin, 15th Alabama

ADAH

for the honor of reaching a stone fence first. Billy paused at Plum Run for a drink of water and was never seen again. His legacy for services rendered was a muster roll inscription which declared he "...was noble and gallant."[42]

Not all the Alabamians displayed the same valor normally associated with the brigade. Feigning a wound Private Joseph Roberson, Company A, 15th Alabama, slipped to the rear and the field hospital. Surprisingly he was not examined and was sent to Staunton, Virginia for treatment. His captain wrote of Roberson, "He was perfectly no account. A miserable apology for a man."[43]

Isaac Feagin, lieutenant colonel of the 15th Alabama, went down with a severe leg wound. Within the 15th Alabama ranks Privates Alsop Kennedy, Company B, and William Trimmer, Company G, fell dead. Private G. E. Spenser of Company D took a severe wound from a shell fragment. He was permanently disabled and honorably discharged from service.[44]

Born in Georgia, Feagin resided before the war at Midway, Alabama, where he was a merchant. Feagin held a captain's commission in Company B and was the second captain in seniority until appointed lieutenant colonel in April 1863. The wound was caused by a Minié ball near the right knee. Feagin was evacuated to a Confederate field hospital and captured when the Army of Northern Virginia left the field. Because the bone was shattered, his leg was amputated. He was exchanged in March of 1864 and retired in December of that year. After the war he became a sheriff and probate judge.[45]

Law's Line—near the Slyder House

The 4th Alabama, 4th Texas, and 5th Texas made a dash through a hayfield, yelling for all they were worth. Coles recalled they were "...firing and running like demons."[46] As the three regiments advanced across a field south of the Slyder dwelling, Stoughton's Sharpshooters kept up a lively fire from behind a stone fence just across Plum Run.[47] Private Mark Smith, Company D, 5th Texas, recalled "men fell out every step."[48] Colonel Scruggs took the precaution for the 4th Alabama to fix bayonets in anticipation of carrying the fence by force. Exhausted, winded and thirsty men tumbled over the wall to find the sharpshooters had disappeared into the adjacent woods.[49]

These elite marksmen were more comfortable firing at long range than fighting at close quarters. When the gray line closed on their position, Stoughton's men began falling back. His left wing sought cover in the woods. Five companies fell back toward Walker's line at Devil's Den. The remaining three moved onto the slopes of Big Round Top.[50]

It now became necessary to halt, realign the ranks and wait for men who had fallen behind to come up. Scruggs collapsed from heat exhaustion, the second regimental commander to fall out since the charge began.[51] Major Coleman assumed command, his first time to command the regiment in battle, but the young officer managed to gather his men and move off in a northerly direction over Big Round Top's lower slopes.

Twenty-seven-year-old Thomas Coleman began his military career as the first lieutenant of Company D, 4th Alabama. A native of Georgia, he lived at Uniontown in Perry County where he pursued farming. He was elected captain in April 1862. When Lawrence Scruggs became lieutenant colonel of the regiment a bitter dispute erupted between Captains Thomas Coleman and E. Jones Glass. Each claimed seniority over the other and thus entitled to the office of major. Longstreet's headquarters finally settled the issue in Coleman's favor.[52] Glass resigned and joined the cavalry service. Coleman went on to lead the regiment at the battles of Gettysburg and Chickamauga.[53]

Coleman sent Adjutant Coles in search of stragglers. He encountered several struggling forward and encouraged them. He found others laying prostrate in

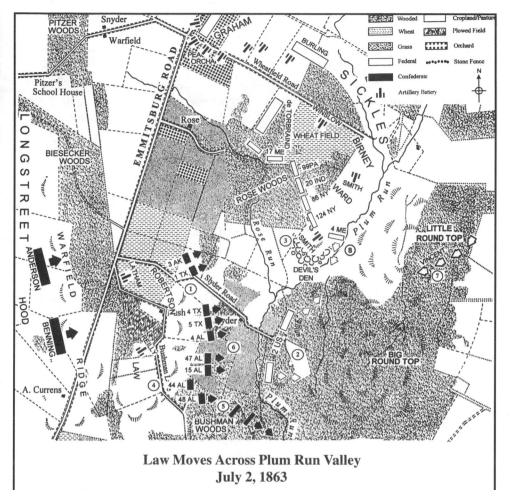

Law Moves Across Plum Run Valley
July 2, 1863

1. A large gap appears in Robertson's Brigade as he tries to hug the Emmitsburg Road.
2. Stoughton's Sharpshooters continue to fire on Law's line as it crosses Plum Run Valley. As Law's men approach Plum Run, Stoughton's force divides and falls back. The right moves north and joins the 4th Maine around Devil's Den. The left falls back on Big Round Top to menace the 15th and 47th Alabama.
3. Smith's battery continues to play on Law's line, inflicting a number of casualties.
4. Law has withdrawn the 44th Alabama from the brigade's right and sent it against Smith's battery.
5. Law orders the 48th Alabama from the extreme right to support the 44th Alabama in its attack on Devil's Den. Skirmishers from the 47th and 48th Alabama are moving south and advance to the eastern side of Big Round Top.
6. The 47th and 15th Alabama continue toward Big Round Top. The 4th, 5th Texas, and the 4th Alabama cross Plum Run, move into the woods, and prepare to assault Little Round Top.
7. Vincent arrives on Little Round Top.
8. The 4th Maine is moving forward to cover an attack from the woods.

the wake of the charge and simply too exhausted to go on. Near the edge of a wheatfield, Coles thought he saw a familiar form lying face down. Prodding with his sword failed to convince a comrade he thought to be Private Charles T. Halsey, Company F, 4th Alabama, to get up. His friend's conduct seemed strange "...because," according to Coles, "he knew Halsey was one of the best fighting men in the regiment and could always be found on the firing line." The men were about to advance over the northwestern slope of Big Round Top when he rejoined the regiment in edge of the woods.[54]

When the 4th Alabama moved out fallen timbers and large boulders scattered about severely hampered progress. Each man freely issued commands to his neighbor as the line made its way through the obstacles. Men assisted each other over the boulders while others passed between them. By chance, Coles saw Halsey to his front, very much surprised at his friend's quick recovery and exclaimed: "How in the world did you get here?" "Get here?" Halsey asked. "I've been here all the time." Coles happily recalled it was a case of mistaken identity. In spite of all the interchange, alignment soon fell apart. Hardened veterans simply fell down, victims of heat exhaustion and lack of water. Officers attempted to put the line in motion, but the soldiers needed more rest before making the climb to the crest of Little Round Top.[55]

47th Alabama—Plum Run Valley

The 47th Alabama's charge also became disorganized while the men were running and crossing fences. Men fainted from exhaustion and heat, leaving a trail of prostrate bodies in the wake of the charge.[56] Bulger became puzzled when it appeared that Jackson did not attempt to control the regiment. Major James McDonald Campbell later attributed the confusion in the ranks to Jackson's absence, because, in his words, "owing to the fact that in the charge the lieutenant colonel expected the colonel to give all necessary commands."[57]

Bulger did not know the colonel had collapsed. Acting on impulse, he ran out in front of the 47th and managed to halt the regiment. Unfortunately, the right of the line had collided with the 15th Alabama, mingled with Oates's left and disrupted the progress of both lines.[58] Stoughton recorded that he saw one regiment thrown into confusion and rally before continuing forward.[59] It is likely that he witnessed the confusion when the 47th ran into the 15th before Bulger halted to regain control. After closing the ranks, Bulger sent it forward again. At a hundred yards from the sharpshooters a shout suddenly rose from the 47th. A moment later it charged the marksmen. Forty paces separated the lines when Stoughton's men disappeared into the woods.[60] A few minutes later Terrell rode up and informed Bulger he now commanded the 47th Alabama.[61]

Michael Bulger came to Alabama in 1823 as a seventeen-year-old apprentice to a gin maker. He prospered in his adopted state, becoming a planter and later serving in the legislature in 1851 and 1857.[62] At the Secession Convention in Montgomery Bulger told his fellow delegates that secession was unwise and refused to vote for secession.[63] When a mob threatened bodily harm, he sent word to the ruffians to do their worst to any man who did not vote the wishes of his constituents. The unyielding stand for his principles probably led them to decide he had been misjudged.[64] At age fifty-five Bulger raised a company of volunteers which became Company A of the 47th Alabama. At the Battle of Cedar Mountain, Virginia, he led Company A in its first fight until two wounds forced him from the field. The first was a nasty arm wound that he tightly bound. A Minié ball then severed a leg artery. Someone quickly applied a crude tourniquet fashioned from two corn cobs and a set of suspenders.[65] Shock and loss of blood almost caused his death, but miraculously the elderly gentleman slowly recovered. He was promoted to lieutenant colonel while on wounded leave.[66]

Lt. Col. Michael J. Bulger, 47th Alabama

CV, v5, n7, 338

James Campbell received very little formal education, but early in life decided his calling was the ministry. When Alabama left the Union, Campbell joined the troops gathering at Pensacola, Florida. There was a stint as chaplain of the First Georgia Regiment which he accompanied to Virginia in the summer of 1861. During the following winter Campbell became torn between his calling to ministry and the desire to become a soldier. In the end he decided to actively participate in the defense of his country.[67]

Campbell came to prominence within the regiment after a nasty encounter with Colonel James M. Oliver. Following a particularly bad drill, an irate Oliver, who was prone to frequent bouts of profanity, singled out Company E. The company may have been deficient in drill, but hurling curses at his men would not be tolerated. Campbell boldly confronted their antagonist. The two men stood nose to nose and angrily shouted at each other. Oliver eventually backed down and the men noted the concern Campbell had shown for them.[68] The regiment elected the former minister major when that position became vacant.

Smith's Battery Causes a Change in Plans

When the Confederates moved into Plum Run Valley, Smith's cannonading proved effective and formations were difficult to maintain. Law decided to eliminate the Federal battery. The line was west of the Slyder house and crossing a fenced area of grass when he began pulling regiments from the right of the brigade. Colonel Perry withdrew the 44th first, then Colonel Sheffield with the 48th Alabama. Both obliqued sharply left.[69] Prior to the advance Law had not communicated the plan of battle to his regimental commanders.[70] This was probably the first indication that any of them had that the intended objective was the Federal left.

As senior colonel, Sheffield would normally have acted as commander of both regiments. However, Perry reported the 44th Alabama "was detached from its place in line, by order of General Law" to capture the battery that had been playing on the line from the moment the charge began.[71] Sheffield only acknowledged command of the 48th and then brigade command in his battlefield report. Because the two regiments operated independently it has to be assumed Law communicated separately with Perry and Sheffield. Both regiments crossed behind the brigade and entered the woods east of the Slyder buildings. A short time later Perry executed a left wheel maneuver toward the sounds of the battery which brought the 44th's left opposite the battery and its right extending toward the base of the mountain.[72]

**Col. William F. Perry,
44th Alabama**

William A. Baugh, *Confederate Faces*, 69

William Perry became a teacher at age 20, and from 1848 through 1853 he served as principal at a school in Talladega, Alabama. After studying the law under Judge Chilton at Tuskegee, he was admitted to the Alabama Bar in 1854, though he did not practice law. In the same year he became Alabama's first state superintendent of education, serving in that capacity until 1858. Perry returned to private life and became principal of the East Alabama Female Institute in Tuskegee, Alabama, and served in that capacity until the war started.[73]

Law's Line—near Plum Run

Law ordered additional skirmishers thrown out on the right flank of the brigade. He may have done so as a result of the persistence of Stoughton's marksmen, or it may have been a precaution against reinforcements from the south of Big Round Top. Companies, A, D, and F, under the command of Captain Henry C. Lindsay, withdrew from the 47th Alabama. Writing of the event, Lindsay said, "My own company was D, of which I was captain and in command, as I was the ranking officer of this battalion. I took command and leaving some considerable distance between the main body of the regiment and my battalion, prolonged the line of both, so as to face little Plum Run Valley. "As soon as this battalion was detached," he wrote in an account of the action, "...we marched hurriedly to the right and front towards the enemy posted in force beyond the bridge across Plum Run."[74]

When he came to Gettysburg, South Carolina native Henry Lindsay was a twenty-three-year-old farmer and a resident of Rough and Ready, Alabama. Only the company's second captain, he had succeeded Albert Menefee, who was killed in the regiment's first battle at Cedar Mountain, Virginia.[75]

15th Alabama—near Plum Run

The 15th Alabama probably advanced just east of Plum Run and fronted the southern slope of Big Round Top when Law found his junior regimental commander. The two would have discussed the current situation. Law wanted to move in the direction of the heights on his left and instructed Oates execute a left wheel.[76] However, neither he nor Oates identified the intended objective, Houck's Ridge above Devil's Den or Little Round Top. When the Alabamians were in that part of Plum Run Valley, Law based his decisions on information his scouts gathered before the charge began. There would be no reason for him to believe the enemy occupied Little Round Top. At that time, Bulger believed his objective was Smith's guns and the infantry defending it.[77] It is reasonable to expect that Bulger acted under the same orders. Therefore, Law probably directed Oates to advance in the direction of Devil's Den.[78]

Law also told Oates that Bulger would be instructed to keep the 47th Alabama closed on the 15th Alabama. However, Oates later claimed he understood Bulger was to act under his command in the event the 47th and 15th Alabama regiments became separated from the remainder of the brigade.[79] Oates did not see Law again until the following day.

There is no indication from Bulger's description of the charge that he at any time considered himself acting under Oates's orders.[80] His actions, after assuming command of the 47th, support this observation. However, the 47th more or less stayed on the left of the 15th Alabama, though it did reach Little Round Top before the 15th.

At this point in the charge, Law's advance divided into four separate thrusts. The 4th Alabama and the 4th and 5th Texas were on a course to take the three regiments over the lower slopes of Big Round Top. The 15th and seven companies of the 47th Alabama would eventually sweep north over the crest of Big Round Top. Perry with the 44th and Sheffield with eight companies of the 48th were about to launch an attack on Smith's guns above Devil's Den.

Both skirmish battalions, which acted independently, crossed Plum Run near a bridge and continued to the southern base of Big Round Top. Those from the 48th went around to the eastern side.[81] Lindsay and his command remained on the brigade's flank until late the following day. The five companies represented the loss of half a regiment from the fighting strength of Law's Brigade.

Chapter 5

Devil's Den

The Federal Position—Devil's Den Area

Colonel Elijah Walker and the 4th Maine waited at the mouth of Plum Run Gorge. He was there to support Smith's 10-pounder Parrotts but firmly believed that mission could best be accomplished from Houck's Ridge. Earlier in the afternoon, Smith discovered his guns could not cover an attack from below Devil's Den and requested the 4th Maine move into the ravine. Walker adamantly declined because he thought it impossible to defend the position against a Confederate attack from the woods to the left of and below Devil's Den. Smith insisted, which drew a blunt retort from Walker that he "would not go into that den unless I was obliged to."[1] The New Yorker realized the two were at a stalemate and took his request to brigade headquarters. General Ward agreed and sent his adjutant with the order to move. Walker continued his argument with Captain John M. Cooney, protesting with all "the power of speech he could command." The suggestion that another brigade would be forthcoming failed to convince him. Walker continued remonstrating against the order but time had run out. Hood's Confederates were already in the fields to his front.[2] As he wrote John B. Bachelder in 1885, "I must obey and suffer the results, or disobey and take the consequence; I obeyed."[3] Walker grudgingly moved his men into position to wait for the inevitable Confederate onslaught.[4]

Company F, some 70 strong, deployed among the rocks of Devil's Den. The rest of his regiment lay in the ravine

Col. Elijah Walker, 4th Maine

MSA

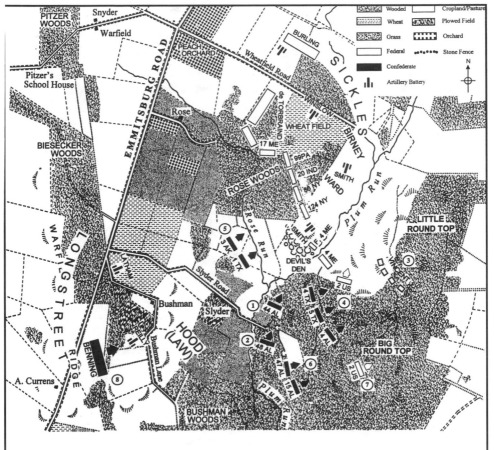

Law Begins His Assault on the Federal Left
July 2, 1863

1. The 44th Alabama arrives before Devil's Den at about 4:30 p.m. and prepares to engage the 4th Maine.
2. The 48th Alabama has withdrawn from the main line and is moving to support the 44th Alabama.
3. Vincent's brigade has deployed on Little Round Top and thrown forward skirmishers.
4. The 4th Texas, 5th Texas, and 4th Alabama enter the woods and advance over Big Round Top's lower slopes toward Little Round Top.
5. The 3rd Arkansas and 1st Texas prepare to assault Devil's Den from the western side.
6. The 15th and 47th Alabama enter the woods on Big Round Top's southern end. The 47th and 15th Alabama are ordered to advance north toward Little Round Top, but Oates is unsure of the Federal strength on his front and decides to move up Big Round Top's southern slope.
7. Stoughton's men fall back and fire on the 15th Alabama as both clamor up the mountain.
8. Benning emerges from the woods along the Emmitsburg Road and mistakes the 3rd Arkansas and 5th Texas for Law's Brigade, which he is supposed to follow, and instead follows them toward Devil's Den.

with the right resting on the eastern edge of the Den.[5] Walker recalled his left was "in line of battle near the woods, or bushes, at the foot of Big Round Top."[6] He had lost sight of the Confederates, but from the sounds of skirmishing in the woods to the south the Rebels were evidently pushing north. To cover his left flank, skirmishers, commanded by Captain Arthur Libby, moved into the woods between the Round Tops.[7]

The surrounding fields and woods below the Den teemed with activity. The Alabama brigade, and the Texas regiments, pressed their advance on Devil's Den and the Round Tops, while a Federal brigade moved over the crest of Little Round Top and began deploying on its southern slopes. Walker felt a little better when a line of skirmishers from the unknown brigade moved up on his left. At first he thought the troops intended to connect with his line and withdrew Libby from the woods.[8]

Smith's Position above Devil's Den

In the meantime, Law's men continued to feel the sting of the Parrotts. Smith used case shot on the column until it entered the woods south of Devil's Den. Shell played on the men while they were in the woods. When the Texans and Alabamians emerged from the woods on Walker's left flank canister crashed into the line. Because of the protection afforded by the numerous boulders and rocks the canister did little harm.[9] A few minutes later they swept past the 4th Maine.

The Confederate presence in the woods below the Den caused Smith's once calm demeanor to disappear. As the Confederate lines drew closer, Private A. W. Tucker, Company B, 124th New York, heard Smith yell at a gunner to give them five-second fuses and then two-second fuses. When Smith expended his supply of case shot and shrapnel, his excited voice rose above the din of battle: "Give them solid shot. Damn them, give them anything."[10]

Line of the 4th Maine

The Federal brigade on Little Round Top was Colonel Strong Vincent's Third Brigade, First Division, V Corps.[11] The skirmishers that Walker thought would connect with his line had been thrown out to cover his front. The large body of troops off to his left were the 4th Alabama and 4th and 5th Texas. After executing a wheel left west of Big Round Top, they were advancing on a line to attack Little Round Top.

The Texans and 4th Alabama drove Vincent's skirmishers back on the main line before Walker became aware that the woods hid more Confederates.[12] Breathless sharpshooters fell back through his skirmishers and reported an enemy column closing in.[13] Some joined the 4th Maine among the boulders of Devil's Den.[14] At least one company fell back on Little Round Top.[15] A body of grayclad troops that Walker described as a strong skirmish line followed a short distance behind.[16] Fear that disaster lay in the ravine surely resurfaced. The Confederate attack materialized in the form of the 44th and 48th Alabama.

Perry Arrives at Devil's Den

Neither Perry nor the rest of his regiment suspected imminent danger. A few scattered shots from the boulders gave the only hint that a Federal line lay nearby. Perry was barely able to yell "down" before a volley ripped into the 44th. As if on cue the entire line went down. Walker thought he had achieved surprise and wiped out an entire regiment. Perry later reported his casualties from the first volley were relatively light.[17] In fact more than one quarter of the line fell dead or wounded.[18]

The 44th lay where it fell for a period of time, then men began seeking cover among the rocks in the woods.[19] Walker concluded the 4th Maine "had no mean foe to contend with."[20] But, he was mistaken about the Alabamians' willingness to fight. The morning's hard march and the demanding advance across the fields under a boiling sun at the quick step and run had exhausted them. Lack of water and rest subsequent to the charge only compounded the problem.[21] Perry knew his men, if called upon, would rush Devil's Den, and he harbored little doubt as to the outcome. He put the situation in perspective, "But then what? There were no supporting troops in sight. A heavy force of the enemy might envelop and overpower us. It was certain that we should be exposed to a plunging, enfilading fire from Little Round Top."[22] Perry elected to bide his time and wait for the right opportunity.

When the 44th Alabama responded a fire fight ensued. Bullets zipped through the den and splattered off the rocks around Company F. Because the main line stood in the open it is logical to assume Perry's Alabamians found the men from the Pine Tree State inviting targets. The teacher from Alabama would later write, "The volume of fire which they [44th Alabama] returned proved they were very much alive."[23]

In the meantime the 48th Alabama emerged from the woods into open ground in front of Little Round Top. Sheffield began deploying in line of battle on Perry's right. To ward off a possible envelopment of his flank, Walker refused his left to face the mountaineers from northeast Alabama.[24] Adjutant Charles F. Sawyer, of the 4th Maine, reported "five to eight rounds being expended before they returned the fire."[25] When the 48th Alabama fired its first volley, the distance between the combatants was on the order of 20 paces. A close quarter fight that lasted 20 to 30 minutes developed.[26]

Before long the Federal line on Little Round Top joined in the attack on the 48th Alabama. Casualties mounted rapidly on the left of Sheffield's line. The woods partially shielded the right and it fared a little better. However, the added weight of the fire from Little Round Top forced the left back to cover.

Fight for Smith's Guns—West Side of Houck's Ridge

While Perry and Sheffield carried the contest to Walker's line, the 1st Texas, and 3rd Arkansas dueled the left center of Ward's brigade. The Confederate objective was Smith's battery.

Work led the 1st Texas across a triangular field enclosed by stone, stake and rider. The Orange Blossoms turned back at least two assaults. The contest on that part of the field ebbed back and forth for the better part of an hour. Work's men fought to within 50 yards of the prized guns and in the process dealt severe punishment on the battery. However, they in turn suffered a heavy number of casualties.[27]

After a time, Smith lacked sufficient men to handle the pieces. He dashed to the Orange Blossoms, and pleaded for help to load and fire. According to J. Harvey Hanford, a sergeant of Company B, 124th New York, the battery captain "would run back to the guns, do what he could, and then back to us, and with tears in his eyes, would say, 'for God's sake, men don't let them take my guns from me.'"[28]

When all seemed lost a desperate charge stalled the Texans' forward momentum and sent them reeling back to the edge of triangular field. The New Yorkers' rush down the hill carried them within a couple hundred feet of the men from the Lone Star State. Here began the contest for the triangular field.[29]

Perry Overruns Smith's Guns

While the New Yorkers engaged in their own war with the 1st Texas, and 3rd Arkansas, Walker became concerned for his right flank and started in that direction.[30] Smith appeared to be in the process of abandoning his guns, or so Walker thought. But, Smith had simply ceased firing when the 124th New York drove the 1st Texas from the southwest face of the ridge.[31] Walker probably saw a gun crew removing a damaged Parrott. In the confusion of the battle it is reasonable to assume he concluded Smith was pulling out.

Meanwhile, Sheffield rallied his men, brought the left forward and volleyed. The volume of fire hit Walker's main line of battle hard and casualties mounted. At the same time Perry's left began working its way around the west side of Devil's Den and threatened Walker's hold on the boulders.

Perry sensed the Federal line wavering. Acting on impulse the forty-five-year-old teacher seized the opportunity. He intended to hasten Walker's retreat. Drawing on all his reserve energy, Perry ran through his line yelling "forward." Though his shouts were barely audible above the din of battle, those around him immediately guessed his intent. Someone repeated the order which raced along each wing. A moment later the Alabamians rose as one and followed.[32]

The right wing scrambled over the boulders while the left, led by Major Cary, scaled the south end of Houck's Ridge and raced for the Parrotts.[33] Company F, 4th Maine, offered little resistance, and could do little more than fall back to the crest of Houck's Ridge. Several of its numbers were caught in the recesses of Devil's Den and became prisoners.[34]

The regimental colors went down. Sixteen-year-old Private James L. Forte picked them up and mounted a gun carriage. A Federal gunner grabbed a gun swab and knocked the young flag bearer senseless.[35] Cary seized the colors and pressed forward. By this time the artillerymen had made good their escape into the woods on the right. With the 44th Alabama swarming into his right rear, Walker realized

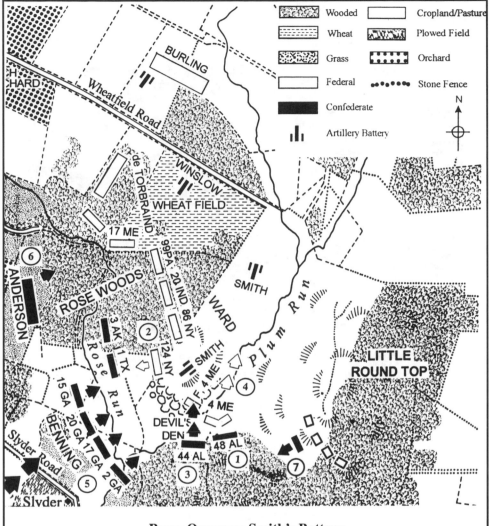

Perry Overruns Smith's Battery
July 2, 1863

1. On deploying the 48th Alabama covers the flank of the 4th Maine. Walker refuses the left of the 4th Maine to meet the threat posed by the 48th Alabama.
2. The 124th New York makes a desperate charge which drives the 3rd Arkansas and 1st Texas from the forward slope of Houck's Ridge. The Confederates fall back to the western edge of the triangular field.
3. At approximately 5:00 p.m. Perry leads the 44th in a charge which drives Company F of the 4th Maine from Devil's Den and overruns Smith's guns.
4. Elijah Walker and the 4th Maine fall back several hundred yards to reform its line of battle.
5. Benning arrives with his brigade of Georgians and moves up on the right of the 1st Texas.
6. Anderson moves up on the left of the 3rd Arkansas. The Georgians will extend the Confederate line north toward the Wheatfield Road.
7. The 4th Alabama, 4th and 5th Texas suffer their first repulse.

Devil's Den—Where the Alabamians Fought July 2, 1863

MC MOLLUS USAMHI

his position had become untenable. He decided to withdraw.[36] About one hour after the charge began, Devil's Den belonged to the Confederates.[37]

Perry reached the base of Devil's Den, but that was as far as his tired legs were able to go. Exhaustion from the heat, lack of water, and the final burst of energy required to make the charge forced him to fall out and seek cover among the boulders. Perry became the third regimental commander of the brigade to collapse.

Cary, regimental flag in hand, led the charge farther up Houck's Ridge. He soon returned and joyfully displayed swords captured from officers of the 4th Maine.[38] Federal and Confederate cannon were lobbing shells onto the ridge and Cary complained about the danger. Just then case shot rained down from the direction of Little Round Top.[39] A shell exploded near Perry's head, throwing its deadly contents against a nearby rock. The missiles of destruction came from a section of battery located on a shelf above the Federal infantry. Small arms fire also opened from the same direction, but owing to the protection provided by the rocks, proved less worrisome. It seemed prudent to move the men to safety and Perry ordered the 44th withdrawn from the brow of the ridge to cover on its sides.[40]

Cary once again disappeared into the smoke but quickly returned with news that a Federal force advanced down Plum Run Valley. Perry became concerned because it appeared the line might overlap the 44th. He struggled to his feet and attempted to scale the rocks for a view of the advancing troops, but the colonel's legs refused to support him and he sank back to the ground.[41] Lieutenant Colonel John Archibald Jones and the survivors of the charge were left to confront the new threat.

Jones was a native of Fayetteville, North Carolina, whose family had moved to Alabama when he was quite young. He graduated from the University of Alabama in 1855 and for the next two years stayed there to teach Latin and Greek. He taught mathematics at the Central Female College in Tuskegee from 1857 through 1858. In 1859, he relocated to Bibb County, Alabama, engaged in farming and served as a corporate officer of the cotton mill at Scottsville.[42]

Ward Throws in Reinforcements

When Captain Smith saw the infantry faltering he sent an urgent message to brigade headquarters for reinforcements.[43] General Ward responded by pulling the 99th Pennsylvania from his right. A courier, carrying a request for two more regiments, dashed off to find General Birney. Though hard pressed at several points, the division commander did what he could. Colonel P. Regis De Trobriand, commanding the Third Brigade, First Division, sent the 40th New York ("the Mozart Regiment"). For his second regiment Birney turned to Colonel George C. Burling, commanding the Second Division's Third Brigade. Ward received the 6th New Jersey.[44]

Walker Retakes Smith's Guns

Cary had encountered the 4th Maine, and they were determined to retake the lost ground. Walker had rallied a hundred yards in rear of Devil's Den and ordered bayonets fixed.[45] In 1885 he wrote, "I shall never forget the click that was made by the fixing of bayonets, it was as one."[46]

Charging forward at a right oblique, the men from the Pine Tree State scrambled up the eastern face of Houck's Ridge. When the regiment drew about even with the position held before entering the ravine, Walker halted and prepared to volley. The charge up Houck's Ridge had left the Alabamians disorganized and ill prepared for the renewed surge. A scattering fire greeted the 4th Maine, but Walker's line quickly got the upper hand. Jones conceded the cannon and pulled the 44th Alabama below Devil's Den. [47]

Benning Moves onto the Field

General Benning emerged from the woods along the Emmitsburg Road to the splendor of the scene before him. Devil's Den and Little Round Top teemed with Federal activity. Smith's battery and his supporting infantry were clearly visible. Vincent's line lay below the crest of Little Round Top. Skirmishers extended Vincent's line to the floor of Plum Run Valley. Six guns on a ledge above Vincent commanded all approaches to Little Round Top. In all, Benning counted 11 guns. About 400 yards ahead he saw a Confederate line he thought to be Law and followed. Actually Law's Brigade was farther right, hidden from Benning's view in the woods. Benning mistakenly followed Robertson's left regiments to the fight for Devil's Den.[48]

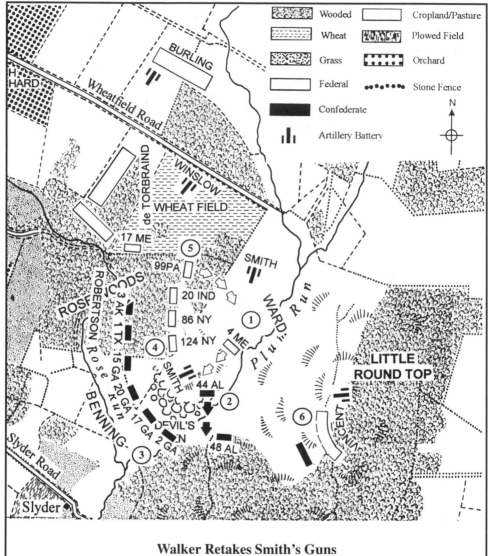

Walker Retakes Smith's Guns
July 2, 1863

1. After being driven north in Plum Run Valley, the 4th Maine charges across the eastern face of Houck's Ridge and clears the 44th Alabama from the southern end of the ridge.
2. The 44th Alabama retires to the shelter of Devil's Den.
3. Benning and Robertson move steadily forward, driving the 124th New York before them.
4. Survivors of the 124th New York return to the main line.
5. The 99th Pennsylvania has withdrawn from Ward's right and is moving to the extreme left of the brigade.
6. The 4th Alabama, 4th and 5th Texas assault Vincent's right center a second time.

One of Benning's biographers described the native Georgian as a "lawyer, judge, soldier and patriot." As a youth Henry excelled in scholarly pursuits and graduated from Franklin College (now the University of Georgia) with first honors. He was admitted to the Georgia Bar at age 21 and at age 39 was elected to the state supreme court, serving a six-year term. By political affiliation he was a Democrat and ardent supporter of the State's Rights movement. Benning actively campaigned for secession, then worked hard to raise and organize the 17th Georgia Infantry. Elected its first colonel, he led the regiment in the bloody fighting around Richmond and subsequently commanded Toombs's Brigade in the fall of 1862. His commission as brigadier was dated April 23, 1863, to rank from January 17.[49]

Brig. Gen. Henry L. Benning, Commanding Brigade

CV, v12, n3, 114

By this time Law knew he was division commander and had joined the fight around Devil's Den. The details of his activities that hot afternoon in southern Pennsylvania are very sketchy at best. Unfortunately, he failed to prepare a report of the action. None of his post-war articles speak in any detail of his direct involvement. After assuming division command he spent most of the afternoon near Devil's Den. However, it appears that communications with his subordinates suffered. Sheffield led three charges before learning he had ascended to brigade command.[50] Robertson did not learn for sometime that Law commanded the division and communicated directly with Longstreet.[51] As Benning and Anderson came up, Law threw their regiments into the fray, and after that disappeared into the smoke and haze around Devil's Den.[52]

Benning Joins the Fray

Benning arrived below Devil's Den while the 1st Texas and 3rd Arkansas were reforming for another assault on the 124th New York. At that time Perry's Alabamians were probably working their way around Walker's right flank. The four Georgia regiments belonging to Benning filled the gap between Work and Perry. To cover the space between the Texans and Alabamians, Benning executed a left oblique. Unfortunately the left of the 15th Georgia overlapped the right companies of the 1st Texans. Sorting out the tangled lines proved no easy task. Work and Benning decided to go forward and almost immediately ran into trouble. The line wavered and fell back under a severe fire from the Orange Blossoms.[53]

The Confederate line renewed its advance but measured forward progress a few yards at a time. Colonel A. Van Horne Ellis, commanding the 124th New York, made a stand half way up the face of the ridge, losing his life in the process. Benning and Work fell back a short distance, but by this time the New Yorkers were fought out and failed to follow.[54]

Benning reported his brigade advanced uninterrupted, although progress was slow.[55] The 124th New York, now under the command of its senior captain, Charles H. Weygant, grudgingly gave ground. Many of its men lay on the western slope of Houck's Ridge, a testament to the severity of the previous fighting. Most of the company officers and all its field officers were down.

As the Georgians inched their way up the ridge, the 20th covered Smith's rifled Parrotts.[56] The 17th Georgia was on a path to carry the regiment over the nose of Houck's Ridge and the path of the 2nd Georgia would carry it into Plum Run Valley.[57] On the Federal side, Captain Weygant led the remnants of his regiments back into line on Houck's Ridge.

Perry's Line—Devil's Den

Perry, Cary, and Jones were discussing the situation when Benning's right wing, composed of the 2nd and 17th Georgia, moved up.[58] As the two Georgia regiments advanced through the woods, they picked up Federal stragglers and sent them to the rear. The Georgians' appearance was good news and one of the trio happily remarked, "There is Benning, we are alright now."[59] Colonel Wesley C. Hodges guided the 17th Georgia up the terminus of Houck's Ridge.[60] Owing to the nature of ground, the 2nd Georgia found "it impossible to preserve alignment. The extreme right of the 2nd Georgia mingled with Perry's left, but Colonel William T. Harris quickly had his men scrambling over the rocks of Devil's Den and moving toward the north end of Plum Run Valley. [61]

Earlier in the day Harris called several friends around him and bid farewell. An uneasy feeling, maybe even a "sixth sense," led the Georgian to believe he would not survive the day. In the charge through Plum Run Valley, death already stalked its prey. Somewhere near the foot of Devil's Den Harris experienced at least one near miss; when his mount was shot from under him.[62]

For Perry, the fighting was over for the day. Exhaustion from the heat and excessive exertion made it impossible for his middle-aged body to go on without rest. His feelings on the subject appeared in an article written in 1901:

> It has always been to me a source of sincere regret that my disability, which continued until after nightfall, prevented me from seeing anything that occurred after the arrival of Benning's line. Buried in the recesses of the rocks, I could only hear. It is seldom that a soldier in the midst of a great battle, in comparative security and perfect composure, can enjoy the privilege of listening.[63]

The Concluding Fight for Smith's Gun

Walker established his line in rear of the battery with his right resting near the 124th New York. At the moment his left was in the air. However, he had precious little time to worry about that. Benning's Georgians appeared and a terrible clash developed on the nose of Houck's Ridge. Walker recalled the 4th Maine had a hot time for a few minutes.[64] This was a bit of an understatement. Both lines pitched in and engaged in vicious hand-to-hand combat. An infantryman from the 20th Georgia overpowered Walker and wrested the colonel's sword from his hand. Only quick action by one of his men saved both sword and colonel.[65]

In the meantime, Benning's right wing, composed of the 17th and 2nd Georgia, began working their way around Walker's left flank.[66] Hodges's 17th Georgia covered the left of the 4th Maine. The 2nd Georgia's move into Plum Run Valley brought it into position to threaten the left. It is not clear from accounts if Walker was fully aware of the danger developing. But just in the nick of time Major John Moore, leading the 99th Pennsylvania, came up at the double quick.[67]

Organized in July 1861 as the 32nd Volunteers, the designation of the unit was later changed to the 99th Pennsylvania. A three-year regiment, it was comprised of veterans of the Virginia campaigns and the Battle of Antietam, Maryland.[68]

Moore went into line on Walker's left when the conflict seemed the most desperate. The Pennsylvanians deployed along the brow of Houck's Ridge and generally faced the 17th Georgia.[69] Moore sent the men from the Keystone State into action with the command "up and charge!"[70] Pausing only for a single volley, the 99th Pennsylvania dashed forward. Above the crack and rattle of muskets and the scream of shells, rose the shout, "Pennsylvania and home."[71] The full weight of the charge fell on the 17th Georgia and pushed it below the brow of the hill, though Hodges did not admit being driven back. On the other hand the Pennsylvanians found it impossible to dislodge the Georgians from their hold on the south end of Houck's Ridge. Hodges gave an indication of the severity of the fighting that late afternoon, reporting seven charges against his line.[72]

Smith's Section—North End of Plum Run Valley

The fate of the guns on Houck's Ridge was sealed when the 124th New York staggered back to the main line. Though Smith had been asked to hold for thirty more minutes, the fighting at close quarters caused him to abandon the pieces. Deciding their presence on the hill "foreboding to the Confederates," Smith elected to trade the time required to remove the pieces to safety for fighting time. Three guns were operational and a short time before Smith had instructed his men to remove all implements for firing the guns.[73] The battery crew also left with horses and caissons.[74]

Smith went to great lengths in post-battle writings to explain his actions and his rationale for abandoning the guns when he did. Probably the most concise account appears in his report of the battle filed July 20, 1863 near Sandy Hook, Maryland. It read in part:

> *When I left three guns on the hill (one having been sent to the rear disabled), I was under the impression we would be able to hold that position, but, if forced*

to retreat, I expected my supports would save the guns, which, however, they failed to do. I could have run my guns to the rear, but expecting to use them at any moment, and the position difficult of access, I thought best to leave them awhile. Again, I feared if I removed them the infantry might mistake the movement for a retreat. In my opinion, had supports been placed in the woods, as I wished, the hill could not have been taken.[75]

The defense and abandonment of the guns became another of those controversial issues much discussed.

Smith moved to the rear guns and opened that section on the Confederate line at the entrance to Plum Run Gorge. Firing obliquely across the valley, the New Yorker began to take the measure of the 48th Alabama, particularly the left wing.[76]

Men on Little Round Top paused to watch the spectacle of Smith's duel with Sheffield and the 2nd Georgia. William J. Johnston, 44th New York, saw the Confederate column pressing the 4th New York Battery. Johnston believed the battery's commander did not realize the perilous nature of his position. Smith gained the admiration of those above him with his rapid and efficient handling of the guns. After each discharge he rushed beyond the voluminous cloud of smoke from the guns, observed the effect of the rounds, and rushed back. The New Yorker personally aimed each shot, seizing the gun trail and slewing either right or left for the desired effect. On command another charge flew down the valley.[77]

Federal infantry on Little Round Top also brought their fire to bear on Smith's target. Johnston reported the Confederates were so intent on firing at the lone section of artillery that few paid attention to the flanking musketry from the mountain. The combined infantry and artillery fire took its toll. Men toppled and pitched from the ranks. Two or three stands of colors seemed to be on the ground at once. Sheffield reported the 48th's flag went down three times.[78] The 48th Alabama and 2nd Georgia lost any semblance of organization.

Sheffield's young adjutant, Henry Figures, assumed a number of roles that afternoon. At one point he saw the flag lying on the ground and became the regimental color bearer. During the hottest part of the engagement he retrieved a musket and fired a few rounds at the opposing line. That accomplished, he turned to the task of assisting his fellow officers in keeping the men in line. But Little Round Top made the most vivid impression on the young soldier, and others as well, that afternoon. Its height grew as the afternoon wore on, and a few days later he wrote home that it was the steepest hill he had ever seen.[79]

Galling fire on Sheffield's left flank and canister charges finally became more than the line could bear. The Alabamians gave way, leaving the 2nd Georgia to face the wrath of Smith's two guns. Sheffield followed his men to the cover of the woods in his rear and began rallying those still able to fight. Though they had endured more punishment than could reasonably be expected of most men, the gritty mountaineers from northeast Alabama mustered fresh energy and re-formed line of battle. Sheffield brought his men to the front as Federal infantry made its appearance in the north end of the valley.[80]

Slaughter Pen—Where the Alabamians and Georgians Fought July 2, 1863

Library of Congress

Fighting in the Slaughter Pen

Lieutenant Colonel Stephen R. Gilkyson, commanding the 6th New Jersey, Third Brigade, Third Division, III Corps, traversed Rose's Wheatfield at the double-quick and led his men through Rose Woods on the north end of Houck's Ridge. Advancing without a guide, he followed the sound of the heaviest fighting on Ward's left. On reaching a fence Gilkyson immediately formed line of battle and opened on the 48th Alabama and 2nd Georgia. After directing a few volleys at the Confederates, Gilkyson moved forward 200 yards under a steady fire. This placed his regiment beyond Smith's Parrotts and directly in front of the 2nd Georgia.[81]

The 6th New Jersey's right rested on the eastern base of Houck's Ridge and extended toward Plum Run. Harris and his Georgians made a stand, absorbing the punishment inflicted by the men from the Garden State. Gilkyson reported he opened with great effect, but the 6th New Jersey lacked the firepower to dislodge the Georgians.[82] However, a number of the 2nd went down, including its colonel. Harris's sixth sense proved correct. He had crossed Plum Run and was 20 yards in advance of the 2nd Georgia when a bullet snuffed out his life.[83] Major W. S. Sheppard proudly recorded the Georgians "fought as gallantly as men could fight, and did not yield an inch."[84]

Colonel Thomas W. Egan and the 40th New York were the last of the reinforcements. Moving from the north end of the Rose Woods and crossing Rose's Wheatfield, Birney's aide-de-camp, Captain J. C. Briscoe, led the 40th New York. Twice before, the 40th New York entered the fighting when it seemed the most desperate. They were first sent to the Peach Orchard and then to Rose's Wheatfield. Going into action at the head of Plum Run, Egan understood his objective was to prevent the Confederates from turning Ward's left and pouring into the valley.[85]

Composed of men from New York City, Pennsylvania, and Massachusetts, the 40th New York traced its origins to early 1861 and an organization known as the "Constitution Guards." At the solicitation of the "Mozart Hall Committee," of New York City, it acquired the name "Mozart Regiment." The state gave the regiment the numerical designation 40th New York. Four companies from Massachusetts were added as were two companies from Philadelphia, Pennsylvania. Three companies from the 38th New York joined the regiment in May 1863.[86]

Not much is known about Egan before the war. Born the son of Irish immigrants in Watervliet, New York, he resided in New York City at the outbreak of hostilities. Commissioned lieutenant colonel of the 40th New York, he served in that capacity until the Battle of Seven Pines, when he placed the colonel commanding the regiment under arrest for misconduct. Egan was promoted to colonel when his superior's discharge became effective.[87]

Egan led the Mozarts through Smith's horses and carriages parked in rear of the guns. Smith beseeched Egan to save the artillery on Houck's Ridge.[88] However, one look down the valley caused Egan to realize he was in for a hot time elsewhere. The matter of Smith's gun would be the responsibility of other regiments.

The 2nd Georgia lay ahead of the main Confederate line and became the first obstacle in the path of the New Yorkers.[89] To the Georgians' right lay the 48th Alabama. The only thing to do was charge, which Egan immediately did. According to Smith, the Mozarts "marched down the valley fighting like tigers."[90] Egan ordered the line move at the double-quick step, but because it straddled Plum Run several found the going difficult. As he later described the charge, men struggled through marshy lowlands up to "their knees in mud and water."[91] Less than a hundred yards separated the opposing lines when the Mozarts halted.

Ward's line now extended nearly across Plum Run Valley, though its left center was badly battered. Benning's line confronted the 124th New York, 4th Maine and 99th Pennsylvania. On Ward's left the 6th New Jersey and 40th New York exchanged volleys with the 2nd Georgia and 48th Alabama. Major Sheppard reported the 2nd Georgia repulsed several charges. But the cost of standing his ground was high. The Federal line inflicted 91 casualties, but the Georgians remained firmly in place. The New Yorkers paid an equally high price, suffering severe losses as they dueled the Georgians and Alabamians. A shot unhorsed

Colonel Egan and he continued fighting on foot.[92] Sheffield was not as fortunate as Sheppard. The combined weight of attacks by the left of the Mozarts, the 6th New Jersey and fire from Little Round Top drove the 48th Alabama back a third time.[93] With the Alabamians gone, Sheppard's 2nd Georgia found itself unable to bear the weight of fighting alone and drifted back to the cover of Devil's Den and the woods surrounding Plum Run Gorge.

At least an hour and a half had passed since Sheffield and the 48th Alabama entered the fight. They were pretty well fought out. Though the men suffered greatly from fatigue and thirst, Sheffield resolved to rejoin the fight. However, a courier found him with orders to take command of the brigade. Because Lieutenant Colonel William McTyiere Hardwick and acting major Columbus B. St. John were wounded, Captain Thomas Eubanks, Company D, reformed the north Alabamians. A short time later the 48th Alabama made its fourth appearance on the front line.[94] Eubanks was not the ranking captain present when the regiment left New Guilford. None that ranked him were wounded or captured that day. The only explanation for Sheffield turning over command to him is that the others fell out before reaching the Devil's Den area.

Federal Position—4th Maine

It was near sunset when the 4th Maine received orders to fall back. Walker's men had fought gallantly, but now all the fight was gone. Walker himself was unable to walk without assistance, the result of a nasty leg wound. His horse had been shot from under him. Once again the colonel required the assistant of his men. Sergeant Mowry, Company B, and Corporal Roberts, also of Company B, assisted their colonel to the rear.[95]

Thirty-two bullet holes and two tears caused by shell fragments were counted in the colors. Its staff was significantly shorter, the result of a hit. All the color guard with exception of its bearer were either killed or wounded. Though the staff had been shot into, Sergeant Henry Ripley "did not let the colors touch the ground."[96] Ripley led a charmed life the afternoon of July 2, 1863, coming through the conflict without a scratch.[97]

Walker and the 4th Maine acquitted themselves admirably in the face of considerable adversity. Very few probably thought the rugged gorge later christened "The Valley of Death" the place to make a stand. But the choice of battle ground was not theirs to make. When the time came to do their duty the 4th Maine gave all that could be expected. It was a testament to their fighting spirit that the area just north of the Devil's Den remained in Federal hands as long as it did. Walker turned the regiment over to Captain Edwin Libby and rode from the field in an ambulance. He had reason to be proud of the regiment.[98]

Elijah Walker returned to service by October 1863 and commanded a brigade in 1864. During the winter of 1864 a group of superior officers and several leading politicians from the state of Maine lobbied to secure him a commission as brigadier general. As he later described it, "In an unguarded moment I expressed my favoritism for George B. McClellan." Walker in effect committed political suicide. All efforts on his behalf were quietly withdrawn.[99] Walker was also denied one of the brevets for higher rank so freely bestowed at the end of the war.

Federal Position—124th New York

During a lull in the fighting Captain Weygant glanced down the slope to his front. Dead and wounded covered the ground. Many of the fallen belonged to the "Orange Blossoms." In the line, little ammunition remained. Muskets were clogged and many unusable. Weygant later recalled, "Every few minutes a man would drop a rifle, bidding those beside him be careful when they fired, rush forward and pick up, in place of it, one that had fallen from the hands of a dead or wounded comrade."[100]

A detail went out to bring in the bodies of their colonel and major. Somewhere in the line a soldier shouted "they are advancing!" Looking to the left, Weygant saw the 40th New York withdrawing. Because the 124th had not received orders to withdraw, he logically assumed the left was falling back before a determined effort from Benning. A few minutes later a courier found Weygant with instructions to withdraw immediately.

He first directed the main line move out, then went after Company A which was posted among the rocks between the 124th and 86th New York. After successfully collecting his men, Weygant left Houck's Ridge a few steps ahead of Benning's Georgians.[101]

Postwar Barbs

In later years Walker and Smith exchanged verbal barbs over the New Yorker's desire to redeploy 4th Maine. Writing in April 1886, Walker stated that Smith "did not want his help." Smith retorted, "I certainly never said that I did not want his help; I was not fool enough to think a battery could maintain a position such as was assigned to the 4th New York [Battery] without a strong force of infantry in support."[102] However, no explanation appeased Walker who remained a harsh critic of Smith and of Ward for his decision to shift the 4th Maine. On January 5, 1885 he wrote, "I always have and ever shall regret that I obeyed the order and moved my command into that den which caused our entire loss of prisoners and most of the other casualties."[103]

Confederate Reminiscences

George Cary, the 44th Alabama's dashing twenty-four-year-old major from Montevallo, Alabama, was a native of the state and before the war a

**Maj. George W. Cary,
44th Alabama**

teacher.[104] He was the son of a physician and grandson of an English architect who migrated to Baltimore, Maryland.[105] After the conflict ended Cary became a partner in a dry goods firm in New Orleans, remaining there until 1880. He then moved to New York City as a cotton broker, becoming one of the better known and respected former Confederates residing in the city. It was reported that he had a unique ability to "administer a rebuke without leaving a sting." In a letter written when both men were in their twilight years, William F. Perry, once more a teacher and shaper of young minds, wrote his friend:

> *To the students of my college classes to whom I often related war stories—your name is as familiar as a household word—how you scaled the cliff at Devil's Den ahead of your line and with flashing sword and blazing face landed among the artillerymen of the battery, demanding and receiving the surrender....*[106]

Chapter 6

Attack on Little Round Top

Warren Finds a Brigade

Daylight of July 2 found the Federal V Corps, under the command of Major General George Sykes, in bivouac three miles from Gettysburg.[1] Though the previous three days proved arduous, the march into Pennsylvania did have its refreshing moments. Of the trek through Frederick, Maryland, Ziba B. Graham recalled "It was a long time since many of the old topers of the army had a chance to step up to a bar, and everyone seemed to be possessed to avail himself of the opportunity of filling up himself and his canteen as the brigade passed through." Renewed energy flowed through the column when it crossed the Maryland-Pennsylvania line. Spirits rose when the color bearers unfurled the flags and the regimental band played patriotic music.[2]

The corps arrived east of the Round Tops near 7:00 a.m. Many took the opportunity for a much needed nap or simply whiled away the early morning hours. Later in the morning the First and Second Division occupied the ground on the right of the XII Corps. As the day wore on the V Corps shifted left in several moves. By mid-afternoon the First and Second Divisions and two brigades of the Third Division were massed near where the Baltimore Pike crossed Rock Creek. Longstreet had completed preparations for the First Corps assault when orders arrived for the V Corps to move forward and go into line on the Federal left.[3]

Sykes, accompanied by Brigadier General James Barnes, commander of the First Division, rode ahead to reconnoiter and select a position.[4] The First Division led the corps and halted east of Rose's Wheatfield. Colonel Strong Vincent's Third Brigade of 1,141 muskets led the division. Having completed the survey Sykes went in search of General Birney and directed Barnes to bring the corps forward. Mackenzie met Sykes a short time afterwards. On learning of the request from Warren, Sykes agreed to occupy Little Round Top and dispatched an aide with the orders.[5]

Vincent sat on his horse at the head of his brigade when the aide appeared off the left flank.[6] He and his standard bearer, Oliver W. Norton, rode out to meet the rider. Norton recalled the following conversation between the pair.

Vincent: "What are your orders?"

The captain: "Where is General Barnes?"

Vincent: "What are your orders? Give me your orders."

The captain: "General Sykes, told me to direct General Barnes to send one of his brigades to that hill yonder," pointing to Little Round Top.[7]

In a fortuitous move that thrust the brigade into a critical role and into history, the young colonel from Pennsylvania took responsibility for occupying the eminence.

Three of the Third Brigade regiments, 16th Michigan, 83rd Pennsylvania, and 44th New York, were seasoned veterans from the campaigns of 1862 and the Battle of Chancellorsville. The 16th Michigan was the smaller of the regiments. The 20th Maine, the largest and latest addition to the brigade, came on the field with troops who were yet to taste the harsh realities of savage combat.

Vincent was not yet a brigadier, but the similarities to Law are worth noting. Like Law, Vincent was a strict disciplinarian, and gaining a reputation as fearless in battle. He was about the same height as Law, if not a bit taller, and a splendid horseman. A native of Waterford, Pennsylvania, he received his early education at the academy in Erie, then learned the trade of an iron molder in his father's firm. In the fall of 1854 the young Pennsylvanian entered Trinity College at Hartford, Connecticut. Two years later he transferred to Harvard College, graduating in 1859. Afterwards he read law in Erie and was admitted to the bar in December of 1860.[8] Just after the start of hostilities he had enlisted in the 83rd Pennsylvania, becoming its first lieutenant colonel, and later colonel.[9]

**Col. Strong Vincent,
Commanding Brigade**

MC MOLLUS USAMHI

James C. "Crazy" Rice, the senior colonel, brought up the brigade while Vincent and his standard bearer rode ahead to examine the area over which they would fight. After two attempts to climb the northwestern slope failed the pair galloped around the eastern side and ascended from the southern end.[10] A few minutes later men of Vincent's brigade saw their flag on the crest of Little Round Top.

Two batteries that had been firing on the signal station quickly found the range. Vincent suddenly realized the brigade standard fluttering in the breeze obviously drew the fire. "Down with that flag! Damn it, go behind the rocks with

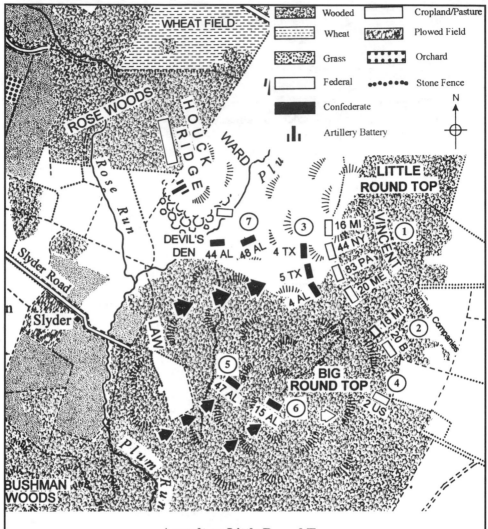

Assault on Little Round Top
Opening Phase—July 2, 1863

1. Vincent has advanced over the eastern slope of Little Round Top and deployed a few minutes ahead of the Confederate advance over the northern slopes of Big Round Top.

2. Captain Morrill, commanding Company B, extends the 20th Maine's left across the valley between the Round Tops. Morrill deploys on the left of the 16th Michigan skirmishers.

3. The 4th Texas, 5th Texas, and 4th Alabama open their attack on Vincent's center and right at about 4:45 p.m.

4. A detachment of Stoughton's Sharpshooters descend Big Round Top's eastern slopes.

5. The 47th Alabama is still in the woods on Big Round Top's western slopes and will advance over the northern face toward Little Round Top.

6. After climbing the southwestern slope of Big Round Top, Oates pauses to give the 15th Alabama a few minutes rest.

7. The 44th and 48th Alabama engage the Federal around Devil's Den. The 44th Alabama will overrun Smith's battery.

it!" he yelled at Norton. The Pennsylvanian then decided to complete preparation for the brigade on foot and a few minutes later placed his mount, "Old Jim," in the care of his standard bearer. Norton did not see his commander the rest of the afternoon.[11]

To the southwest, Vincent saw part of Hood's battle line making its way across the fields east of the Emmitsburg Road. However, he could not, at the moment, see Law's Alabamians in the woods on Big Round Top's western slopes. Vincent turned his attention to the task of determining where his line of battle would lay.[12]

In the meantime, the brigade's four regiments, with each man carrying 60 rounds of ammunition, worked their way past Little Round Top's northern slopes, moved down the eastern side, turned right and ascended the wooded slopes.[13] Near the summit shells exploded and filled the air with missiles of destruction. Metal fragments ripped branches from trees and flying rock fragments produced whirring and humming sounds. Like the brigade commander before them, officers dismounted and sent their horses to safety.[14]

Vincent Deploys for Battle

The brigade probably marched in column of fours by the right flank and formed line of battle from the right.[15] Vincent personally supervised the deployment of each regiment. "Crazy" Rice and the 44th New York went into position on the extreme right. The 83rd Pennsylvania, organized at Erie in September 1861 of men from Erie, Crawford and Warren, followed the New Yorkers. The 20th Maine was making its way around the eastern side when the 16th Michigan reached the southern base. Lieutenant Colonel Norvell E. Welch noted the right of the brigade circled the hill when the 16th Michigan formed on the left of the Pennsylvanians.[16]

Vincent ordered each of the regiments to throw out skirmishers onto the lower slopes.[17] These were the men that Walker had thought were about to connect with his left. The right center of Vincent's line had directed fire on Sheffield which contributed to forcing back his left.

Captain Lucus S. Larabee, Company B, drew the assignment for the 44th New York.[18] Like many men about to meet their fate, the captain had a premonition that he shared with several captains: "Since our last battle I have known I would be killed the next time I was under fire." He requested a friend retrieve his watch, money, and other valuables and send them to loved ones. Companions endeavored to cheer him up, but to no avail. Larabee departed with the comment, "I shall never see you again."[19]

A relatively flat valley separated the Round Tops and in 1863 brush and trees covered its floor.[20] Because of the vicious fighting which occurred there later in the afternoon, the historian of the 83rd Pennsylvania referred to it as the "Valley of the Shadow of Death."[21] On the opposite side of the valley lay the heavily wooded northern slopes of Big Round Top. Welch posted two of his largest companies in the edge of these woods. Company A came from the right of the regiment and Brady's Independent Company of Sharpshooters from the left.[22]

Little Round Top—July 1863

Library of Congress

In the meantime Vincent elected to entrust the security of the right flank to the 16th Michigan.[23] None of the participants revealed the rationale for the move, therefore we can only speculate as to the cause. Vincent could see the fight developing around Devil's Den. A Confederate success there would threaten his right. The pending assault by the 4th and 5th Texas and the 4th Alabama would hit his right. Therefore, placing the 16th Michigan on the extreme right extended his line to prevent that flank from being turned. The 20th Maine would occupy the ground vacated by Welch. The anchor of the Federal army's left and thus its fate fell to the 20th Maine.[24]

Joshua Lawrence Chamberlain was an unlikely hero, though he became one that day. Though the family heritage included a long line of volunteer soldiers, his education and chosen profession did little to prepare him for his eventual place in history. Born in Brewer, Maine, the name Joshua came from his father and grandfather and Lawrence was in honor of naval hero Captain James Lawrence.[25] Chamberlain received his grade school education at a military academy and graduated from Bowdoin College, class of 1852. After receiving a degree from the Theological Seminary at Bangor in 1855, he returned to Bowdoin College as a lecturer the same year. At the outbreak of hostilities the college refused him leave of absence to volunteer for military service. In 1862 the school granted him leave, ostensibly to study in Europe. Apparently Chamberlain entertained little, if any, intention to depart the country. His next position was lieutenant colonel of the 20th Maine.[26]

The 20th Maine was one of the last units organized under the 1862 call for 300,000 volunteers. There was precious little time to train and acquire arms. The raw recruits left the state with little knowledge of drill and there were only adequate arms for two companies. Their baptism of fire occurred at Antietam, though only that portion of the regiment that was at Blackford's Ford on September 19 and 20 became engaged. It participated in the fighting at Fredericksburg, but the first major test in combat would not come until the afternoon of July 2, 1863.[27]

Somewhere on the crest of the hill Warren climbed a large boulder for a better view of the valley below. Fighting raged around Devil's Den. Hood's Confederates were now visible in the woods east of the Devil's Den and closing on the Federal extreme left. Warren thought it doubtful one brigade could hold the line and decided to seek reinforcements. Before departing he made sure Vincent clearly understood his mission. Adjutant Rufus W. Jacklin of the 16th Michigan stood a short distance away when the army's chief engineer ordered the Pennsylvanian to "hold this point at all hazards, if you sacrifice every man of the Third Brigade."[28]

Chamberlain, Rice, and Vincent initially stood near the brigade's right and had a good view of the fighting around Devil's Den. Vincent then accompanied Chamberlain to the left as shells exploded among the rocks and trees. As the brigade commander departed to make his way back to the center of the line his parting words were: "Hold at all costs."[29] Those few words were the last communications between the two.[30]

The 20th Maine had ducked beneath the crest of Little Round Top to avoid the shelling and approached the line of battle from a northern direction. However, that portion of the line designated for the regiment ran in an east to west direction. At the moment Chamberlain had precious little time to spare because the Confederates were already on the lower slopes of Big Round Top. He decided on an unusual move and issued the command "On the right by file into line."[31] According to Chamberlain, this maneuver required more time to form the entire line, but he believed more rifle muskets went into action earlier.[32] When the 20th Maine completed deploying the brigade formed a huge quarter circle that wrapped southward

**Capt. Walter G. Morrill,
Co. B, 20th Maine**

MSA

around Little Round Top and terminated near the northern end of the valley between the Round Tops. That portion of the line occupied by the 20th Maine faced
slightly southwest.[33]

It is not clear if Vincent directed Chamberlain to extend his line or whether
Chamberlain acted on his own initiative and sent Company B across the valley.
Captain Walter G. Morrill led his men into the woods across the valley. Because
the two companies from the 16th Michigan were already there Morrill went into
line on the left of the skirmishers.[34]

Regimental commanders mustered every available man. The 83rd Pennsylvania drum corps grabbed muskets and found a place in line. Every able-bodied
pioneer and musician of the 20th Maine went into the ranks. Footsore soldiers
and the sick struggled forward. Chamberlain even relieved several men from
arrest and put them into line.[35] Oliver Norton left the brigade standard and his
horse with mounted orderlies, fetched a musket and found a place on the right of
the 44th New York.[36]

Known as the "People's Ellsworth Regiment," the 44th New York was raised
in honor of Colonel Elmer E. Ellsworth, one of the first Union volunteers to fall
in the service of the Union. Each town or ward contributed one man. To qualify
for membership, candidates were unmarried, temperate, able-bodied, and measured at least five feet eight inches in height. Each applicant had to provide proof
that he represented some town or ward. More important, a twenty dollar membership fee went into the regimental fund.[37]

To determine the condition on his left Vincent had sent his acting assistant
inspector general, Captain Eugene A. Nash, over to Big Round Top to observe the
Confederate movements. As he departed, Nash saw two or three lines advancing
without skirmishers in Plum Run Valley. The fight in Devil's Den was just getting under way at the time and Colonels Oates and Bulger were in the woods on
the lower slopes of Big Round Top. Therefore, he probably saw Benning's and
Anderson's Brigades. On Big Round Top he mounted a large boulder for a better
view of the western side. To the right, the Texans and Alabamians were in view.
The line of the 47th Alabama was visible through the trees on the lower slopes.
As he observed the Confederate movements, random shots began to zip in and
crash among the rocks scattered about, so Nash hastened down one hill to join the
fight for the other.[38]

Attack on Vincent's Center

Vincent's brigade had been in place less than fifteen minutes when the
Alabama and Texas lines emerged from the woods. Company F, 2nd U.S. Sharpshooters, scrambled out of the woods a few steps ahead of the Confederate line of
battle. The marksmen darted from boulder to boulder for protection. Several paused
to fire.[39] Farther up the mountain the Federal line braced itself for the Confederate onslaught. The 83rd Pennsylvania color bearer, having planted the regimental flag staff in the crevice of a rock, gripped a musket and awaited the order to
fire.

Captain Larabee had just completed his dispositions when the 4th Alabama, and 4th and 5th Texas stormed out of the woods south of Little Round Top.[40] Major John P. Bane, 4th Texas, described the ensuing exchange with the skirmishers as a "sharp contest."[41] A rebel bullet ripped through Larabee's body. The young warrior became the first officer from the 44th New York to die in battle.[42]

Musket fire erupted from the mountain, taking a heavy toll on the front rank of the 4th Alabama. Sergeant Ward and two companions on either side went down together. Ward's wound was in the lower part of his body, causing a sharp pain. A few seconds later he fell unconscious to the ground.[43] Lieutenant Colonel King Bryan, 5th Texas, reported similar conditions in the ranks of the Texans. In his words, "many of our officers and men fell in passing the open space between the heights."[44]

Men from the second rank rushed over their comrades and struggled around and over boulders scattered over the slope. The brunt of the assault fell on the 83rd Pennsylvania and 44th New York.[45] According to Captain William McKendre Robbins it was difficult to determine which Confederate regiments fought a given regiment in Vincent's line, as all regiments on both sides were connected. He later concluded the 4th Alabama's initial attack was against the 83rd Pennsylvania and the 4th and 5th Texas fought the 44th New York and 16th Michigan.[46]

The Confederate lined staggered under a galling fire. Several paused and shot into the Federal ranks above them, but most pushed on through the brush and rocks until within a few yards of the Federal line.[47] Fighting "Indian Fashion," behind rocks and the few trees on the slope, they began "popping away at the enemy whenever a head was exposed." The left of the 16th Michigan and the 83rd Pennsylvania responded with a vengeance, "pouring volley after volley into the gray line."[48] Private Decimus Barziza, 4th Texas, recalled "The trees were barked and thousands of bullets blew to atoms against the hard rocks."[49] Private J. Mark Smither, Company D, 5th Texas, thought the idea of scaling the fortifications ludicrous. In his words, "We could hardly have gone over them if there had been no Yankees there."[50]

Men sought shelter, such as it was, among the rocks below Vincent's line. Major Coleman found it difficult to hold the 4th Alabama in position. To the left, Major Bane struggled to hold the 4th Texas in line as did Major Jefferson C. Rogers of the 5th Texas.[51] Coleman's Alabamians gave way first, but the Minié balls rained down with such frightful effect the Texans followed the Alabamians.[52]

When Ward regained consciousness he knew from the sound of musket fire that his companions had discovered the main Federal line. His legs were useless, but he managed to drag himself to the cover of a four- or five-feet-high boulder. A private from Company A stopped and offered assistance, but was told to go on. A severe chest wound took him out of action. A second private, without a weapon, stopped to help and departed with Ward's rifle. Sergeant John W. Mosely, Company G, 4th Alabama, came up and took shelter behind the same boulder. The sixteen-year-old soldier had become too exhausted to keep up and was probably one of the stragglers that Coles had seen on his trip to the rear. After being admonished for not moving on, Mosely mustered sufficient strength to struggle forward and eventually took his place in line. The young Alabamian was struck down within 50 yards of the Federal line.[53] His fate would lie in the hands of the Federals.

Vincent's Line—the Brigade's Center

Many of the Confederates sought shelter directly in front of Company E, 83rd Pennsylvania. Five of the Pennsylvanians volunteered to go out and bring in prisoners. Yelling for their comrades not to fire, five brave souls dashed forth. Taken by surprise several Texans were easy prey and soon prisoners on their way to the rear.

The slaughter below shocked the Federals. Oliver W. Sturdevant wrote, "The scene where our volley first struck the enemy's line was one of sickening horror. Their dead and wounded tumbled promiscuously together, so that it was difficult to cross the line where they fell without stepping on them." As he searched among the bodies for the living one fellow begged to have the strap cut from his cartridge box as it lay across his wound. Sturdevant never regretted the time he spent rendering some comfort to the wounded nor speaking a few kind words. His fervent wish was: "I pray to God that I may never witness such a scene again."[54]

Second Charge—4th Alabama, 4th and 5th Texas

From the available accounts it is unclear how the second charge developed. Though he was not present for that one, Colonel Powell claimed, "The soldiers all, or someone saying, lets charge them again,"[55] Private Smither reported that "General Law came up and gave the order to charge."[56] In any event the Texans and Alabamians found new courage and scrambled up the lower mountain slopes. Men fired, sought cover behind a boulder, and then ran up the mountain to the next boulder. Captain Robbins stood at the 4th Alabama's right flank while a leaden hailstorm rained down on his position. Grit and gravel chipped from surrounding boulders felt like needles jabbing the skin. Dust particles filled the eyes and brought a flow of tears.

**Capt. William M. Robbins,
Co. G, 4th Alabama**

UDAH

Through sheer determination the Texans and Alabamians drove within several yards of Vincent's line. Had it not been for the thick smoke floating over the

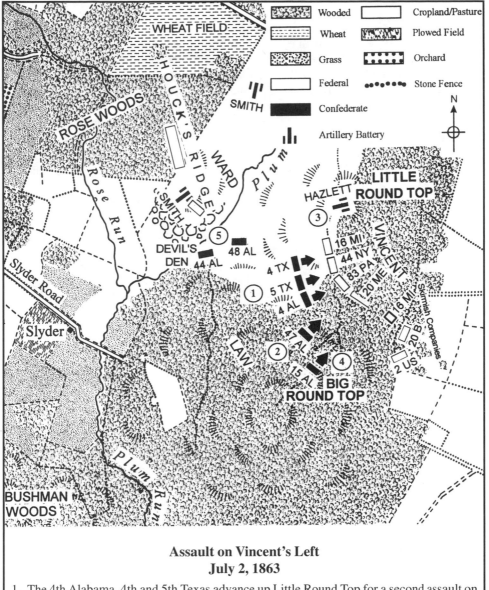

Assault on Vincent's Left
July 2, 1863

1. The 4th Alabama, 4th and 5th Texas advance up Little Round Top for a second assault on Vincent's line.
2. The 47th Alabama enters the valley between the Round Tops and prepares to attack Vincent's left.
3. Hazlett's battery has gone into action and is firing on Confederate positions around Devil's Den.
4. The 15th Alabama is advancing down the northern end of Big Round Top.
5. The 44th Alabama has overrun Smith's guns and in turn is driven back by a Federal counterattack. The 48th Alabama is engaged with Ward's left.

combatants, one of the 2nd U.S. Sharpshooters thought it would have been possible to see the "whites of their eyes."[57] A courier found Major Rogers, and yelled over the din of battle, "General Law presents his compliments and says hold at all hazards." "Compliments, Hell!" roared Rogers, "Go back and ask Law if he expects me to hold the world in check with the 5th Texas."[58] After wavering a few moments, the Confederate line broke in confusion. Private Rufus K. Felder, 5th Texas, wrote his mother that Little Round Top would have been impossible to take "had the enemy only been armed with rocks."[59] Some of the men chanced a hasty retreat. A few held up handkerchiefs or hats to signal surrender. Others chose to take cover behind boulders and a slight elevation not far from the Federal line and fire on the defenders.[60]

Private Rufus Franks of the 4th Alabama suddenly stood up and still holding his rifle started for the rear. As he passed Adjutant Coles, the young soldier quietly pleaded for Coles to persuade Major Coleman to retreat. Coles thought that Franks might be suffering from a minor wound and had subsequently lost his courage. Then he noticed Franks's face had turned deathly white. Without looking back, Franks said he was wounded and continued on. He made his way to the base of the mountain and was placed in an ambulance wagon. Wounded in the abdomen, Franks suffered greatly with spasms and severe nausea as the wagon bounced its way toward the division field hospital where he died a painful death.[61]

Hazlett Brings on the Artillery

A short time after the 4th Alabama began its assault Battery D, 5th U.S. Artillery, Lieutenant Charles E. Hazlett commanding, went into position on Little Round Top and opened on the Alabamians, Texans, and Georgians fighting around Devil's Den. Pioneers hastily cut a narrow path through the woods on the east side while men struggled to move the guns up the hill.[62] Drivers vigorously applied spurs and whips. Cannoneers and infantry alike labored to turn wheels and lift the carriages over rough spots. Lieutenant Benjamin F. Rittenhouse believed the guns went into place without touching a single tree. Hazlett, wearing a white hat, remained on horseback as he guided each piece to its place. He chose to leave the caissons in the rear because of rugged terrain and they were easy targets on the hill.[63]

When Hazlett fired his first round the infantry paused momentarily from their work. The 44th New York's historian wrote that "No military music ever sounded sweeter." A loud cheer erupted along the line as the first shell exploded near Devil's Den.[64] A cannoneer of the fourth gun dipped his sponge into a bucket and made ready to fire his own piece. At the same instant a rebel bullet ripped a large hole in the container. He paused, faced the foe, gritted his teeth, and muttered "damn." Rittenhouse believed from the look on his face the artilleryman thought more colorful thoughts. He rammed the sponge home with vengeance and the piece fired. A rather satisfied gunner sent his compliments to the rebels, saying, "Take that damn you."[65]

After the battle James Smith, 4th New York Battery, in a conversation with Rittenhouse, revealed his anxiety over his tenuous hold on Devil's Den. "I kept looking back," was the way Smith put it, "wondering if we would ever occupy the Top. The report of the first gun fired from there was the sweetest music I ever heard."[66] This was probably the fire brought to bear on Perry after the 44th Alabama overran Smith's guns.

Rally the Broken Lines

The 5th reformed on open ground when the Texans fell back, and the 4th in a skirt of wood.[67] The 4th Alabama retired to a position farther to the right of the Texans and fronted some companies of the 20th Maine's right.[68] Major Coleman rallied the survivors for a third attempt to break Vincent's line.

From this point in time the 4th Alabama and Texans fought more or less independently. Coleman brought the 4th Alabama forward for another attempt to scale the mountain. The 47th went into line on their right, but there was little fighting spirit left in the 4th. Colonel Vincent easily repulsed the third attempt of the 4th Alabama and the 4th retired.[69] Lieutenant Colonel Scruggs attributed the failure to exhaustion and the roughness of the mountain side.[70] After drifting back to the cover of the woods, its men lay prostrate among the rocks and boulders.

Coleman attempted another rally, but nearly 25 percent of the regiment were casualties. Many others were scattered around the battlefield, victims of the sustained march in the morning. One of Longstreet's staff officers rode up and in a loud voice inquired for the person in command. No one within the sound of his voice responded. Someone eventually pointed in the direction of Coleman, but the staff officer mistook Coles for the 4th's commanding officer. With his foot pressing hard on the adjutant's shoulder, he loudly ordered the regiment to charge Little Round Top. Coles politely informed the staff officer of his mistake and directed the man to Coleman. The officer decided the task of finding the commander too difficult and rode into the woods.[71] In the meantime Coleman's men raised a brisk fire from the cover of rocks and trees. [72]

Oates Occupies Big Round Top

After crossing a fence beyond Plum Run, Oates noticed a few stragglers from Stoughton's Sharpshooters making their way up Round Top. The main body had disappeared into the woods, and Oates was trying to decide his next course of action. He was under orders to turn left. However, at the moment his primary concern was for the force he perceived to be somewhere in the woods to the east. It was necessary, he concluded, to deal with this enemy. He decided to disobey the order. In later years he tried to justify the decision by complaining that the 47th Alabama pressed his left and caused confusion in the ranks of the 15th. He further explained that in order to obey he would have had to turn into the 47th Alabama. In addition, the maneuver would expose his right flank to an enfilading fire from the enemy on his right.[73] The 15th Alabama continued forward in search of the sharpshooters and began climbing the rugged slopes.

It was not an easy climb. Men held onto rocks, bushes, and tree limbs or crawled over boulders. Stoughton's men moved up a short distance, fired at the 15th Alabama, though most of the shots whizzed harmlessly overhead. Return fire from the 15th Alabama also failed to find its mark. Shots striking the rocks around Nash as he observed the fighting below were probably from the 15th Alabama. About halfway up the mountainside Stoughton divided his command into two squads. One moved to the eastern side of the mountain, while the other fell back around the right of the 47th Alabama. Departing shots from the men in green uniforms caused Oates to detach Company A to protect his right flank. Oates then scrambled onto the crest of Big Round Top.[74]

Bulger Encourages His Men

Colonel Bulger halted on the lower slopes of Big Round Top to realign the 47th Alabama. The boulders and thick woods gave his men protection and he took the opportunity to explain the task ahead. He intended to drive the enemy as ordered, but he was also concerned for the safety of his men, particularly from the battery posted above Devil's Den. Bulger instructed his men to employ the boulders for protection and at the same time use the Federal infantry as a shield against the Federal battery. At the appropriate moment he intended to turn on Smith's battery and overrun it. His plan was simple: move cautiously, get behind a boulder, carefully select a target and fire, then advance again.

Suddenly, Private Benjamin F. Russell, the regimental color bearer, stepped forward and informed his lieutenant colonel: "get someone else to carry these

Breastworks on Little Round Top—Big Round Top in the Distance—July 1863

colors." "Why?" Bulger inquired. "I can't carry them anymore," came the reply. Wasting little time with an unneeded irritant, the elderly gentleman snatched the colors from Russell's hand, faced the regiment and loudly asked, "Boys, who will carry these colors?" Private David J. Smith stepped forward and volunteered, "I'll carry them colonel." The 47th Alabama had itself a new color bearer.[75]

Bulger turned his attention to finding the Federal left. A moment later the 47th Alabama renewed its advance.

Oates Proposes a New Plan

During the brief rest period before the charge, someone from the 15th Alabama discovered a well several hundred yards to the rear. Oates knew most of the canteens were empty, and sent out two men from each company to replenish their supply. Unfortunately the regiment moved out before they returned. The detail followed the path of the charging line across Plum Run Valley and entered the woods on Big Round Top's slopes. They were searching for the 15th Alabama when they stumbled onto a detachment of Stoughton's Sharpshooters. The regiment's supply of water and 22 men fell into Federal hands.[76]

Exertion from the climb, heat exhaustion, and lack of water caused many of Oates's men to fall out. When the regiment reached the crest Oates decided to pause for a rest. Through the veil of smoke and haze, he caught a glimpse of the battle raging about Devil's Den. From the rattle of musket fire farther to the right he guessed the Federal left had been located. Oates quickly concluded the road to success lay in occupying Big Round Top. In his words, "It was higher than the other mountain and would command the entire field." He believed artillery placed on the top would wreak havoc on the Federal left.

Adjutant Terrell found Oates observing the battle unfolding below, and inquired why the regiment had halted. Oates retorted the 15th Alabama could fight better after some rest. He then learned of Hood's wound, and that Law was in command of the division. The adjutant's responsibility was to keep the line moving and as Oates recalled reminded him that "General Law's order was for me and Colonel Bulger to lose no time, but to press forward and drive the enemy before us as far as possible."

Oates was never one to hesitate when he thought the situation demanded a change, and presented his new idea. "Within half an hour," he informed Terrell, "I could convert it Round Top into a Gibraltar that I could hold against ten times the number that I had." Law's adjutant had precious little time to spare for a regimental commander with new plans of battle; besides he was merely a messenger with no authority to act on his own. Oates persisted and inquired as to where Law was at that particular time. Terrell knew only that he was somewhere to the left. The adjutant was in no mood to act on Oates's behalf or waste more time with talk of fortifying the hill. The orders were clear, which he reiterated: "Lose no time, but press forward and drive the enemy as far as possible." This time Oates obeyed and put his regiment in motion. The tired Alabamians obliqued to the left and clambered down the rugged northern slope in search of the Federals.[77]

The 47th Alabama Attacks the 20th Maine's Center

The 4th Alabama's final assault against the 83rd Pennsylvania and 20th Maine was in progress when the 47th and 15th Alabama joined the fight. Bulger arrived ahead of Oates and emerged from the woods onto the valley floor between the Round Tops. The 4th Alabama was to their left, but there is no evidence that Bulger attempted to connect with it. Turning right, the 47th began filing east. Its line was in good order and roughly parallel to the 20th Maine's right. At the order "Forward," the regiment moved out at a quick step. A hundred feet or so above, the 20th Maine waited behind a low rock ledge.

The 47th Alabama crossed the valley floor without incident and began climbing the southwest slope. Halfway up Lieutenant Thomas L. Christian, adjutant and inspector general for the brigade, rode up with an order from Law. It was simply "Charge." At that moment Bulger entertained little interest in exchanging pleasantries nor adhering to military protocol. He quickly came back with, "Tell Law I am charging to the best of my ability. Put the 15th Alabama on my right and we will drive them when we come to them."[78] Christian turned to ride off only to have his horse shot from under him. Rider and horse tumbled to the ground. Bulger later recalled the incident, saying that "it was only by a miracle that Christian escaped with his life."[79]

Bulger and his men stormed up the hill as far as the ledge protecting the Federal defenders. Chamberlain recalled the Alabamians "...burst upon us in a great fury."[80] The fight turned into hand-to-hand combat among the rocks. Muskets were used for clubs, and for a few moments it looked as though the Alabamians just might break the Federal line.[81]

His fighting blood was up and Bulger surged through the line to the front of his regiment. Jumping onto a nearby rock, he defiantly waved his sword at the Federals while urging his Alabamians to stay in the fight and charge. The show of courage reinforced the fighting spirit of his men, but he also presented an easy target. A ball tore through his left lung and lodged in the muscle of his shoulder.[82] By sheer force of willpower he stayed on his feet. He carefully returned his sword to its scabbard, then struggled down the hill some distance to cover behind a large boulder. It was only then that he eased to the ground and rested his back against a tree that jutted from the rocks.[83] For a time, at least, the menace of flying Minié balls ceased to be a problem. At the moment he could do nothing more than listen to the din of battle. Blood gushed from his mouth and nostrils while his strength slowly ebbed.[84]

The 15th Alabama Joins the Fight

The 47th engaged in its struggle with Chamberlain's right, when Oates descended to the base of the north slope of Big Round Top. His heartbeat probably jumped when he saw a Federal wagon train two hundred yards ahead. The 15th Alabama was close to the Federal rear and in position to turn the Federal left. Oates decided to go around the mountain. He detached Captain Francis K. Shaaff with Company A to capture the ordnance train and bring them to the cover of a spur of Big Round Top. However, the appearance of Federal troops east of the wagons presented a problem. Shaaff became concerned for the safety of his company and withdrew to the woods on the northeast side of Big Round Top.[85] Unfortunately for Oates and the rest of the 15th Alabama, he remained there while the fighting raged around him.

The 83rd Pennsylvania and 20th Maine saw the 15th Alabama emerge from the woods and file by the right flank. Both gave the 15th a volley.[86] From his position on the 20th Maine's extreme left Major Ellis Spear realized that the Confederate flanking maneuver would overlap the 20th Maine or at least strike the left flank. To cover the flank he believed a couple of companies on the left should be refused.[87] But, this required the line be extended and hence Chamberlain's approval. Chamberlain was farther up the hill near the regiment's center and mounted a large boulder behind the line to survey the situation for himself.[88] What he saw made his blood run cold.

The 15th Alabama was moving by the right flank at the quick step. From his position in rear of the 83rd Pennsylvania Captain Orpheus S. Woodward, commanding the regiment, also saw the danger to Chamberlain's left and sent a courier to inquire about the condition of Chamberlain's line. When the courier returned with a request for a company, Woodward declined because he, at the time, was under attack by the 4th and 47th Alabama. Instead, he suggested Chamberlain extend to his left and Woodward would fill the gap.[89]

Calling the captains together, Chamberlain quickly outlined his plan. First, he wanted the men to keep up a lively fire. At the same time each company would take side steps until the line came into a single rank. He then guided the colors with their guard to the left where a huge boulder gave some cover.[90]

While the 15th Alabama filed to the right, the 20th Maine extended the line down the hill by going into single rank on the right. Spear refused two companies on the extreme left to follow the natural contour of the lower slope. Company K lay on the left of Company F, the color company, and so that its line was parallel to the direction that the 15th Alabama would attack. When Chamberlain completed extending his line it roughly resembled a horseshoe with the color company at the apex.[91] His left wing now lay concealed behind a rocky ledge and waited for the fury of the fighting to burst upon it.

Oates was unaware of the impending danger until his line came

Col. Joshua L. Chamberlain, 20th Maine

MSA

within 40 or 50 paces of the Federal line. The men from Maine suddenly rose up and volleyed. The Alabamians halted but did not break ranks. The 20th Maine kept up the fire, and although a number of Alabamians went down, the ranks, quickly closed.[92] The 15th Alabama stood its ground, opened fire at close range, and quickly took the measure of Chamberlain's left causing it to give way.[93] Oates ordered a charge that only partially succeeded. The portion of the line that confronted the two left companies of the 15th Alabama held.[94]

William Jordan, Company B, 15th Alabama, fired only one round during the charge, preferring to make each shot count. Just as he reached the edge of the valley, Jordan squeezed off a deliberated round, then dashed behind a tree to reload. Several members of his company had crossed the valley and though Jordan was clearly visible to the Federals he ran to join them. Jordan made it to the base of Little Round Top, but three companions following in his tracks were not as lucky. Sandy McMillan and Benjamin E. Kendrick fell dead 30 feet from Jordan. R. Samuel Kendrick received a nasty wound to a foot, but managed to reach cover.[95]

As the 15th Alabama struggled toward the 20th Maine, the fire intensified. Oates recalled the line "...wavered like a man trying to walk against a strong wind." Company G took the brunt of the fire, losing three officers within a few minutes. Lieutenant Barnett Cody went down, mortally wounded. Captain Henry C. Brainard fell, and his last words were of his mother in Alabama and his desire to see her one more time. Lieutenant John Oates, a younger brother of Oates, was shot eight times during one volley.[96] Captain James H. Ellison stood a short distance from Oates and cupped his hand around his ear to hear the commands. Through the smoke and haze Oates saw the gesture and repeated the order to go forward. Ellison never heard the words. A bullet pierced his skull, killing him instantly.

Chamberlain's line held. The 15th Alabama fell back among the rocks and trees in the valley.[97]

The 47th Alabama Retires

When Colonel Bulger fell Campbell assumed command and did his best to push the regiment forward. He enjoyed some measure of success until the 4th Alabama retired after its third and last charge.[98] The departure uncovered his left. Captain Woodward immediately took advantage of the opportunity. The 83rd Pennsylvania directed a destructive volley into the left flank of the 47th Alabama. When the right companies of the 20th Maine joined in, Oates recalled the "...men were mowed down like grain before the scythe."

Captain Joseph S. Johnston Jr. received a mortal wound in the side, dying on 19 July. Though at one time charged with cowardice, Johnston proved his detractors wrong. He fell as any gallant officer should, at the head of his men, urging each to the front. Captain James Whitaker received a severe wound and Lieutenant John G. Adrian fell dead a short time after Bulger fell. His companions at the time thought Whitaker mortally wounded, but he survived and became a prisoner. He was later exchanged. In Company B, the extreme left company of the regiment, four died outright. Twelve suffered wounds of varying severity. There were three captured. Over 60 percent of the wounds were to the individual's left side. In the space of a few minutes Company B sustained almost 50 percent casualties. Though he gave up the flag, Sergeant Benjamin Russell "did his duty as soldier." He too went down with a wound.[99]

After Companies A, D and F went out on the flank as skirmishers, Company E became the center company, and very likely the color company. Fourteen of its members went down, including Lieutenants Joseph N. Hood and Andrew Ray.[100]

The men from eastern Alabama traded rounds until the Federals got the upper hand. The regiment's fighting spirit faded. In spite of Campbell's efforts to hold the line, squads drifted rearward to the woods on the southern edge of the valley.[101] From the cover of rocks and trees, men settled in to fire on the 83rd Pennsylvania and 20th Maine.

When the 47th Alabama began falling back Oates attempted to relieve the pressure on Campbell. He attempted to change front to his left in order to deliver an enfilade fire.[102] It did not work. He found the regiment alone in the attack on Chamberlain's left. The men from Maine were fighting with the benefit of cover. Oates recalled that to "...stand there and die was sheer folly; either retreat or advance became a necessity."[103] He chose the charge. Waving his sword and yelling for his men to follow, Oates rushed through the line. According to Chamberlain the 15th Alabama came "...with a shout, firing as they came."[104]

Oates mounted a rock and discharged the contents of his pistol at the opposing line. The Alabamians managed to reach a ledge and slowly pushed the defenders toward another one farther up the slope.[105] Theodore Gerrish, Company H, 20th Maine, described the scene as a "terrible medley of cries, shouts, groans, cheers, curses, bursting shells, whizzing rifle bullets and clanging steel."[106]

Frustrated with the smoke and lack of visibility, Private William R. Holloway, Company G, 15th Alabama, stepped up beside Oates and remarked, "Colonel I can't see them." His commander suggested he look under the smoke. Holloway kneeled, fired once and was preparing to reload when a bullet snuffed out his life. After laying the lifeless private on the ground, Oates picked up his musket and fired a few rounds before returning to his duties as colonel.[107]

A short distance above the combatants, Hazlett's guns blasted away at targets in the Devil's Den area. At the same time, bullets flew into the left and rear of the battery. The gunners remembered it as a very trying time. But they ignored the close quarter fighting between the men from Maine and Alabama. Lieutenant Benjamin Rittenhouse later recalled the gunners' "duty was to take care of our front, and trust to our people at other points to take care of theirs, as they are trusting us."[108]

The men from Maine now took the initiative. Five assaults would be launched against the Alabamians. Four were hurled back. Two were repelled with bayonets.[109] Oates would later say his adversaries fought like devils.[110] During one charge, Oates stood by a large boulder and steadied his men. John G. Archibald stood nearby with the regimental colors. When a Federal lunged for the flagstaff, Archibald deftly stepped aside while Sergeant Patrick "Pat" O'Connor drove his bayonet home. Chamberlain reported the fighting, which rolled backward and forward like a wave, was "...literally hand to hand...Dead and wounded were now in the front and then in the rear."[111] "At times," Chamberlain recalled, "I saw around me more of the enemy than of my own men, gaps opening, swallowing, closing again with sharp convulsive energy; squads of stalwart men who had cut their way through us, disappearing as if translated."[112] The fifth charge finally dislodged the 15th Alabama, then pushed it down the hill.[113]

Somewhere at the foot of the hill, an Alabamian twice had Chamberlain in his sights, and twice failed to fire. Years later Chamberlain received a note from the would-be sniper. The Confederate was unable to fire, claiming a strange feeling enveloped his body.[114] Apparently the individual did not learn the lessons of Second Manassas. Under similar circumstances, Isaac Feagin severely rebuked Captain Shaaff for drawing down on a major in the front of his men. Stonewall Jackson heard the rebuke and ordered Shaaff to fire, saying, "Kill the brave ones, because they lead the others."[115]

Every regiment had its share of stragglers, and there were many on this afternoon. Though most had legitimate reasons, there were a few who sought to slip away. One example was a private in the 15th Alabama. John Nelson, Company K, was an Irishman by birth and seemed to take great delight in a good fight, especially when bare knuckles were involved. However, when bullets flew in battle the desire to fight quickly disappeared. Nelson would go into line when the shooting started, then at the first opportunity nearly always managed to slip to the rear. His company commander, Captain William J. Bethune, was a stern disciplinarian. At the beginning of the charge, Bethune ordered Sergeant O'Connor to keep a close eye on Nelson, and use whatever means necessary to hold the man in line. Sure enough, somewhere on the slopes of Little Round Top Nelson slipped out of line. O'Connor grabbed Nelson and held him until a bullet snuffed out the Irishman's life. The sergeant let the lifeless form down with words: "I guess you'll stay in line now."[116] Sometime in the fight Bethune also fell, severely wounded by a shot in the face.[117]

Company B, 15th Alabama was on the regiment's extreme left, and had less cover than some of the other companies. There were eight of the company behind one of the larger boulders. Chamberlain's men saw every move, and easily fired down while the Alabamians awkwardly raised muskets to return the fire.[118]

While Oates regrouped, Chamberlain took advantage of the lull in fighting to collect wounded and gather ammunition from his fallen men. He also ordered arms collected from the wounded to replace those that were no longer serviceable. Loose stones were piled up in the more exposed areas of the defense line. Even then, the works were no more than 18 inches high and barely covered a man lying on the ground.[119]

During the lull in fighting Adjutant DeBernie B. Waddell worked his
way out to the right where he discovered the Federal flank in the air. The
situation presented an unexpected opportunity to deliver an enfilade fire. He
sought out Oates and requested 40 or
50 men for that purpose, to which his
commander consented. A few minutes
later Waddell and his men were doing
splendid work. Bullets flew into the rear
of the 83rd Pennsylvania. Captain
Woodward became concerned for his
left because the only avenue of escape
was a small space between the 83rd
Pennsylvania's line and a large rock in
his rear. He sent his adjutant to assess
the situation and as a precaution, short-
ened the line by moving the center back
10 or 12 spaces. When he had satisfied

**Capt. Orpheus S. Woodward,
Commanding 83rd Pennsylvania**

MC MOLLUS USAMHI

himself that the Pennsylvanians' line of retreat was relatively secure, Woodward
returned to the business of directing the regiment's fire.[120]

Attack on Vincent's Right

After the Confederates secured Devil's Den and while Oates engaged in his
private war with the 20th Maine, fighting spread north through Plum Run Valley.
The 44th and 48th Alabama joined the Texans led by Banc, 4th Texas and Rogers
of the 5th Texas, as Law mounted a last effort to carry Vincent's right.[121] The
Texans had barely "recovered their breath" from the last charge when orders
came to go forward. Walking over ground littered with the carnage and wreckage
from two previous assaults, Rogers led the 5th Texas in on the right of the 4th. In
a manner characteristic of the Civil War commander, Sheffield delivered a short
speech to the Alabamians.[122] Then advancing north from Devil's Den, using the
rocks between Plum Run and the western face of Little Round Top for cover,
Law's next assault on Little Round Top was directed toward the right flank of the
16th Michigan.

The Texans and Alabamians achieved some initial successes when the right
flank of the 16th Michigan gave way. Benjamin F. Partridge claimed that the
companies fell back when Colonel Welch withdrew the colors.[123] Welch laid the
blame on Lieutenant Kydd, reporting the subordinate acted with "unwarranted
assumption of authority."[124] Rice did not officially investigate the matter. Norton
and Partridge, who was at the time a captain in the 16th Michigan, later talked
about the incident.[125] Immediately after the war, Partridge wrote that Welch left
the field with the colors and remained in the rear until the following day. Norton

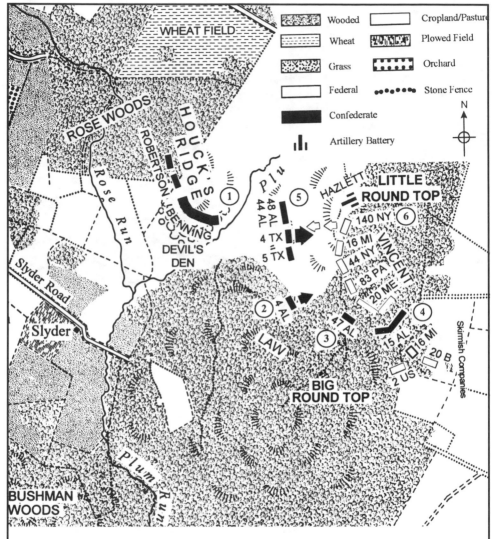

Assault on Vincent's Right
July 2, 1863

1. The Confederate attack on Devil's Den succeeds in driving the Federal defenders from the southern end of Houck's Ridge and Plum Run Valley.
2. The 4th Alabama makes its third assault against Vincent.
3. The 47th Alabama moves up on the right of the 4th Alabama and attacks Vincent's left center.
4. Oates extends Law's line to the right and attack's the 20th Maine's left flank. Chamberlain extends his line and refuses the left to meet the Confederate threat.
5. With Devil's Den secured, the 4th and 5th Texas, 44th Alabama, and 48th Alabama move north in Plum Run Valley and assault Vincent's right.
6. The 140th New York moves into line on Vincent's right and aids in repelling the attack by the Texans and Alabamians.

claimed that after the fighting ended on July 2 he saw Welch near the Bushman house with the regimental flag and 40 or 50 men. Partridge, Captain Elliot, Adjutant Jacklin, and several other officers on the following day refused to leave the field until Rice ordered Welch to return with the colors. It was only then that the Michigan volunteers, under their banner, marched away from the line they had defended with their life's blood.[126]

Regardless of the cause, the fate of Vincent's Third Brigade hung in the balance. His flank was in serious danger of being turned. Vincent thrust his sword in the air and rushed into the breech. According to Chamberlain, the Pennsylvanian believed "All was lost, unless the very gods should intervene." He was able to restore a portion of the line while exhorting the more timid to "Don't yield an inch now men or all is lost!"[127] A shot to the groin mortally wounded the young Pennsylvanian. He had been a favorite target of sharpshooters. As stretcher bearers prepared to carry him from the field Vincent remarked: "This is the fourth or fifth time they have shot at me, and they have hit me at last."[128] Vincent died July 7, 1863.[129]

Command of the brigade fell on Rice, a thirty-seven-year-old native of Worthington, Massachusetts. Educated at Yale College, he spent the first year after college in Natchez, Mississippi in charge of a seminary. Returning north after one year, Rice settled in New York City, read law, and pursued that profession until the war began. Enlisting in the 39th New York, he received a first lieutenant's commission and served as the regiment's adjutant. He later became a captain and served in that capacity when commissioned lieutenant colonel of the 44th New York.[130] Known in the ranks as "Old Crazy," Norton described him as "brave enough, but in a fight too excitable to do anything right."[131]

Once in command of the brigade, Rice exhibited none of the qualities that Norton described. Demonstrating the coolness of a veteran commander, he first turned command of the 44th New York over to the lieutenant colonel. The historian of the 83rd Pennsylvania recounted that Rice "passed at once along the line and notified the officers and men he was about to assume command of the brigade and they must hold the position to the last."[132] He then sought out each of the regimental commanders and in his words "assured them of my determination to hold the line to the last."[133] With the orderly transition accomplished Rice moved on to direct the fire of his new command.

Col. James C. Rice,
44th New York

MC MOLLUS USAMHI

Before the Confederates could exploit the advantage gained, Federal reinforcements arrived. Warren found the 140th New York, commanded by Colonel Patrick H. O'Rorke, preparing to move into line farther to the right.

O'Rorke belonged to the Third Brigade, commanded by Brigadier General Stephen H. Weed, Third Division, V Army Corps. Weed's brigade moved to support the III Corps when Warren approached Captain Joseph M. Leeper, Company E, 140th New York, and O'Rorke, who were riding in front of the 140th. Warren, riding a gray charger, addressed O'Rorke in an excited tone: "Paddy, give me a regiment," to which O'Rorke replied, "General Weed has gone to the front to select a position." Warren, determined to have this regiment for Little Round Top, said, "Is this the 140th? If so, take your command and secure the hill before the enemy reaches it, that position must not be lost." A few minutes later the 140th New York, conspicuous by its jaunty Zouave uniforms, marched in column of fours up the northeast slope.[134]

Captain Leeper thought Paddy O'Rorke a "congenial and easy going" sort of man. Before the fighting commenced on July 2, he recalled how O'Rorke and General Weed sang a chorus of the song, "Someone to Love, Someone to Cherish."[135] Porter Farley noted that West Pointers were men of little words when it came to delivering speeches, and "O'Rorke was no exception." Astride his little brown horse, wearing a soft felt hat, long white gloves, and a military cape, the young colonel gave his first and only speech to the regiment. It was, according to Farley, short and to the point. His closing words left no doubt the fate awaiting the faint of heart. "I call on the file closers to do their duty, and if a man this day leaves his company, let him die in his tracks—shoot him down like a dog."[136] A

few minutes later the 140th New York, apparently accompanied by Warren, scrambled over and around the rocks toward Little Round Top's crest. At the summit a horrific sight greeted the New Yorkers. Smoke floated over Plum Run Valley. Riderless horses milled about. "The wild cries of charging lines, the rattle of musketry, the booming of artillery, and the shrieks of the wounded were orchestral accompaniments of a scene," was the way Porter Farley described it, "—like very Hell itself."[137]

Colonel O'Rorke prepared to dress the regiment when Warren rode up and exclaimed, "No time now, Paddy, for alignment; take your men immediately into action."[138] The terrain was too rough for horses, so O'Rorke dismounted. Drawing his sword, the 1861 graduate

**Col. Patrick H. O'Rorke,
140th New York**

MC MOLLUS USAMHI

of West Point and top cadet in his class, yelled, "Face to the rear; Forward, follow me!" and rushed down the western slope.[139]

The line of the 140th New York slightly overlapped the 16th Michigan's right, but the Federal line was extended sufficiently to hold against the Confederate assault.[140] A few rods separated the opposing lines when O'Rorke turned and uttered his last words, "Here they are men. Commence firing."[141] From 40 feet away a Texan fired a fatal shot at Paddy O'Rorke. He fell from a wound in the throat. Companies A and G, 140th New York, instantly directed a volley at their colonel's assailant. Afterward 17 bullets holes were counted in the gallant Confederate's body.[142]

Hand-to-hand combat broke out in a few places. Each side fired and loaded as fast as it could for a few minutes.[143] Men toppled from the ranks. However, the 140th New York, with aide of flank fire from the 44th New York and 16th Michigan, began to get the upper hand.[144] A charge down the hill sent the Alabamians and Texans reeling back and into Plum Run Valley.[145] The Zouaves were content to take cover behind rocks while their recent foe retreated to safety.[146]

The fight for Vincent's right was over. The 44th and 48th Alabama Regiments engaged the enemy over one and one-half hours, both losing slightly over one-quarter of their complement. Sheffield led a charmed life, being struck three times by spent balls in four assaults and escaping without a scratch.[147] The 44th and 48th withdrew southward to positions on the lower slopes of Round Top.[148]

Neither Perry nor Sheffield mentioned an attack by their regiments on Little Round Top. Coles said the Texans were the only regiments that advanced up Little Round Top with the 4th Alabama. However, Major John P. Bane commanded the 4th Texas during its last charge against Vincent and reported the 44th and 48th Alabama accompanied his regiment. The apparent discrepancy in the accounts as to whether the 44th and 48th participated in the charge deserves an examination.

Neither Perry nor Sheffield was in command of their regiments when the 4th Texas made its last charge, which explains the absence of comment on their part. However, the 44th and 48th Alabama saw fighting after Perry and Sheffield relinquished command. The 48th Alabama made four charges. Sheffield only accounts for three, none against Little Round Top. It is clear from Sheffield's description that the 48th Alabama rested on a line perpendicular to Little Round Top. Sheffield moved up to command Law's Brigade after the third assault and reported that Captain Thomas Eubanks took command of the 48th Alabama and brought it to the front. Private John Anderson of Company K wrote on July 17, 1863, that the 48th Alabama "...charged on top of a mountain to the enemy's breastworks," obviously referring to Little Round Top.[149] There were no breastworks, as such, around Devil's Den, but Anderson had the charge etched in his mind when he wrote home. Anderson could only be referring to Little Round Top. Therefore, two eyewitnesses place the 48th Alabama on Little Round Top.

The most likely scenario is the 44th and 48th Alabama fought around Devil's Den until the Confederates overran and secured it. Both then participated in the last charge made by the 4th Texas. This does not discredit Coles because the 4th Alabama became separated from the Texans. Coles would not have known the 44th and 48th Alabama joined the 4th Texas.

Should We Stay or Retreat

Oates sent Sergeant Major Robert Cicero Norris to find the 4th Alabama. He found the regiment had retired and discovered Federals moving up the mountainside. Captains Park and Hill reported the presence of Federals to the rear. Each thought there were two regiments. Oates went to the rear and thought he saw at least two battle flags. Two different uniform colors were visible.[150]

Captain Ziba B. Graham of the 16th Michigan recalled that Company A and Brady's Sharpshooters remained on detached duty on the brigade's left.[151] It is reasonable to assume these companies made an appearance with Morrill's company. Morrill later wrote that a detachment of sharpshooters, under the command of a non-commissioned officer, joined his company. Oates thought a body of dismounted cavalry had moved up on his left. Some of the troops closing in on the Confederate left were probably from the 83rd Pennsylvania that pushed forward skirmishers when the 4th and 47th Alabama retired. It is probable the Federal strength on the flanks and rear of the 15th Alabama approached half a regiment. Oates described the situation: "While one man was shot in the face, his right hand or left hand comrade was shot in the side or back. Some were struck simultaneously with two or three balls from different directions."[152] Under the circumstances Oates concluded Park and Hill were correct in their assessment of the strength suddenly confronting the 15th Alabama.

Both Hill and Park suggested the time had come to fall back. Oates declined for the moment and instructed the two captains: "Return to your companies; we will sell out as dearly as possible." Hill did not reply, but Park, smiling, saluted and said: "All right, sir." Oates briefly thought that reinforcements might materialize, but then realized the men were fought out. He began to consider the merits of retreat and went so far as to advise the men to run at his signal.[153] Norris went to the company commanders and informed each the regiment would retreat on signal. Their orders were simple: "Run in the direction from whence they came and halt on the top of Big Round Top."

Sgt. Maj. Robert C. Norris, 15th Alabama

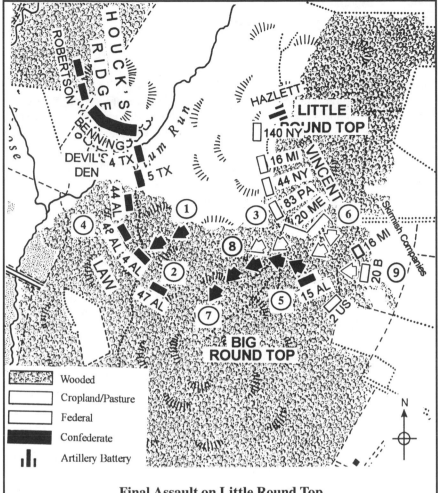

Final Assault on Little Round Top
July 2, 1863

1. After its last assault against the 83rd Pennsylvania and 20th Maine failed, the 4th Alabama has retired to the woods on Big Round Top's northern slope.
2. The 47th Alabama retired from Little Round Top when the departure of the 4th Alabama uncovered its left.
3. The 83rd Pennsylvania throws forward skirmishers after the 47th Alabama retires.
4. The 4th and 5th Texas and 44th and 48th Alabama retire to the cover of Houck's Ridge and eventually move south of Devil's Den.
5. After repeated assaults against the 20th Maine, Oates discovers that both of the 15th Alabama's flanks are threatened and considers withdrawing.
6. Chamberlain, fearing that the 20th Maine cannot withstand another assault by the 15th Alabama, orders a charge.
7 The 15th Alabama makes a disorderly retreat before the 20th Maine's charge and retraces its route up Big Round Top.
8. The 20th Maine sweeps the valley between the Round Tops and returns to its original position on Little Round Top.
9. Morrill follows the 15th Alabama up Big Round Top until stopped by fire from Oates.

Norris either did not know that Oates had sent Waddell to the right with a detachment, or in the excitement of the moment simply forgot to tell him. In either case, Waddell remained ignorant of Oates's plan.

On the Federal side, Chamberlain was just as unsure of his regiment's fighting condition. Members of his color guard were either dead or wounded, and the same was true for most of his color company.[154] Many of the regiment's muskets were unusable. Holman Melcher, Company F, 20th Maine, reported the strength was hardly more than a strong skirmish line and the 60 rounds of cartridges each man carried in the fight had been fired.[155] Men scavenged ammunition from fallen comrades. His anxiety increased when bullets flew into his rear from the opposite side of Little Round Top. These were probably from the attack on the 16th Michigan by the Texans and Alabamians. But his most immediate fear was that the Confederates may have surrounded Little Round Top. Men were firing their last round and "...getting ready to use their muskets as clubs."[156]

Chamberlain looked across the valley and believed he saw two lines, en echelon on the far side of the valley and felt sure his adversary was preparing for one final assault. Actually, Oates was probably covering his withdrawal from the field. Waddell's detachment was forward of the main line and off to the right. Therefore it's easy to see how Chamberlain concluded Oates was forming his regiment en echelon for his next assault. Chamberlain's men opened on the Alabamians with their remaining rounds, but he knew it would be impossible to fight off another assault.[157]

This scholarly man from Maine decided on a bold move. He gave the order to fix bayonets and later recalled "The word was enough. It ran like fire along the line."[158] At the word "charge" a shout rose from the center and right of the regiment. Spear recalled he had just returned from the colors to his place on the left when he heard the shout, "Forward." Though the center was advancing, those on the left hesitated because there were no orders directing the advance. His men saw the colors move out and heard the shout and acting on impulse, Spear decided "if any part must charge, all must." Without a moment's hesitation he joined in the charge. The companies on the left made a mad rush down the hillside and burst on the 15th Alabama.[159]

Oates faced a critical decision. His men were exhausted and had suffered a great number of casualties on the slopes of Little Round Top. His support had retired. Fire hit the Alabamians from the rear and right flank as well as from Chamberlain's soldiers. The young colonel believed "...the entire command was doomed to destruction."[160] When the New Englanders rose up with a shout and began to charge down the hill, Oates concluded it was time to give the signal to withdraw.

The 15th Alabama Leaves the Field

The 15th Alabama did not withdraw in an orderly fashion. At Oates's signal the men bolted and ran like "...a herd of stampeding cattle." On the right flank, Morrill yelled loud commands to deceive the Alabamians into thinking a large body of troops pursued them. Some of the sharpshooters on Oates's left made the mistake of getting in the way. For their trouble, the reward was a trip to the Confederate rear as prisoners.[161]

John Keils, Company H, ran past Oates as blood spurted from a severe throat wound which cut through his windpipe. A hissing noise came from his throat as the wounded private attempted to breathe. He made it to the rear and a field hospital where he died two days later.[162]

Waddell saw the retreat begin and correctly surmised that the regiment was withdrawing. However, Spear and his men overran Waddell and his detachment before they could move. Oates later contended that only a few of Waddell's men escaped, but the records do not support that claim. According to the casualty figures the captured came to 12 men from the four right companies. Waddell supposedly had about 50 men. Removing those captured on the water detail from the count indicates that most of Waddell's detachment escaped.[163]

Toward the center of the charge Chamberlain rushed up to Lieutenant Robert H. Wicker and demanded his surrender. Wicker calmly aimed his pistol at Chamberlain's head, fired, and missed. With that bit of business over with, the Alabamian surrendered his sword and pistol.[164]

On the left, several members of Company B declined to make a run for it, fearing the attempt meant sure death. However, William Jordan resolved he would not become a prisoner and ran for all he was worth. A familiar voice caused him to stop and there was Elisha Lane, hobbling along. It was then Jordan saw six of his companions behind the rock he had just left surrender. Lane, with Jordan's assistance, made good his escape. Of the retreat, Jordan believed it "required more courage and determination to get out of than to get in."[165]

As Waddell reached the valley floor he met Captain Shaaff and Company A emerging from the woods on the east side of the valley. Waddell took command of Shaaff's company and went to find the rest of the regiment.[166]

When Spear came abreast of the main line, Chamberlain executed a maneuver he termed "...an extended right wheel." His right company acted as a pivot while the remainder of his line "...swung like a gate upon a post." The 15th Alabama's main line retraced its approach route through the valley. Those in the rear were forced to fall back, fighting from tree to tree.[167] Some fought, some chose to run, was the way Theodore Garrish and Holman Melcher remember the situation at the foot of the hill, but a great many begged to be spared. Few of Chamberlain's men paused to invoke the formalities of a surrender, choosing instead to direct the Alabamians to the rear and pressing ahead.[168]

A squad from the 15th Alabama found Bulger's familiar form slumped against a tree and attempted to rally around the wounded officer. They were no match for the 20th Maine. Bulger, choking in his blood, remained behind. When a Federal soldier passed by, Bulger called for water. The soldier cut his canteen strap and tossed it to the old man. To his surprise Bulger found the liquid was not water. The Federal's canteen contained whiskey, which the Federal volunteered was "...a great deal better for you." His good deed done for the day, the Federal returned to fighting. He positioned himself behind a boulder and commenced firing at the retreating Alabamians.[169]

After clearing the valley, the men from Maine were so charged with excitement that Chamberlain found it difficult to bring them under control. From the ranks men declared "...they were on the road to Richmond." Chamberlain found himself in a rather exposed position and became concerned about his ability to fight off an attempt to retake the ground just lost by the Confederates. Despite his men's enthusiasm to continue the charge, he regained control over the regiment and returned it to his original position.[170]

In the meantime Morrill followed the 15th Alabama as it climbed Big Round Top. Because most of his men were scattered and some were helping the wounded, Oates could not reform until the regiment reached the crest of the mountain. The few available men joined Waddell and Company A, and fired several shots at Morrill's men. Two of his men were quickly wounded. Since Morrill was unsupported, caution seemed a wise course of action. He sought cover and waited for the Alabamians' next move.[171] It would be 9:00 p.m. before relief came.

In the charge, an officer of the 20th Maine and two of his men became separated from the main line. As they made their way around the brow of Big Round Top the trio encountered Lieutenant Joseph R. Breare, Company E, 15th Alabama, with 15 men. They surprised the rebels and demanded their surrender. With Breare and his men under guard the Federal officer began making his way toward the 20th Maine's last known position. Breare quickly surmised the Federal force was only three strong and that he surrendered too easily. Before the group entered the Federal lines he confirmed his suspicion with the enemy officer. In Breare's mind the Federal's exploit demanded a token of recognition. He retrieved a silver cup from his haversack and presented it to his captor.[172]

Somewhere on the crest of Big Round Top, Oates fainted from exhaustion. He became the fourth regimental commander of Law's Brigade to fall out. Command of the 15th Alabama was turned over to Captain Blanton Hill, while a stretcher was found for Oates. Four hours after it began its charge, Hill led the 15th Alabama into position along the southwestern base of Big Round Top. Jordan and John W. Hughes met Samuel J. Ming, and a litter bearer of Company B, and received their first water since early morning.[173]

Oates remained convinced that had Shaaff returned from his mission and joined the 15th Alabama, he could have turned the Federal left—but the premise is doubtful. Even with Shaaff's company of 28 men, the 22 men lost of the abortive water detail and the addition of the estimated 100 men who fell out from exhaustion, it is unlikely that Oates could have accomplished the feat. Had Oates managed to get in Chamberlain's rear, Federal reinforcements would probably have driven them off Little Round Top. Both regiments were almost evenly matched. The 20th Maine went into line with 358 rifles. When Oates engaged Chamberlain his strength was about 380. Chamberlain enjoyed the advantage of fighting behind rocks. Even with that advantage, the 15th Alabama inflicted about as many casualties as it sustained. Chamberlain suffered 136 killed and wounded, while inflicting 178 casualties on the 15th Alabama.[174] The 47th Alabama caused some of Chamberlain's casualties, but it is impossible to know the number.

It is with justified pride that Oates later wrote of the fighting prowess shown by the Alabamians that afternoon in July 1863. They were terribly fatigued when the assault began and worse still, they were forced to fight without water. When the 15th fell back the last time, its men were exhausted. In the final analysis, the Federal left was secure.

Chapter 7

Night—July 2, 1863

Night Finally Ends the Fighting

As daylight turned to dusk Hood's Division settled down behind boulders, logs, or trees to exchange fire with Vincent's and Weed's reinforced line.[1] Anyone exposing himself for too long became a target. Opposing Federals enjoyed the advantage of looking down on the opposing line and all too often an unfortunate Confederate became an easy mark.

John Cussons ventured out to the forward positions and seemed oblivious to the fire as he moved from boulder to boulder. A private from the 4th Texas observed the Englishman's calm demeanor and marveled at his bravery. When he reached the Texan's position Cussons advised those around him to aim well. A shower of Minié balls suddenly rained down on the position. Men made a headlong leap for cover and immediately realized that the balls were directed at Cussons. Several angrily yelled for the scout to move on.[2] As on other battlefields, Cussons led a charmed life and escaped unharmed. A private from the 5th Texas recalled that he only saw two men standing in the open that late afternoon. One was the major of the 5th Texas who stood on top of a boulder delivering a speech to anyone who would listen. Cussons was the other.[3]

Sometimes called "Law's Wild Man" or "Hood's Indian," the twenty-six-year-old Englishman from Horncastle

Capt. John Cussons, Aide-de-Camp, Law's Alabama Brigade

CV, v5, n9, Sept. 1897

had emigrated to the United States as a youth of 18. Cussons roamed the west, lived with the Sioux Indians, and hunted buffalo four years before becoming editor and half owner of the Selma *Reporter*.[4] A big man with long hair worn in the style later popularized by Buffalo Bill Cody, he possessed a disregard for danger. Before joining Law's staff as captain and aide-de-camp, he served as chief of scouts in Whiting's division in 1862. After the war Law wrote that Cussons was an "experienced frontiersman whose skill and nerve were equal to any emergency." He believed the Englishman to be "one of the most daring and successful scouts in our army." In fact, his exploits as a scout became legend among the Alabama troops.[5]

Occasionally men from Vincent's brigade—now led by Colonel Rice—brought in wounded Confederates. Joseph Nellis, 83rd Pennsylvania, went out twice before becoming too fatigued to go out alone. One or two men volunteered to accompany him, but quickly retreated when shots whizzed their way. Nellis moved only to be shot dead in the act of assisting a wounded Confederate to his feet. Both were found the next day lying side by side.[6]

Night brought a merciful end to the slaughter of the late afternoon. Hood's Division held Devil's Den, the southern end of Houck's Ridge, and the northwestern slopes of Big Round Top. With few exceptions, Law elected to leave the regiments in the positions held when the day came to a close. By Lieutenant Colonel Scruggs's judgment the 4th Alabama, still under the command of Major Coleman, spent the night about 200 yards from the Federal line.[7] Oates and the 15th Alabama would have been on Coleman's right. After the firing died down Sheffield deployed the 47th Alabama as a skirmish line on his right.[8] Companies A and H of the 48th Alabama rejoined the brigade.

**1st Lt. Alvin O. Dixon,
Co. A, 48th Alabama**

ADAH

Alvin O. Dixon of Company A recalled the companies passed around Big Round Top and drove in some pickets, but failed to identify landmarks or mention specific encounters with Federal units.[9] Two eyewitnesses place Confederates on the eastern side of Big Round Top near the Jacob Weikart house.[10] From the descriptions given the approximate time would be late in the afternoon and one of the eyewitnesses, Tillie Pierce, described an encounter with the Pennsylvania Reserves.[11] The only possibilities for the Confederates are the two companies of the 48th Alabama, Captain Lindsay's three companies from the 47th Alabama, or Captain Shaaff's company from the 15th Alabama. Lindsay indicated he remained south of Big Round Top. Oates maintained that Shaaff did not venture out of the woods covering Big Round Top. Therefore the Confederates near the Jacob Weikart farm dwellings were probably skirmishers from the 48th Alabama. Colonel Joseph W. Fisher's brigade of Pennsylvania Reserves was on the east side of Little Round Top toward the close of the fighting for that eminence and moved to the west side. Tillie probably saw a regiment of the Reserves in action. After exchanging a few shots with the Pennsylvanians, the Alabamians disappeared into the woods on Big Round Top's eastern slopes.[12] As Dixon later wrote "...we had nothing to do but hold our position which we did till night. We then rejoined the regiment about half way up the mountain."[13]

A bright moon bathed the bloody battlefield, and immediately after darkness fell, Lieutenant Colonel Work detailed Companies E and I of the 1st Texas to run Smith's three captured 10-pounder Parrotts to the rear. He knew where three other pieces were, but because they were between the lines, the guns were inaccessible. Armed with the knowledge that the guns were also denied the Federals, Work was content to let the artillery remain in view of both sides.[14]

Collecting Arms and the Wounded

Darkness began settling over the field by 8:00 p.m. and Colonel Rice ordered detachments from the 44th New York and 83rd Pennsylvania forward to "...secure all fruits of the hard earned victory."[15] The scene on Little Round Top's lower slopes was appalling. The dead and wounded lay about in great numbers, while the wounded called for water.[16] A line of dead and wounded marked the location where Vincent's first volley ripped into the Alabama and Texas line. It proved difficult to cross the area without stepping on a lifeless or wounded body.

As the Federals moved over the field a sergeant from the 44th New York discovered a severely wounded Confederate who begged to have the strap attached to his cartridge box cut because it rested on his wound. After responding to the man's request the sergeant moved on and found another man asking not to be stepped on.[17] Among the wounded Alabamians were Colonel Bulger and John Mosely.

Bulger lay motionless and waited for either death or assistance. His wound looked fatal, and his men certainly thought so. Campbell reported Bulger's death.[18] The elderly Alabamian drifted in and out of consciousness and eventually pulled his hat over his face. A private from the 44th New York walked by and noticed Bulger's motionless form propped against the tree. He too thought Bulger dead and on inspection discovered the lieutenant colonel's sword and belt, both prized trophies. So the Federal bent down over the motionless form and proceeded to remove the dead officer's hat, sword, and belt. Bulger suddenly revived and reacted by slapping the offending hand away. A surprised Federal jumped back, raised his musket, and demanded the Confederate surrender.

The old gentleman might have been seriously wounded, but he still managed to retain a strict sense of military protocol. An interesting exchange followed, going something like this:

Bulger: "My good fellow it seems strange to me that a U.S. soldier doesn't know he has no right to disarm an officer. You should direct me to a person as near as possible to my rank."

The Federal private responded: "But you are unable to go."

Bulger quickly retorted: "Then you should find an officer."

Bulger made a convincing argument. A rather amused private trudged off to find an officer suitable to take the old gentleman's surrender. In the meantime Bulger contemplated escape. At the moment it was unlikely that he could walk, let alone run. The desire was there but his body proved too weak to respond; he waited for the inevitable.[19]

A short time later the private returned with an officer who introduced himself as Colonel Rice of the 44th New York. After an exchange of pleasantries Rice informed Bulger that his duty as an officer of the U.S. Army required him to demand the Confederate's arms. The old gentleman's sense of military protocol had been satisfied. Sword and pistol were dutifully handed over. Bulger remarked that he "...had a short loan of the sword, which had been taken from the lieutenant colonel of the 22nd Maine a short time ago and presented me yesterday."[20]

Rice directed a private to find a litter. None were available. The New Yorker then caused the private to secure a strong blanket and three men. With Rice leading the way Bulger was carried to a makeshift field hospital somewhere in the rear.[21] Rice also made sure a doctor examined his captive's wound and then led the litter bearers to a barn where a bed of hay was prepared. A man from the 83rd Pennsylvania remembered Bulger as courteous and pleasant in manners. At midnight the elderly officer lay shivering from the chill in the night air.[22] Rice returned the next morning with Dr. Augustus M. Clark of New York. Though a surgeon in the Regular U.S. Army Clark was acting surgeon in chief, First Division, V Army Corps at Gettysburg.[23] At Rice's instruction, Bulger received special attention from the Federal physician until sent on to a Federal hospital. After the war Bulger remained convinced that the compassion shown by Rice saved his life.[24]

In later years Oates described Bulger's capture in his history of the 15th Alabama. However, Oates and Chamberlain, at the time, were embroiled in a heated debate over how far Oates had advanced up Little Round Top. Chamberlain immediately took issue with Oates's account. In 1903 Chamberlain wrote Colonel John P. Nicholson, Gettysburg Military Park Commissioner, that Bulger had surrendered his sword to him and that he, Chamberlain, ordered Bulger sent to a Federal hospital.[25] Chamberlain's report of the battle, dated July 6, 1863, does mention that two field officers and several line officers were sent to the rear.[26] When Rice prepared the brigade report of the battle, dated July 31, 1863, he obviously utilized information from his regimental commanders and identified the two field officers as colonels and the line officers as 15 commissioned officers. He did not identify either colonel by name.[27] Oliver W. Norton, who was on Vincent's staff, said the incidents of the fight were much discussed around brigade headquarters. He claimed that if the capture had been as Oates described in his history it would have been the subject of conversations and he thus would have heard about it. Norton further stated that if Chamberlain had not taken Bulger's surrender, Rice would have required Chamberlain correct his report. Norton, therefore, accepted Chamberlain's version.[28] But, since Chamberlain did not mention Bulger by name there would have been no reason for Rice to correct Chamberlain's report. It is possible that Chamberlain saw Bulger and ordered him taken to the rear. But, in the excitement of the charge which carried well past the fallen Bulger, it does not appear that Chamberlain stopped to formally accept the wounded lieutenant colonel's surrender. Bulger's description corresponds to the events described by the Federal participants and identifies his captors as being from the 44th New York. The more probable explanation is that Bulger surrendered his sword to Rice.

John Mosely was another hapless Confederate. He and his captors knew his wound to be fatal. Somewhere in the Federal rear the dying boy requested a note be sent home to his mother in Alabama. The next day a short letter found its way through the lines. It read:

Battlefield G'burg Penn
July 4, 1863

Dear Mother:
I am a prisoner of war and mortally wounded. I can live but a few hours more, at best; was shot within 50 yards of the enemy's line. They have been exceedingly kind to me. I have no doubt of the final result of the battle and hope I may live long enough to hear the shouts of victory yet before I die. I am very weak. Do not morn my loss, I had hoped to have been spared, but a righteous God had ordered it otherwise and I feel prepared to trust my case in his hands. Farewell to you all. Pray that God may receive my soul.

Your Unfortunate Son
John[29]

Occupying Big Round Top

On the Federal side men of the 20th Maine were exhausted. Many had fallen asleep when the regiment returned to its position. However, Colonel Rice worried about Big Round Top and because of the importance of the hill feared Oates and the 15th Alabama might renew an attack from that direction. When asked if his men could occupy the hill on his front, Chamberlain readily assented. The 20th Maine, barely 200 strong, made its way up the northern slopes of Big Round Top about 9:00 p.m. In his report to General Barnes, the scholarly colonel described his advance onto Big Round Top: "Not wishing to disclose my numbers and in order to avoid, if possible, bringing on an engagement in which we should certainly have been overpowered I went silently with only the bayonet."[30] Here and there squads of Law's men contested the advance, but there was little resistance and Chamberlain soon occupied the crest of Big Round Top.

Chamberlain immediately set out to establish a line. As many as possible positioned themselves behind boulders. A detail retraced its steps down the mountain for ammunition. Two companies pushed forward to reconnoiter the ground in front.[31] A courier scrambled back to report the enemy in force in Plum Run Valley. The distance he estimated at 200–300 yards. As a precaution Chamberlain decided to leave the two companies forward with orders to watch the Confederates while the main line maintained its position near the crest.[32] Afterwards pickets were sent forward with instructions to report every half hour.

A Confederate Reconnaissance Turns Sour

Sometime after Chamberlain completed his dispositions Captains Thomas Christian and Jeremiah Edwards moved onto Big Round Top with a squad of 24 men which they intended to post as pickets. Unfortunately the group stumbled into the 20th Maine picket line. All were captured.[33] They proved talkative, informing their new hosts that Hood's Division was massed in Plum Run Valley.[34]

Eleven of the men were from Captain Edwards's Company F, 48th Alabama. Accompanying him were Second Lieutenant John B. Eubanks, a corporal named James Smith, and nine privates. The remainder were privates from the 4th Alabama.[35] James Smith was sent to Fort Delaware, dying there on December 8, 1863. Private Benjamin H. Baker, Company F, 4th Alabama, remained a prisoner until October 1864 when he decided the cause he had volunteered to defend had been lost. He took the Oath of Allegiance and joined the U.S. Army.[36]

Lieutenant John Eubanks was a thirty-two-year-old farmer from Blountsville, Alabama, when he entered the service in 1862. He spent much of his time in prison thinking about his plight and contemplating alternatives to get out. Escape proved impractical, so he eventually decided amnesty offered the most viable avenue to freedom. In his petition, Eubanks stated he had always been a strong Union man and only joined the Confederate army because he lived too far from the Federal lines to escape. He volunteered to join the Federal army if necessary and closed by lamenting he had not attempted an escape from the Confederate army because of the great danger of being recaptured. The Federal authorities did not believe him. Maybe it was because Eubanks had been elected by his company to the office of junior second lieutenant and then promoted to second lieutenant. It could easily be assumed his peers would not elect a Union sympathizer to lead them in battle. In actuality, Eubanks resided in a region with considerable Union sympathy. Had he chosen to seek sanctuary he would have been relatively safe a few miles west of his home. In any event Eubanks spent the remainder of the war a Federal prisoner. He finally took the Oath of Amnesty on May 12, 1865.[37]

Reinforcements Arrive on Round Top

Later in the night a regiment from Colonel Joseph W. Fisher's Third Brigade, Third Division, V Army Corps started up the mountain to join Chamberlain. Men lost their way in the darkness. Numerous boulders hindered progress. The line almost immediately became broken and officers became separated from their companies. Before long any semblance of order disappeared.[38] A brisk fire erupted from the Confederate line, throwing the newcomers into confusion. Fisher disappeared into the night. One Pennsylvania infantryman thought the retrograde movement resulted from a misunderstanding of orders.[39] A member of Company C, 12th Pennsylvania Reserves recorded in his diary that when they encountered the enemy, someone discharged a rifle and the regiment fell back down the hill.[40] The historian of the 12th Pennsylvania Reserves attributed it to the officers and men deciding "to return to the starting position."[41]

As the night wore on Chamberlain began feeling insecure in his isolated position. A courier was sent, found Rice's headquarters, and requested reinforcements. The 83rd Pennsylvania was promptly dispatched. The Pennsylvanians went into position on the 20th Maine's right about midnight.[42] Satisfied that he had taken every precaution to secure the line from surprise assault, Chamberlain permitted the men to sleep on their arms.[43]

Shortly thereafter, Fisher brought the 5th and 12th Pennsylvania Reserves up on Chamberlain's left and rear and went into position near the summit. Colonel Martin D. Hardin's 12th Pennsylvania Reserves became the Federal extreme right while the 5th Pennsylvania Reserves under the command of Lieutenant Colonel George Dare connected on the right. Skirmishers from the 5th and 12th were thrown forward on a line with the 20th Maine. The 9th and 10th Pennsylvania Reserves were left in the valley between the Round Tops.[44] Convinced that Hood's men were not a threat from the south, Chamberlain did not bother to connect with the Pennsylvanians.[45] Because he commanded a brigade, Fisher insisted he was senior and thus exercised command over Chamberlain, which Chamberlain did not accept, and later disputed. In a letter dated January 25, 1884, he wrote: "I had nothing to do with Fisher nor he with me.[46] Thus was born another dispute that was never resolved.

The Confederates Collect Their Wounded

The wounded from Hood's Division were carried to a makeshift hospital on the John E. Planck farm. Litter bearers brought in Captains William W. Leftwich, Company F, 4th Alabama. Wounded from Law's Brigade totaled 14 officers and 287 privates and non-commissioned officers. They were sorted out as they came in. Surgeons tried to look after the more seriously wounded first, but the number was so large many were forced to wait hours or days before receiving medical attention. Sergeant Ward lay in agony until well after midnight when a surgeon administered a sleep-inducing drug. He woke to the thunder of the cannonading which preceded "Pickett's Charge." Hunger caused him to reach for his haversack, only to find that it and the rations prepared at New Guilford were gone. Some rascal, he sadly concluded, thought he was dead or would die, and walked away with his food.[47]

Several men from Company H, 15th Alabama went out in search of John Oates and Lieutenant Cody. They managed to pass through the Federal line on Big Round Top, but were discovered near Little Round Top and driven back before the wounded could be located. Unfortunately very few wounded were retrieved. Most of the severely injured lay where they fell. One picket from the 44th

New York spent his time on duty attending to them, giving water, cutting off shoes and otherwise helping the wounded in whatever way he could.[48]

The Horrible Cries of the Wounded

The historian of the 83rd Pennsylvania wrote that Vincent's men brought in as many of the wounded as they could. Because the Confederates fired at anything that moved a number of the wounded were left where they fell. In the historian's words: "...many had received severe and painful wounds, and their ceaseless cries for help, breaking upon the stillness of the night, sent a thrill to the heart of many a brave soldier of the 83rd Pennsylvania."[49]

Private John Anderson, 48th Alabama, vividly recalled for his wife, "...it was an awful scene to see and hear the shrieks and groanings of the poor dying soldiers on my right and on my left and before and behind and all around me."[50] Private A. C. Sims, Company F, 1st Texas, stood for two hours on picket duty and listened to the groans of the wounded. "Water, give me water," was the most frequent plea. A man just in front of Sims begged, "Oh, pardner, bring me a drink of water, I'll assure you no one will hurt you. My leg is shot off or I would come to you. I'll give you a dollar for a drink of water. I'll give you all the money I have for a drink of water." Sims stared into the darkness and made no reply. He had no water and besides he felt duty bound to remain at his post.[51] A wounded soldier from the 4th Alabama called for a friend named John. Others prayed and groaned in agony. Some begged for death.[52]

Men of Hazlett's battery lay by the guns and listened to cries of the wounded drifting up from the valley. The gunners, Thomas Scott recalled, clearly heard "some praying, some were swearing, and some were preaching and exhorting the men to forgive their enemies."[53] Though the moon lit the night, Lieutenant Rittenhouse envisioned spirits of those so recently departed souls "flitting from Round Top to Devil's Den and back all night."[54] The 16th Michigan completed the task of retrieving its wounded about midnight. Weary and exhausted survivors of the afternoon's fighting dropped to the ground and slept.[55]

Law Realigns the Division

It was about 2:00 a.m., on July 3, when Law ordered Colonel Work to

**Pvt. John M. Anderson,
Co. K, 48th Alabama**

William Simpson, Holly Pond, Alabama

withdraw the 1st Texas and 3rd Arkansas from the crest of Houck's Ridge. Speaking of the eerie nature of the moonlit night, Work later described his feelings as they inched along, "This weird, rocky glen destitute of vegetation, appeared as the habitation of witches, hobgoblins, ghosts and devils to the Texans passing through it in the night to join the 4th and 5th Texas, one quarter of a mile distant."[56]

After establishing a new line about halfway up the western face of the mountain, the Texans and Alabamians hastily constructed a crude breastworks. The works, made from loose stones stacked between boulders, stretched from the north end of Big Round Top to near its southern base. Major Bane, 4th Texas, reported the fortifications along his front were two feet high.[57] Based on the battlefield map prepared under the direction of Brevet Major General Gouverneur Warren after the war, there were two lines of Federal breastworks at the summit of Big Round Top. Law's line ran roughly parallel to the Federal works. About 500 feet separated the opposing lines on the southern end of Big Round Top. The distance between them increased to about 1,000 feet at the north end.[58]

The opposing lines were so close that each side could hear the other. Law's Alabamians listened to the distinctive sounds of rocks dropping into place as the Federals constructed fortifications. On the crest of Big Round Top men listened to Confederate officers giving commands.[59] Exhausted soldiers on sides rested as best they could. A few managed to sleep. All waited for the dawn.[60]

Chapter 8

Morning—July 3, 1863

Dawn July 3—Confederate Right

As dawn broke over the battlefield Law directed his brigade commanders to throw forward scouting parties, reconnoiter the Federal line, and determine its strength. In the twilight, breastworks higher up the mountain materialized. Federals on the division's front had been just as active as the Confederates. On examination the scouts found the Federal presence in strength and behind strong defensive positions.[1]

John Cussons ventured forth at first light. This was not unusual for Law's scout and trusted aide, for he had often been seen on similar missions on other battlefields. He walked into the Federal lines, as in times past. But this time, the Englishman's luck ran out and he was captured. Later in the day, Cussons sat on the crest of Big Round Top, watching the splendor of "Pickett's Charge."[2]

Though he was not in command of the brigade, "Aunt Pollie" Robertson directed Captain F. L. Rice, his assistant adjutant general, to conduct a reconnaissance along the Texans' front. Rice departed with instructions to report back as soon as possible. The Texan disappeared into the woods and was not heard from again.[3]

Line of Hood's Division—Big Round Top

Law's line followed the crest of Houck's Ridge, running in a southerly direction. It curved sharply east to cross Devil's Den, then snaked its way well up the northwestern slope of Big Round Top, turned south and terminated near the southern base of Big Round Top. Sheffield commanded the Alabama brigade, which occupied the division's right. Oates and the 15th Alabama were on the extreme right. Campbell with the 47th Alabama was in line on Oates's left. Scruggs had sufficiently recovered from the exhaustion suffered the previous afternoon to resume command of the 4th Alabama.[4] He was on Campbell's left. The 48th Alabama, commanded by Captain Eubanks, was next in line. Perry's 44th Alabama lay on the extreme left.

Robertson's Texans were next in line, connecting with Sheffield's left. Benning, and Anderson lay on the extreme left of the division.[5] Robertson's left rested on the north point of Big Round Top next to the "gorge," as Hood's men called it. Benning lay along the southern end of Houck's Ridge. A gap between Benning and Robertson, caused by the gorge, was filled with skirmishers from both brigades. Anderson connected with McLaws's right.[6] The 7th Georgia came in from skirmish line duty shortly after dawn and rejoined Anderson's Brigade.[7]

Henry Lindsay and his battalion Companies A, D, and F, 47th Alabama, spent the night south of the Bushman Woods. When Law began re-arranging his lines in the early morning hours he chose to leave Lindsay in that vicinity.

1st Lt. Nathan C. Kimball,
Co. D, 47th Alabama

Louise Holmes, Woodland, Ga.

From the scanty information available one company probably picketed the valley separating the southern base of Big Round Top from Bushman Hill. This was likely Company D, under the command of First Lieutenant Nathan C. Kimball, a twenty-four-year-old native Alabamian and farmer from Desoto. Companies A and F, also commanded by lieutenants, probably picketed the area between the J. Meyers house on the southwestern side of Bushman Woods and the Emmitsburg Road.[8] Company F was probably near the Meyers house and Company A east of the road. Captain John Ham commanded Company A.[9] A native of Georgia, age 25, Ham resided near Dadeville, Alabama before the war where his occupation was farming.[10] Twenty-five-year-old Third Lieutenant (also called Brevet Second Lieutenant) Elisha Mayo of New Site, Alabama led Company F. He was the only commissioned officer present in the company.[11]

Sharpshooters

At first light opposing sharpshooters began firing at targets of opportunities. About 6:00 a.m. two companies of Berdan's crack riflemen appeared on the crest of Little Round Top in the rear of Battery D, 5th U.S. Artillery. In response to "Boys, do the Reb sharpshooters trouble you this morning?" came the reply that one of the cannoneers was already a victim. Eager to ply their deadly trade marksmen moved forward and began deploying. After counting down, even numbered sharpshooters dropped to their knees and crawled through the guns to the brow of Little Round Top and found shelter behind the rocks. Those drawing odd numbers then did the same, except when they reached the brow of the hill each worked his way down the west side and south toward Big Round Top. That was the last Battery D saw of the marksmen. Only an occasional crack from their weapons gave away their hiding place among the rocks and trees.[12]

Firing played over the lines all day. Law's Alabamians for the most part were content to stay concealed. Exposure often meant death or a painful wound. Among the officers were Lieutenants Henry D. Simmons, Company B, 47th Alabama, and John H. Sheppard, Company B, 48th Alabama. Simmons fell victim early in the morning, and it is presumed Sheppard did also.[13] Private John Young, Company I, 4th Alabama, became a victim on a scouting detail when he paused to rest near a boulder. Young only partially concealed himself and a ball struck his right hand, severing three fingers. This could have posed a major problem because his trade of printer required the ability to set type. He was relieved to discover that his thumb and forefinger remained intact. A little while later he returned to the company and happily remarked to comrades that when the war ended he would be able to set type as well as ever.[14]

Skirmishers from Law's Brigade took their own measure of the Pennsylvanians. A private from Company A of the 12th Pennsylvania Reserves was shot in the head and expired instantly. Several others from the 5th and 12th Reserves also became victims.[15]

Longstreet's Headquarters

At First Corps headquarters Longstreet, the recent recipient of a "rag-tag" band of invalids and wagon drivers from the cavalry, decided to send the new arrivals to serve as pickets for Law's batteries on the extreme right. They were led by John Logan Black, colonel of the 1st South Carolina Cavalry. A native of York, South Carolina, Black was 33 years of age and before the war a resident of Ridgeway, South Carolina. He had attended West Point from 1850–1853. While there during the superintendency of Robert E. Lee he was roommate of the future renowned international artist, James A. Whistler. Several of Black's books contained sketches by the young artist. Enlisting in the Confederate service in October 1861, Black was elected lieutenant colonel of the 1st South Carolina Cavalry and promoted colonel of the regiment in July 1862.[16] It was said of him that his views on prohibition were so adamant he refused a portion of whiskey when severely wounded by saying, "A drink of cold water, please, Doctor."[17]

Col. John L. Black,
1st South Carolina Cavalry

CV, v35, n6, June 1927

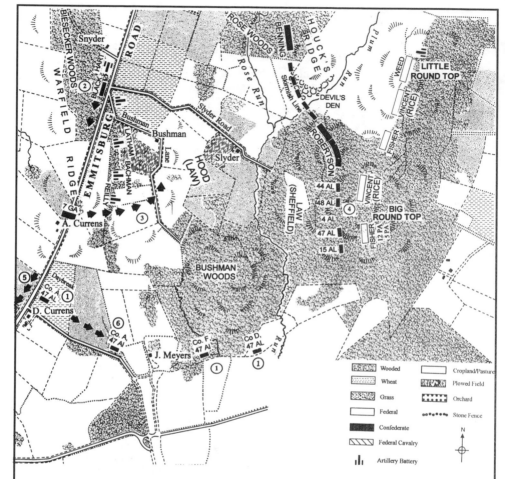

Situation on the Extreme Confederate Right
Early Morning—July 3, 1863

1. At daybreak Companies A, F, and D of the 47th Alabama are deployed along a skirmish line between Plum Run and the D. Currens house.
2. Colonel John Black's command of dismounted cavalry, accompanied by Hart's South Carolina battery, moves south on the Emmitsburg Road shortly after sunrise.
3. The 7th Georgia has withdrawn from its position near the A. Currens house and is moving to join Anderson's Brigade.
4. Law's Brigade is deployed on the western slope of Big Round Top. Its skirmishers exchange fire with the 5th and 12th Pennsylvania.
5. Black will deploy south of the D. Currens house. Members of his command will be posted as sharpshooters in the second story of the Currens house.
6. Company A of the 47th Alabama will move to the left after Black arrives and occupy a position near the Meyers house.

When he fought in the Battle of Gettysburg, Black was still recovering from a nasty head wound inflicted during the cavalry engagement at Upperville on June 21. Unable to accompany his regiment on the march into Pennsylvania, the South Carolinian followed as soon as he was able to ride. Black found several detachments of cavalry near Williamsport. One was a company of his own regiment, one came from the 2nd South Carolina, and the last was a small band of 1st North Carolina Cavalry commanded by Lieutenant Robert H. Maxwell.[18] The cavalryman pushed on toward Chambersburg with a force that now numbered about 100 men.

Black reported to General Lee and received orders from the army's commander to collect casual cavalry from the countryside. Lee then ordered him to Fairfield and finally to Gettysburg. A battery of horse artillery, the Washington Artillery of South Carolina, under the command of Captain James F. Hart, was also placed under Black.[19] By the time it reached Gettysburg the command numbered about 200.

The physical condition of Black's command varied. Some he considered good men. However, many were lame and not fit for hard marching nor fighting. Some he called "wagon rats." Discipline was not the best, yet Black said he was able to keep them in tolerable order. His true feelings were expressed when Black later recounted his fervent wish at the time was that he and his command were each back at their own regiments.[20]

Arriving at Lee's headquarters, Black found Longstreet and A. P. Hill in conference with the commander of the army. To the South Carolinian, Lee looked the most perfect specimen of manhood found in the universe. He had a slightly different opinion of Lee's two companions. In Black's words: "Longstreet was fat and full. A. P. Hill was rather slender." He said nothing of their military bearing. As the conference ended, Black approached the trio and saluted, which Lee returned and then warmly grasped the colonel's hand. Turning to Longstreet, the commanding general, after introducing him, informed his "Old Warhorse" that Black was a cadet under Lee at West Point. Noting that Black had a small command of cavalry and a battery, Lee assigned the Carolinian to the First Corps.[21]

Black still felt the effects of his wounds and slept soundly the night of July 2. Ordered to report to Longstreet at dawn, the South Carolinian found the First Corps commander east of the Emmitsburg Road. The pair, with an aide accompanying, rode slowly toward the Confederate right. Colonel Moxley Sorrel soon joined the group and after a brief discussion accompanied Black to the extreme right to locate a position. At the same time Black learned he would be placed under Law's command.

Sorrel was obviously concerned about the strength of Black's "rag-tag" band and its ability to ward off a serious attack. Before departing he made sure that Black understood that if attacked and overpowered he would fall back on the Confederate flank. Black received additional instructions to send a courier to Law's headquarters with news of the attack. However, Sorrel cautioned the South Carolinian to hold his ground as long as possible, and then fall back in good order.[22]

Law Places His Artillery

As the morning wore on Porter Alexander prepared for the bombardment that would be a prelude to the Confederate charge on the Federal center. Batteries were pulled from the flanks and placed in position. Latham's and Captain Hugh R. Garden's batteries were transferred from Law's to Alexander's command. Law still retained 10 guns under Reilly and Bachman.[23] Reilly mustered six pieces and Bachman four. Hart brought two guns onto the field which brought Law's complement of artillery pieces to 12.[24]

During the early morning hours sporadic cannonading erupted between opposing batteries. On Little Round Top Hazlett's battery, now commanded by Lieutenant Rittenhouse, on at least one occasion dueled Law's batteries. Most of the Confederate shells flew over Law's line and crashed in enemy territory. However, as smoke began filling the valley and obscuring targets, rounds began falling on the lower western slope of Big Round Top. When two men from Company F of the 1st Texas were hit, Work sent a courier to Reilly and Bachman with an urgent request to raise the elevation of their guns.[25]

About mid-morning Longstreet visited the right and instructed Law to ready his men to renew the attack. Law thought the idea nothing short of madness.[26] He considered a defensive posture the division's only viable alternative. Federal infantry held the rugged high ground and their breastworks afforded good protection against an assault. Considering his own substantial losses the previous afternoon, Law believed the opposing Federal forces were vastly superior to his own. Though it had not yet materialized, he was also concerned about the threat of cavalry.

It is not known when Law became aware he had inherited fresh troops or discovered their true fighting condition. Perhaps Sorrel brought that news after his dispositions. It is reasonable to expect Law would have conducted his own reconnaissance of the extreme right and may have encountered the ad hoc cavalry force then. However, it is not evident from events later in the day that he met Black. Law obviously preferred his own cavalry to counter Federal horse should it appear. The Carolina contingent should have fulfilled that need. Unfortunately the command mustered only about 200 mounted men. In Law's words, they were "the 'ragtag and bobtail' of the hospital and wagon trains, which proved a nuisance rather than a benefit." Law would have to rely on his own infantry to defend the Confederate right flank.[27]

Federal Line—Big Round Top

On top of the mountain Chamberlain and Fisher maintained two lines. Fisher reported, "In the morning I discovered that the hill was of immense importance to us, inasmuch as that if we had not taken it the enemy most undoubtedly would have done so, and in that event our left would have suffered very much, if, indeed, it could have held its position at all."[28] After examining the line Fisher concluded the troops were not adequately posted to defend against an attack. Two more regiments from the Third Brigade were brought up to join the 5th and 12th Pennsylvania Reserves. The line was then extended to cover the valley between the mountains. To add a measure of protection in the event of an attack, Fisher also ordered a stone wall constructed across the valley and up Big Round Top[29]

Shortly before noon General Barnes told Colonel Rice that William S. Tilton would relieve Rice's command with his First Brigade.[30] The saviors of Little Round Top were moving north toward the Federal left center. They would spend the afternoon in the second line.[31]

Law Relocates His Headquarters

The exact time cannot be determined, but Law located his headquarters near Reilly's batteries after mid-morning. The pieces were carefully positioned to fire on the Federal left center when Alexander's bombardment began, or if need be, direct fire south should a threat materialize on the right flank. In the first of his defensive moves of the day, Law brought a regiment from Anderson's brigade to the Emmitsburg Road. Captain George Hillyer came with the 9th Georgia, which Law placed near the Alexander Currens house, a stone frame structure west of the Emmitsburg Road.[32]

Hart's Washington Artillery and its supports were stationed south of the D. Currens residence, a two-story stone structure, on the southwestern slope of a knoll on the east side of the Emmitsburg Road.[33] Earlier in the morning Sorrel had placed Lindsay's two companies near the J. Meyers house under Black's command. The Carolinians deployed on the west side of the road and perpendicular to it.

Federal infantry on Big Round Top seemed content to wait for the Confederates to make the first move. There was still no sign of the Federal cavalry. With his dispositions made Law could do little more than wait for the events of the afternoon to unfold.

Law's Position—1:00 p.m.

At 1:00 p.m. the double boom of the signal guns from the Washington Artillery Battalion signaled the beginning of the great cannonade prior to "Pickett's Charge." Porter Alexander wrote, "It was indeed a grand and exciting moment to hear our long line of guns break loose." Federal artillery responded almost immediately. According to Alexander, "The whole line from Cemetery Hill to Round Top seemed in five minutes to be emulating a volcano in eruption."[34]

Law looked in that direction and saw that the hills on either side of Plum Run Valley were "...capped with crowns of flame and smoke." Great clouds of smoke soon enveloped the infantry positions and settled in the valley separating the opposing lines. Law recalled that the shells exploding over the lines "...lit up the clouds with their snakelike flashes." He would remember the cannonading as "...one of the most magnificent battle scenes witnessed during the war."[35]

A correspondent for the *Richmond Enquirer* related the splendor of Alexander's duel with the Federal artillery. Writing under the pen name Tyler Allegre, the byline of July 8 read in part:

I have never yet heard such tremendous artillery firing. The very earth shook beneath my feet. The shrieking of shells, the crash of falling timber, the fragments of rock flying through the air shattered from the cliffs by solid shot, the heavy mutterings from the valley between the opposing armies, the "splash" of bursting shrapnel, and the fierce neighing of wounded artillery horses, made a picture terribly grand and sublime.

Private Sims, Company F, 1st Texas, called it the "the heaviest cannonading ever heard on the American continent." According to the Texan, "The air was alive with hissing bomb-shells and the hills and mountains fairly trembled."[36]

The Federal Cavalry Makes Its Appearance

While Law and his men watched the spectacle of the cannonading, Federal cavalry, a brigade of the Third Division of the Cavalry Corps, commanded by Brigadier General Hugh Judson Kilpatrick, began massing in the Bushman Woods on Law's right flank. Five days before, Major General Alford Pleasonton implemented a major re-organization of the cavalry, which gave Kilpatrick two volunteer brigades.[37] In an unprecedented move three junior officers were, at the same time, given brigadier commissions.

Writing in 1879, Pleasonton described his first meeting with Meade as commander of the Army of the Potomac as pleasant. He took the opportunity to renew a previous request for the appointments: "I called his attention to a division of cavalry near Frederick City, which he might place under my command, and I would like to have officers I would name specially assigned to it, as I expected to have some desperate work to do. The General assented to my request, and upon my naming the officers, he immediately telegraphed to have them appointed brigadier generals." This was his first dispatch to Washington, and in the afternoon he received the reply "making the appointments, and directing the officers to be assigned at once."[38] Elon J. Farnsworth and Wesley Merritt leaped three ranks from captain. George A. Custer, the third young officer promoted, jumped from the rank of first lieutenant to brigadier.[39] Merritt reported to Brigadier General John Buford, commanding the First Division Cavalry Corps, where he was assigned command of the Reserve Brigade of regulars.[40] Custer and Farnsworth were assigned command of the Second and First Brigades, respectively, in Kilpatrick's First Division.[41]

Kilpatrick reached Gettysburg the afternoon of July 2 and moved on to Hunterstown. After participating in fighting against Wade Hampton's cavalry Kilpatrick retired from the field and made camp at dark.[42] At 11:00 p.m. the troopers, still weary from the day's activities, were called "to horse." Under orders to march for Two Taverns on the Baltimore Pike, Kilpatrick rode all night, reaching his destination in the pre-dawn twilight.[43] The Third Division turned off the road and made camp facing the road. Weary troopers unsaddled, fed and watered their mounts, and then grabbed a few moments rest themselves. Some made coffee, others stretched out on the ground for some sleep, a few simply took the opportunity to lounge and reflect on their thoughts.[44] While the men rested a

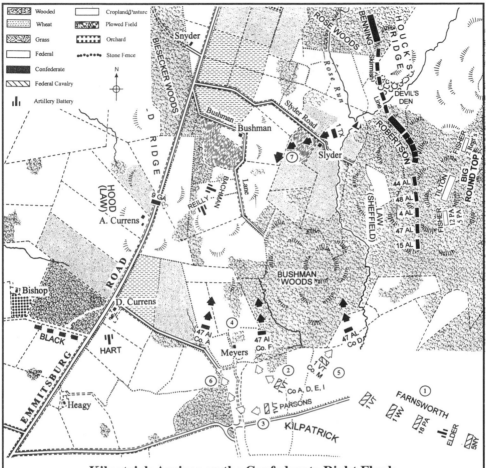

Kilpatrick Arrives on the Confederate Right Flank
July 3, 1863

1. Farnsworth approaches the battlefield south of the Bushman Woods about noon.
2. Dismounted detachments from the 1st Vermont Cavalry are thrown forward. Companies A, D, E, I and M engage the Alabama skirmish line.
3. A mounted squadron, commanded by Captain Henry Parsons, supports Companies A, D, E, and I.
4. After exchanging fire with the Vermonters, Captain Henry Lindsay's Alabama skirmishers fall back toward the Confederate batteries.
5. Company M of the 1st Vermont drives forward and locates the main Confederate line.
6. Parsons moves past the Meyers house and advances along the farm lane toward the D. Currens house. His command comes under fire from sharpshooters posted in the second story of the D. Currens house and from Hart's battery.
7. When Farnsworth begins massing in the Bushman Woods the 1st Texas withdraws from the main line and advances south in Plum Run Valley.

steady stream of wounded passed by on the way to field hospitals. Sergeant Horace K. Ide, of Company D, 1st Vermont Cavalry, recalled the houses and barns were filled with the wounded.[45] Because of the heavy demand numerous field hospitals placed on the local water supply guards were stationed at each well. Horse soldiers from the Third Division were forced to venture more than a half mile to fill their canteens and bring back water for cooking. In the early morning hours of July 2 the horsemen first learned of the severe fighting the previous two days. The death of Major General John F. Reynolds was sadly reported and word spread that Dan Sickles had been severely wounded the previous afternoon.[46] Sergeant Thomas Grier, 18th Pennsylvania Cavalry, then saw General Sickles brought by on a stretcher.[47]

Kilpatrick was known as "Kil-Cavalry" because of his disregard for his men and a reputation to ride his mounts until they were completely broken down.[48] A native of New Jersey, he was born in 1836 near Deckertown in the Clone Valley, the youngest child of Judson Kilpatrick. The elder Kilpatrick was reportedly an affluent citizen and respected farmer of the region. As a young boy the junior Kilpatrick was fond of athletics and readily participated in anything related to a military endeavor.[49] At age 18 he secured an appointment to West Point, entering a class which pursued a five-year curriculum. Classmates included John Pelham, later called by Lee the "Gallant Pelham," and Charles Hazlett whose battery gave much needed confidence to hard-pressed defenders of Little Round Top the previous afternoon.[50]

With the firing on Fort Sumter, South Carolina, Kilpatrick became eager to get to war and cover himself in glory. A number of his classmates shared the same enthusiasm. Kilpatrick became the spokesman for those in the class of '61 who sought early commissions as "officers and gentlemen." He is reported to have prepared a petition to the president of the United States, soliciting the army's commander in chief to permit the petitioners "to take the final examination in the presence of the enemy." Lincoln approved. Kilpatrick, ranked 17th in his class, and 44 of his comrades were graduated May 6, 1861. In June of the same year Kilpatrick became the first regular officer wounded in the conflict. Ruthless, ambitious, and impulsive, Kilpatrick was either adored or hated. With Judson Kilpatrick there was no in between.[51] Recognizing very early in the war that the volunteer service offered the easiest

Brig. Gen. H. Judson Kilpatrick, Commanding Cavalry Division

MC MOLLUS USAMHI

path to promotion and glory, the West Pointer had secured a commission as a captain in the 5th New York Infantry. With a wound to his credit, he made lieutenant colonel in September 1861, colonel in December 1862, and brigadier general of cavalry in June 14, 1863.[52]

In the early morning hours of July 3, Pleasonton decided on the cavalry dispositions for the day. Brigadier General David M. Gregg's Second Division, Cavalry Corps, would cover the Federal right flank. Kilpatrick drew responsibility for the left. Merritt's Reserve Brigade, then at Emmitsburg, would join Kilpatrick and cooperate with him. Sometime after daybreak a courier appeared with orders for Custer to join Gregg. A short time later Custer's brigade of Michigan volunteers rode off into the early morning haze.[53] Citing the order to detach Custer as "a mistake," Kilpatrick reported his objective was "to attack with my whole command and the Reserve Brigade."[54] Shortly before 8:00 a.m. a courier arrived at Third Division headquarters with orders to proceed to the Federal left.[55]

Farnsworth wasted little time preparing the First Brigade of four regiments, almost 2,000 strong, to ride.[56] All too quickly the bugler sounded "boots and saddles." Troopers, worn out from the hardships of the previous two days, rubbed the sleep from their eyes, formed up, and in column of fours rode toward the Federal left. On the morning of July 3 Lieutenant Colonel Addison W. Preston's 1st Vermont led the brigade.[57]

Raised in the fall of 1861, the 1st Vermont Cavalry was the first mounted regiment raised in New England. It was also the second largest regiment, cavalry or infantry, from the state of Vermont. Because no state law authorized raising a mounted regiment, the 1st Vermont Cavalry was recruited under U.S. authority. Mustered into service November 19 for three years, it left the state December 14, 1861 with a roster numbering 1,966 officers and men. With baggage and men aboard, the regiment required 150 cars for the trip to Washington, D.C. The Vermonters' uniforms were dark blue jackets trimmed with yellow braid. Their trousers were light blue; the hat was made of black felt, with the brim turned up on one side.[58]

Next in line came the 1st West Virginia and then the 5th New York. The 18th Pennsylvania brought up the rear.[59] Lieutenant Samuel S. Elder accompanied Kilpatrick with Battery E, 4th U.S. Cavalry, First Brigade, Horse Artillery. Elder fielded four three-inch Rodman rifled guns.

Farnsworth rode north on the Baltimore Pike as far as a church (probably Mark's German Reform Church)[60] which sat on the east side of the pike. After turning left onto White Run Road, the column slowly made its way south over the narrow byway. Before crossing Rock Creek just south of the confluence of White Run, Farnsworth paused to water the horses, then turned northeast toward the Taneytown Road.[61] A considerable number of infantry were seen hurrying eastward. Sergeant Grier, 18th Pennsylvania Cavalry, concluded the front line was not far away.[62] When the column struck the Taneytown Road, Farnsworth guided it south past the James Rider and Jacobs farms.[63] Continuing south on the Taneytown Road, the column rode past Little Round Top and the south end of Big

Round Top before turning west near the J. Keefauver farm.[64] After traveling over open fields and through patches of timber, the head of the column, about the noon hour, took a farm road which crossed Plum Run. As it approached the meandering stream Farnsworth halted the column.[65] He and Kilpatrick probably surveyed the terrain and discussed the appropriate line of advance.

The ground they were about to contest was less than ideally suited for maneuvering cavalry. Generally wooded and with frequent knolls, the ever present granite boulders and outcroppings made it virtually impossible to maintain any semblance of a formation during a cavalry operation. To their front Bushman Woods covered a small ridge comprised of two distinct knolls. The higher elevation, which rose 180 feet above the valley floor, lay on the east side where the woods were fairly dense. The second crest rose 166 feet above Plum Run Valley. About the only ground suitable to mount a cavalry charge lay toward the Emmitsburg Road. The available ground, such as it was, John B. Bachelder described as open fields, interspersed with occasional thickets or small pines. Numerous fences of stone and rail construction divided the cleared areas into individual plots, hardly a place to mount a cavalry charge.[66]

When the conference concluded Farnsworth sent his horsemen across Plum Run. Sometime between 12:30 and 1:00 p.m. the column turned northwest toward Bushman Woods.[67] The 1st Vermont led the advance and as it approached Bushman Woods thunder from the artillery barrage before "Pickett's Charge" rolled across the countryside. A few minutes later the Vermonters ran into Lindsay's skirmishers.[68]

Opening Skirmish

Lieutenant Colonel Preston threw forward two squadrons, which he ordered dismounted. Companies A, D, E, and I deployed in a skirmish line and advanced in the direction of the J. Meyers house on the western edge of Bushman Woods. Companies F and L, commanded by Captain Henry C. Parsons of Company L, rode in support of the skirmish line.[69] Both companies were led by lieutenants. Stephen A. Clark was in command of Company F and Alexander G. Watson, Company L.[70]

With a few men from Company L Watson charged the men from the 47th Alabama. The Alabamians got off at least one volley before the Vermonters overran the position. Several troopers pitched from their saddles, including Private George S. Brownell who probably became the first Federal cavalryman to die on the Federal left flank. Lindsay's men stubbornly held their ground, and began falling back only when "the revolvers flashed in their very faces."[71] In the ensuing melee Third Corporal William G. Johnston, Company D, 47th Alabama, and seven privates became captives.[72]

Preston's skirmishers likely discovered Black's skirmish line posted at a two-story stone house on the east side of the Emmitsburg Road which was occupied by the D. Currens family. When the Confederate skirmishers near the Emmitsburg Road were reported, Farnsworth took the precaution to look after his left flank. Preston sent Parsons toward the Emmitsburg Road.[73] The Vermonters rode west along a farm lane before turning northeast at a skirt of woods. When they were uncovered from the woods Hart's Washington Artillery, about 600 yards away, opened on the squadron. Parsons raced several yards to the north and sought cover under the nose of the Warfield Ridge. Owing to the elevation of the guns, the shells passed harmlessly over the cavalry, but the Federal horsemen were kept at bay by sharpshooters posted in the D. Currens house. Lieutenant Colonel Preston reported the men "suffered considerably" from the musketry.[74] In elevation the D. Currens house was about 20 feet above the nose of the ridge. The west side of the nose dropped about 40 feet to a small valley which separated Bushman Hill from Warfield Ridge. This was the most logical place for Parsons to seek cover.[75]

Parsons later indicated Companies F and L rode to the Bushman house. This is not consistent with Preston's battlefield report, nor with the accounts by Sergeant Horace Ide of Company D and G. G. Benedict. None of the Confederate accounts report Federal cavalry near the Bushman house until late afternoon when Farnsworth made his charge into Plum Run Valley. It does not seem reasonable that Law would have permitted two companies of Federal cavalry to remain unmolested that far in the Confederate rear and passing within a few hundred feet of his headquarters. Preston probably discovered Black's skirmish line when he drove the skirmishers from the Meyers house. Therefore, it is logical to conclude that Parsons was placed on the brigade's left to look after Black's line near the D. Currens house.[76]

Farnsworth Deploys in Bushman Woods

In the meantime Preston pushed north through Bushman Woods, easily driving Lindsay's skirmishers which fell back toward Reilly's battery.[77] Vermonter Ide recalled the Confederates were pushed back a half mile, which corresponds fairly well with the distance from the Meyers house to the stone wall later defended by the 1st Texas.[78] Captain John H. Woodward, commanding Company M, was sent forward to reconnoiter on the right. After crossing Plum Run, Woodward led his men toward the southern base of Big Round Top. Swinging east of Oates's right flank the Vermonters found the left of the Federal line and a short time later located the 15th Alabama behind rock breastworks. Woodward now knew where the Confederate right flank lay and reported back to Preston and Farnsworth.[79] Preston began deploying below the crest of Bushman Hill.

The 1st West Virginia and the 5th New York came into line after Preston. Elder's two sections went into battery on a knoll in a clearing. In his rear the ground dropped off sharply, creating a small cliff. The 1st West Virginia lay to the right of Elder, while one squadron of the 5th New York, on the same line with the battery, anchored on Elder's left.[80] Sergeant Grier believed the remainder of the regiments were hidden in the woods off to the right.[81] Kilpatrick established his headquarters near the battery.[82] In the meantime Farnsworth halted the 18th Pennsylvania south of Bushman Woods while Elder unlimbered and setup. On signal from the brigade commander, Lieutenant Colonel William P. Brinton, commanding the regiment, led his men into position to the left of the 5th New York. Brinton formed in a clearing on the western edge of the woods.[83]

Known as the "First Ira Harris Guard" at its organization, the 5th New York Cavalry came into existence October 1, 1861 at Staten Island, New York Harbor. Its first inspection occurred on October 31 and the 5th New York departed for Annapolis, Maryland in November. A large number of its personnel were from New York City, though several companies and parts of companies were raised in Essex, Wyoming, Allegheny and Tioga counties. At Gettysburg, the New Yorkers were seasoned veterans, having served in the campaigns of 1862 and Chancellorsville. They claimed the honor of being the first regiment "to exchange shots and cross sabers on free soil with the daring and desperate invaders who fought under the justly celebrated leader of the Confederacy, Major General J. E. B. Stuart. This incident occurred at Hanover, Pennsylvania on June 30.[84]

Law's Headquarters

Reacting quickly to the developing cavalry threat, Law first directed Bachman and Reilly to open upon the horseman.[85] Couriers spread out with urgent messages. Lieutenant Colonel Work received orders to send a regiment. The 1st Texas drew the assignment and formed in column for the march to the south end of Plum Run Valley.[86] Oates had already extended his line westward toward the Emmitsburg Road. It is likely that Lindsay deployed Companies A, F, and D of the 47th Alabama along an extended line between Oates and the left of the 9th Georgia.[87] Company A, 47th Alabama probably connected with Oates's skirmish line. It is likely Company D joined the 9th Georgia near the A. Currens house.

The rumble of Hart's guns near the Currens house was certainly worrisome. At the time, Law would not have known the size of the force defending the right flank. Anticipating the need for additional troops in the near future, Law sent for two regiments from Anderson's Brigade. Lieutenant Colonel William Luffman would send the 7th and 8th Georgia.[88]

Finding the range after a few rounds, Reilly worked his pieces effectively, inflicting considerable punishment on the Federal battery and its supports.[89] One of the first shells struck a horse. Another exploded in the limber park, wounding several men and horses. Hammond asked for and received permission to move his men in rear of the battery. A few minutes later the New Yorkers were scrambling down the declivity.[90] To the left Brinton's 18th Pennsylvania ducked into the woods as Reilly's shells began finding the range. While his support sought cover, Elder responded to his antagonists. However, because of the trees to the front, his gunners were forced to elevate their pieces. There is good reason to expect that Elder's fire was little more than an annoyance to Reilly.

Skirmish Line—1st Vermont Cavalry

In the meantime a squadron of Vermont skirmishers worked their way to the edge of the woods. Reilly's southernmost section was visible and presented an appealing target. Subsequent carbine fire caused the cannoneers to divert their fire from Elder's battery. Sergeant Ide was sure "we annoyed them some as they favored us with several charges of canister."[91] The Vermonters were more comfortable charging Confederate cavalry than exchanging shots with Reilly's section. Farnsworth retired to a line several hundred yards from the northern boundary of the woods.

Born at Athlone, Ireland in 1823 and migrating to America when quite young, James Reilly made military service his life's pursuit. He resided first in New Jersey and later Maryland, where he joined the Second Regiment of Artillery. After service in the Second Seminole War, Reilly fought in the War with Mexico, where he was severely wounded at Chapultepec and promoted orderly sergeant for bravery. In 1857 he was promoted ordnance-sergeant. Just before the outbreak of the Civil War Reilly transferred to Fort Johnson on the Cape Fear River. In January 1861 he and a party of local citizens confronted each other over an attempt to secure the fort's stores from the Federal government. Resistance proved futile and Reilly reluctantly turned over the stores. However, the governor condemned the action and Reilly reclaimed possession the next day. Not long after the incident Reilly separated from service with the United States by special order dated May 3, 1861. At age 30 Reilly tendered his services to the state of North Carolina and was assigned to a camp of instruction.[92] On May 31 he became first lieutenant of Company A, 1st Regiment of North Carolina Artillery. A month later he received an appointment to captain and transferred to the command of Company D of the same regiment. Raised primarily in Rowan County, the battery was known by two names; Reilly's battery for its commander and the Rowan (North Carolina) Artillery for the county where it was organized and where most of its personnel resided.[93] The official name used by the Army of Northern Virginia appears to have been the Rowan (North Carolina) Artillery. After joining the army in Virginia the Irishman quickly gained a solid reputation as an excellent artilleryman.

As his skills developed Reilly sought promotion to higher rank. General Joseph E. Johnston had written he "would rather have Reilly's battery with him than any other in the Confederate States." In May 1863, Major General Chase Whiting recommended him for promotion.[94] His promotion would not be realized until after the Gettysburg Campaign.

The 1st Texas—Bushman Woods

With a courier guiding the regiment, Major Frederick S. Bass and the men of the 1st Texas splashed across Plum Run and headed toward Bushman Woods. Advancing at the double quick, the column crossed the open fields and meadows east of the Bushman house. The Texans thought at the time their purpose was to protect the wagon trains.[95] It is reasonable to assume Law pointed out the regiment's intended position. The most logical choice was a stone wall in front of Bushman Woods. On reaching the Bushman farm road Bass turned toward an open field adjacent to the woods and began deploying at the stone wall. The Alexander Currens house stood about 200 yards to their right. A section of Reilly's battery was in position on Warfield Ridge about 200 yards in rear of the 1st Texas.[96] To their left the rock wall ended at the edge of a stand of timber which jutted forward from the body of woods. A light rail fence extended into the woods. From the field's western edge a worm fence snaked its way to the Emmitsburg Road.[97] Private Thomas L. McCarty, Company I, wrote, "We took down the rail fence and rebuilt it at an angle of 40 degrees, connecting with the stone fence."[98]

A graduate of the Virginia Military Academy and prewar instructor of military science at Marshall, Texas, Bass was about to put his military training to practical use.[99] The commander of the 1st Texas had the unenviable task of establishing a strong skirmish line more than a half mile in length with a single regiment. Using the low stone wall and rail fence as cover, the Texan's line connected with Lindsay's skirmishers in the woods to the left and the 9th Georgia on the right. Hillyer, from his position behind the 9th Georgia, observed the Texas line deployed in a single rank and must have seriously doubted the Texans could put up much of a fight should the cavalry charge. According to Hillyer, the 1st Texas line did not have a man more than every five or six feet.[100]

Shortly after establishing his line, Bass ordered a detail out for water. Captain John N. Wilson, Company K, drew the assignment and selected a man from each company. After collecting the canteens, Wilson and his men headed toward Plum Run and disappeared into Bushman Woods.[101]

The Texans were hardly in place before Kilpatrick began feeling the Confederate line again and extending his own line to the left. While the main line remained concealed some distance back in Bushman Woods, scouting parties were sent forward. Wilson's water detail ran into a squad of Farnsworth's skirmishers. Upon interrogation, Farnsworth learned the First Brigade's adversary was Hood's famed Texas brigade.[102] Kilpatrick reported Farnsworth became engaged with the Confederate skirmishers about 1:00 p.m.[103] This corresponds fairly closey to Law's account. He knew of the Federal cavalry approach south of Bushman Woods shortly before noon. Lindsay's encounter with the 1st Vermont would have been reported. Porter Alexander wrote that he noted the time as 1:00 p.m. when the signal guns fired to start the bombardment.[104] Law later recalled the "grand artillery" duel was under way when Farnsworth began massing in Bushman Woods.[105] Therefore, it appears the skirmishers became engaged between 1:00 and 1:30 p.m.

Chapter 9

Law Counters Merritt

Squadrons of Wesley Merritt's Reserve Brigade searched unsuccessfully for Stuart's cavalry during the last days of June 1863.[1] On the 29th Merritt rode to Frederick and bivouacked near Mechanicstown (present day Thurmont). The next two days found the Reserves spread out over the countryside. Detachments of varying strength were either posted on picket duty, detailed as scouting parties, or patrolled roads through the mountains. Among other places, the troopers visited Hagerstown and Cavetown.[2]

On July 2 the Reserve Brigade marched to Emmitsburg, Maryland and camped about two miles north of town.[3] Though it was called a brigade of regular cavalry, that was not precisely correct. Of the five regiments, four were regulars and the fifth was a volunteer regiment of Pennsylvanians, formerly known as the Rush Lancers and designated the 6th Pennsylvania Cavalry. The regulars were the 1st, 2nd, 5th, and 6th U.S. Cavalry. Three of the these, the 1st, 2nd and 5th, came from the "old army," having served in the west just prior to the outbreak of war. The 6th was formed after the outbreak of the conflict.

At age 27, Wesley Merritt's commission as brigadier general was just 5 days old. He was described by his biographer as tall, having brown hair, and "baby-faced," which for many years made him appear much younger.[4] A West Point graduate, class of 1860, his was the only class to pursue and complete a

Brig. Gen. Wesley Merritt, Commanding Reserve Cavalry Brigade

five-year curriculum. Ranked 22nd out of 41 classmates, Merritt was one year ahead of Judson Kilpatrick. He engaged in his first fist fight at the academy with the impulsive Kilpatrick. His first army assignment sent him west to Utah as a brevet second lieutenant in the Second Dragoons. In the early days of the war, Merritt was promoted in quick succession to second lieutenant and then first lieutenant. The Dragoons were ordered east in July 1861.[5]

Before the war, the army's mobile arm consisted of two regiments of Dragoons, one regiment of mounted rifles and two regiments of cavalry.[6] By an act of Congress in early August 1861, additional cavalry regiments were authorized and the designations of the cavalry units were standardized. The First and Second Dragoons became the 1st and 2nd Cavalry. The Second Cavalry received the designation 5th U.S. Cavalry.[7]

After his arrival in the east, Merritt drew an assignment in Washington, D.C. In February 1862 he became aide-de-camp to the commander of the Cavalry Corps, Brigadier General Phillip St. George Cooke, who had been his commander when Merritt was attached to the Second Dragoons. While serving on Cooke's staff, he was appointed captain of the 2nd U.S. Cavalry in April 1862. When George Stoneman succeeded Cooke, Merritt continued in the same capacity and also served as ordnance and mustering officer. He was suddenly thrust into command at Chancellorsville. Though only a captain, he commanded the Reserve Brigade. After spending two weeks on Pleasonton's staff, he returned to his old regiment. Expecting to command a company, he found himself instead in temporary command of the 2nd U.S. Cavalry.

Merritt's qualities as cavalry commander and coolness under fire were evident during the June 9 cavalry fight at Brandy Station. Pleasonton, in praising Merritt's performance wrote, "It is necessary to have a good commander for the regular brigade of cavalry, and I earnestly recommend Capt. Wesley Merritt to be made a brigadier-general for that purpose. He has all the qualifications for it, and has distinguished himself by his gallantry and daring. Give me good commanders and I will give you good results."[8] On June 29 he was appointed brigadier general and given command of the Reserves. In Salem, Illinois his father, editor of the *Advocate*, proudly announced the promotion: "General Wesley Merritt ... appointed Brigadier General of Volunteers solely on the grounds of merit, the honor having been entirely unsolicited."[9]

Sometime in the early morning hours of July 3, the Federal network of scouts and lookouts reported a Confederate wagon train moving from Cashtown toward Fairfield. Merritt decided to go after the prize and sent Major Samuel H. Starr with the 6th U.S. Cavalry to intercept the train. A Union spy brought news the train was guarded by a single regiment of mounted infantry.[10]

Starr failed to find the wagon train. But about two miles from Fairfield his regiment of regulars ran into the 7th Virginia Cavalry, Brigadier General William E. "Grumble" Jones's Brigade, Stuart's Division of the cavalry, which he easily repulsed. Encouraged by his initial success, Starr continued to hold his roadblock, which was bounded on both sides by post and rail fences. Here he was struck by the remainder of Jones's Brigade.[11] Starr found himself outmanned and outflanked.[12] "The regiment," according to Private William Carter, 6th U. S. Cavalry, "was caught in a bad plight."[13] The results were predictable. In the ensuing one-sided fight Starr lost heavily and was driven from the field. Federal casualties were high, with 34 killed and wounded and 208 captured, including Starr himself.[14]

In the meantime, a courier from Pleasonton found Merritt's headquarters about two miles north of Emmitsburg. The Reserves were ordered to join Kilpatrick on the Federal left at Gettysburg. Several of his companies were on assignment at Meade's headquarters. Companies E and I were detailed from the 6th Pennsylvania.[15] Each of the regular units had contributed a detachment.[16] The brigade, less the 6th U.S. Cavalry and the companies at Meade's headquarters, moved out by noon.[17]

The column crossed Marsh Creek as it approached Gettysburg from the south.[18] Between 2:00 and 2:30 p.m., with the 6th Pennsylvania Cavalry leading, the Federal horsemen encountered Black's outposts about a mile south of the D. Currens house. Merritt reported to division headquarters while the 6th Pennsylvania, meeting little resistance, pushed forward.[19] Kilpatrick ordered him to demonstrate against the Confederate right flank. "Pickett's Charge" against the Federal center was well under way.

Rolling farmland, broken by scattered wooded plots, bordered either side of the Emmitsburg Road. Fields and farm lanes were enclosed by rail fences. Sergeant Samuel J. Crockett, Company A, 1st U.S. Cavalry, recalled the horsemen were forced to dismount.[20] Merritt probably deployed along the W. Currens farm lane with the 6th Pennsylvania astride the Emmitsburg Road.[21]

Major James H. Hazeltine led the Pennsylvanians forward to the edge of a wooded plot, deployed in a skirmish line, and advanced into a large open field. Captain W. W. Frazier commanded Hazeltine's left wing and Captain J. Hinckley the right.[22] On the opposite side of the field lay the Confederate line.

Black's Line—D. Currens House

The Pennsylvanians saw Hart's battery and Black's "rag-tag" band which was probably in a single rank and lying behind a rail fence along the edge of the woods. Two of Hart's guns were posted on the crest of a small slope south of the house. Black's dismounted cavalry extended the line several hundred yards west of the road. A number of his men were posted as sharpshooters on the second floor of the house. From this vantage point the South Carolinians enjoyed a good view of the cavalry as it moved up and deployed. By this time Black realized he was facing at least a brigade of cavalry.

Black did as Colonel Sorrel instructed earlier in the morning. A courier, with an urgent request for support, mounted a horse and galloped toward Law's headquarters. In the meantime, Black gave the order to open fire on the Pennsylvanians.

As the Pennsylvanians appeared on the crest of the ridge and started into the field a sheet of flames raced down the line. The ensuing rattle of musketry

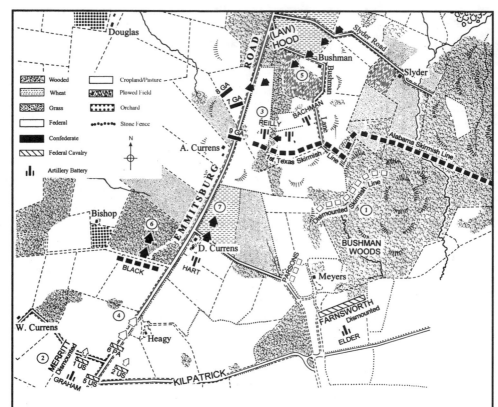

Merritt Arrives on the Confederate Right Flank
July 3, 1863

1. Between 1:00 and 1:30 p.m. Farnsworth pushes forward a skirmish line and exchanges fire with Law's skirmishers.
2. Merritt's Regulars approach the battlefield between 1:30 and 2:00 p.m. and deploy along the W. Currens farm lane as dismounted cavalry.
3. Law moves a section of Reilly's Battery several hundred yards west to support the 9th Georgia.
4. The 6th Pennsylvania advances along the Emmitsburg Road.
5. The 7th and 8th Georgia arrive to strengthen Law's skirmish line.
6. Black's dismounted cavalry falls back under pressure from Merritt's advance.
7. Hart in turn falls back to a position north of the A. Currens house.

signaled the opening round of the skirmish.[23] Sharpshooters positioned in the windows of the Currens house peppered Hazeltine's line while rounds from Hart's guns crashed into the advancing line. "We were saluted by a storm of balls," wrote the historian of the 6th Pennsylvania, which inflicted "great mischief" on the line and "checked our advance."[24] Frazier's line suffered considerably before return fire answered the challenge from the stone house.[25]

Merritt sent a courier to hurry William M. Graham, commanding the 1st U.S. Horse Artillery, Battery K, onto the field. The Reserves' artillery escort un-limbered on a knoll a short distance south of the line. Though he lacked the credentials of West Point, Graham came on the field a seasoned artillery officer. His commission as second lieutenant dated June 7, 1855. He had attained the rank of first lieutenant in March 1861 and captain in October of that year.

Graham's first target was the D. Currens house. Three or four direct hits on the second story put an end to the sharpshooting. The South Carolinians abandoned the stone house.[26] Undaunted by the incoming projectiles, Hart and Black's line west of Emmitsburg continued to fire on the Pennsylvanians, who were now in the swale of the field.[27]

Law's Headquarters

Law heard the rumble of the cannon and musketry to the south and correctly surmised Black's line had come under attack. Though he likely did not know the strength of the force, he had already decided on a course of action before the courier from Black arrived. A section of Reilly's battery moved several hundred yards to the east to support the 9th Georgia. The 7th and 8th Georgia were making their way from the north end of Houck's Ridge. These he intended to place in support of the 9th Georgia.

Since Law did not accompany the regiments to the Emmitsburg Road, it is reasonable to assume the Georgians were given instructions to support Captain Hillyer. Because they were placed on the road, Law's force was in position to counter a move by Merritt to either side. Should he attempt to punch through on Hillyer's left, the 7th and 8th could easily reinforce the line and block such a thrust. On the other hand if Merritt attempted to turn Law's right flank, the Georgians were also in position to easily extend the right. Merritt chose the latter course of action.

Merritt's Position—South of the D. Currens House

As his remaining regiments came up, Merritt ordered each dismounted. The 1st U.S. Cavalry halted in a wooded plot near a schoolhouse and the horses were led to the rear.[28] Their commander was a native of Ohio and a West Point graduate. Richard S. C. Lord graduated 40th in the class of 1856 and served on the western frontier from 1857 until 1861. Owen Kenan McLemore, who had been major of the 4th Alabama, was ranked 39th in the same class and Fitzhugh Lee 45th of 49 cadets. Lord had been captain in the 1st U.S. Cavalry since October 1861.[29]

When Reilly's section in rear of the 9th Georgia opened the Confederate firepower doubled. Exploding shells sent deadly fragments ricocheting through the lines. Here and there men toppled from the ranks. Reilly and Hart continued to play on the Pennsylvanians as the line pushed forward. But the fire proved too much to endure and the Pennsylvanians advance ground to a halt. In response, Merritt sent the 1st U.S. Cavalry and the 2nd U.S. Cavalry forward.

Captain Lord guided the regiment up on the left of the 6th Pennsylvania. Sergeant Crockett described the formation as a strong skirmish line.[30] Captain Theophilus F. Rodenbaugh deployed the 2nd U.S. Cavalry east of the Emmitsburg Road. Merritt placed the 5th U.S. Cavalry, commanded by Captain Julius Mason, in reserve.

The 1st U.S. Cavalry advanced through the line of the 6th Pennsylvania, driving through a skirt of woods and out into a large field of grass and hay. About 500 yards away lay a field of corn in tassel. The regulars thrust against the opposing line was not to be denied. Black's thin line was able to offer little resistance before melting into the woods.

Black's Position

With the Carolina cavalry falling back, Hart's battery became uncovered. To save the guns, Black resorted to a clever delaying tactic. Since Hart only had two pieces in action, one fired while the other limbered up and moved some distance to the rear.[31] That gun was then unlimbered and several rounds directed at the Federal skirmish line. The sequence was thus repeated until the section was north of the A. Currens house.[32] Black proudly wrote of the affair, "Thus I had a battery firing from one gun at a time, but it was served rapidly and before the enemy was aware I had moved the battery 500 or 600 yards."[33]

Merritt's left emerged from the woods to find the Confederate line firmly anchored across the Emmitsburg Road.[34] Captain Hillyer's grayclad 9th Georgia lay in two ranks in rear of the A. Currens house. When it became apparent the Federal line overlapped the Confederate line west of the road, the 7th and 8th Georgia moved to Hillyer's right.

Merritt's Position—South of the D. Currens House

The 1st U.S. Cavalry, 2nd U.S. Cavalry, and 6th Pennsylvania pushed out into the open fields. The Reserves were inviting targets and the Georgians let loose a volley. The Federal cavalrymen promptly responded. A Pennsylvanian recalled "carbines and rifles were rattling on both sides of the pike."[35] Participants described the ensuing contest for the A. Currens house as a considerable fight.[36]

In the meantime, Merritt began extending his left. The regulars probably worked their way along a rail fence which separated a field of grass and hay from a large cornfield. One squadron of the 5th U.S. Cavalry, under Captain Edward H. Lieb, moved through a large wooded plot and entered a large cultivated area, southeast of the Douglas house where individual plots were marked by rail fences. All but two squadrons of the 1st U.S. Cavalry remained connected with the 6th Pennsylvania. Captain Eugene M. Baker followed Captain Lieb with the two squadrons from the 1st U.S. Cavalry and a squadron of the 2nd U.S. Cavalry deployed in a weak skirmish line to fill the gap between the main body of the 1st U.S. Cavalry and the 5th U.S. Cavalry.[37]

Graham's battery, in supporting distance of the 6th Pennsylvania, occupied a position astride the Emmitsburg Road. On the right of the road detachments of the 1st U.S., 2nd U.S., and the 5th U.S. Cavalry were positioned as skirmishers in a wooded area. Captain Julius Mason commanded one squadron of the 5th U.S. Cavalry; Lieutenant Isaac Dunkelberger commanded a squadron of the 1st U.S. Cavalry. A squadron of the 2nd U.S. Cavalry was under Lieutenant Michael Lawless.[38]

On the Confederate side Hart's two gun section moved to its third position of the day in rear of Bachman and Reilly and near the Synder house.[39] Captain Hillyer shifted left to cover an advance by the regulars east of the road. The 7th and 8th Georgia remained on the west side of the road.

Black's Position—West of the A. Currens House

Black saw the danger developing on his right. A line that was weak from the beginning had been extended to the limit and reinforcements would be needed to hold. Once again a courier departed for Law's headquarters. This time the need was urgent. The colonel of South Carolina cavalry believed that only part of his command could be relied on to stand against the Federal threat. These he ordered dismounted and deployed as skirmishers. Hart came up with his two guns and unlimbered. Because of the urgency of the situation, Black sent word for the battery to fire directly over his line.[40]

A graduate of the Citadel in Charleston, South Carolina, Hart had been a schoolmate of Law, graduating in 1857. Upon entering the service in 1861, he was appointed a lieutenant in the Washington Light Artillery of Charleston, then captain in November of that year. The unit transferred to Hampton's Cavalry as horse artillery in 1862 where it was unofficially known as Hart's Battery.[41]

Hart's new position, his fourth of the day, was southeast of the Douglas house.[42] Unfortunately the first shell exploded prematurely over the Carolinians' line. When the second went off at the muzzle, Black hastened to the section and ordered the firing ceased. A lieutenant assured the colonel the rest of the fuses were more reliable. Black hesitated. However, a glance over his

**Capt. James F. Hart,
Washington Light Artillery**

Brooks, *Stories of the Confederacy*

shoulder convinced him the need for the artillery fire was worth the risk. Hart opened on the advancing line and Black recalled the guns were never served better.[43] In the meantime the 7th and 8th Georgia extended the right to the west. Like the dismounted cavalry before them, the Georgians were extended to the limit and presented little more than a line of skirmishers."[44] According to Law, "Black's line was too weak to offer resistance." But the timely fire from the South Carolina artillerist bought valuable time while Law decided on the next course of action. He later complimented Hart saying that "the guns were well handled."[45]

Hart's battery was part of Stuart's Horse Artillery, commanded by Major R. F. Beckman. After being damaged and rendered unserviceable during the Battle of Brandy Station on June 9, the pieces needed considerable repair before entering another fight. Because of the condition of his guns, Hart did not accompany Stuart on his ride into Maryland and Pennsylvania. As Hart recalled, "I was directed to follow the wagon trains with debris of a battery, into Pennsylvania, and remain idle until I could get new equipment." Three guns were repaired at the railroad shops in Martinsburg. From there Hart moved on to Chambersburg and reported to Lee for orders.[46] It was at Chambersburg that Hart was placed under Black's command.

Law's Headquarters

When the day began Law's line ran along the western slope of Big Round Top. By mid-afternoon a weak skirmish line, running perpendicular to the main line, extended to the Emmitsburg Road. Now, as the clock approached 4:00 in the afternoon, the weak skirmish line was rapidly becoming a line of battle.

The Confederate hold on the Emmitsburg Road had became tenuous. Previous withdrawals from Big Round Top had seriously depleted the strength of the line there. "My supply of men to meet the demand began to seem very low," commented Law.[47] After concluding Merritt's objective was to stretch the Confederate line till Farnsworth could easily punch through and menace his rear and the batteries, Law decided his only viable alternative was to draw from the line on Big Round Top. Lieutenant Colonel Luffman was ordered to come with the 11th and 59th Georgia.[48]

The Georgians, less Luffman, approached Law's headquarters on the run. Two days with little sleep took its toll on the lieutenant colonel, who fell out somewhere in Plum Run Valley. Major Henry D. McDaniel of the 11th Georgia assumed command over the regiments and placed his own under Captain William M. Mitchell. As McDaniel passed Reilly's battery Law joined the column and personally led it toward the extreme right.[49]

Born at Monroe in Walton County, Georgia, McDaniel graduated with honors from Mercer University and began the practice of law in his hometown. Though he opposed secession, McDaniel accepted the inevitable and as the youngest member of the Georgia secession convention, voted for and signed the ordinance.[50]

McDaniel would be critically wounded at Funkstown, Maryland after Gettysburg. When told his wound was fatal, McDaniel replied in Latin that "Southern Soldiers know how to die." He survived and later became governor of Georgia.[51]

Black's Position—Confederate Extreme Right

Part of Black's line ran through a field of head high oats. The remainder rested in a skirt of woods. He was unable to see the entire Federal line and became concerned for his right. A friend, "old Parson Johnson," scaled a nearby tree for a better look. His report back was not good. Merritt was turning the right flank. "Things," according to Black, "were quite blue."[52] If help did not arrive soon, the right flank would certainly be driven back on Reilly and Bachman.

Glancing to his rear Black breathed a sigh of relief when he saw the head of a grayclad column not more than 75 yards away. It was Law and the last of Anderson's Georgians. Though Black's men were giving ground, Law's infantry must have looked at the "rag-tag" band with some admiration. The South Carolinians were, for the moment at least, making the contest interesting. A Georgian wrote of the action, the "cavalry was fighting for every inch of ground."[53]

In Black's view the pace of the column coming to his relief marched much too leisurely and he spurred his horse toward the Georgians. He was in a highly excited state and rather irritated as he approached the person he assumed to be in command. Black did not recognize Law, believing him at the time to be a colonel. The cavalryman quickly described the situation and then pointedly suggested the column form on his right. Law agreed. As the Georgians filed past, Black and Law, whose rank he still did not recognize, rode toward the flank. The cavalryman still thought the pace too slow to meet the danger and blurted out, "Damn it colonel, our flank will be turned if you don't hurry up!" "Oh no, I don't think so," came the calmly directed answer.[54] Just then someone rode by and addressed the supposed colonel as General Law.[55] A red-faced and much embarrassed Black apologized. In spite of the seriousness of the situation, Law saw a bit of humor in the preceding lecture and gave out a good-natured laugh. Law informed Black that as soon as the 11th and 59th Georgia were in line on the right of the South Carolinians the line would charge.[56]

Law knew the hazards of fighting a mobile force in open country. But his spirits rose when he saw that the Federal cavalry were dismounted. He later said of the situation, "It is not an easy task to operate against cavalry with infantry alone, on an extended line, and in open country where the former, capable of moving much more rapidly, can choose its own point of attack and can elude the blows of its necessarily more tardy observers. But Merritt's brigade was now dismounted and deployed as skirmishers and I lost no time in taking advantage of this temporary equality as to the means of locomotion."[57]

Law's plan was simple. The right flank would execute a left wheel and drive on Merritt's left while Hart's cannon moved in support of the line. Law placed McDaniel in command of the two Georgia regiments and Black's little force.

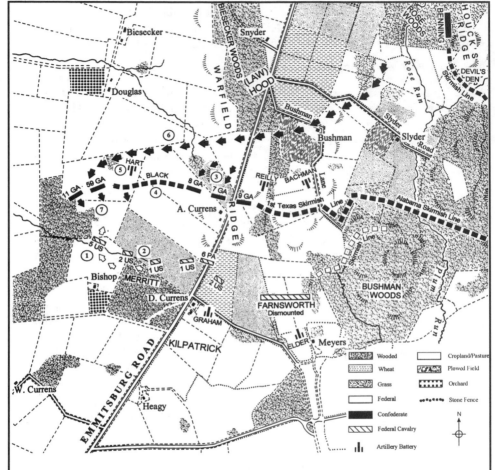

Merritt Demonstrates Against the Confederate Right Flank
July 3, 1863

1. The 5th U.S. Cavalry extends Merritt's line west in an enveloping move that threatens Law right flank.
2. Two detachments from the 1st and 2nd U.S. Cavalry fill the gap between the 5th U. S. Cavalry and the main body of the 1st U.S. Cavalry.
3. The 7th and 8th Georgia go into line and extend Law's right flank to the west.
4. Black's dismounted cavalry form a weak skirmish line.
5. Hart's battery goes into position and fires over Black's line into the advancing 5th U.S. Cavalry.
6. Law arrives with the 11th and 59th Georgia.
7. The 11th and 59th Georgia and Black's command of dismounted cavalry mount a charge against the flank of the 5th U.S. Cavalry.

Black's "rag-tag" band was in poor condition to fight. Many were physically unable to charge; others were low on ammunition. But Black intended to participate in the left wheel and ordered his men to keep up with the Georgians. When one man complained his ammunition had run out, he was bluntly told to move out and yell for all he was worth.[58]

As soon as Law was satisfied that the Georgians and Black were ready, he ordered the charge.[59] To the north Pickett's ill-fated charge against the Federal center was in its final stage.[60]

Caught by surprise, Captain Lieb's left flank gave way when the Georgians stormed out of the fields of oats and tall grass. Sergeant Samuel Crockett was unaware of impending danger until a portion of McDaniel's line suddenly rose up on his front. His 70-man squadron withstood the initial volley and put up a stubborn resistance. Crockett saw the opposing colors go down three times. However, superior numbers overwhelmed the 5th U.S. Cavalry. "Though everyone fought like a tiger, Crockett wrote in his diary, "We had to fall back."[61]

Black was in the woods when the charge began. As he entered the field "the Yankee Blue Coats (were) mounting the big rail fence and over."[62] The "rag-tag" band joined in the chase, but the real pressure came from the 11th and 59th Georgia which caused Crockett to relate, the "balls came like hail."[63] With Captain Lieb's squadron on the run, the left flank of Merritt's line disintegrated. As Law described it, the charging Confederates "struck Merritt's skirmish line 'on its end and doubled it up' as far as the Emmitsburg Road."[64]

Though McDaniel's Georgians were driving the dismounted cavalry splendidly, Law did not want to bring on a general engagement. Captain Leigh Terrell found McDaniel with orders to stop the pursuit.[65] The Georgians found much pleasure in the chase but McDaniel reformed his line behind a rail fence that was on an extension of the skirmish line to his left.[66] James Hart unlimbered and went into battery roughly on a line between the A. Currens and W. Douglas houses.[67]

Law now felt his right flank sufficiently secure to turn his attention to the cavalry massed east of the Emmitsburg Road. As he stated, "This reduced my front to manageable dimensions and left some force at my disposal to meet any concentrated attack that the cavalry might make."[68] Skirmishing and occasional demonstrations near the road continued two more hours. But for all practical purposes Merritt had ceased to be a threat.[69] Law's parting words to the cavalry commander were that he hoped Black "would hold his ground."[70]

Chapter 10

Farnsworth's Charge

Kilpatrick's Headquarters—Bushman Woods

By 4:00 p.m. skirmishers from both sides were closing in on the timber line of Bushman Woods. Henry Parsons recalled they were within speaking distance of each other. Though the firing had become sporadic, Confederate and Federal alike concealed himself behind rocks and trees. "Picketts Charge" was over. The rattle of musketry in its aftermath had died down. Only an occasional shot between the opposing batteries now disturbed the silence falling over Bushman Woods. The first news of the Federal success came when an orderly dashed by shouting, "We turned the charge! Nine acres of prisoners."[1]

Kilpatrick was in a foul mood. The infantry had covered itself in glory while he languished on the left flank. Harboring thoughts of grandeur, he conceived the idea for a charge. The plan was simple. He wanted Farnsworth to ride north through Plum Run Valley and cause as much havoc as possible. For some unexplained reason Kilpatrick did not see the need to communicate his plan to the infantry, or else, he simply failed to do so. Apparently he thought the infantry would see the obvious opportunity, and seize the initiative to finish the job. Kilpatrick explained his thought process: "instead of a defeat, a total rout would occur."[2]

Farnsworth's Skirmish Line—Bushman Woods

Captain John W. Bennett, a Newberry, Vermont resident and captain of Company D, crouched behind a large boulder in the edge of the woods and looked over Plum Run Valley. From his position the perils of operating in Plum Run Valley were painfully clear. Stone and rail fences presented formidable obstacles to cross. Maintaining any semblance of order during a charge would be nearly impossible. Big Round Top, a quarter mile to his right, formed a natural barrier on the valley's east side. One terrain feature made a lasting impression. A five-or six-acre plot atop a 100-foot hill jutted from the southwestern slope of Big Round Top. A stone fence that was probably three and a half to four feet high enclosed the field, which has been described as "D-shaped."

Large boulders covered the hill's west wall. Earlier in the day Company M discovered the main Confederate line lay between the "D-shaped" plot and the crest of the mountain.[3] Bennett looked at the imposing terrain and probably dreaded a charge into the valley.

Presently, a whistle came from his rear. Kilpatrick and Farnsworth, oblivious to the threat of sharpshooters a short distance away, casually rode forward. Farnsworth waved for the captain to join them. Just at that moment the prospect of a trip to the rear brought nothing but dismal thoughts. The Texans and Alabamians, ever alert for targets of opportunity, plied their deadly trade a few rods away. As a result, the captain had already experienced several near misses. "A slight blister on each cheek," was how Bennett recalled the experience, "while endeavoring to keep a watch of what was being enacted in my front by peeking around first one side of a tree and then the other."[4] On signal from Bennett, a companion slowly raised his hat on top of a stick. Confederate sharpshooters took the bait and blazed away at the decoy. Bennett dashed for a tree 30 feet to his rear. Even then, a hail of Minié balls filled the air before he arrived at the place of safety. Deadly balls whizzed in chipping bark from both sides of the tree and dirt splattered in all directions. The trip required several more similar adventures before the Vermonter was out of range.[5]

Kilpatrick and Farnsworth engaged in serious conversation when Bennett approached. Addressing his subordinate, Farnsworth informed him that "General Kilpatrick thinks there is a fair chance to make a successful charge. You have been up there all day, what do you think?" Kilpatrick interrupted before Bennett could respond: "The whole army is in full retreat. I have just heard from the right. Our cavalry there is gobbling them up by the thousands. All we have to do is charge and the enemy will throw down their arms and surrender." Bennett did not share that opinion. He knew from the 1st Texas water detail and Lindsay's skirmishers that they faced a tough veteran division. "Sir," Bennett deliberately replied, "I don't know about the situation on the right, the enemy in our front are not broken and retreating." Numerous huge boulders dotting the terrain and the walled field on top of the 100-foot hill were also much on the Vermonter's mind. He expressed a strong opinion that there was not a horse in the division capable of jumping the wall surrounding the "D-shaped" field from the lower side.[6]

Kilpatrick appeared annoyed at the officer's reluctance and demonstrated his quick temper. Though he angrily expressed his displeasure, the division commander probably recognized the perils of the mission. According to Bennett, "He chose not to challenge the junior officer's opinion."[7] However, Kilpatrick remained determined to go through with the charge.

It was then that Farnsworth requested Bennett accompany him on a final reconnaissance. The pair carefully noted the position of Hood's infantry. Unlimbered batteries were trained in their direction. The rocky terrain presented formidable obstacles for men on horseback. At the conclusion of their excursion Farnsworth paused and turned to Bennett. The brigade commander put into words what each believed: "I don't see the slightest chance of success."[8] At Kilpatrick's

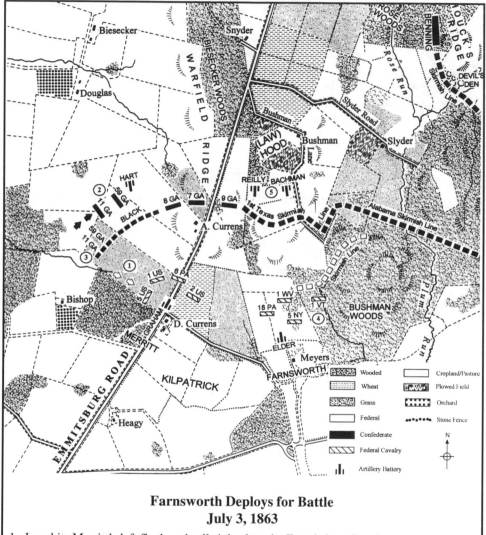

Farnsworth Deploys for Battle
July 3, 1863

1. Law hits Merritt's left flank and rolls it back to the Emmitsburg Road.
2. The 11th and 59th Georgia, pulled from the Confederate extreme right, are moving to support the line near the Emmitsburg Road.
3. Black is ordered to hold the Confederate right with his skirmish line.
4. Farnsworth prepares to charge Law's skirmish line.
5. Law returns to his headquarters near the batteries a short time before Farnsworth mounts his first charge.

headquarters Farnsworth carefully explained the situation. Once again he expressed serious doubt the charge would succeed.

Kilpatrick's anger flared up again. Several of the Texans and Vermonters claimed they heard a heated argument. Law referred to the argument, though he probably based his information on conversations with the Texans and with Alabamians.[9]

John Bennett claimed only he, Kilpatrick, and Farnsworth were present. He reported that Kilpatrick yelled: "General Farnsworth, well somebody can charge." The accusation was clear. The insult cut to Farnsworth's very soul. His body went rigid. According to Bennett, "His set lips turned white." After a lengthy pause, Farnsworth retorted, "General Kilpatrick, if anybody can charge, we can sir."[10]

Stephen Clark remembered that "Gen. Farnsworth informed Gen Kilpatrick of the situation saying it would be a desperate undertaking to charge mounted men. This nettled Kilpatrick, who replied that the charge must be made, and if he (Gen. Farnsworth) did not want to lead it, he (Kilpatrick) would lead it himself. Gen. Farnsworth's reply was characteristic of the man: I am not afraid to go as far as any man, and no man can take my men further than I can." Joseph W. Allen, bugler of the 1st Vermont, claimed to be close to the pair and that Farnsworth "protested against the hopelessness of the charge, saying the 1st Vermont had been cut to pieces already and that the men should not be sacrificed."[11]

Parsons's account is more dramatic. In his version Farnsworth exclaimed, "Shall I throw my handful of men over rough ground, through timber, against a brigade of infantry? The 1st Vermont has already been fought half to pieces, these are too good men to kill." Kilpatrick retorted in a loud voice, "Do you refuse to obey my orders? If you are afraid to lead the charge, I will lead it." Farnsworth shot back, "Take that back." Gaining control of himself, Kilpatrick said, "I did not mean it; forget it." After a lengthy pause, Farnsworth spoke in a calm voice: "General if you order the charge, I will lead it, but you must take the responsibility." Parsons heard little of the remaining conversation. Farnsworth departed with, "I will obey your order."[12]

Bennett claimed Kilpatrick did not say he would lead the charge.[13] On the other hand Parsons claimed he was within earshot of the pair and overheard the conversation between the two generals, as did Captain Elder.[14] There is one common thread in the accounts of the incident. Farnsworth thought the plan of attack senseless and most likely would result in a useless waste of men. But Kilpatrick had ordered a charge. In the end Farnsworth led it.

Born in Green Oak, Michigan, Farnsworth was removed at an early age to Rockton, Illinois. He entered into the study of law at the University of Michigan. But in 1858, he and several classmates left the university after their involvement in an "unfortunate affair" was discovered. Farnsworth joined Albert Sidney Johnston's Mormon Expedition as a civilian forager. Answering the call for volunteers, he enlisted in the 8th Illinois, which was a cavalry regiment raised by his uncle. Rank came quickly to the young man from Illinois, first attaining the position of adjutant and by December 1861 a captain's commission. After serving in

41 engagements, Farnsworth was for a time acting chief quartermaster of the IV Corps. In the spring of 1863 he was an aide-de-camp on Pleasonton's staff. Custer served at Pleasonton's headquarters at the same time.[15] The pair dressed like their mentor, wearing broad-brimmed hats similar to Pleasonton's as they rode about camp.[16] Henry Parsons described Farnsworth as taller than Custer and Kilpatrick; perhaps more soldierly in his demeanor; pale in complexion and the possessor of a determined look and manner.[17]

Farnsworth Prepares for Battle

The First Brigade's alignment remained essentially the same as in the early afternoon. The 18th Pennsylvania maintained its position on the extreme left. Major Charles E. Capehart's West Virginians were next in line. On the

Brig. Gen. Elon J. Farnsworth, Commanding Cavalry Brigade

MC MOLLUS USAMHI

mountaineers' right Preston's 1st Vermont were pretty well hidden in the Bushman Woods.[18] Major Hammond and the 5th New York were to the rear of the 18th Pennsylvania.[19]

Farnsworth selected the 1st West Virginia and the 1st Vermont to lead the charge. Preston organized the Vermonters in three battalions and formed them in columns by fours. Major William W. Wells, with the Second Battalion (Companies B, C, H and G, 1st Vermont), went into column on Richmond's right.[20] Captain Henry Parsons commanding the First Battalion (E, F, I, L) was next in the column. Captain Andrew J. Grover, Company K, brought up the rear with a portion of the Third Battalion. These were probably Companies A and K.[21] Farnsworth detailed the remainder of the battalion under Bennett to look after his right.[22]

Wells, a merchant from Burlington, Vermont, enlisted as a private in September 1861. He steadily progressed through the ranks and at Gettysburg had held the rank of major since December of 1862.[23] Bennett was from Newbury and enlisted as first lieutenant in Company D. He would rise to the rank of lieutenant colonel with the regiment.[24]

Before the column departed, Kilpatrick placed Parsons and Grover behind a stone wall as reserves. Lieutenant Colonel Preston remained with the reserves. It was between 4:45 and 5:00 p.m. when Farnsworth placed himself at the head of the West Virginians and Vermonters. The young brigadier of just five days had been unable to procure a proper uniform for his new rank. His mentor and former commander, Major General Alfred Pleasonton, had willingly shared his own wardrobe.

On the afternoon of July 3, Farnsworth wore Pleasonton's blue coat with a single star.[25]

Preston's fighting spirit was up as the rear column rode by. In an impulsive moment, the colonel ordered the cavalrymen to horse. But, Kilpatrick was not ready to sacrifice his reserves and brought the battalion back.[26]

Born in Burke, Vermont, Addison W. Preston spent most of his youth in Danville. Entering Brown University at age 21, he quickly gained a reputation as a scholar. But then illness struck one and a half years short of graduation. On advice of his physician, Preston undertook an extended sea voyage, visiting, among other places, Australia and California. In 1861 he resided in Danville where he answered the call for volunteers. In September of that year Preston enlisted in the 1st Vermont Cavalry, becoming captain of Company D.[27]

**Lt. Col. Preston W. Addison,
1st Vermont Cavalry**

MC MOLLUS USAMHI

The Texans Stand Their Ground

Following a rough wood lane, Major Wells led the Second Battalion through a skirt of timber. The head of the column emerged from the darkness of the woods just to the right of the 1st Texas. Farnsworth and Wells turned sharply right and skirted the woods. At the dedication of the Vermont monument on the Gettysburg Battlefield, Bennett said of the parting scene: "Away into the jaws of death and into the mouth of Hell rode that splendid body of brave men."[28]

The West Virginians formed line of battle in full view of the 1st Texas.[29] When Colonel Richmond became satisfied with the line, the bugler sounded the charge. Across an open field, approximately 200–300 yards away, the 1st Texas hunkered down behind the stone fence and waited.[30]

Earlier in the afternoon several Texans and Alabamians were thrown forward as skirmishers. When the cavalry began forming, the men scurried for their own line. Private H. W. Berryman, Company I, 1st Texas reached the safety of the stone wall in time to position himself to fire.[31] Private Theophilus F. Botsford, Company D, 47th Alabama found the situation more harrowing. He lay in an old field when the cavalry bore down on him, then fled over a high fence and raced for cover. An exhausted and winded Alabama private tumbled over the stone fence a scant few moments ahead of the 1st West Virginia Cavalry.[32]

In the meantime, Bass steadied his men. Thundering hoofs gobbled up the yards between the antagonists. At 50 or 60 yards the command, "Fire!" rang out.

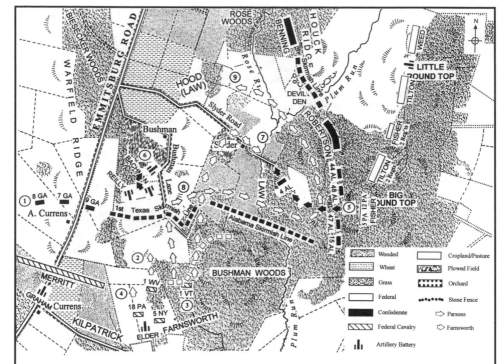

Farnsworth's Charge North through Plum Run Valley
July 3, 1863

1. At 4:00 p.m. Law's skirmish line extends west from the main line to just past the Currens house. Law has his headquarters flag near Riley's and Bachman's batteries.
2. A charge against the 1st Texas by the 1st West Virginia Cavalry fails.
3. Between 4:45 and 5:00 p.m. Farnsworth leads a squadron of the 1st Vermont Cavalry against the Confederate skirmish line and easily breaks through.
4. The 18th Pennsylvania Cavalry, supported by the 5th New York, mounts a charge about 5:00 p.m. and is easily repulsed.
5. Law sends a staff officer to order a regiment from the main line. The 4th Alabama withdraws and advances toward the Slyder house to confront Parsons.
6. Bachman moves a section to cover Plum Run Valley below Devil's Den.
7. Parsons, leading a second squadron, breaks through and rides as far as the Slyder house before turning east. His troop then advances along the farm lane toward Big Round Top.
8. Farnsworth initially rides parallel to and west of Parsons's line. After passing Law's skirmish line Farnsworth turns sharply to the east, riding almost parallel to Law's skirmish line, then turns and races north behind the Confederate line.
9. Farnsworth turns west as he nears Devil's Den and comes under fire from Benning and from Bachman on Warfield Ridge. Farnsworth's horse is killed but a trooper gives his horse to the young general.

An instant later, a sheet of flame leaped at the charging mountaineers.[33] Before voluminous smoke obscured the view, the Texas defenders saw several horses and riders go down.[34]

Richmond's charge came to an abrupt end a few yards in front of the rock fence. Major Capehart described the charge as "one of the most desperate during the present rebellion."[35] The West Virginians lost formation, becoming little more than a mass of mounted horsemen milling around. While the officers attempted to rally the broken line, Bass's Texans loaded and fired. In the space of a few minutes, Berryman claimed that he killed a captain, wounded a lieutenant, and captured five or six horse soldiers.[36] Richmond collected a few men and dashed for the

Capt. William K. Bachman,
Rowan (North Carolina) Artillery

CV, v10, n6, June 1902, 274

Texans' right flank. A few rounds were randomly fired at the defenders as the troopers rode past. These shots "did us no harm," Private James O. Bradfield, Company E, happily recorded, "as the rock fence protected us perfectly."[37]

On turning the flank, Richmond led the band north. As they rode, bullets zipped in from the Emmitsburg Road.[38] The 9th Georgia was probably visible as it marched toward Reilly's and Bachman's batteries. It is logical to assume Reilly turned at least one section toward the intruders. The Texans had sustained little damage and certainly posed a threat should a retreat be attempted. The tiny band found themselves surrounded.[39] The West Virginians did little more than ride aimlessly in a box. Richmond concluded the ride had accomplished its purpose. Time had come to leave the field. The dilemma now was to determine the best avenue of retreat. He decided to tackle the Texans again and so ordered the "Officers and men to cut their way through."[40]

Law's Headquarters—Reilly's Battery

Law stood near the division's batteries when Farnsworth launched his cavalry attack against the 1st Texas.[41] His first thought was to support the batteries. The 9th Georgia would take care of that. The men from the Lone Star State also needed reinforcements. For this task Law ordered the section of Reilly's battery near the A. Currens house moved 300 yards to the east. Two ten-pounder Parrotts went into battery about where the marker and guns stand today on the eastern edge of Warfield Ridge. Law also took the precaution to change Bachman's front to the east and move forward on the crest of Warfield Ridge to a position where the guns easily covered the valley.[42]

The Pennsylvanians Give the Texans a Try

It was about 5:00 p.m. or a little after when the 18th Pennsylvania skirmishers moved to a clearing in the woods and formed line of battle.[43] A new fighting unit, the 18th Regiment of Cavalry (also designated the 163rd Regiment of the Line) had been recruited during the fall and winter of 1862. Its men came from Greene, Crawford, Dauphin, Washington, Allegheny, Lycoming, Cambria, Philadelphia, and Montgomery counties. The 18th Pennsylvania received horses about December 15 and moved to the vicinity of Bladensburg, Maryland where the men were armed with sabers and carbines. Its first serious engagement occurred at Hanover, Pennsylvania on June 30 when it was attacked by Stuart's column.[44] This would be its second serious fight.

The 5th New York divided into two battalions and supported either flank of the Pennsylvanians. William P. Bacon commanded the right battalion and Major John Hammond the left.[45] Colonel William P. Brinton led the regiments forward, riding first across an open field, then through boulder strewn dense timber.[46] Reilly's and Bachman's batteries played on the charging cavalry while it was still in the timber. The historian of the 18th Pennsylvania wrote that "shells were flying, thick and fast over our heads." An occasional limb, cut from a tree, fell into their path. As the Pennsylvanians and New Yorkers approached the timber line, the rattle of musketry filled the air. Confederate infantry were then discovered lying behind the stone fence, which at this point, skirted the woods.[47] The 1st Texas was about to receive another charge.

Maj. John Hammond,
5th New York Cavalry
MC MOLLUS USAMHI

Owing to the boulders and dense timber, the cavalry had difficulty maintaining formation. According to one trooper the line became an "irregular mass."[48] The Texans' first volley went high, passing harmlessly over the heads of the Pennsylvanians. Federal horse soldiers forced their horses "up to the very muzzles" of the Confederate rifles.[49] Texas musketry, however, took its toll. Several Pennsylvanians fell in short order. One had a horse shot from under him and became a prisoner.[50] Because the charge lacked organization, the Texans easily repulsed the Federal horse. W. T. White wrote, "We felt we could almost whip all the cavalry the enemy had."[51]

The 18th Pennsylvania and 5th New York fell back to an open field where the line had first formed.[52] Hammond took up position in rear of Elder's battery and "stood to horse during the remainder of the fight."[53] Brinton's men dismounted and formed a skirmish line.[54] The Confederate artillerists discovered the Pennsylvanians and shells began bursting around the troopers.[55] From the tone of the accounts of this particular action, the shelling amounted to little more than an annoyance and inflicted little damage.

The Pennsylvanians extended the skirmish line to the left, reaching almost to the Emmitsburg Road.[56] The line ran through a field of high grass and weeds. The A. Currens house stood to the left. A "stake and rider" fence bordered a wheatfield on their front. A lively skirmish developed with the Georgians. According to Thomas Grier, "While in this position the men covered themselves in various ways and the puffs of smoke from their guns was the only way of locating many of them."[57]

After the Pennsylvanians deployed General Merritt pushed his line forward. Squadrons of the 2nd and 5th U.S. Cavalry came into position on Brinton's left. The Pennsylvanians were unaware of the Regulars presence until carbine fire zipped overhead and into the grass.[58] Angry shouts announced the displeasure of the men from the Keystone State. Firing between the lines continued until near sundown when a furious rainstorm rolled in.[59]

Farnsworth Breaks Through

From their position on Big Round Top the 5th Pennsylvania Reserves were witnesses to the splendor of a cavalry charge against infantry.[60] Bennett's battalion skillfully executed a diversionary thrust against the skirmish line. With sabers drawn, Farnsworth's column rode parallel to the skirmish line a short distance, then made a sharp turn left. Early in the ride a weak cheer rose from the ranks of the cavalry, but the expectation of a volley at close range dampened the men's enthusiasm. Most chose to ride in silence.[61] A few scattering shots proved ineffectual. Then a volley cracked harmlessly over the heads of the Vermonters.[62] Lead riders worked furiously to tear down the fence. Amazingly very few horse soldiers fell, which Bugler Joe Allen attributed to dense smoke shrouding the attacking column. The Vermonters charged a thin skirmish line of Alabamians to the left of the 1st Texas.[63] Brandishing sabers and slashing at the defenders, blue uniforms mingled with the Confederate butternut. After a brief fight Farnsworth and his men easily broke through.

Law Lays a Trap

Law would later say he watched the fight between the Texans and West Virginians with "intense interest and no small degree of anxiety."[64] Use of artillery to support the Texans was out of the question. The combatants were so close, friendly shells would inflict damage on the Confederate side. There was a brief moment of relief when the Texans sent the West Virginians reeling. When Farnsworth broke into the clear, Law sensed a critical moment had presented itself.[65] This was a battalion of four companies, but an attack by Kilpatrick's entire force might produce disastrous results. Or, an equal disaster might occur if the cavalry charge overran the batteries.

Fortunately for the Confederates, Farnsworth and Wells turned right at the northern end of Bushman Woods. Law now had the time he needed to bring up infantry support for the batteries. He also breathed a sigh of relief when it became apparent that Farnsworth's command rode unsupported.

Farnsworth splashed across Plum Run and rode for the "D-shaped" field. Parsons noted Wells was "a young officer who bore a charmed life and was destined to pass through many daring encounters."[66] On reaching the base of the 100-foot hill Farnsworth put spurs to his horse and raced up the slope, guiding his men between the walled field and Law's line of infantry. A participant described the ride as a "swift resistless charge over rocks, through timber, under close enfilading fire."[67]

"The situation demanded," as Law related it, "the utmost promptness and decision."[68] Upon ascertaining the cavalry's general direction, he decided to pull a regiment from Big Round Top. He also wanted Oates to strengthen his skirmish line and close toward the 1st Texas.[69] The 9th Georgia was already on its way to support Reilly and Bachman.[70] He started Lieutenant E. B. Wade of his staff across the valley to detach the first regiment he found. In effect, Law was closing the door on Farnsworth. From his vantage point above the valley floor Law marveled at their bravery. But he now believed the horsemen were no match for his infantry.[71]

Kilpatrick's Position—Bushman Woods

On observing the West Virginians' repulse, Kilpatrick and Preston knew Farnsworth's small column was cutoff and unsupported. To relieve the pressure on the isolated column Kilpatrick ordered Preston to ride to support the Second Battalion. Preston took with him the First Battalion, under Captain Parsons, and Captain Grover with a portion of the Third Battalion.[72]

Captain Oliver T. Cushman, Company E, and Alexander A. Watson of Company L rode with Parsons. Twenty-year old Oliver Cushman, of Hartland, Vermont, left Dartmouth in his sophomore year to join the 1st Vermont.[73] On the morning of July 3, he wore a "duck fighting jacket trimmed with gold braid." Before the charge Parsons and Cushman stood near Elder's battery and engaged in idle conversation. Responding to a comment about his dress, Cushman informed his companion the garment was the gift of a

**Capt. Oliver T. Cushman,
Co. E, 1st Vermont Cavalry**

MC MOLLUS USAMHI

lady friend. Her correspondence conveyed the warm reassuring gesture, "my own hands made it, and no rebel bullet could pierce it." Cushman decided the present day might be a good occasion to test the garment's magic powers.[74] The pair stood near Elder's battery when Cushman retrieved a silk handkerchief from his pocket, threw it over his cap, and pinned it to the visor. He wore the silk cloth when the charge began.[75]

As the First Battalion rode through the dismounted skirmish line, troopers called out for the mounted men to halt. On exiting the woods, Parsons's men saw the 1st West Virginia to their left and retiring in disorder. The First Battalion crossed Bushman hill slightly north of the track followed by the Third Battalion. Parsons hit the skirmish line north of the point where Farnsworth and Wells broke through, and like Farnsworth a short time before, easily overran the line.

Preston then divided the column. Parsons rode north toward the Slyder house. Preston followed the same general route as Farnsworth. Crossing the fields and fences, the First Battalion turned east at the house into Slyder farm lane. Thinking the lane might lead to Little Round Top, Parsons headed for the base of the 100-foot hill.[76]

Fight Below the 100-Foot Hill

Wade found the 4th Alabama and sent it scrambling through the woods toward the west. Men broke into a sprint with the fleet of foot leading the way. They emerged from the woods east of the Slyder buildings, scrambled over the walls enclosing the "D-shaped" field and raced for Slyder lane. A moment later Parsons's First Battalion bore down on them.

A new recruit from Company C, 4th Alabama, who was small in statue became particularly unsettled. But he resolved to do his duty and "let the consequence be what it may." "With pallid cheeks and trembling limbs," Adjutant Coles wrote, "he advanced with us, determined to stand by his colors."[77]

At his first glimpse of the Alabamians, Cushman cried out, "an ambuscade!"[78] Lieutenant Vaughan, Company C of the 4th Alabama, exclaimed, "Cavalry boys, cavalry! This is no fight, only a frolic, give it to them!" The little fellow, who only a few minutes before trembled with fright, suddenly found courage and enthusiastically shouted, "Well, I will be dog-goned, if we ain't got the best lieutenant in the whole army." [79]

The Vermonters were only 30 or 40 paces away when the 4th fired its first volley, which enveloped the cavalry in smoke.[80] When the smoke cleared Captain James Taylor Jones, on the right of the 4th, was disappointed to see only one horse down. Parsons turned in the saddle for a glance at the rear and was equally surprised. So far luck was with the Vermonters.[81]

A private in the Alabama line turned and pointed proudly to the horse, explaining: "Captain, I shot that black." Jones chastised the private for not shooting the horse's rider. The thirty-year-old lawyer from Demopolis, Alabama, received a quick reply that they would get the rider anyway. The private claimed he had not seen a deer for three years and was not about to miss the opportunity to bring down some game.[82]

There was not a second volley as such. Each man loaded and fired as fast as he could. Vermonters, with swords drawn, drove their horses forward and slashed at the Alabamians. On the 4th's flank several horsemen were shot from the saddle in the act of striking a blow to someone's head.[83] One of the Vermonters escaped with the 4th's guidon.[84]

During the attack Private Sam Whitworth, Company F, stood to the rear of Coles. Sam, a thirty-year-old teacher, forgot that Coles stood in front.[85] When a trooper rode by Whitworth, with musket pressed firmly against his shoulder, turned to draw a bead on the man. At the instant he pulled the trigger, the musket barrel struck a blow to the left side of Coles's head.[86] Just then Parsons's Vermonters were not more than 10 paces away. A Federal near Coles went down with his horse. Instead of surrendering, the trooper jumped over the animal, fired a shot at the Alabamians, and attempted to get away. Unfortunately for the Vermonter, a well-aimed shot brought him down.[87]

Parsons realized that the infantry held the upper hand and guided the front companies away. He regrouped southeast of the Slyder house. The small band was under cover of the 100-foot elevation and temporarily out of harm's way. In the meantime the rear companies fell back toward the Slyder house. This group reformed in some timber between the house and Plum Run.[88]

Farnsworth's Ride—near Devil's Den

Farnsworth's ride through the eastern edge of Plum Run Valley turned into a trip through hell. Word raced along the Confederate line that Federal cavalry was loose in the rear. Men ran for the edge of the woods and shot at the intruders. The Vermonters galloped past the right flank of Law's Alabamians before they could react. The 15th and 47th Alabama could do little more than give the column a parting shot. Undaunted, the Federals, with sabers drawn, galloped forward in near perfect formation.[89] Further on Alabamians and Texans stood behind rocks and trees and fired with deadly accuracy. All would look quiet and peaceful until puffs of smoke suddenly appeared. An instant later bullets whistled past.[90] A telltale "spat" marked each time a rebel bullet found its mark. At the moment of impact, the victim noticeably tensed, then a frightened look appeared as the trooper either pitched from the saddle or struggled to ride on.[91]

Bugler Joe Allen saw a lone Confederate in the open and gave chase, intending to cut the man down with his saber. Fortunately for the butternut-clad rebel, a nearby tree afforded good protection. Allen rode on, but a moment later heard a thud as a Minié ball buried itself in the neck of his mount. A glance to the rear revealed his former prey reloading for another shot.[92]

Nearing Plum Run Gorge, Farnsworth turned abruptly left and came under fire from Benning's right. The Vermonters also came into view of Bachman and Reilly and quickly felt the sting of Confederate shells. They were on the west side of Rose Run when Farnsworth's horse went down. At the direction of Major Wells, Private David P. Freeman, Company C, gave the general his horse.[93] By this time the charge was in disarray and the horsemen hesitated, as if trying to determine the next move.

In the meantime, Preston joined Parsons's command. On seeing the small band near Devil's Den under fire, Preston ordered a detachment under Captain Cushman to support it. A few minutes later Cushman placed himself at the head of a small unit, raised his saber, and dashed forward.[94]

Farnsworth's battalion now divided into three groups. Cushman rode with Farnsworth. He, Farnsworth, Wells, and a few others retraced their route through the valley. The second group swept southwest toward Bachman's and Reilly's batteries.[95] The third group rode south through Plum Run Valley toward Law's skirmish line.

Action at the Batteries

The second group of Vermonters were less than 100 yards away from the guns when the 9th Georgia arrived in rear of Bachman's battery. Captain Hillyer faced right and advanced at the quick time through the guns. Meanwhile, the Federal horse formed line of battle and made a dash for the artillery. Just then, the Georgians' battle flag, flying in the breeze, moved in front of the guns. As Hillyer explained it, "The mass of men and horses were right in front and in easy range. I gave the command, Fire!"[96] One volley emptied several saddles and a blast from one of Bachman's cannon cut a trooper in half.[97] Even so, some were able to get among the cannon.[98] Gunners, wielding rammers for weapons, unhorsed two Vermonters while the others escaped.[99] Survivors rode through the skirmish line connecting the Texans and Georgians.[100]

A fine looking riderless Morgan horse, possessing a black mane and tail, came through the volley unhurt. In the confusion and excitement of the moment, the animal shied away from the whine and neighing of wounded horses. It broke from the cavalry troop and galloped toward the artillery horses in the Confederate rear. On seeing the loose mount, Captain Hillyer, who was then in need of a good horse, ran to the front and caught the steed.[101]

The Texans Tangle with the Cavalry Again

While the ill-fated charge on the batteries took place, the third body of Farnsworth's battalion bore down on the 1st Texas skirmish line. Colonel Richmond's West Virginians probably joined this group. At the stone wall someone shouted, "Look behind you. Here they come!" Major Bass resolved to make every shot count and held his fire until the last moment. No more than 30 yards separated the lines when the Texans volleyed. "Horse and riders went down in piles," recalled Private Bradfield.[102] Those remaining in the saddle covered the distance to the wall before the Texans could reload. A few got off shots by firing ramrod and all at the charging line. An instant later weary cavalrymen, welding their sabers, slashed at the Texans. Several of the Texans thought the Vermonters intoxicated because of abnormal swaying and lurching in the saddle.[103] One historian attributed their behavior to exhaustion from the demanding schedule in the days immediately preceding the battle.[104] "The firing," recalled McCarty, "was front, rear and toward the flanks." One of Reilly's batteries fired a shot and shell that whistled a few feet overhead.[105] In a vicious fight that was over in a few minutes, Bass's men fought back with bayonets, butts of rifles, and rocks.[106] Once through the Texas line the battered band limped to the cover of the Bushman Woods. Major Capehart spoke for all the West Virginians when he wrote, "Any one not cognizant of the *minutiae* of this charge upon infantry, under cover of heavy timber and stone fences, will fail to form a just conception of its magnitude."[107]

Fight for the "D-Shaped Field"

On the east side of the valley Farnsworth approached the walled field at a gallop. At the north end he guided the column left to pass between the field and the main line of Law's Alabamians. In the meantime Oates approached the south end of the field, and blocked Farnsworth's route of escape. A detachment of the 47th Alabama bolted from the woods and took up position near the east wall of the field. Several Alabamians appeared in the rocks above the Federal cavalry and opened fire as the horse soldiers rode past.[108]

On the west side of the field Preston ordered Parsons to lead the remainder of the First Battalion across the field from that side. Parsons and Farnsworth were in sight of each other as they raced toward the Confederate skirmish line. Near the end of the field Parsons turned sharply, reversed his route after a short distance, then spurred his horse over the wall and into the field. By this maneuver, Parsons's little command came up in rear of a group of Alabamians.[109]

Smoke from a volley at close range filled the short distance separating the lines. Mounts ridden by Lieutenant Alex Watson and Sergeant Willard Farrington, both from Company L, fell dead. Corporal Ira E. Sperry, Company L, though mortally wounded, rode from the field under his own power. As the troopers burst from the smoke, Sergeant George W. Duncan of Company L raced past Parsons. Duncan waved his saber, turned toward his commander, cried, "Captain, I'm with you."[110] An instant later a fatal bullet found its mark. The hard-charging sergeant, jerked, threw up his left hand and pitched from the saddle. Parsons's horse stumbled as it ran over the dead trooper and stopped, leaving Parsons momentarily alone in the rear. A brief hand-to-hand combat developed in which Preston reported sabers were effectively used.[111] In the melee the Confederate line lost any semblance of organization. Stephen Clark and Preston claimed the Southerners "surrendered in squads."[112] Clark did qualify the statement by saying, "Very few, however, saw fit to go."[113] The 15th Alabama reported three men captured on the 3rd, and it is assumed these occurred during the skirmish. None of the 47th's men reported as captured could be attributed to the fight in the "D-shaped" field.[114]

A detail from the 47th Alabama ran up and attempted to make Parsons a prisoner. His fighting blood was up and the cavalry officer pressed the issue. Brandishing his saber, Parsons spurred his horse forward. A bullet fired at close range buried itself deep in his chest. More shots in quick secession severely wounded his mount, sending it into a momentary frenzy. Somehow Parsons managed to stay in the saddle while the animal jerked about. It then bolted through the ranks of the 47th Alabama and to safety.[115]

When the foray into the field began, Lieutenant Clark commanded the third company from the front. As the troopers rushed forward they became easy targets for the Alabamians. In a few seconds the leading companies melted away. Clark saw Parsons and Duncan hit. Acting on instinct, he gave the order "charge" and dashed for the south wall of the field. At the wall, which Clark described as a stone and rail fence, the Vermont horse soldiers began slashing at the defenders behind the obstruction with their sabers.[116]

The Death of Farnsworth

Meanwhile Farnsworth, Wells, and Cushman rode at the head of their small battalion. Cushman's silk handkerchief waved in the wind. From some distance away, the 4th Alabama thought the silk handkerchief a flag of truce.[117] But Farnsworth harbored no thought of surrender. He was on a collision course with the 15th Alabama and boldly charged. A canister round whizzed harmlessly over the horsemen and fortunately the 15th Alabama too. Oates later recalled the shot made a sound like a covey of partridges in flight as it passed overhead.[118]

Oates's skirmishers were under the command of Lieutenant John D. Adrian of the 44th Alabama. A native of Alabama, Adrian enlisted in the 4th Alabama with the first call for Alabama volunteers. He listed his nearest post office as Arbacoochee in Calhoun County. After transferring to Company K of the 44th Alabama, its members, in October 1862, elected him third lieutenant. He held that rank at Gettysburg.[119]

Adrian needed a horse and thought the skirmish line a good place to acquire one. The skirmishers were just ascending the hill when the Vermonters bore down on them. Farnsworth waved his pistol and demanded those nearest him surrender. Adrian and his companions volleyed. Farnsworth pitched from his saddle and, although not killed outright, suffered from multiple wounds, any one of which would probably have proved fatal.[120] Cushman went down with a horrible face wound. The fearless trooper refused to surrender, drew his pistol, and blazed away at anyone in the vicinity. Though several men quickly pinned him to the ground, the young man from the Green Mountain State continued to struggle until he fainted.[121]

Adrian related that Farnsworth still grasped his pistol when the Alabamians approached. Several muskets were trained on the Federal general. He probably knew his wounds were fatal and resolved to fight to his death. On impulse he demanded the Alabamians surrender. Adrian demanded Farnsworth surrender instead. Farnsworth defiantly responded "he would never surrender to a rebel" and with the strength remaining in his dying body, attempted to open fire.[122] It was his last act on this earth.

Private Craig, 9th Georgia, had followed the flight of the horsemen and arrived in time to witness the scene. He recalled that Farnsworth retorted, "...he would die before he would surrender, turned the pistol and shot himself."[123] Oates saw the encounter but did not pay much attention to the group gathered around Farnsworth until someone brought him a shoulder strap. They thought at first

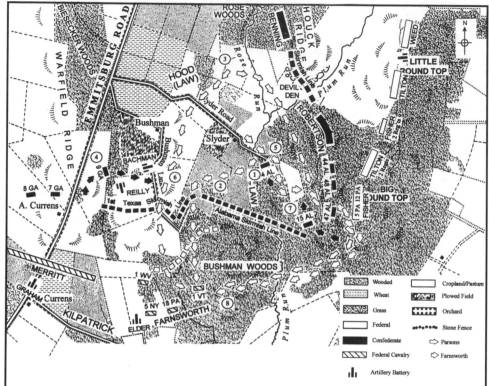

Law Breaks Farnsworth's Charge
July 3, 1863

1. Parsons encounters the 4th Alabama southeast of the Slyder house. Several troopers are shot from their saddles. Parsons's battalion splits into two groups.
2. One group turns southwest, reforms under cover of some woods, and eventually fights its way through Law's skirmish line to safety.
3. Farnsworth's battalion also splits into two groups. Farnsworth leads one group south along the original route north. The second group gallops southwest toward Bachman and Reilly.
4. The 9th Georgia arrives to support the artillery as Farnsworth's troops approach.
5. Parsons initially rides east, then turns south and rides parallel with Farnsworth.
6. Farnsworth's men are easily repulsed by the 9th Georgia and Law's artillerymen. The Federals continue south and after a sharp encounter pass through Law's skirmish line.
7. The 15th Alabama blocks Farnsworth's escape route. Parsons and several troopers are severely wounded. Farnsworth is mortally wounded.
8. Survivors from the encounter with the 4th and 15th Alabama return to their original position.

that Farnsworth was a major because he wore a star on each shoulder strap. Oates concluded that Farnsworth was a brigadier and went to the body. The dead man's pockets contained several letters, at least one being from his wife. In an act of compassion for the Federal, Oates subsequently destroyed all of them to keep his personal correspondence from falling into the hands of souvenir hunters.[124]

Several versions of Farnsworth's death circulated throughout the brigade that night. Oates said at one time that Farnsworth blew his brains out. In later years he recalled that Farnsworth shot himself through the heart. Adrian and Craig steadfastly maintained that Farnsworth took his life by turning his pistol on himself.[125] The Confederates accepted the story of Farnsworth's suicide which the Federals disputed.[126] The issue remains unresolved.

Escape through the Lines

Away from the fight, Corporal Walker, an orderly to Farnsworth, saw Parsons struggling to stay in the saddle. Overtaking the captain, Walker supported the wounded man and related the account of how Farnsworth and Cushman fell.[127]

In the meantime, Oates's struggle with Farnsworth relieved the pressure on Lieutenant Clark. Even then it became every man for himself, but most managed to escape. Clark had not ridden far when he happened on Major Wells. The regiment's major greeted him with, "Clark, where are you going?" In response the lieutenant pointed west toward the Confederate batteries on Warfield Ridge. Wells sensed the time had come to call off the ride, and countered with, "We must get out of this."[128] By now only a few remained to continue the ride. Wells col-

lected as many survivors as he could. A thunderstorm rumbled over South Mountain when he led the remnants of Farnsworth's battalion through the Federal line on Big Round Top.

In the ride through Plum Run Valley Parsons rode his bugler's sorrel horse, which he described as "scarred and stiff from long service." But the mount served him well. Although blood gushed from the sorrel's side, the ride was gentle and reassuring. Before drifting into unconsciousness, Parsons remembered gentle hands lifting him from the saddle and seeing the horse's "great eyes turned upon his as if in sympathy and reproof."[129]

Perley C. J. Cheney, second lieutenant of Company E, 1st Vermont Cavalry, and his mount received wounds. A shot ripped through Chaney's body. His horse, though fatally wounded,

Maj. William Wells,
1st Vermont Cavalry

faithfully bore the wounded man from the field. Before entering the troopers body, the bullet struck his watch, stopping the hands at 5:27 p.m.[130] Farnsworth's charge was over.

Celebration of the Repulse

After the fighting ended a detail from the 4th Alabama went over to the battery where the artillerists were in good spirits. One recounted that they had "...a hot time defending their guns." As the Alabamians roamed the field, dead Federal horse soldiers were found lying in a number of places. Private Reuben Nix spotted one and climbed over a fence to investigate. He returned with a roll of greenbacks.[131]

The Worth of the Charge

Colonel Scruggs's losses were relatively light, totaling two captured, one killed and one wounded.[132] The ill-fated charge by Farnsworth cost the brigade 112 casualties. Sixty of these were missing on the battlefield and there were 19 reported killed.[133] In the end the charge contributed nothing to the Federal cause. Meade's infantry had been content to watch the cavalry's adventure from the sidelines. A Pennsylvanian on Big Round Top had a clear view of the event and described it as one of the grandest sights on the battlefield. Law cleverly boxed Farnsworth in by maneuvering the 15th Alabama and then correctly anticipated Farnsworth's moves. He agreed with others at the scene that Farnsworth's charge was foolhardy. Felix H. Robertson, a son of General Robertson and an artillerist with the Army of Tennessee, put it more bluntly, calling it an "...inexcusable military blunder."[134] When Longstreet visited division headquarters he found the cavalry repulse the only favorable action of a rather dismal afternoon. In Law's words he "...warmly congratulated me on the manner in which the situation had been handled."[135]

Federal Recollections of the Charge

In later years Captain Parsons corresponded with many of the survivors in an attempt to identify the course and events of the afternoon. Though there were good recollections from earlier in the day, Farnsworth's men recalled little of the desperate ride through Plum Run Valley. One horse soldier wrote, "If you rode in a cyclone, how could you describe the scenery." Another said of the ride, "I was fighting, not looking." "The excitement was so intense, it was so mad a gallop, the spirit of action rose so high," as Parsons remembered it, "that the ordinary impression left no effect."[136]

There were, however, some occurrences that memories retained. Parsons summarized some of these:

> *For instance: a man at the battery was cut through by a cannon ball; where we received the first volley; where we struck the Alabama regiment at the foot of the lane, and where we went over the blazing wall on the hill; but none of the intervening places, the ditches and fences we cleared, the houses and barns we passed, nothing was remembered.*

In his own case Parsons clearly recalled "the brown eyes and honest face of the man who planted his gun against my breast and fired."[137]

The Generals Remember a Comrade

Meade considered the cavalry actions on his flanks the afternoon of July 3 a means of harassing and occupying the enemy's attention.[138] Though he had lost a promising young brigadier the sacrifice of Farnsworth was not mentioned. That was not Meade's style. None of the other generals who fell were mentioned either.

Twenty-seven years after the Battle of Gettysburg, Henry Parsons lashed out at Meade because he perceived the commanding general had not properly recognized the contribution made by Farnsworth and his men. In a *National Tribune* article the former captain lamented: "It is proper to say the charge which drew the admiration of the enemy, drew no admiration from Meade; that he refused to mention in his report the name of the only general officer who fell in the Battle of Gettysburg within the enemy's lines."

Praise from the cavalry hierarchy was more generous. Pleasonton was generous with his praise, calling Farnsworth's charge a "brilliant engagement." Referring to his protégé as the "gallant and noble Farnsworth," Pleasonton went on to say:

> *Gifted in a high degree with a quick judgment and remarkable for his daring and coolness, his comprehensive grasp of the situation, on the field of battle and rapidity of his action had already distinguished General Farnsworth among his comrades in arms. In his death was closed a career that must have won the highest honor of his profession.[139]*

In his own way Kilpatrick mustered a few kind words for the man who was surely sacrificed on the altar of glory. A fitting epitaph in his report of the action read: "A general on June 29, on the 30th he baptized his star in blood, and on July 3, for the honor of his young brigade and the glory of his corps, he gave his life."[140]

The Rains Must Fall

General Merritt reported the Reserves were engaged four hours before rain brought an end to the fighting. On previous occasions a good downpour fell shortly after cessation of hostilities. More than one Confederate attributed the rain to the effects of heavy cannonading. Of the affair at Gettysburg, Adjutant Coles wrote, "We knew it would come." And it did. The heavens opened up and rain came down in torrents, drenching the Pennsylvania countryside.[141]

Somewhere on Big Round Top, Sergeant William N. Johns, Company B, 15th Alabama suffered from a severe wound inflicted the previous day. He was unable to turn himself over and lay on his back all night and the day of July 3. He nearly died of thirst the night of July 2, but the heavy rain from the severe thunderstorm almost caused him to drown. John managed to survive by placing his hat over his face until the rain subsided.[142]

Chapter 11

Aftermath of Battle

A Case of Poor Communications

From his vantage point near the Emmitsburg Road, General McLaws watched Pickett's, Pettigrew's, and Trimble's lines hurl themselves against the Federal center and the subsequent destruction. As he prepared to cover their withdrawal, McLaws saw that the Federals made no move to follow. Because wooded terrain between his division and the Federal artillery afforded good protection McLaws felt sufficiently secure to stay in position and observe the Federal line. A short time later a staff officer from Law requested a brigade to replace Anderson in his main line. McLaws told the man to inform Law that "...Pickett had been thoroughly routed" and advised Law to close left because they might be called upon to meet a Federal advance. Fifteen minutes later Colonel Moxley Sorrel rode up, and McLaws proceeded to inform him of Law's request and his reply. "Never mind that now," Sorrel interrupted, "General Longstreet directs that you retire to your position of yesterday." When McLaws asked who would tell Law, Sorrel indicated he would. McLaws then launched into a lecture on the ill-advised nature of the order, the importance of the position, and the fact it had only been won after a hard struggle. Sorrel felt compelled to interrupt again: "General, there is no discretion allowed, the order is for you to retire at once."[1]

As McLaws withdrew, his men came under artillery fire which did little damage. Sorrel reappeared after McLaws reached his new position and countermanded the previous order to retire. McLaws immediately asked, "Why?" "Because," replied Sorrel. "General Longstreet had forgotten that he had ordered it, and now disapproved the withdrawal."[2] McLaws declined to move, and later recalled that Sorrel "gave no orders to try and retake the position, and I did not attempt it."[3] Law saw the danger in McLaws's withdrawal and sent a courier to inform "Rock" Benning that he wished a regiment moved to an elevation to the left to replace McLaws. Benning did not know which hill, and neither did the courier, because when Law gave the order he had simply waved his hand in the general direction he wished the regiment placed. Unfortunately the courier left without a clear understanding of the order. Benning assumed Law meant for him to occupy the ground vacated by McLaws, and ordered the 15th Georgia to move farther left.[4]

Law then sent for McLaws to join him in a discussion of the situation. Benning also joined the two and as the trio conversed, Federal infantry advanced toward McLaws's old position. Law's flanks were now in the air and the generals decided that Law's position had become untenable. However, Law had not received an order to retire.[5] Any doubts about the merit of withdrawing were soon removed from their minds. Colonel William McCandless's Federal brigade attacked the 15th Georgia on the front and both flanks, driving it back with considerable loss.[6] After the 15th Georgia rejoined Benning's main line, Law quietly withdrew his division to the Emmitsburg Road.[7]

Law's Brigade left its position without the 15th Alabama, which held the Confederate extreme right opposite the enemy cavalry. Sheffield had sent Thomas J. Sinclair, Company B, 4th Alabama, who was serving as courier, to order the 15th Alabama to rejoin the brigade. However, in the failing light and heavy rainstorm he had been unable to find the Alabamians. Oates later claimed Sinclair was captured. However, the records do not support this statement.[8] As darkness fell, Oates became concerned for the regiment's safety and started toward the brigade's last known location. On the way, he discovered another Federal skirmish line, presumably more cavalry as skirmishers. Although Oates had no orders to leave his position, the presence of Federals on both his front and rear caused him much concern and he immediately decided to move. Marching in single file by the right flank, Oates led the 15th Alabama through torrential rain toward the Emmitsburg Road. After reaching an open field, Oates marched in a direction he believed to be north. As he walked through the dark, the sounds of breastwork construction were discernible and Oates moved in that direction. When he discovered the sounds were made by members of Hood's Division, he happily placed the 15th Alabama in the Confederate works. Just over 24 hours after it advanced, Hood's Division occupied the same position where it entered the fight at Gettysburg.[9]

Their Best Was Not Enough

Law's Brigade did its best to turn the Federal left and almost succeeded. Most of the officers and men did their duty and courageously faced the foe. Colonel Scruggs said all his officers and men behaved with coolness and gallantry, while Colonel Perry applauded the efforts of Lieutenant Colonel John Jones, Major George Cary, and Adjutant Winns Becker.[10] He refrained from mentioning others because the list would be too long. Major Campbell stated all the officers, with the exception of Jackson and Adjutant Keller, acted well.[11] Campbell did not elaborate, nor has a record of any action against either individual been found. It can be assumed the negative remarks directed at Jackson resulted from the colonel falling out soon after the charge began. Little doubt remained as to Sheffield's ability to instill discipline. He proved himself an able regimental commander at Gettysburg. In his report of the battle Lieutenants Reuben Ewing and Francis Burk received their commander's plaudits while Captains Thomas Eubanks and Jeremiah Edwards were specifically cited for their gallantry during the hottest part of the conflict. He closed by saying that, before being wounded, Lieutenant Colonel William Hardwick and Major Columbus St. John performed their duties very efficiently.[12]

Oates was uncharacteristically quiet in praise of his men. He placed Lieutenant William D. Wood of Company H under arrest, charged with conduct unbecoming an officer. Wood tendered his resignation July 16, 1863, which Oates accepted as "the most expedient means to rid the army of an unworthy officer."[13] Many years later, Oates wrote a short biography about his former lieutenant, and either did not remember, or chose not to mention that day at Gettysburg. Wood, according to Oates, had been a fair soldier.[14]

In the aftermath of Gettysburg, perhaps more than any other battle of the Civil War, the focus has been to determine who most directly caused the Confederate reverse. Even as the Confederate army prepared to leave the Gettysburg battlefield, the seeds of discord were already sown. Longstreet and Law would soon be engrossed in a bitter dispute about which one of Law's aides traced to the battle on the Federal left. After the war Longstreet's enemies sought to place the blame on him, alleging negligence for not promptly carrying out Lee's order on July 2. It is true that Longstreet could have deployed the First Corps before noon. He could have captured the Peach Orchard and the high ground west of Little Round Top before the Federals occupied it.[15] Longstreet did not have to wait for the arrival of Law to do this. Law could have found Longstreet on the Emmitsburg Road. That premise has been studied in considerable depth by Douglas Southall Freeman, Edwin Harry Coddington, and Pfanz. None of the commanders wanted to deliver the assault as it was envisioned by Lee. Law and Hood were well within their right, as division and brigade commanders, to offer protests when the Federal position was found to be significantly different from what they anticipated. If there is any fault to be found with either, it is that Hood continued the discussions about the turning movement too long. While the generals talked, Federal preparations were under way to occupy Little Round Top, which did not occur until the charge had commenced. Had they attacked a half hour earlier, the Confederates would have reached the summit of the famous hill before Vincent.

As Hood began deploying, he was ordered to attack up the Emmitsburg Road and strike the Federal left. The original plan was modified to conform to the reality on the battlefield. It seems probable therefore that Hood on his own initiative altered his instructions to use the Emmitsburg Road as his axis of attack. Hood would have been under enfilade fire, and fire from the rear, if he had held his left to the road during the attack. The alignment of Hood's Division nearly parallel to the Emmitsburg Road gave him the best opportunity to strike the Federal left. Unexplained is why Robertson attempted to maintain his left on the Emmitsburg Road. When it became impossible to both hold his left to the road and maintain his right close upon Law, Robertson made the decision to stay with Law. A gap appeared in the middle of the Texas brigade, nonetheless. Law probably gave no thought to the Emmitsburg Road after he deployed his men in battle line, as it lay some distance to his rear. The Federal left was Law's target. To get to that objective, which Hood and Law believed to be at Devil's Den, it was necessary to pass across the Federal line under heavy and effective fire. Law then attempted to front his brigade to the north and turn the Federal left. Perhaps the terrain, the long slope down into Plum Run Valley, and the enemy fire from the base of Big Round Top all combined to force Law's Brigade to the east. Much of the enemy musketry was from Stoughton's eight companies of sharpshooters. They did effective work against Law's men. In addition, they probably appeared to Law to be a skirmish line for a stronger force which he could not ignore. Law strove to obey his order to roll up the Federal left. He moved the 44th and 48th regiments from the right of his line to the left. He ordered Oates to turn his regiment to the north and inflict as much damage as possible on the enemy's flank. Scruggs faced the 4th Alabama to the north, probably under the same order. All these maneuvers served to put his brigade in line opposite the enemy's left. As events unfolded, Law's Brigade did attack the Federal left with considerable striking power.

Once the charge got under way, Law displayed the same boldness and aggressiveness that caught Lee's eye at Gaines's Mill. While his lines were being swept by artillery and musketry, he moved two Alabama regiments, in a flawless execution under fire, from the right of the line to the left by an oblique maneuver, which put more men at the point of the heaviest fighting at the moment. He was forced to shift the 44th and 48th to the left to attack Smith's cannon. Since Benning filled the gap, had Law left the Alabama regiments on the right, he would have found a greater opportunity for success there because the fight for Little Round Top was a toss up. With two more regiments, even two as small as these, the Confederates may have wrested the hill from Union hands. Unfortunately the five regiments which did assault Little Round Top did so without benefit of unified command, attacking the hill piecemeal. To make matters worse the most junior regimental commander in the Alabama brigade was entrusted to turn the Federal left. It is certainly a tribute to the fighting ability of the Alabamians and Texans that the Federals were almost thrown off Little Round Top. On July 3, with only a day's experience in division command, Law performed with the competence of a veteran division commander as he skillfully maneuvered his regiments to defeat Farnsworth's cavalry attack.

It has not been the subject of discussion by historians, but the absence of Benning's Georgians on the right was critical to the Confederate failure to roll up the Federal left. In the fog of battle, Benning mistakenly followed the two left regiments of the Texas brigade toward Devil's Den. Had he followed Law as planned, the Confederate strength on the right would have been vastly superior. In addition, the Confederates would have had another general officer in that sector. As it was Law tried to control the nine regiments of Hood's front line virtually alone. Of course, lack of adequate staff was not new to Confederate commanders. Law experienced an almost identical situation at Chickamauga. Discussing Confederate staff problems, Porter Alexander wrote after the war, "Scarcely any of our generals had half of what they needed to keep a constant and close supervision on the execution of important orders."[16]

The Valley of Death

Sometime during the day of July 4, Federal units began venturing onto the ground that had been the scene of terrible conflicts. William Brown, 44th New York, described the wreckage on the battlefield as "a dreadful sight...heaps of men laying on the field. In some spots behind one of the larger rocks there would be laying dead around in squads where they were killed from our fire."[17]

The 118th Pennsylvania—the Corn Exchange Regiment—moved forward to occupy the Confederate positions near the Devil's Den. A pitiful and horrifying sight greeted them. Squads of dead lay shielded by the rocks, probably killed by shell bursts. Some were still kneeling behind rocks and boulders, their sightless eyes turned toward the Federal positions. Others managed to crawl behind boulders before succumbing to their wounds. Many, unable to move after being shot, had dug shallow trenches for some protection. Several were killed instantly in the act of firing and fell clutching their muskets. For many their last hours on earth were agonizing as death came slowly. Bits of grass and twigs held between clenched teeth attested to the agony they must have suffered. Most of the dead perished with lavish chews of tobacco in their mouths. Just south of Devil's Den, a neat row of dead marked Perry's line where the 4th Maine's first volley sent it to the ground. Among the slain were Captain William Dunklin. Even in death, it was obvious the Alabamian, being of large proportions and handsome features, had been a fine specimen of southern manhood.[18]

Men from Battery D, 5th U.S. Artillery also saw evidence of the hard fighting on July 2. Limbs of trees were shot away. Several dead men were scattered along Plum Run. The Federal gunners concluded the Confederates must have been wounded, crawled to the stream for water and died there. Mutilated bodies gave evidence of the work done by Smith's guns from the north end of Plum Run Valley.[19]

Casualties—Law's Brigade

Brigade casualties totaled 533 killed, wounded and missing. The 4th Alabama lost four officers killed, four wounded, and one missing.[20] There were 14 men killed, 51 wounded and 18 missing for a total of 92. The 15th Alabama incurred the largest number of casualties, sustaining 178 killed, wounded and missing. Four of its officers lay dead on the field, one was wounded, and two were missing. Fourteen of its men were killed, 76 wounded and 81 were missing. The 44th Alabama lost three officers killed and two wounded. Twenty-two of its men lay dead in front of Devil's Den, 56 were wounded and five missing. The 47th Alabama lost four officers killed and one wounded. Six of its men died on the slopes of Little Round Top, 45 were wounded and 13 were reported missing. The 48th Alabama counted eight officers wounded and two missing. Eight of its men were killed, 73 wounded, and 15 were missing.

Law's Brigade left 274 of its officers and men behind, either wounded and hospitalized or missing on the battlefield. Four of the officers left in field hospitals died before they could be removed to prison camps. Five of the missing officers were wounded and eventually recovered. Of the eleven officers captured, eight would be exchanged but only one, Thomas Christian, would return to duty. Seven of the 14 wounded officers would eventually return to duty. Therefore, when the number of captured and wounded that would not be returned to duty are considered, the brigade effectively lost 38 officers or 21 percent of its officer strength present at Gettysburg.[21]

From the brigade perspective, a total of 124 men and officers succumbed to battle-related wounds; 53 died in crude field hospitals around Gettysburg, 26 more died of other causes after incarceration in Federal prisons, bringing the total fatalities to 203 or a 16 percent permanent reduction in strength.[22]

Many, like Sergeant George Thomas, Company D, 4th Alabama, would have harrowing stories of near brushes with death to tell their children and grandchildren. Thomas came to Gettysburg with a Bible, picked up from a distant battlefield, tucked safely in his haversack. Inside the Bible an inscription read:

> *Presented to Harrison Preston Reid on April 27, 1849, by his affectionate mother.*
> *May it be a lamp to his path and may he live that at last he be gathered among*
> *the saints in heaven.*

Somewhere on the battlefield a bullet struck the haversack and ripped into the Bible. Part of the Bible was destroyed, but fortunately Thomas was spared a potentially serious wound.[23]

Several of those left behind did not survive the Gettysburg field hospitals. Barnett Cody died July 22 and John Oates just as the sun dipped behind South Mountain on July 25. Though Oates suffered terribly, his last days on earth were made a little easier by the friendship of Dr. G. A. E. Reed, the doctor's wife, sister-in-law and a lady friend. A few days after the battle the women visited Reed at the hospital. By chance their attention turned to the two Alabamians. A friendship was quickly cemented which led to small acts of kindness. A short while before he died Oates requested a song which was followed by the Lord's Prayer. Sensing the end was near, the young officer's last words were, "Tell my friends at home that I died in arms of friends." Cody and Oates were buried in a field near the hospital.[24]

Near the end of August Colonel Oates knew the sad fate of his brother and several close friends left in the hands of the Federal army. It then became his painful duty to inform friends and parents that loved ones had gone to a better life. In a letter penned August 30, 1863 Oates wrote Cody's father. It read in part:

> *I have not only lost my dearest relative on earth, but my dearest friends. Captain Brainard, one of the most honest and gallant men I ever knew, ever deported himself as a gentleman and soldier. He was one of those friends of mine whose name will ever be treasured up in my memory as one dearly loved. Barnett, my dear boy friend, I loved him with the tenderness of feeling I have for my brother. Noble and manly in bearing, brave, honest, reliable and true, he challenged the admiration of all who knew him. Strict in discipline, accurate in drill and obedient and respectful to superiors, he was unsurpassed as an officer by any in the Confederate army of his age.[25]*

Junior Second Lieutenant Andrew Ray died July 4. Captain Joseph Johnston succumbed to his wounds July 18.[26] Captain William Leftwich, a twenty-one-year-old bachelor, and druggist from Huntsville, Alabama, also died from his wounds.[27] Because he had been a strict disciplinarian most in his company disliked him personally. Few mourned his passing.[28]

Left in a field hospital, sick and in a weakened condition, Private John J. Davis, 44th Alabama, was sent to West's Building Hospital in Baltimore, Maryland. On recuperating from his illness, Davis began scheming to get out of prison. Petitions to the authorities cited his occupation as physician and claimed that he "... was sickly and not fit for service." The wily Confederate sought to take the Oath of Allegiance, citing as his reasons being a conscript, "always in opposition to secession," and he assured his captors that he wished to remain in the northern states. On August 13, 1863, military authorities released him from prison on his oath. Instead of heading north, as one would expect under the circumstances, the Alabamian traveled south. By September 1863 he had made his way back to the regiment and was present for duty.[29]

Private William Penny, Company E, 47th Alabama, was an ordinary private. He could also be described as the son of a typical Confederate family with a deep-rooted Southern heritage. His family traced its origins to the 1680s in southern Virginia. The Penny family migrated to North Carolina and on to Alabama as the lands were opened. William and three brothers joined the Confederate armies. An older brother, Riley, met his death at the 47th Alabama's first battle at Cedar Mountain, Virginia. William had just turned eighteen when he marched into Pennsylvania. Gettysburg was his first and only battle, where he received several serious wounds during the assault on Little Round Top. William languished in a makeshift field hospital until he succumbed to his wounds.[30]

Prison Bound

A few days after the armies departed the field, captured Confederates, under heavy guard, began arriving at Westminister, Maryland. From there the prisoners were transported to Baltimore by train and temporarily housed in Fort McHenry until sent to prison camps. On August 8 the Richmond *Dispatch* reported 120 prisoners arrived at Baltimore for transfer to Johnson's Island, Ohio. Most of the prisoners from Law's Brigade were sent to Fort Delaware. For them the next leg of their journey to prison was by steamer down the Chesapeake via Fort Monroe and then to Fort Delaware, the count being at least 87. From the direction of the trip, some thought they were going to be exchanged at City Point, Virginia, but that proved to be a false hope. Once in prison 44 were detained until June 14, 1865. Twenty died in prison and the remainder were exchanged at various times. At least six men from the brigade were left as nurses and administered whatever comfort they could for the suffering and dying. Most were exchanged in the fall and early winter of 1863.[31]

In late August the officers were sent to Johnson's Island on the shores of Lake Erie. The camp was three miles from Sandusky, Ohio, and covered five or six acres of land.[32] John Cussons did much to enliven the camp and provide entertainment for his fellow prisoners. A theatrical company put on a number of productions throughout the winter months of 1863–64. Cussons managed to solicit sufficient contributions from his audiences to procure needed goods for the camp's sick and wounded. The audiences were not only Confederate prisoners, but Federal soldiers and the local populace as well.[33]

Several brigade officers were exchanged in the spring of 1864, including Cussons and Christian on March 17, 1864. Christian returned to the brigade and assumed his duties as adjutant and inspector general, but Cussons never seriously considered returning to active service.[34] He was a British subject and immediately applied for leave to return to England. When he returned, Law was on wounded leave and Cussons applied for additional leave, using Law's absence as his reason. The leave was granted and Cussons elected not to return to Confederate service.[35] Instead, he married and settled in Glen Allen, Virginia.

For some time after the battle soldiers of the 47th Alabama thought that Colonel Bulger had perished on the field of battle. By late July he was able to travel and was transferred to a hospital in Baltimore. After spending the winter in a Federal prison he was selected, in February 1864, to be exchanged and transferred to Point Lookout, Maryland.

It was by sheer luck that First Lieutenant John P. Breedlove, Company B, 4th Alabama, survived his wound. A bullet entered the left side of his lower abdomen, near the groin, tearing a hole in the lower intestine.[36] He lay in a field hospital six weeks before receiving any attention.[37] An examination on August 29, 1863, revealed the wound was discharging heavily. A special diet was prescribed and by November 9 Breedlove was transported to West Building Hospital in Baltimore.[38] He was then sent to Fort Delaware, Maryland, remaining there until August 1864. Breedlove became one of 600 Confederate prisoners sent to Morris Island in the Charleston, South Carolina, harbor and placed under fire of Confederate guns from James Island.[39] The prisoners were placed in open camps next to the Federal batteries in retaliation for Federal prisoners being placed in private homes along the Ashley River waterfront shelled by the Federal batteries. From there he was sent to Fort Pulaski, Georgia, and finally exchanged in January 1865.[40] After the war Breedlove farmed a few years near Tuskegee, Alabama, then entered the mercantile business. He later served as tax assessor for Macon County.[41]

Captain Jeremiah Edwards, 48th Alabama, spent the remainder of the war at Johnson's Island and was not paroled until July 3, 1865. Lieutenant Robert H. Wicker, 15th Alabama, endured his imprisonment at Fort Delaware.[42] Oates described Wicker as a fine soldier and as "brave as any man in the regiment."[43] His bravery, however, did not compensate for the necessary leadership qualities to fulfill the duties of captain. Prior to the Battle of Gettysburg, military examining boards twice refused Wicker promotion to captain of Company L. Captain Shaaff, commanding the 15th Alabama on December 17, 1864, explains what happened afterwards:

> *There being no one in the company in any way competent to fill the office of captain, an election was ordered by the brigade commander which resulted in*

*the election of Lieutenant Hatcher of Company D. Lieutenant Wicker most cheer-
fully and willingly wavered his claim verbally in favor of Lieutenant Hatcher.
His written waiver could be readily procured if he was not in the hands of the
enemy. Lieutenant Hatcher was his own choice for a captain and he acknowledged himself not competent to fill the office.*

Wicker finally gained his released June 12, 1865, upon his Oath of Allegiance to
the Union.[44]

Lieutenant Joseph Breare, 15th Alabama, secured his freedom March 17,
1864 when exchanged, obtained leave for 30 days, and returned to Alabama.
When he did not return to the 15th an order was issued for his arrest.[45] He managed to avoid that unpleasant experience when, as Oates later reported, Breare,
an Englishman by birth and lawyer by profession, raised a company of cavalry in
the conscript service.[46]

The Case of James Jackson

Colonel Jackson tendered his resignation June 23 at Millwood, Virginia.
Though his body was racked with pain, he remained with the regiment and attempted to lead the 47th on July 2. By mid-July 1863, Colonel Jackson's health
was broken, and his resignation from the 47th Alabama was effective July 16.
Adjutant Keller accompanied his brother-in-law to Georgia. However, Major
Campbell still held Jackson accountable for the regiment breaking formation during
the charge across Plum Run Valley. On August 7, 1863 he wrote of Jackson, "The
colonel remained so far behind that his presence on the field was but a trammel
on the lieutenant colonel." He went on to state, "...out of 21 officers...all acted
well. The colonel and adjutant are not included in this number."[47]

Jackson also left the regiment on bad terms with at least one of his officers.
Captains John V. McKee, Company G, and Joseph S. Johnston, Jr., Company B,
had been appointed by the regiment to buy Jackson a horse as a gift. The rank and
file donated $850 for the purchase. Unfortunately, the price of a quality mount
was $1,000. The two officers paid the difference from their own funds in the
belief the regiment would reimburse the expense. Johnston was killed at Gettysburg.
McKee died of disease, leaving a widow in need of money. Isaac Newell suggested the colonel pay the $75 due McKee to McKee's widow. Jackson refused,
believing the regimental officers should make up the difference. The officers declined. In a letter to McKee's widow, Newell said, "I once thought him a fine
man, but after acting in such a manner I have no more use for him."[48]

Jackson went to his father's plantation near Greenville, Georgia, where his
wife resided during his absence. In April 1865 Jackson was still bedridden when
a Federal raid swept through Greenville and the surrounding area. Jackson's father hid his cattle in a wooded area about five miles from the plantation. Upon the
approach of Federal horsemen Jackson put on his uniform once more. On his way
to the hidden livestock, Jackson rode to a hill about a mile from the house where
he saw Federal soldiers. Jackson thought he was undetected, but unfortunately he
was not. Some of the Federals went to the house, others went after Jackson. At the

house the Federals threatened to kill Jackson, but his elderly blind mother told the officer in charge that Jackson had served his country just as the Federal had served his. With grief in her voice the elderly lady informed the Yankee her son had come home to die. The group departed with the officer's word that Jackson's life would be spared. A short time later two servants arrived with news that Jackson was captured and probably dead. His mother and wife were grieving for their loved one when Jackson walked up. The Federal officer proved a man of his word. Jackson was released, but his horse had been confiscated. His captors provided transportation part of the way home, then forced him to walk. Jackson arrived exhausted and returned to bed, never to rise again. James W. Jackson died July 1, 1865. Before dying he called his aged father to the bedside and asked the elder Jackson to look after his wife and two little children. Jackson was buried on Sunday, July 2. His father collapsed and was buried the next Sunday.[49]

Shattered Careers

Military careers of the Federal and Confederate antagonists at Little Round Top and Devil's Den took drastically different paths. Out of Law's Brigade Perry became the only regimental commander to advance beyond the rank held at Gettysburg, receiving a brigadier's commission February 21, 1865.[50] James Sheffield remained in temporary command of the brigade through the early winter of 1863, at which time he returned to Alabama and eventually resigned from the service. Lawrence Scruggs still held the rank of lieutenant colonel and commanded the 4th Alabama when it surrendered at Appomattox Court House. Major James Campbell repeatedly tried, but always in vain, to secure an appointment to lieutenant colonel of the 47th Alabama. Law insisted the regiment suffered under his leadership and blocked each attempt. Campbell went directly to the War Department, but it took a sniper's bullet at the Spotsylvania to settle the issue.[51]

The competent William Oates experienced an unpleasant miscarriage of justice. Unfortunately for Oates, Law failed to follow all the procedures when he unilaterally dropped Major Alexander Lowther from the rolls and promoted Oates and Feagin to field rank. Lowther argued his case in the War Department and the halls of Congress. After considerable effort and lobbying the original commissions were revoked. Lowther received a colonel's commission and command of the 15th Alabama. A commission as major went to Oates and the rank of lieutenant colonel to Isaac Feagin, both in the 15th Alabama. At the time a number of close associates and admirers tried unsuccessfully to secure Oates a colonel's commission. In his later years Oates believed Generals Charles W. Field, commanding the division, and Richard H. Anderson, commanding the First Corps, recommended his appointed to brigadier. Oates claimed Law initiated the recommendation, and that his friendship with Law caused Longstreet, in the summer of 1864, to disapprove the recommendation.[52] At the time in question, Longstreet was on convalescent leave and hardly in position to interfere in the business of running the corps. Congress had just overturned Oates's appointment to colonel.

Perry outranked him, and it seems unlikely that a highly political body such as the Confederate Congress would consider Oates's appointment after the Lowther affair.[53] It is a testament to Oates's sense of duty that he never entertained the idea of resigning the service, though he could have. He also never considered the idea of serving under Lowther and informed Adjutant and Inspector General Samuel Cooper:

> *Having ever performed my duties as an officer faithfully and to the best of my humble ability I have but to request Genl that I be relieved from my present unpleasant position. I have the very best reasons of a private character for not desiring to serve in a subordinate position in the regiment I have so long commanded.*[54]

In the end Oates, still a major, assumed command of the 48th Alabama. On August 16, 1864 at Second Deep Bottom, Virginia he received a career-ending wound which resulted in the loss of an arm. He was in the process of securing another position when the war ended, but in reality his military career ended at Second Deep Bottom.

Law's career, which before Gettysburg held such promise, sadly took a turn for the worse. Within weeks after the great fight, Law was engaged in a bitter dispute with Longstreet over a perceived promise on his commander's part to promote Law to commander of Hood's Division. Unfortunately for Law, Longstreet wanted his protégé Micah Jenkins, who ranked Law by a few months, to command the storied division. Before the end of 1863 the dispute turned into a bitter feud, wrecked a once elite division, led to Law's arrest by Longstreet, and drew General Lee and President Davis into the affair. Sadly, in the summer of 1864 Law left the brigade and Army of Northern Virginia for good. His military career in shambles and the esteem of his superiors, once high destroyed.

On the Federal side, Joshua Chamberlain received a brigadier's commission and was breveted a major general. Given the honor of receiving the surrender of the Army of Northern Virginia's infantry at Appomattox Court House, he mustered out in 1866 and was elected governor of his state.[55] Congress bestowed the county's highest honor on the aging campaigner in 1893 with the award of the Medal of Honor. The citation read: "for daring heroism and great tenacity in holding his position on the Little Round Top against repeated assaults, and carrying the advance position on the Great Round Top."[56]

Though he was on his death bed when told the news, Strong Vincent received a brigadier's commission for his heroic defense of Little Round Top. For his efforts James Rice, in August 1863, was made brigadier and fought with the Army of the Potomac into the fighting at Spotsylvania Court House. As fate would have it he on May 10 was shot in front of Law's Brigade, which resulted in the amputation of a leg. Before he could be removed from the field hospital, his condition deteriorated. Rice grew restless, but was unable to move himself. An aide asked which way the dying man wanted to be turned. His response was barely above a whisper: "Toward the enemy. Let me die with my face to the foe." A few minutes later he passed into eternity.[57]

Richard S. C. Lord, 1st U.S. Cavalry, Judson Kilpatrick, and William Graham, 1st U.S. Artillery, Company K were breveted for "gallant and meritous service at Gettysburg."[58] William Wells of the 1st Vermont Cavalry bcame the recipient of brevets for brigadier and major general. John Hammond of the 5th New York Cavalry, and Orpheus Woodward of the 83rd Pennsylvania, and Benjamin Partridge of the 16th Michigan, each received brigadier general brevets.[59] On September 8, 1891 Wells was awarded his nation's highest honor for "leading the second battalion of his regiment in a daring charge" on July 3, 1863.[60] Thomas Egan earned a promotion to brigadier in 1864 and later had the honor of receiving a brevet to major general. By the end of the war Wesley Merritt advanced to the rank of major general of volunteers.[61] He would render many years faithful service to the United States before retiring June 16, 1900 as the second ranking officer in the U.S Army.

Chapter 12

Return to Virginia

Retreat to Virginia

Hood's Division remained in position on Warfield Ridge throughout much of July 4. Word came down to make preparations to leave the field. Brigadier General John D. Imboden's cavalry brigade drew the assignment to accompany the wounded. Their route back to Virginia would take them through Greencastle. Lee ordered the infantry to travel by way of Fairfield to act as a screen between Meade's army and the ambulance train. A severe thunderstorm rolled over the battlefield near noon, and the rain continued all afternoon and most of the night. Men began loading the wounded about the time the rain began. These hapless individuals were forced to lay on a bed of wet straw. None of the wagons were equipped with springs. As a result all endured a tortuous ride back to Virginia. By necessity the badly wounded were left behind. Some of the injured refused to go, preferring a Federal prison to the trip back to Virginia.

The wagon train consisted of ambulances and supply wagons. It extended more than 17 miles and moved out around 4 p.m. Rain fell in torrents, transforming the roads into bogs. As darkness settled over the countryside occasional lightning flashes and accompanying loud thunderclaps startled the horses. When a team bolted, the wagon's wounded occupants were either jolted or sent tumbling into the mud. At Greenwood the train followed a shortcut to Greencastle. The head of the column arrived there near dawn July 5. Local civilians gathered and attacked several wagons. A few wagons were disabled when the spokes were cut.[1] The 1st New York Cavalry charged a portion of the train, capturing 134 wagons, 600 horses, two guns, and 653 prisoners.[2] Officers took an oath to remain where they were until moved, while the privates and noncommissioned officers were paroled.[3] First Lieutenant James S. Ridgeway, Company D, 48th Alabama, was among those captured. He was exchanged October 31, 1864, but did not return to service.[4]

The Infantry Withdraws

The infantry began its withdrawal from the battlefield late in the evening of July 4.[5] The order of march was Hill's Third Corps, Longstreet's First Corps and

Plaque for Law's Brigade—Warfield Ridge, Confederate Avenue
Located where Law formed his line of battle July 2, 1863

Ewell's Second Corps. Longstreet, being the center of the column, guarded Federal prisoners. Those in the ranks knew the army had fought well and did what was asked of them, but they also knew the army had suffered a repulse. Some would return many years later as old men to relive memories of the fight at Gettysburg and once more charge the Federal positions. A battlefield commission would be established to preserve the field of conflict and sort out the various positions of the combatants.

Before departing, several members of the 4th Alabama visited the wounded at the field hospital on the Planck farm. Someone removed John Breedlove's cap because the gold braid indicated his rank. An older, well-worn hat was placed over the wounded officer's face. Colonel Scruggs exchanged the braid on Henry Roper's hat with his own. Some of the more seriously wounded would stay in the hospital several months. Every day there was someone to bury, usually in a shallow grave in the nearby Peach Orchard. Yard and garden fences and wood from the dwelling and surrounding buildings became fuel for campfires. All the poultry and livestock in the immediate area disappeared.[6]

Private John Anderson considered it a blessing to be among the living. He was positive the battle had been the "bloodiest fight of the war." In a somber reflection to his wife, the 48th Alabama private "thought I was doing well to get off the field alive while others were falling around me dead and dying."[7] Private Charles McEachern, Company I, 44th Alabama, watched his comrades leave the field. Though suffering from a severe wound, he resolved to follow at the first opportunity. On September 3, McEachern slipped away from his captors and made his way through the lines. A short time later he joined friends and fellow soldiers in the 44th.[8]

Law's Brigade departed in a downpour about 2 a.m. on July 5.[9] The march took the Alabamians across the mountains to Hagerstown by way of Fairfield. Camp the night of July 5 was on a damp and chilly road at Monterey Springs. Law's Brigade reached Hagerstown about midnight July 6 and took up position a few miles from town. Rations were distributed and cooked in a steady rain that continued throughout the day of July 7 and most of the night.

Major Coleman participated in an engagement with cavalry near Funkstown. A courier, chased by Federal cavalry, arrived July 8 with the division's mail. On July 10, Law's Brigade left its camp at 7 a.m. and marched toward Williamsport. They went into line of battle at 9 a.m. fronting Antietam Creek. After several hours Law marched toward Dam Number 4 and made camp near Downsville. Next day the brigade moved a mile nearer to the Potomac and threw up rifle pits.[10]

Law's Brigade remained in the fortifications near Downsville until the night of July 13 when orders were received to recross the Potomac. They took up the line of march about 10 p.m., slogging along all night in the rainstorm. Small farm roads that were rough, narrow, and hilly in good weather, turned to mud five or six inches deep in most places. It was the dark period of the moon and the clouds shut out the starlight. An artilleryman remembered that he had been unable to see his hand in front of his face.[11] Artillery carriages and wagons dug muddy trenches in the already bad roads. All too often, shoes sank up to their tops. Ten hours after it started for the Potomac, Law's Brigade struggled across the pontoon bridge at Falling Waters.[12]

The 4th Alabama brought up the rear at the crossing. They were met by General Lee with instructions to remove the bridge as soon as the squadron of cavalry crossed. Part of the 4th entered rifle pits, receiving an ineffective artillery and rifle fire. The remainder began to dismantle the bridge. Lieutenant Colonel Thomas H. Carter's Artillery Battalion of Major General Robert E. Rodes's Division, Second Corps, supported the 4th. Federals appeared in the distance a short time after the bridge was cut loose and caused a few anxious moments. A detachment of Confederate skirmishers appeared on the opposite bank. For a few moments it appeared they might be stranded and face certain capture. Fortunately, a few shots from the artillery drove the Federals back some distance while several boats retrieved the stranded soldiers.[13] This ended the Alabamians excursion onto Northern soil.

On Virginia Soil

After crossing into Virginia, Law's Brigade marched toward Martinsburg, and camped the night of July 14 along the road. About 1 p.m. on July 15 they resumed the march, passing through Martinsburg and making camp below Darkesville where they cooked their first rations in five days. At daylight on the 16th, Longstreet's corps marched for Bunker Hill. Law's Brigade encamped a mile north of the village. The brigade remained in camp four days and enjoyed a much needed rest.

Law's men returned from Gettysburg exhausted, their clothes reduced to tattered rags.[14] Many had walked miles over roads without shoes and their feet were in terrible condition.[15] They were veterans, however. They were expected this late in the war to march through ankle deep mud, or on dry roads which covered them with dust. They had signed on for "three years or the war" and expected to fight for the duration. Lieutenant Isaac M. Newell of the 47th Alabama Regiment, a veteran who had enrolled on May 2, 1862, at Loachapoka, Alabama, was one such soldier. He wrote his sister, the widow of his former captain, John V. McKee, that "I don't expect to get to come home myself till the war closes without I get wounded."[16]

Hardened veterans or not, the Alabamians realized the significance of the retreat from Pennsylvania and the fall of Vicksburg. Newell expressed concern about morale in a letter home. "If there ever has been a dark and gloomy time since the war commenced, I think it is just at this time. The fall of Vicksburg and the Gettysburg affair," he added, "has greatly discouraged the soldiers."[17] Reuben Kidd, 4th Alabama, also felt "things in our little Confederacy begin to look blue," after Gettysburg.[18] James Daniel, Company H, 47th Alabama, wrote home that "our boys is [*sic*] in mighty low spirits."[19]

It is not known when Private Seaborn O. Hobby, 44th Alabama, decided the cause was lost. Sustaining a serious wound July 2 he received a furlough to recover in Alabama. By the fall of 1863 he was in Federal hands. On December 14, 1863 Hobby took the Oath of Allegiance to the United States and went north of the Ohio for the remainder of the war.[20]

While the regiment camped at Bunker Hill, a military court sentenced Private Benjamin Ryan, Company B, 15th Alabama, to an unspecified punishment for disobedience. Oates described him as prone to bouts of heavy drinking, a gambler, and possessor of a turbulent disposition. He began military service as fourth corporal, but because of his behavior was soon reduced to the ranks. Ryan had grown weary of army life and to avoid punishment left camp, taking with him James B. Hill, also of the same company. Both were in Union hands by July 23. Hill disappeared into the Federal prison system and was never heard from again. Ryan went to Camp Chase, Ohio. Federal authorities released him on oath December 1, 1864, with the stipulation he too remain north of the Ohio until the war's end. Oates claimed to have seen him in 1867 working as a laborer on the construction of the railroad from Troy to Union Springs, Alabama.[21]

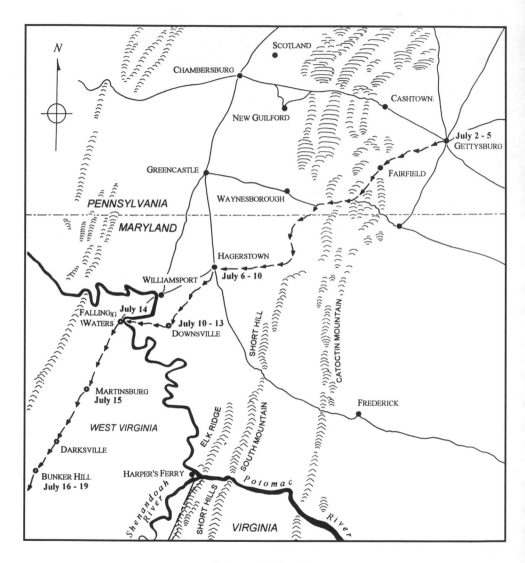

**Return to Virginia
July 1863**

Then there was the ever present sad duty to inform someone at home of a son's or husband's passing beyond this life. Frank Park was obviously heavy of heart when he wrote the Gardner family, "...in the death of your son (Samuel H. Gardner, second corporal, Company I) I have lost a pleasant associate and friend, the service of a faithful, vigilant and brave soldier, and your noble boy. I am afraid I thought too much of Sam."[22]

Securing the Mountain Gaps

Lee suspected that Meade planned to cut him off from his railroad link to Richmond, and on the morning of the July 20 he sent the First Corps to gain possession of Ashby's Gap. With Longstreet and the other corps in control of the gaps through the Blue Ridge Mountains, future movements of the Army of Northern Virginia up and down the Shenandoah Valley could be secured.[23]

The First Corps marched up the Shenandoah Valley at dawn, through Winchester, taking the turnpike which passed through Ashby's Gap en route to Culpeper. Law's command camped the night of July 20 four miles southeast of Berryville. Arriving at Millwood the next morning, Longstreet's troops found the Shenandoah River too high to ford. The Federal army had crossed the Potomac River east of the Blue Ridge Mountains, advancing through the Loudoun Valley toward the mountain gaps through which the Confederates must pass to reach safety. Brigadier General George A. Custer's cavalry reached Ashby's Gap ahead of Longstreet's infantry. Ashby's Gap and the road beyond were occupied down to the river by the 5th and 6th Michigan Cavalry regiments of Custer's command.[24]

Longstreet turned his column up the Shenandoah Valley toward Manassas and Chester Gaps, the next two passes through the Blue Ridge. The First Corps, with Pickett in the van, hurried along the western slope of the Blue Ridge while the Union cavalry on the east side of the range raced them for possession of the gaps.[25]

At Front Royal, opposite Manassas Gap, Brigadier General Montgomery D. Corse, of Pickett's Division, crossed his brigade over the two forks of the Shenandoah River.[26] Corse detached the 17th Virginia to hold a position at the west end of the gap against the Federal horsemen who had already entered it from the east, and sent the rest of his Virginians to Chester Gap, still farther south in the Blue Ridge.[27] Corse's Brigade secured Chester Gap before the Union cavalry could reach it. Brigadier General John Buford's horsemen on June 30 had reached Gettysburg ahead of the lead elements of Lee's army, holding the town until infantry could arrive, but on this occasion the Confederates were faster.[28]

Hood's Division, under Law's command, crossed the Shenandoah at Berry's Ferry near Millwood on July 22 and relieved the 17th Virginia at the west approach to Manassas Gap. The task assigned to the division was to protect the Confederates from the Federal cavalry and artillery occupying the gap.[29] Law deployed his infantry to drive the Union cavalry back into Manassas Gap, away from the Confederate column.[30] Two roads passed through Manassas Gap, one next to the tracks of the Manassas Gap Railroad, the other over the mountain

through the village of Wappen.[31] "Rock" Benning's Georgia Brigade was positioned on the road through the gap with Robertson's Texans on his left, the 4th
Alabama on his right, and Anderson's Georgia Brigade on the extreme right. The
rest of Law's Brigade, commanded by Sheffield, was in reserve. Enemy cavalry
was visible in the gap and on the heights above. The division moved eastward
into the gap, turning the flank of the Union horsemen and pushing them about a
mile into the gap which provoked, according to a member of the 4th, "a dozen or
more shells" from Federal artillery.[32] As Longstreet reported to Lee, the enemy
"gave but little trouble" to Law's veterans.[33]

That evening, Law marched the other brigades of the division to Chester
Gap, already in Pickett's possession, leaving Benning's Brigade and the 4th Ala-
bama, commanded by Lieutenant Colonel Scruggs, to block Manassas Gap until
relieved by the Third Corps.[34] During the night, the vanguard of the Federal III
Corps relieved the Union cavalry. The Union infantry launched several attacks
during the daylight hours of July 23 in the action known as the Battle of Manassas
Gap (Wapping) Heights, which began only an hour after Brigadier General A. R.
"Rans" Wright's Third Corps brigade relieved Benning at 9 a.m.[35]

Benning's Georgians and the detached Alabamians hastened to rejoin their
division. It was necessary to pass A. P. Hill's column on the narrow mountain
road through Chester Gap, which delayed Benning.[36] Benning and the 4th Alabama bivouacked the night of July 23 two miles south of Flint Hill, 15 miles from
Front Royal, well behind the rest of Law's command.[37]

An Ambush Badly Sprung

Law had marched through Chester Gap, and detached the 15th Alabama to
picket the Warrenton Road near Gaines's Cross-Roads. The 15th was ordered to
get astride the road to prevent a surprise attack on the column. About noon, on
July 23, after his soldiers had eaten their last rations, Oates marched his regiment
down the Warrenton Road about a mile and a half before stopping at a defensible
position near a clear stream. As the situation was calm, Oates allowed his men to
bathe in the mountain creek, half the regiment at a time, but this pleasurable
experience was interrupted by firing on the road toward Warrenton. The shooting, explained a Confederate cavalryman who rode into Oates's line, was by a
Federal cavalry brigade pushing up the road, and his squadron was retreating
before it.[38]

Oates laid an ambush, using the Confederate cavalry to lead their pursuers
into the concealed line of the 15th Alabama. Most of the regiment was near a
fence on the crest of an elevation which bisected the road. Between this small hill
and a bridge over the stream in which the Alabamians had bathed was an open
field. When the Union riders entered the field the trap would be sprung.[39] Oates
planned to bag the lot.

Company A was concealed near the open ground, lying on an elevation
below the bridge with instructions to rush to the bridge to cut off the Federals
retreat after the head of the enemy column had been stopped at the fence. Con-
trary to orders, however, the men of Shaaff's company opened fire when only the

head of the cavalry column was on the bridge. This was too soon to trigger the ambush, and most of the Federals escaped. Oates captured one prisoner whose horse had been shot from under him, and the Alabamians identified their opponents as members of the 1st West Virginia Cavalry, not a brigade as had been reported by the Confederate trooper.[40]

The 15th Alabama marched back to the Culpeper Road on the morning of July 24 to join Benning's Brigade and the 4th Alabama. Oates allowed his hungry men to stop for breakfast at a blackberry patch. At least one soldier, Orderly Sergeant Billy Jordan, credited the combination of short rations and berries with curing his chronic diarrhea, which he thought was caused by the lingering effects of typhoid.[41]

Benning had halted within two miles of Gaines's Cross-Roads to allow time for the 15th Alabama to catch up.[42] He was not pressing his brigade, for the entire column was moving slowly to prevent its stretching out and giving the enemy cavalry the opportunity to cut off isolated Confederate wagons.[43] When the 15th Alabama arrived, the march was resumed, with the Third Corps close behind. As his column neared Newby's Cross-Roads, Benning met two cavalrymen who reported advance riders of Custer's Second Brigade, Third Division, on the road between Newby's Cross-Roads and Amissville. The two Confederates were going to Amissville to have their horses shod, and were unaware the town had been occupied by Custer the previous night.[44]

Fight for Battle Mountain—near Newby's Cross-Road

The 15th Alabama was the vanguard of Benning's command, and Oates was quick to volunteer his regiment to make a reconnaissance toward Battle Mountain, an elevation about half a mile from the crossroads. Benning accepted his offer. Oates led the 15th Alabama to the foot of Battle Mountain, where he found the Union cavalry arrayed on the mountain with its artillery covering the road. Oates's skirmishers exchanged fire with Custer's Michiganders. Benning waited but was unimpressed with the volume of fire. Word arrived from A. P. Hill that he would relieve Oates, so Benning gave the order for his brigade and the 4th Alabama to resume the march to Culpeper.[45]

Custer, commanding the Third Division while Kilpatrick was on leave, ordered his brigade to attack up the Amissville Road, intending to halt the Confederate column moving toward Culpeper.[46] He sent forward to Battle Mountain the 1st, 5th, and 6th Michigan Cavalry regiments and Battery M of the 2nd U.S. Artillery to engage the Confederates. The 5th Michigan had the advance of the Federal column, fighting the 15th Alabama on the right of the road as dismounted skirmishers while the 1st Michigan supported the artillery positioned on the crest of the hill to the left of the Amissville Road. The 6th Michigan reinforced the 5th Regiment on the right.[47]

Four companies of the Alabama regiment moved against the Federals deployed on the mountain. Lieutenant Edmond P. Head, of the "Ft. Browder Roughs," was killed and three men wounded while making the ascent of the mountain. All

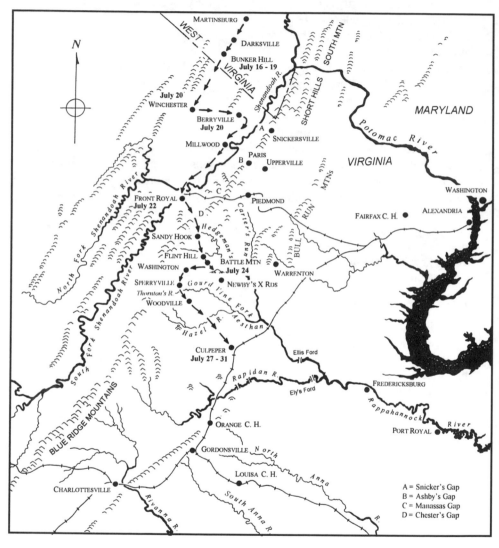

Travel in Virginia
July 1863

four were taken by ambulance to Culpeper Court House where Head, a favorite of his colonel, was buried with military honors.[48]

Learning of the arrival of A. P. Hill, Oates halted the attack and rode to the general's headquarters for the loan of an artillery piece. Oates placed his borrowed cannon where it could enfilade the Federal battery.[49] Hill also placed artillery in position to fire upon the Federal cavalry. The situation remained in stalemate for an hour or more, the Federals holding the high ground and the Alabamians firing case and canister that forced the Union cavalrymen to keep their heads down.[50] Oates was prepared to attack with his regiment when the Federals were driven off by Benning's surprise appearance at their rear.[51]

Benning had almost reached the Hazel River when a courier from A. P. Hill stopped him with the request that he wait for Hill's artillery. Before any artillery arrived, however, Hill sent another courier asking Benning to return to the area of Battle Mountain to block the retreat of the Union cavalry as Hill drove them from the mountain. Lieutenant Robert C. Stanard of Hill's staff and an elderly civilian led Benning through the Federal picket line. If the Confederates got possession of the road to Amissville, Benning believed they could capture the entire enemy force. But Benning's guides had been mistaken when they told him there was no escape for the Union cavalry.

Benning came up behind the artillery and the 1st Michigan, but the artillery quickly retreated to the Amissville Road while the 5th Michigan withstood a volley before making a hasty retreat to the same road. When Benning executed his flank movement against the Union left, Oates saw an opportunity to attack and ordered the 15th Alabama, supported by at least two of Hill's artillery pieces, to advance against the Union right, splitting the force on the right of the road. But Oates and Benning did not move in concert, and although surprised by the Confederate flanking movement, the Union horsemen eluded the trap.[52] The 15th gave only token pursuit as Custer's riders retreated from Battle Mountain.[53] Custer reported only 15 casualties in the engagement, though it was a near disaster for his command.[54]

Since the route of their flanking movement put the Georgians and Alabamians between the Federal pickets and their main body, Adjutant Coles joined Lieutenant William F. Turner and another soldier of the 4th Alabama in a plan to capture the pickets. Expecting the pickets to attempt to rejoin their regiments as quickly as possible, the enterprising Confederates ran to the point where they believed they could intercept the Federal horsemen. The three captured one rider at a gate, although Coles admitted they succeeded due to negligence on the part of the Union cavalryman. Coles obtained the horse and saddle as spoils, the other two divided the contents of the saddlebags. In the bags was a toothbrush which Turner boiled and used for himself, declaring to Coles, ..."that he valued it more than any other trophy we had captured which fell to his lot."[55]

From Battle Mountain, the 4th and 15th Alabama marched with Benning's Georgians unmolested into Culpeper. Law's Brigade encamped on the same grounds they had occupied before the Pennsylvania Campaign.[56]

In a letter dated August 16, 1863, John Anderson penned a few words to his wife in Alabama: "I thought I would write to you about my tricks in Maryland and Pennsylvania and what a beautiful country it is, but I do not feel like doing so." He went on to describe the hardships endured and likened the Confederate thrust onto Northern soil to the Federal drive on Richmond by saying "Gettysburg was a hard road to travel as Richmond was to the Yankees." Anderson surely spoke for his fellow Confederates when he concluded, "I never want to travel it anymore."[57]

Epilogue

Second Battle of Little Round Top

After the war William Oates became a prominent figure in the state of Alabama, serving in the state legislature, U.S. Congress, and later as governor. In the Spanish-American War the old campaigner was commissioned a brigadier general.[1] While serving in the U.S. Congress, Oates supported the bill which appropriated funds for the Gettysburg National Military Park.[2] Because of his political influence Oates secured his fellow Alabamian, William H. Forney, an appointment as the lone Confederate representative on the three-man park commission. When Forney died Oates successfully lobbied to have William M. Robbins, his old friend, appointed to fill the vacancy.[3] In his twilight years Oates decided it appropriate to erect a monument on the battlefield in memory of his brother and the others of the 15th Alabama who fell at Gettysburg.[4] Oates wanted the monument placed at the most advanced point reached by the 15th Alabama on Little Round Top, which violated a commission rule stipulating monuments to units should be placed where the unit formed its line of battle. Though an earlier commission frequently waived the rule Robbins and his fellow commissioners decided there would be no exceptions and informed Oates that the monument could be placed along Confederate Avenue, a road built after the area became a national military park in 1895 to make the battlefield more accessible.[5] Oates's application to place the monument on Little Round Top was returned to him. Oates replied he would never consent to placing a monument to his men on Confederate Avenue.[6]

When Oates pressed the issue the Federal members deferred to Robbins to act as intermediary for the commission and explain their position. Robbins wrote Oates he deferred to his colleagues on the commission.[7] Oates concluded Robbins was the primary obstacle to a favorable action on his request.[8] Federal commission members clearly wanted to avoid direct communication with Oates and continued to place Robbins between themselves and Oates. Colonel John P. Nicholson, Gettysburg National Military Park Commissioner, and chairman of the Gettysburg Battle Commission, went so far as to write Oates that the commission deferred to

Robbins on Southern matters.[9] Robbins became the man caught in the middle. Distressed over the position in which they placed him, Robbins expressed his displeasure to his fellow commissioners. He felt they had implied he was the principal reason why Oates's request was refused.[10] Commission members, however, did nothing to dispel the idea. Oates, in a letter dated July 4, 1903, accused Robbins of personally blocking his application to place a monument on Little Round Top. Robbins maintained his position that the commission was not granting exceptions.

In an effort to overturn the commission's decision Oates sent a barrage of letters to commission members, U.S. congressmen, the War Department, and Joshua Chamberlain.[11] Oates informed Robbins that he only "wanted to leave a little stone on the spot" where his brother was killed. He offered to use his own funds to place the monument on Little Round Top.[12]

The War Department deferred to the commission which in turn sought Chamberlain's opinion on the matter.[13] Though he did not object to the monument, Chamber did specify it be correctly located. Oates contended his men pushed the Maine defenders back. In earlier years Chamberlain acknowledged the Alabamians thrust carried them well up the hill.[14] But as the years wore on Chamberlain's memory of the events changed and he refused to admit giving ground. He and Oates could never agree on how far the 15th Alabama advanced on that hot July afternoon.[15]

As he grew older, Oates did not always correctly remember the events as they occurred on Little Round Top. His quest was doomed when he wrote Secretary of War Elihu Root that the 15th Alabama had turned the 20th Maine's right and rolled up the 83rd Pennsylvania's left.[16] When he was informed of Oates's statement Chamberlain withdrew any support he may have had for Oates's request. Oates had lost the second battle of Little Round Top.

Oates made a last futile effort to force the commission to honor his request. On November 4, 1903, Oates informed Chairman Nicholson that the Alabama legislature had "passed a joint resolution requesting the senators and nine representatives from this state to investigate and see why it is that permission is not given to me to erect the monument."[17] But the damage to Oates's cause was irreparable. The issue dragged on another two years but the commission continued to refuse Oates's request.[18] Today a monument to Law's Brigade stands on South Confederate Avenue where Law formed his line of battle July 2, 1863. Another small iron tablet on Warren Avenue, south of Little Round Top, identifies the brigade's approach from the direction of Round Top.[19]

The combative Oates died September 9, 1910, at Montgomery, Alabama. On his tombstone is an epitaph probably written by Oates himself. It reads:

Born in poverty; reared in adversity, without education advantage. Yet by honest individual effort he obtained a competency and the confidence of his fellow man, while fairly liberal to relatives and to the worthy poor. A devoted Confederate soldier. He gave his right arm to the cause. He accepted the result of the war without a murmur, and in 1898–9 he was a Brigadier General of the United States volunteers in the war with Spain.[20]

The battle for the Round Tops was finally over.

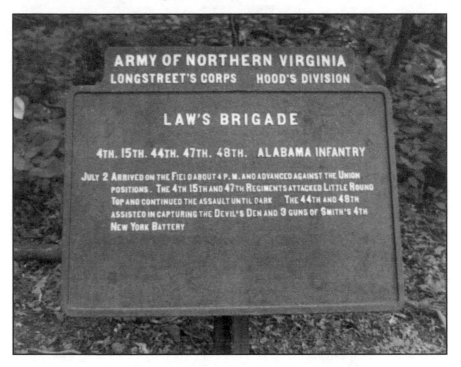

Plaque for Law's Brigade, Warren Avenue

Appendix A

Opposing Forces—Round Tops and Devil's Den[1]

Army of the Potomac and the Army of Northern Virginia
July 2–3, 1863

Organization of the Army of Northern Virginia, Gen. Robert E. Lee, Commanding[2]

FIRST ARMY CORPS
Lt. Gen. James Longstreet

Hood's Division
Maj. Gen. John B. Hood
Brig. Gen. Evander M. Law

Law's Brigade
Brig. Gen. Evander M. Law
Col. James L. Sheffield

4th Alabama, Lt. Col. Lawrence H. Scruggs
  Maj. Thomas K. Coleman[3]
15th Alabama, Col. William C. Oates[4]
  Capt. Blanton A. Hill
44th Alabama, Col. William F. Perry
  Lt. Col. John A. Jones
47th Alabama, Col. James W. Jackson[5]
  Lt. Col. Michael J. Bulger
  Maj. James M. Campbell
48th Alabama, Col. James L. Sheffield[6]
  Capt. Thomas J. P. Eubanks

Robertson's Brigade
Brig. Gen. Jerome B. "Aunt Pollie" Robertson

3rd Arkansas, Col. Van H. Manning
  Lt. Col. R. S. Taylor
1st Texas, Lt. Col. Phillip A. Work
4th Texas, Col. John C. G. Key
  Maj. John P. Bane
5th Texas, Col. Robert M. Powell
  Lt. Col. King Bryan
  Maj. Jefferson C. Rogers

Anderson's Brigade
Brig. Gen. George T. "Tige" Anderson
Lt. Col. William Luffman

7th Georgia, Col. William W. White
8th Georgia, Col. John R. Towers
9th Georgia, Lt. Col. John C. Mounger
  Maj. W. M. Jones
  Capt. George Hillyer
11th Georgia, Col. F. H. Little
  Lt. Col. William Luffman
  Maj. Henry D. McDaniel
  Capt. William H. Mitchell
59th Georgia, Col. Jack Brown
  Capt. M. G. Bass

Benning's Brigade
Brig. Gen. Henry L. "Rock" Benning

2nd Georgia, Lt. Col. William T. Harris
  Maj. William S. Shepherd
15th Georgia, Col. Dudley M. DuBose
17th Georgia, Col. W. C. Hodges
20th Georgia, Col. John A. Jones
  Lt. Col. James D. Waddell

Artillery[7]
Maj. Mathis W. Henry

Branch (North Carolina) Artillery, Capt. Alexander C. Latham
German (South Carolina) Artillery, Capt. William K. Bachman
Palmetto (South Carolina) Light Artillery, Capt. Hugh R. Garden
Rowan (North Carolina) Artillery, Capt. James Reilly

CAVALRY[8]
Stuart's Division
Maj. Gen. J. E. B. Stuart

Hampton's Brigade	*Stuart Horse Artillery*
Brig. Gen. Wade Hampton	Maj. Robert F. Beckham
Col. Laurence S. Baker	
1st South Carolina, Col. John L. Black[9]	Washington Light Artillery, Capt. James F. Hart

Organization of the Army of the Potomac, Maj. Gen George G. Meade, Commanding[10]

Third Army Corps
Maj. Gen. Daniel E. Sickles
Maj. Gen. David B. Birney

First Division	*Third Brigade*
Maj. Gen. David B. Birney	Col. P. Regis De Trobriand
Brig. Gen. J. H. Hobart Ward	40th New York, Col. Thomas W. Egan
Second Brigade[11]	*Second Division*
Brig. Gen. J. H. Hobart Ward	Brig. Gen. Andrew A. Humphreys
Col. Hiram Berdan	
	Third Brigade
20th Indiana, Col. John Wheeler	Col. George C. Burling
Lt. Col. William C. L. Taylor	
4th Maine, Col. Elijah Walker	6th New Jersey, Lt. Col. Stephen R. Gilkyson
Capt. Edwin Libby	*Artillery Brigade*
124th New York, Col. A. Van Horne Ellis	Capt. George E. Randolph
Lt. Col. Francis M. Cummins	Capt. A. Judson Clark
Capt. Charles H. Weygant	
99th Pennsylvania, Maj. John W. Moore	New York Light, 4th Battery
2nd United States Sharpshooters	Capt. James E. Smith
(Eight Companies)	
Maj. Homer R. Stoughton	

Fifth Army Corps
Maj. Gen. George Sykes

First Division	*Second Division*
Brig. Gen. James Barnes	Brig. Gen. Romeyn B. Ayres
Third Brigade	*Third Brigade*
Col. Strong Vincent	Brig. Gen. Stephen H. Weed
Col. James C. "Crazy" Rice	Col. Kenner Garrard
20th Maine, Col. Joshua L. Chamberlain	140th New York, Col. Patrick H. O'Rorke
16th Michigan, Lt. Col. Norval E. Welch	Lt. Col. Louis Ernst

Third Brigade (continued)
44th New York, Col. James C. Rice
  Lt. Col. Freeman Conner
83rd Pennsylvania,
  Capt. Orpheus S. Woodward

Third Division
Brig. Gen. Samuel W. Crawford

Third Brigade
Col. Joseph W. Fisher

5th Pennsylvania Reserves, Lt. Col. George Dare
12th Pennsylvania Reserves (9 companies), Col. Martin D. Hardin

Artillery Brigade
5th U.S., Battery D
  Lt. Charles E. Hazlett
  Lt. Benjamin F. Rittenhouse

CAVALRY CORPS[12]—July 3, 1863
Extreme Federal Left
Maj. Gen. Alfred Pleasonton

First Division
Brig. Gen. John Buford

Reserve Brigade[13]
Brig. Gen. Wesley Merritt

6th Pennsylvania, Maj. James H. Haseltine
1st United States, Capt. Richard S.C. Lord
2nd United States, Capt. T. F. Rodenbough
5th United States, Capt. Julius W. Mason

Third Division
Brig. Gen. H. Judson Kilpatrick

First Brigade
Brig. Gen. Elon J. Farnsworth
Col. Nathaniel P. Richmond

5th New York, Maj. John Hammond
18th Pennsylvania, Lt. Col. William P. Brinton
1st Vermont, Lt. Col. Addison W. Preston
1st West Virginia, Col. Nathaniel P. Richmond
  Maj. Charles E. Capehart

Horse Artillery

First Brigade
Capt. James M. Robertson

4th U.S. Artillery, Battery E, Lt. Samuel S. Elder

Second Brigade
Capt. John S. Tidball

1st U.S. Artillery, Battery K, Capt. William M. Graham

Appendix B

Organization—Law's Alabama Brigade[1]

July 2–3, 1863

Commanding Brigade
Brig. Gen. Evander M. Law

Brigade Staff
Assistant Adjutant General
Thomas L. Christian
Leigh R. Terrell

Quartermaster Staff
Quartermaster: William H. Scruggs
Thomas H. Hopkins, Co. D, 4th AL

Commissary Staff
Commissary: Amzi Babbitt,
Virgil A Nuckols, Co. I, 4th AL

Ordnance: Richard Drake

Couriers
E. M. Ervin, Co. B, 4th Alabama
Thomas J. Sinclair, Co. B, 4th Alabama
Mims Walker[3], Co. D, 4th Alabama

Aide–de–Camp
John Cussons

Ambulance Driver
W. A. Haynes, Co. L, 15th AL

Brigade Blacksmith
Annanias Perdue, Co. B, 4th AL
John W. Chandler, Co. I, 44th AL

Brigade Mail Carrier
George M. Wright, Co. C, 4th AL

Staff[2]
B. F. Johnson, Co. G, 48th AL

4th Alabama[4]

Field & Staff
Col.: Pickney D. Bowles (AA)[5]
Lt. Col.: Lawrence H. Scruggs
Maj.:Thomas K. Coleman

Adjutant: Robert T. Coles
Quartermaster Department
QM: Joseph W. Hudson
QM Sgt.: Richard M. Taylor, [B]
Staff: James H. Kornegay,[6] [D][7]

Scout: Phinias K. McMiller
Pioneer: Jesse B. Nave
Provost Guard: John R. Hawkins,
Samuel R. Norton
Signal Corps: Sidney Porter (division)
Teamsters: Archibald C. Graham, [G]
Lott R. Smither, [I]
George C. Story, [B]
John T. Story, [B]
Thomas Warren, [K]

4th Alabama (continued)

Commissary Department
    Com.: John D. Brandon
    Com. Sgt.: Patrick S. Wheelan, [E]
    Staff: Jerome Hill,[8] [I]
Sgt. Maj.: John L. Brown[9]
Color Bearer: Gilchrist R. Boulware[10]
Ordnance
    Ord. Sgt.: Frank R. Lamson, [C]
    Driver: Francis S. Rutherford,[12] [B]
       James M. Drake,[13] [F]
       William T. Hammer, [F]

Courier—General Longstreet:
    Oliver H. Spenser, [G]
Musicians: John Fried, [B]
    Charles T. Halsey, [F]
Regimental Staff[11]
    James E. D. Hines, [H]
    William F. McElroy, [G]
    John M. McIntosh, [D]
    Robert Q. Pryor, [E]
    William F. Scott, [H]

Company Organization

	Company[14]	Commanders
A	Governor's Guards	Capt. Jason M. West
B	Tuskegee Zouaves[15]	Capt. Bayless E. Brown
C	Magnolia Cadets	Capt. Frank C. Robbins
D	Canebrake Rifles[16]	Capt. James T. Jones
E	Conecuh Guards	Capt. William Lee
F	Huntsville Guards	Capt. William W. Leftwich
G	Marion Light Infantry	Capt. William M. Robbins
H	Lauderdale Guards[17]	Capt. William F. Karnser
I	North Alabamians	3 Lt. Henry B. Roper
K	Larkinsville Guards	2 Lt. William S. Harwell

15th Alabama[18]

Field & Staff
Col.: William C. Oates
Lt. Col.: Isaac B. Feagin
Maj.: Alexander A. Lowther[19]

Adjutant: DeBernie B. Waddell
Quartermaster Department
    QM: Edmond P. Head, [A], [D]
    QM Sgt.: T. J. Bass, [B]
Commissary Department
    Com.: Cornelius V. Morris
    Com. Sgt.: Jeptha P. Hill
    Staff: Charles V. Smith,[20] [A]
Sgt. Maj.: Robert C. Norris
Pioneer Corps
    J. H. Bell, [E]
    W. J. Tillery, [F]
Provost Guard: Young M. Edwards, [E]
Courier: William Youngblood,[24] [I]

Teamsters
    William Edson, [D]
    B. Galloway, [F]
    Newton A. Currenton, [A]
    F. P. Rucker, [A]
    H. M. Wicker, [K] (division)
Musicians
    Patrick Brannon, [K]
    Joshua C. Harrell, [K]
    Richard Harris, [I]
    G. F. Hartsfield, [B]
    A. H. Kirkland, [G]
    Julian C. Kersey[21] (drummer)
    James P Newberry, [A] (drummer)
    Robert S. Warlick[22]
Regimental Staff[23]
    Irwin Hicks, [G]
    J. T. Rushing, [I]
    S. B. Smith, [I]

15th Alabama[18] (continued)

Company Organization

	Company	Commanders
A	Cantey Rifles	Capt. Francis K. Shaaff
B	Midway Southern Guards	2 Lt. Henry H. Glover
C	Macon County Commissioners	Capt. James H. Glover
D	Ft. Browder Roughs	Capt. Blanton A. Hill[25]
E	Dale County Beauregards	Capt. William A. Edwards
F	Brundidge Guards	Capt. Dekalb Williams
G	Henry Pioneers	Capt. Henry C. Brainard
H	Glennville Guards	Capt. William D. Wood
I	Quitman Guards[26]	Capt. Frank Park
K	Eufaula Guards[27]	Capt. William J. Bethume
L	Pike Sharpshooters	Capt. James J. Hatcher[28]

44th Alabama[29]

Field & Staff

Col.: William F. Perry
Lt. Col.: John A. Jones
Maj.: George W. Cary

Adjutant: Thomas A. Nicoll
Quartermaster Staff
   QM: Robert Lapsley
   QM Sgt.: Thomas B. Sommerville
Commissary Staff
   Com.: Gardner W. McConnico
   Com. Sgt.: Thomas Boothe, [G]
Ordnance Sgt.: James J. Garrett, [G]
Musicans: Henry M. Schaad[32], [E]
   William Albritton[34], [C]
   Leonard M. Chandler, [E]
Hospital Steward: Thomas W. Hendree, [G]
Ambulance Driver: Walter M. Martin, [H]
   Hugh Latimer, [I]

Provost Guard: Jacob B. Hudson[30], [G]
Signal Corps: William S. Neal, [G]
   Patrick H. Shivers, [G]
Teamsters: John H. Allen[31], [G]
   Thomas J. Creel, [H]
   Theophilius Miller, [H]
   Robert B. Paul, [C]
   George W. Rogin, [D]
   Davil L. Smith, [K]
   John C. Tew, [C]
   Leonidia Whatley, A; [G]
   John J. Wilson, [G]
Pioneer Corps: John C. Soger[33], [C]
Secretary to Col.: William C. Lewis [G]
Staff: Enoch A. Allbritton, [C]
   James Wade, [K]

Company Organization

	Company[35]	Commanders
A	James M. Calhoun Guards	Capt. David L. Bozeman
B	Scottsville Guards	1 Lt. Virginius W. Jones
C	Cedar Grove Guards[36]	Capt. Robert Powers
D	Kenan Musketeers	Capt. Thomas L. Morrow
E	Sallie Ratcliffe Guards	2 Lt. Thomas Ferguson
F	Dan Steele Guards	Capt. William N. Green
G	Wash Smith Guards	Capt. William A. Dunklin
H	Dawson Warriors[37]	1 Lt. John S. Gardner
I	Aberchroche Guards	Capt. Absalom W. Denman
K	Cynthia Border Greys[38]	Capt. John M. Teague

47th Alabama[39]

Field & Staff
Col.: James W. Jackson
Lt. Col.: Michael J. Bulger
Maj.: James M. Campbell

Adjutant: William H. Keller
Quartermaster Department
 QM: Lemuel H. Dawson
 QM Sgt.: Porey F. Lawes
Commissary Department
 Com: Wade A. Herren
 Com. Sgt.: James V. Sewell
Ordnance Staff
 Ord. Sgt.: Porey R. Lawes, [K]
 Sgt. Maj.: Able L. Robinson
Color Bearer: Benjamin F. C. Russell,
 David J. Smith
Butcher: R. M. Grimmel, [A]
 P. E. Harris, [A]
Blacksmith: Jesse B. Haney, [B]
Teamsters: Walter T. Allen,[40] [K])
 L. J. Bankston, [A]
 John W. White, [F]

Musicans: J. H. Campbell (drummer)
 Thomas J. Hickman
 Carter W. Walls (fifer)
Hospital Stewards: Richard L. Bassett, [I]
 Reuben E. Jordan, [K]
Ambulance Driver: Troy Harris, [A]
Staff: James R. Chrisman, [F]
 John M. Harris, [K]
 William H. Jordan, [I]
 William H. Sexton, [H]
 Wyatt Woods, [F]
 S. C. Parker, [H]
 Richard Winbles, [E]

Company Organization

	Company	Commanders
A	———	Capt. John A. Ham
B	Tallapoosa Tigers[41]	Capt. Joseph S. Johnston, Jr
C	Jeff Holly Guards	1 Lt. William Ballard
D	———	Capt. Henry C. Lindsay
E	———	Capt. Francis T. J. Brandon
F	———	3 Lt. Elisha Mayo
G	———	1 Lt. James Whitaker
H	———	Capt. Joseph Q. Burton
I	Chambers Infantry	2 Lt. Joel F. Burgess
K	Goldwaithe Guards	Capt. James A. Sanford

48th Alabama[42]

Field & Staff
Col.: James L. Sheffield
Lt. Col.: William M. Hardwick
Maj.: Columbus B. St. John, [A][43]
Adjutant: Henry S. Figures
Sgt. Maj.: William F. Robbins
Color Bearer: James M. Parrish,[44] [C]
Quartermaster Department
 QM: William P. Golightly

Teamsters
 J. B. Brown, [K]
 T. J. Cromer, [H]
 R. R. Howard, [A]
 Robert Hurley, [A]
 G. W. McDaniel, [G]
 W. T. Owens, [K]
 G. S. Reaves, [K]

48th Alabama[42] (continued)

Quartermaster Department (continued)
    QM Sgt.: W. C. Hammond, [G]
    Staff: Charles Kingsberry, [G]
Commissary Department
    Com: William F. Robbins
    Com. Sgt.: Elijah S. Hardwick, [H]
    Butcher: A. J. Hall, [G]
Ordnance Staff
    Ord. Sgt.: John D. Taylor
Pioneer: James Keating, [G]
    S. T. Osborn, [K]
    S. C. Parker, [H]
    Richard Winkles, [E]

Teamsters (continued)
    J. P. Reynolds, [K]
    J. T. Slatten, [K]
    F. M. Smallwood, [D]
Musicians: James A. Hallet,[45] [H]
    Joseph S. Harris, [H]
    E. S. Smith, [K] (fifer)
Blacksmith: A. G. Davis, [G]
Ambulance Driver: William Crosby, [E]
Hospital Stewards
    James M. Belew, [G]
    R. W. Cain, [B]
    G. M. Phillips, [K]
    G. M. Phillips, [K]

Company Organization

	Company	Commanders
A	Jackson Boys	Capt. Randolph Graves
B	Mills Valley Guards	Capt. Jerome N. DeArmond
C	Mountain Rangers	2 Lt. W. J. G. Barton
D	Sheffield Guards[46]	1 Lt. James S. Ridgeway
E	Jacksonians	Capt. Issom B. Small
F	Jeff Davis Boys	Capt. Jeremiah Edwards
G	Elisha King Guards[47]	Capt. Norman H. McDuffie
H	Cherokee Grays[48]	Capt. Thomas J. Lumpkin
I	Newman Pound Guards[49]	1 Lt. Reuben T. Ewing
K	Moore Rifles	Capt. John B. Hubbard

Appendix C

Roster of Officers[1] —Law's Alabama Brigade

July 2–3, 1863

Name	Regt	Co	Rank	S	Bn	Age[2]	Trade	Resided
Adrian, James F.	48 AL	F	3 Lt.	P	AL	26	Farmer	Center, AL
Adrian, John D.	44 AL	K	3 Lt.	P	AL	21	Lawyer	Arbacoochee, AL
Adrian, John G.	47 AL	E	2 Lt.	KIA	GA	34	Farmer	Coloma, AL
Alford, Pierce L.	47 AL	C	3 Lt.	P	–	–	–	–
Appleton, Thomas N.	48 AL	E	3 Lt.	P	SC	37	Carpenter	Van Buren, AL
Babbitt, Amzi	BRGD	BS	Maj.	P	–	–	–	–
Baker, Eli A.	47 AL	B	2 Lt.	P	NC	37	Farmer	Real Town, AL
Ballard, William	47 AL	C	1 Lt.	P	GA	31	Farmer	Fish Pond, AL
Barton, W. J. G.	48 AL	C	2 Lt.	P	GA	2	Farmer	Aurora, AL
Bass, Washington P.	15 AL	A	3 Lt.	P	GA	21	Teacher	Dover, AL
Beaty, William A.	48 AL	K	2 Lt.	Wd	AL	–	–	–
Becker, Winns P.	44 AL	G	2 Lt.	Wd	NY	24	Merchant	Selma, AL
Bentley, John T.	47 AL	H	3 Lt.	P	AL	17	Student	Mill Town, AL
Berry, Thomas D.	47 AL	H	1 Lt.	P	GA	25	Mechanic	Dadeville, AL
Bethune, William J.	15 AL	K	Capt.	Wd	GA	17	Clerk	Eufaula, AL
Billingsley, Martin T.	4 AL	G	1 Lt.	P	MS	21	Farmer	Ullden, MS
Boothly, Frank L.	15 AL	H	3 Lt.	P	VA	23	Book Keeper	Norfolk, VA
Bozeman, David L.	44 AL	A	Capt.	P	AL	28	Merchant	Farmersville, AL
Brainard, Henry C.	15 AL	G	Capt.	KIA	–	21	Student	Lawrenceville, AL

Name	Regt	Co	Rank	S	Bn	Age	Trade	Resided
Brandon, Francis Thomas J.	47 AL	E	Capt.	P	GA	30	Minister	Gaylesville, AL
Brandon, John D.	4 AL	RS	ACS	P	MS	–	Lawyer	Huntsville, AL
Brazile, John H.	48 AL	A	2 Lt.	P	AL	24	Farmer	Blountsville, AL
Breare, Joseph R.	15 AL	E	2 Lt.	C	EG	28	Lawyer	Newton, AL
Breedlove, John P.	4 AL	B	1 Lt.	WC	AL	20	Clerk	Tuskegee, AL
Brodnax, Joseph W.	4 AL	A	2 Lt.	Wd	AL	21	Student	Marion, AL
Brown, Baylis E.	4 AL	B	Capt.	P	AL	25	Clerk	Tuskegee, AL
Brown, James H.	4 AL	F	2 Lt.	P	AL	23	Mechanic	Huntsville, AL
Bulger, Michael Jefferson	47 AL	RC	Lt. Col.	WC	SC	56	Farmer	De Soto, AL
Bulger, William D.	47 AL	A	1 Lt.	P	AL	19	Farmer	De Soto, AL
Burgess, Joel F.	47 AL	I	2 Lt.	P	GA	32	Farmer	Roanoke, AL
Burns, John P.	47 AL	A	3 Lt.	P	AL	30	Lawyer	Dadeville, AL
Burson, Elkanah	44 AL	C	3 Lt.	P	AL	30	Merchant	Snow Hill, AL
Burton, Joseph Quarterman	47 AL	H	Capt.	P	GA	19	Student	Lafayette, AL
Campbell, James McDonald	47 AL	RC	Maj.	P	TN	31	Minister	Gaylesville, AL
Carter, John E.	15 AL	I	2 Lt.	P	GA	24	Merchant	Troy, AL
Cary, George Walton	44 AL	RC	Maj.	P	AL	22	Teacher	Montevalo, AL
Cary, Robert E.	44 AL	E	3 Lt.	P	AL	16	Student	Montevalo, AL
Christian, Alfred	4 AL	E	2 Lt.	P	VA	34	Clerk	Evergreen, AL
Christian, Thomas L.	4 AL	D	2 Lt.	C	VA	23	Clerk	Uniontown, AL
Clifton, Francis M.	48 AL	H	3 Lt.	P	GA	24	Farmer	Blue Pond, AL
Cody, Barnett H.	15 AL	G	2 Lt.	MWC	GA	17	Student	Abbeville, AL
Coggins, Ebernezer B.	47 AL	H	2 Lt.	P	AL	29	Farmer	Mill Town, AL
Coleman, John W.	47 AL	D	3 Lt.	P	AL	28	Overseer	Rough and Ready, AL
Coleman, Thomas K.	4 AL	RC	Maj.	P	GA	25	Farmer	Uniontown, AL
Coles, Robert Thompson, Jr.	4 AL	RS	ADJ	P	AL	18	Student	Huntsville, AL
Collins, William W.	48 AL	D	2 Lt.	P	AL	27	Farmer	Guntersville, AL
Cox, Samuel W.	48 AL	B	2 Lt.	Wd	AL	18	Farmer	Duck Springs, AL

Appendix C

Name	Regt	Co	Rank	S	Bn	Age	Trade	Resided
Cussons, John	BRGD	BS	Capt.	C	EG	26	Editor	Selma, AL
Darby, James W.	4 AL	E	3 Lt.	P	AL	21	Clerk	Garland, AL
Dawson, Lemuel H.	47 AL	RS	AQM	P	GA	34	Farmer	Ridge Grove, AL
DeArmond, Jerome N.	48 AL	B	Capt.	Wd	TN	22	Teacher	Lebanon, AL
Denman, Absalom W.	44 AL	I	Capt.	P	GA	42	Farmer	Chulafinnee, AL
Dickson, Alvin O.	48 AL	A	1 Lt.	P	GA	22	Farmer	Brooksville, AL
Drake, Richard	BRGD	BS	ORD	P	–	–	–	–
Dunklin, William A.	44 AL	G	Capt.	KIA	AL	30	Lawyer	Selma, AL
Edwards, Daniel B.	44 AL	A	1 Lt.	P	AL	25	Farmer	Benton, AL
Edwards, Jeremiah	48 AL	F	Capt.	C	AL	30	Farmer	Summit, AL
Edwards, William A.	15 AL	E	Capt.	P	GA	26	Farmer	Westville, AL
Ellison, James H.	15 AL	C	Capt.	KIA	GA	24	Farmer	Enon, AL
Eubanks, John B.	48 AL	F	2 Lt.	C	GA	32	Farmer	Blountsville, AL
Eubanks, Thomas James P.	48 AL	D	Capt.	P	GA	26	Printer	Guntersville, AL
Ewing, Reuben T.	48 AL	I	1 Lt.	P	GA	36	Farmer	Center, AL
Feagin, Issac Ball	15 AL	RC	Lt. Col.	WC	GA	28	Merchant	Midway, AL
Ferguson, Thomas	44 AL	E	2 Lt.	P	AL	17	Student	Selma, AL
Fields, Hugh	15 AL	A	1 Lt.	P	AL	19	Student	Villula, AL
Figures, Henry Stokes	48 AL	RS	ADJ	P	AL	–	Student	Huntsville, AL
Fowler, Martin H.	44 AL	K	2 Lt.	P	SC	32	Farmer	Wehega, AL
Frazer, John A.	47 AL	I	3 Lt.	P	AL	23	Farmer	Lafayette, AL
Gardner, John S.	44 AL	H	1 Lt.	P	AL	21	Clerk	Centerville, AL
Gary, William P.	15 AL	B	3 Lt.	P	GA	21	Farmer	Spring Hill, AL
Glover, Henry H.	15 AL	B	2 Lt.	P	GA	24	Farmer	Pine Grove, AL
Golightly, William P.	48 AL	H	2 Lt.	P	SC	28	Farmer	Center, AL
Graves, Randolph	48 AL	A	Capt.	P	TN	36	Mechanic	Summit, AL
Gray, James H.	15 AL	K	2 Lt.	P	CT	25	Mechanic	Eufaula, AL
Gray, John	47 AL	B	1 Lt.	P	GA	27	Farmer	Walnut Hill, AL
Green, William N.	44 AL	F	Capt.	P	AL	32	Farmer	Six Mile, AL

Name	Regt	Co	Rank	S	Bn	Age	Trade	Resided
Grice, Henry Floyd	4 AL	C	2 Lt.	P	AL	20	Farmer	Benton, AL
Guerry, Lagrand L.	15 AL	C	1 Lt.	P	GA	28	Farmer	Midway, AL
Ham, John	47 AL	A	Capt.	P	GA	23	Farmer	Dadeville, AL
Hardwick, John B.	48 AL	H	1 Lt.	P	AL	19	Farmer	Cedar Bluff, AL
Hardwick, William McTyiere	48 AL	RC	Lt. Col.	Wd	AL	24	Merchant	Cedar Bluff, AL
Harris, Watkins	4 AL	I	Capt.	P	AL	18	Student	Huntsville, AL
Harwell, William S.	4 AL	K	2 Lt.	KIA	TN	21	Farmer	Larkinsville, AL
Hatcher, James J.	15 AL	L	Capt.[3]	P	GA	31	Merchant	Ft. Browder, AL
Head, Edmond P.	15 AL	D	1 Lt.	P	AL	31	Farmer	Ft. Browder, AL
Heaton, John L. F.	44 AL	I	2 Lt.	P	GA	32	Merchant	Arbacoochee, AL
Herren, Wade A.	47 AL	RS	ACS	P	GA	26	Farmer	Camp Hill, AL
Hill, Blanton Abram	15 AL	D	Capt.	P	GA	24	Farmer	Ft. Browder, AL
Hinds, James M.	48 AL	D	3 Lt.	P	AL	19	Farmer	Warrenton, AL
Hood, Joseph Nathaniel	47 AL	E	1 Lt.	Wd	TN	24	Farmer	Spring Garden, AL
Horton, Wylie Hill	44 AL	D	3 Lt.	P	AL	32	Farmer	Columbiana, AL
Hubbard, John B.	48 AL	K	Capt.	P	GA	25	Farmer	Kemp Creek, AL
Hudson, Joseph Warren	4 AL	RS	AQM	P	VA	29	Merchant	Uniontown, AL
Hunnicutt, William R.	44 AL	K	1 Lt.	P	AL	28	Farmer	Oaklevel AL
Jackson, James Washington	47 AL	RC	Col.	P	GA	31	Physician	Fayette, AL
Jamison, William W.	47 AL	D	2 Lt.	P	SC	37	Physician	Rough and Ready, AL
Johnston, Joseph S., Jr.	47 AL	B	Capt.	MWC	GA	31	Merchant	Wynn Creek, AL
Jones, James Taylor	4 AL	D	Capt.	P	VA	27	Lawyer	Demopolis, AL
Jones, John Archibald	44 AL	RC	Lt. Col.	P	NC	31	Cotton Mgr	Scottsville, AL
Jones, John E.	15 AL	E	1 Lt.	P	GA	21	Teacher	Westville, AL
Jones, Richard Channing	44 AL	C	2 Lt.	P	VA	21	Lawyer	Camden, AL
Jones, Robert P.	4 AL	K	3 Lt.	P	AL	28	Teacher	Larkinsville, AL
Jones, Virginius W.	44 AL	B	1 Lt.	Wd	AL	–	Student	Camden, AL
Karsner, William F.	4 AL	H	Capt.	P	AL[4]	22	Sheriff	Florence, AL
Keller, William Henry	47 AL	RS	ADJ	P	Ga[4]	29	Farmer	Newnan, GA

Name	Regt	Co	Rank	S	Bn	Age	Trade	Resided
Kidd, Reuben Vaughan	4 AL	A	1 Lt.	P	AL	19	Merchant	Selma, AL
Kimball, Nathan Crawford	47 AL	D	1 Lt.	P	AL	22	Farmer	De Sota, AL
Kunzie, John L.	4 AL	B	3 Lt.	P	AL	19	Clerk	Tuskegee, AL
Lamar, John H.	4 AL	C	1 Lt.	P	AL	22	Farmer	Benton, AL
Langley, Edmond B.	47 AL	A	2 Lt.	P	SC	28	Farmer	Dudleyville, AL
Lapsley, Robert	44 AL	RS	AQM	P	Ma	22	Clerk	Selma, AL
Law, Evander McIver	BRGD	BC	BG	P	SC	27	Mil Instruct	Tuskegee, AL
Lee, William	4 AL	E	Capt.	KIA	AL	26	Lawyer	Sparta, AL
Leftwich, William W.	4 AL	F	Capt.	MW	AL	21	Druggist	Huntsville, AL
Lindsay, Henry C.	47 AL	D	Capt.	P	SC	21	Farmer	Rough and Ready, AL
Lloyd, William P	15 AL	C	2 Lt.	P	GA	18	Farmer	Creek Stand, AL
Lumpkin, Thomas J.	48 AL	H	Capt.	P	GA	22	Physician	Cedar Bluff, AL
Lusk, John M.	48 AL	I	2 Lt.	P	GA	30	Farmer	Wehega, AL
Mathews, George A. C.	15 AL	I	3 Lt	P	GA	23	Farmer	Brundige, AL
Mayo, Elisha	47 AL	F	3 Lt.	P	GA	25	Farmer	New Site, AL
McCaghren, P. T. G.	48 AL	I	3 Lt.	P	GA	30	Farmer	Kemp Creek, AL
McConnico, Gardner W.	44 AL	RS	ACS	P	AL	43	Clerk	Selma, AL
McDuffie, Norman H.	48 AL	G	Capt.	P	GA	33	Farmer	Gadsden, AL
McInnis, Archibald D.	4 AL	E	1 Lt.	Wd	CA	21	Telegrapher	Evergreen, AL
Morgan, Lewis A.	4 AL	D	3 Lt.	P	AL	23	Merchant	Uniontown, AL
Morris, Cornelius V.	15 AL	RS	ACS	P	–	44	Merchant	Franklin, AL
Morrow, Thomas L.	44 AL	D	Capt.	P	MS	32	Farmer	Montevalo, AL
Moseley, Henry H.	4 AL	G	3 Lt.	P	AL	19	Student	Marion, AL
Newsome, William O.	4 AL	H	2 Lt.	P	AL	20	Clerk	Tuscambia, AL
Nickolson, P. W.	15 AL	F	2 Lt.	P	GA	24	Merchant	Brundige, AL
Nicoll, Thomas A.	44 AL	RS	ADJ	P	AL	23	Clerk	Mobile, AL
Norred, Preston B.	44 AL	I	3 Lt.	MW	GA	36	Farmer	Arbacoochee, AL
Oakes, Jonas	44 AL	D	2 Lt.	P	AL	28	Clerk	Columbiana, AL
Oates, John A.	15 AL	G	1 Lt.	MWC	AL	23	Clerk	Newton, AL

Name	Regt	Co	Rank	S	Bn	Age	Trade	Resided
Oates, William Calvin	15 AL	RC	Col.	P	AL	25	Lawyer	Abbeville, AL
Park, Frank	15 AL	I	Capt.	P	GA	33	Physician	Oaks, AL
Parton, Joseph J.	4 AL	F	3 Lt.	Wd	TN	26	Mechanic	Huntsville, AL
Perry, William Flake	44 AL	RC	Col.	P	GA	30	Teacher	Tuskegee, AL
Peterson, Battle D.	4 AL	B	2 Lt.	P	AL	20	Student	Tuskegee, AL
Pettit, H. L.	48 AL	K	1 Lt.	P	AL	35	Merchant	Mount Polk, AL
Porter, Fred M.	15 AL	K	1 Lt.	P	GA	24	Clerk	Eufaula, AL
Powers, Robert	44 AL	C	Capt.	P	AL	27	Farmer	Monterey, AL
Ray, Andrew	47 AL	E	3 Lt.	MWC	GA	32	Farmer	Goshen, AL
Reese, George	44 AL	A	2 Lt.	P	SC	26	Merchant	Benton, AL
Renfroe, Thomas M.	15 AL	G	3 Lt.	P	GA	21	Farmer	Franklin, AL
Rice, Erwin Foster	48 AL	K	3 Lt.	P	NC	32	Farmer	White Plains, AL
Ridgeway, James S.	48 AL	D	1 Lt.	Wd	AL	30	Farmer	Warrenton, AL
Robbins, Frank C.	4 AL	C	Capt.	P	NC	–	Teacher	Trinity, NC
Robbins, William McKendre	4 AL	G	Capt.	P	NC	31	Lawyer	Marion, AL
Roper, Henry Bently	4 AL	I	3 Lt.	WC	AL	22	Clerk	Huntsville, AL
Samuels, Thomas L.	4 AL	A	3 Lt.	P	MS	24	Clerk	Cherabula, MS
Sanford, James A.	47 AL	K	Capt.	P	GA	24	Mechanic	Dadeville, AL
Scoggins, William H.	15 AL	E	3 Lt.	P	GA	21	Carpenter	Daleville, AL
Scruggs, Lawrence Houston	4 AL	RC	Lt. Col.	P	AL	25	Merchant	Huntsville, AL
Scruggs, William H.	BRGD	BS	QM	P	AL	33	Conductor	Huntsville, AL
Shaaff, Francis Key	15 AL	A	Capt.	P	DC	28	Soldier	Columbus, GA
Sheffield, James Lawrence	48 AL	RC	Col.	P	AL	48	Farmer	Guntersville, AL
Sheppard, John H.	48 AL	B	1 Lt.	P	SC	22	Farmer	Duck Springs, AL
Simmons, Henry D.	47 AL	B	3 Lt.	P	GA	22	Farmer	De Sota, AL
Small, Issom B.	48 AL	E	Capt.	P	AL	26	Teacher	Van Buren, AL
Smith, Otterson	48 AL	G	2 Lt.	P	GA	26	Farmer	Gadsden, AL
Smitherman, Thomas F.	44 AL	H	2 Lt.	P	AL	28	Lawyer	Centerville, AL
St. John, Columbus B.	48 AL	F	1 Lt.	Wd	AL	18	Student	Summit, AL

Name	Regt	Co	Rank	S	Bn	Age	Trade	Resided
Stewart, James H.	4 AL	I	1 Lt.	P	AL	27	Merchant	Summit, AL
Strickland, William H.	15 AL	I	1 Lt.	P	AL	25	Clerk	Troy, AL
Sutton, James T.	48 AL	G	1 Lt.	Wd	SC	25	Farmer	Gadsden, AL
Teague, John M.	44 AL	K	Capt.	KIA	SC	33	Farmer	Corn Grove, AL
Thorton, Dozier	15 AL	D	2 Lt.	AD[5]	AL	24	Farmer	Ft. Browder, AL
Todd, James A.	47 AL	K	2 Lt.	P	GA	27	Farmer	Lafayette, AL
Turnbow, James M.	4 AL	G	2 Lt.	KIA	AL	20	Student	Hambug, AL
Turner, Daniel H.	4 AL	I	2 Lt.	Wd	AL	18	Farmer	Madison X Roads, AL
Tweedell, John F.	44 AL	I	1 Lt.	P	GA	22	–	Gold Ridge, AL
Vaughan, Paul Turner	4 AL	C	3 Lt.	P	AL	20	Farmer	Summerfiled, AL
Waddell, DeBernie B.	15 AL	RS	Adj.	P	NC	27	Clerk	Seal Station, AL
Walker, Mims	BRGD	BS	Pvt.	P	AL	22	Farmer	Uniontown, AL
Walls, Willis W.	47 AL	G	3 Lt.	P	AL	30	Farmer	Bluff Springs, AL
West, Jason M.	4 AL	A	Capt.	P	AL	28	Merchant	Selma, AL
Whitaker, James	47 AL	G	1 Lt.	WC	GA	28	Farmer	Wedowee, AL
Wicker, Robert H.	15 AL	L	3 Lt.	C	AL	21	Farmer	Perot, AL
Williams, Dekalb	15 AL	F	Capt.	P	AL	28	Farmer	Brundige, AL
Wood, William D.	15 AL	H	1 Lt.	P	AL	25	Lawyer	Glenville, AL

Appendix D

Operations July 2–3, 1863— Extreme Confederate Right

Operations July 2—Devil's Den and Little Round Top

Approximate Time	Events[1]	Events
	Emmitsburg Road	
11:45–12:00	Law's Brigade arrives at Herr Tavern[2]	
3:00 p.m.	Law's Brigade arrives before Big Round Top[3]	
3:30 p.m.	Warren arrives on Little Round Top[4]	
4:00 p.m.	Hood sends his division forward[5]	
	Devil's Den	**Little Round Top**
	Walker moves the 4th Maine into Plum Run Gorge	
		Vincent arrives on Little Round Top
	Law's Brigade advances through Plum Run Valley	
		Vincent deploys and throws forward skirmishers
		4th Alabama, 4th and 5th Texas pass Walker's left flank en route to assault Little Round Top
4:30 p.m.	44th Alabama opens the attack on the 4th Maine	
4:45 p.m.	48th Alabama joins the fight for Devil's Den	
		4th Alabama, 4th and 5th Texas began their assault on Little Round Top[6]
5:00 p.m.	44th Alabama overruns 4th New York Battery[7]	
		Hazlett opens on the Confederates around Devil's Den
		4th Alabama, 4th and 5th Texas suffer their first repulse
	Walker and the 4th Maine drive the 44th Alabama from the southern end of Houck's Ridge	

<u>Approximate</u> <u>Time</u>	<u>Events</u>	<u>Events</u>
	Benning arrives in front of Devil's Den	
		4th Alabama, 4th and 5th Texas make a second assault on Little Round Top
	Heavy fighting spreads into Plum Run Valley above Plum Run Gorge	
		47th Alabama arrives in the valley between the Round Tops
		4th Alabama, 4th and 5th Texas suffer their second repulse
5:30–5:45 p.m.	Federals retire from Plum Run Valley[8]	
		4th and 47th Alabama attack left of 83rd Pennsylvania and right of 20th Maine
		15th Alabama arrives in valley between the Round Tops and attacks center and left of the 20th Maine
		4th and 5th Texas, 44th and 48th Alabama move north in Plum Run Valley[9]
6:00–6:15 p.m.		Vincent is mortally wounded[10]
		4th Alabama suffers its third repulse
		47th Alabama is repulsed
		4th and 5th Texas, 44th and 48th Alabama repulsed by Vincent's right
6:45–7:00 p.m.		The 20th Maine charges the 15th Alabama and clears valley between the Round Tops[11]
7:29 p.m.	Sunset[12]	
8:00 p.m.		In falling twilight, Vincent sends out detachments to collect arms and wounded[13]
9:00 p.m.		Chamberlain moves onto Big Round Top[14]

Operations July 3—Extreme Confederate Right[15]

11:45–12:15	Farnsworth's brigade of cavalry arrive south of Big Round Top and turn west[16]
12:30–1:00 p.m.	Farnsworth approaches Bushman Woods from the south
1:00 p.m.	Alexander opens the bombardment prior to "Pickett's Charge"[17]
1:00–1:30 p.m.	Farnsworth pushes his skirmish line forward and begins massing in Bushman Woods
	Law withdraws the 1st Texas from the main line[18]

<u>Approximate</u> <u>Time</u>	<u>Events</u>	<u>Events</u>
1:30–2:00 p.m.	Merritt approaches the battlefield along the Emmitsburg Road	
2:00 p.m.	"Pickett's Charge" is underway[19]	
	Merritt drives Colonel Black's command back on the main skirmish line	
3:00 p.m.	Merritt moves up on Farnsworth's left	
3:15–3:30 p.m.	"Pickett's Charge" is over[20]	
3:30 p.m.	7th and 8th Georgia skirmish line has been extended west to cover Merritt's flanking move[21]	
	Law attacks Merritt's left flank and doubles it back on the Emmitsburg Road	
4:00 p.m.	Law's skirmish line extends from the main line on Big Round Top west past the A. Currens house	
4:45–5:00 p.m.	Kilpatrick orders Farnsworth to charge into Plum Run Valley	
	1st Texas repulses 1st West Virginia Cavalry[22]	
	Farnsworth hits the Confederate skirmish line and rides north into Plum Run Valley	
	Parsons breaks through the skirmish line	
5:00–5:15 p.m.	18th Pennsylvania Cavalry launches an assault against the 1st Texas[23]	
	Parsons leads a squadron of 1st Vermont cavalry in a skirmish with the 4th Alabama skirmishers	
	Farnsworth skirmish with the 15th Alabama	
5:27 p.m.	Perley C. J. Cheney, second lieutenant of Company E, 1st Vermont Cavalry is wounded[24]	
	Vermont cavalry charges Law's batteries	
	Farnsworth is killed in the skirmish with the 15th Alabama	
	Wells leads survivors of Farnsworth's charge from the field	
	A heavy thunderstorm rolls in[25]	

Notes

Introduction

1. Law, *B&L*, v3, 319.
2. Sommers, *Richmond Redeemed*, xii, xiii.

Chapter 1—Prelude to Battle

1. *OR*, v27, pt2, 284.
2. McIver is pronounced "Ma-Keev-er." Although known as McIver, Law's cousin and classmate at the Citadel, Tom Law, called him "Keever." Thomas Law, *Citadel Cadets*, 22.
3. Evander McIver Law was the first son of Ezekiel Augustus Law and Sarah Elizabeth McIver of Society Hill, South Carolina. Judge Gus Law was a graduate of Yale Law School, member of the legislature, and for many years Chancellor in Equity, J. Law, *Adger–Law Notebook*, 85. Society Hill was a satellite community of Darlington, SC. The Laws lived a comfortable plantation life where McIver enjoyed the gentlemanly pursuits of riding and hunting. He attended the Common School and St. John's Academy at Darlington, Law, Surname File, ADAH.
4. 8th U.S. Census, 1860; ADAH; Citadel Alumni Office Records; *Dictionary of American Biography*, v11, 38–39. Law's partner in the school was Robert Parks.
5. First Manassas refers to the Battle of First Manassas fought July 21, 1861; also referred to as Battle of First Bull Run.
6. The first colonel died of wounds received at the Battle of First Manassas.

7. Laine, *Law's Alabama Brigade*, 10, 16, for a discussion of Davis's position.
8. Brigadier General William H. C. "Chase" Whiting's Third Brigade composed of the 2nd and 11th Mississippi, 6th North Carolina and 4th Alabama.
9. Laine, *Law's Alabama Brigade*, 10, 11.
10. Ibid., chapter 1, for a complete discussion of Law and his quest for a brigadier's commission. Second Manassas refers to the Battle of Second Manassas or Battle of Second Bull Run fought Aug. 29–30, 1862. Battle of Sharpsburg is also known as Battle of Antietam fought Sept. 17, 1862.
11. Clopton to Davis, July 23, 1862; Dargan to Randolph, July 24, 1862, CGSO.
12. Watts to Randolph, Aug. 2, 1862, CGSO. Watts became governor of Alabama in 1863.
13. Hood to Randolph, June 30, 1862; CSR, CGSO.
14. Officers' petition to Randolph, about Sept. 1, 1862, CGSO. This was the brigade's second petition on Law's behalf.
15. Officers' petition to Randolph, about Sept. 20, 1862, CGSO.
16. *Journal Confederate Congress*, v2, 414.
17. *OR*, v21, 540. The North Carolina regiments were the 6th, 54th and 57th.
18. Ibid., 1031, 1099. Lee was responding to an executive order to create state brigades.
19. Richard, *Alabama Encyclopedia*, v1, 353. Companies F, I, H, K were from the Tennessee Valley; Company E came from the

coastal plains of Conecuh County. The remainder were from Perry, Lowndes, Dallas, Macon, Bibb and Marengo counties.

20. Commanders contributing to the early development of the 4th Alabama were Egbert J. Jones, veteran of the war with Mexico, McIver Law, military instructor, and Owen Kenan McLemore, graduate of West Point and professional soldier.

21. Oates, *The War*, 775.

22. Laine, *Law's Alabama Brigade*, chapter 1 for a discussion of the 4th Alabama in the first two years of the war. The term "little Gamecock" was used in *Daily Huntsville Confederate* Sept. 11, 1863.

23. Laine, *Law's Alabama Brigade*, 39, 63 for a discussion.

24. Owen, *History of Alabama*, v4, 192, 193; Dubose, *Notable Men*, 17; *CMH*, v8, 724, 725. In his introduction to the Morningside Reprint of Oates, *The War*, relates that Oates, in self-defense, struck a man in the head with a mattock and left the state because he thought the person was dead; however, that part of Oates's background was never recounted in the biographies written while Oates was a prominent and influential politician in the state of Alabama.

25. Laine, *Law's Alabama Brigade*, 28.

26. Ibid., 28–37, for a discussion of the twin regiments.

27. *OR*, v27, pt3, 880–881.

28. Ibid., pt3, 305, 868.

29. Alexander, *Fighting for the Confederacy*, 221.

30. Longstreet, *Manassas To Appomattox*, 335–337.

Chapter 2—Route to Gettysburg

1. *OR*, v27 pt2, 357; "Coles, Gettysburg Campaign," 1; REC, Co. D, CSR, 48th AL Inf; Company A, CSR, 47th AL Inf, NA; Vaughan, "Vaughan Diary," 585.

2. Houghton, *Two Boys*, 59.

3. Coles, "Gettysburg Campaign," 1, refers to Washington as Little Washington; Vaughan, "Vaughan Diary," 585.

4. Vaughan, "Vaughan Diary," 585, 586; *OR*, v27, pt2, 428.

5. REC, Co. D, CSR, 47th AL Inf, NA, Coles, "Gettysburg Campaign," 2; Youngblood, "Unwritten History," 312.

6. Anderson to E. P. Anderson, July 17, 1863, APJSU. John used the local colloquialism "a–tall" for the expression "at all."

7. Youngblood, "Unwritten History," 313.

8. Coles, "Gettysburg Campaign," 2; Vaughan, "Vaughan Diary," 586.

9. REC, Co. D, 47th AL Inf, NA.

10. Coles, "Gettysburg Campaign," 2; REC, Co. E, CSR, 4th AL Inf, NA; Vaughan, "Vaughan Diary," 586; McDaniel, *With Unabated Trust*, 175.

11. McDaniel, *With Unabated Trust*, 175; Figures to his mother, June 21, 1863, FC; TLW.

12. Coles, "Gettysburg Campaign," 3.

13. Ibid., 3; Vaughan, "Vaughan Diary," 587.

14. TLW.

15. Coles, "Gettysburg Campaign," 3; Vaughan, "Vaughan Diary," 587.

16. Youngblood, "Unwritten History," 313.

17. Houghton, *Two Boys*, 58, 59.

18. REC, Co. B, CSR, 44th AL Inf, NA; Vaughan, "Vaughan Diary," 587.

19. TLW.

20. Coles, "Gettysburg Campaign," 4; Vaughan, "Vaughan Diary," 587 indicates they were four miles from the Potomac River.

21. TLW.

22. "Incidents at Gettysburg," The *Register*, Sept. 8, 1901.

23. Jordan, *Events*, 40; REC, Co. D, 47th AL Inf, NA.

24. Houghton, *Two Boys*, 31, 32.

25. Jordan, *Events*, 40.

26. Vaughan, "Vaughan Diary," 587.

27. Sturgis, "War Record," ADAH.

28. Powell, "Recollections."

29. McLaws, "Gettysburg," 66.

30. Ward, "Incidents," 345.

31. Polley, *Hood's Texas Brigade*, 146–147.

32. Collier, *They'll Do to Tie to*, 127.

33. TLW.

34. Sturgis, *War Record*, ADAH.

35. CSR, 15th AL Inf, NA; Oates, *The War*, 759.

36. REC, Co. D, CSR, 44th AL Inf, NA; Vaughan, "Vaughan Diary," 587.

37. Coles, "Gettysburg Campaign," 5; Reese, "Family Sketch," 111.

38. Co. H, HM, 44th AL Inf, ADAH.

39. Coles, "Gettysburg Campaign," 5; Vaughan, "Vaughan Diary," 587.

40. "Incidents of Gettysburg," The *Register*, Sept. 8, 1901.

41. Pierrepont, *Reuben Kidd*, 329.

42. Daniel to Mat, June 28, 1863, DCSU.

43. Figures to his parents, July 18, 1863, FC.

44. Powell, "Recollections."

45. Ward, "Incidents," 345.

46. REC, Co. C, 44th AL Inf, Co. D, CSR, 47th AL Inf, NA; Coles, "Gettysburg Campaign," 5; Vaughan, "Vaughan Diary," 587.

47. Ward, "Incidents," 345.

48. "Incidents at Gettysburg," The *Register*, Sept. 8, 1901.

49. Ward, "Incidents," 345.

50. Ibid., 346.

51. Vaughan, "Vaughan Diary," 587.

52. Coles, "Gettysburg Campaign," 6.

53. Ward, "Incidents," 346.

54. Houghton, *Two Boys*, 38.

55. Yeary, *Reminiscences*, 451; Love, a twenty-two-year-old resident of Madison Station, AL, was wounded three times during the war. He transferred to the 4th AL Cav. in Feb. 1865, CSR, 4th AL Inf, NA.

56. Daniel to Mat, June 28, 1863, DCSU.

57. Anderson to E. P. Anderson, Aug. 16, 1863, APJSU.

58. Powell, "Recollections."

59. Parsons, "How Farnsworth was Killed."

60. Coles, "Gettysburg Campaign," 6; Longstreet, "Lee's Invasion," 250; Longstreet, *Manassas to Appomattox*, 346–347; *OR*, v27, pt1, 358; Sorrel, *Recollections*, 155.

61. REC, Co. E, H, CSR, 48th AL Inf, NA; Figures to his parents, July 18, 1863, FC.

62. Figures to his sister, July 18, 1863, FC.

63. CSR, 48th AL Inf, NA.

64. Duncan, *Marshall County*, 50–51; *Northern Alabama*, 619.

65. Smith, *History of Debates*, 356–358.

66. Owen, *Alabama Dictionary*, 156; Duncan, *Marshall County*, 51; *Northern Alabama*, 619.

67. CSR, 48th AL Inf, NA.

68. Ibid., 48th AL Inf, NA; HMR, 48th AL Inf, ADAH.

69. Ibid., 48th AL Inf, NA; HMR, 48th AL Inf, ADAH; CSR, 44th AL Inf, NA; HMR, 44th AL Inf, ADAH.

70. CSR, 9th AL Inf, NA; John Rayburn to Samuel K. Rayburn, Feb. 22, 1862, RFP, ADAH; Duncan, *Marshall County*, v1, 65; LRCAI, roll 56, NA; CSR, 48th AL Inf, NA.

71. Ibid., 44th AL Inf, NA.

72. Figures to his parents, July 18, 1863, FC; TLW.

73. Coles, "Gettysburg Campaign," 7.

74. Law, "Round Top," 319; Vaughan, "Vaughan Diary," 588; Coles, "Gettysburg Campaign," 7.

75. 15th AL Inf, ADAH.

76. Oates, *The War*, 649.

77. Ibid., 632; 15th AL Inf, ADAH.

78. Houghton, *Two Boys*, 34.

79. Ibid., 35, 36.

80. Oates, "Gettysburg," 173.

81. CSR, 44th AL Inf, NA.

82. Ibid.

83. Oates, "Gettysburg," 173; Vaughan, "Vaughan Diary," 588.

84. CSR, 4th AL Inf, NA; Bowles to E. P. Alexander, AP. The nature of the sentence is unknown.

85. Law's Pension Application, 1909.

86. *Northern Alabama*, 342; 8th U.S. Census, 1860, Madison County, Alabama, 215; Williams, *Huntsville Directory*, 81.

87. Brigade strength is estimated from an examination of the muster rolls for June 30, the next rolls taken after the battle and the Historical Muster Rolls compiled near the end of the war. The estimated strength represents the strength at the time of the muster.

88. Stevens was a Pennsylvania congressman, uncompromising abolitionist and a leader of the Radical Republicans, a group he helped organize. Boatner, *Civil War Dictionary*, 797.

89. Oates, *The War*, 684, 704; CSR, 15 AL Inf, NA; HMR, 15th AL Inf, ADAH.

90. CSR, 15th AL Inf, NA; Oates, *The War*, 750.

91. Purifoy, "Horror of War," 254; Ward, "Incidents," 346; Longstreet, *Manassas to Appomattox*, 365; *OR*, v27, pt2, 394.

92. Oates, *The War*, 206.

93. Longstreet, *Manassas to Appomattox*, 365.

94. Coles, "Gettysburg Campaign," 7; Law, "Round Top," 319; *OR*, v27, pt2, 394.

95. REC, Co. D, 47th AL Inf, NA.

Chapter 3—Before the Round Tops

1. Purifoy, "Horror of War," 254; Perry, "Devil's Den," 161.

2. Purifoy, "Horror of War," 254.

3. Georg, "Principal Loss," 1.

4. Ward, "Incidents," 346.

5. Ibid.

6. Figures to his parents, July 18, 1863, FC.

7. *OR*, v27, pt2, 308, 318.

8. Longstreet, *Manassas to Appomattox*, 365; Alexander, "Artillery at Gettysburg," 358; *OR*, v27, pt2, 318. Pickett's Division was not yet up.

9. Ibid.; Pfanz, *Second Day*, 113.

10. *OR*, v27, pt2, 308, 318.

11. McLaws, "Gettysburg," 68.

12. Longstreet, "Lee's Right at Gettysburg," 30; McLaws, "Gettysburg," 68, was an eyewitness to the conversation between Lee and Longstreet. For detailed analyses of this issue and Longstreet's subsequent behavior see, for example, Pfanz, *Second Day*, chapter 6; Coddington, *Gettysburg Campaign*, chapter 14; and Freeman, *Lee's Lts*, v3, chapter 7.

13. *OR*, v27, pt2, 308; see also Pfanz, *Second Day*, 28, for a discussion.

14. Longstreet, *Manassas to Appomattox*, 365.

15. Alexander, "Artillery at Gettysburg," 358, 359.

16. McLaws, "Gettysburg," 69.

17. Law, "Round Top," 320.

18. *OR*, v27, pt2, 396.

19. McLaws, "Gettysburg," 69.

20. Pfanz, *Second Day*, 120, for the route from Herr's Ridge to the Emmitsburg Rd.

21. *OR*, v27, pt2, 396, 397.

22. McLaws, "Gettysburg," 71.

23. *OR*, v27, pt2, 367.

24. Longstreet, *Manassas to Appomattox*, 366.

25. McLaws, "Gettysburg," 70.

26. *OR*, v27, pt2, 367.

27. Longstreet, "Lee's Right Wing at Gettysburg," 340, 341; Longstreet, *Manassas to Appomattox*, 367; Hood "Letter From General John B. Hood," 149. See also Pfanz, *Second Day*, 113, for a discussion of Lee's orders.

28. Kershaw to Bachelder, Mar. 20, 1876, *BP*, v1, 454, 453.

29. *OR*, v27, pt2, 367.

30. Hood, *Advance and Retreat*, 58.

31. Scott, "The Texans at Gettysburg."

32. Hood, *Advance and Retreat*, 57.

33. Scott, "Texans at Gettysburg"; J. Mark Smither to his mother, July 29, 1863, CRC. It is obvious the rank and file knew of Hood's protest and his desire to go around the Federal left flank; see also McLaws "Gettysburg," 70.

34. Scott, "Texans at Gettysburg."

35. Ibid.

36. Hood, *Advance and Retreat*, 58

37. Law, "Round Top," 323; *OR*, v27, pt2, 412.

38. McLaws, "Gettysburg," 73.

39. Robertson to Bachelder, May 11, 1882, *BP*, v2, 860.

40. *OR*, v27, pt2, 407; Robertson to Bachelder, Apr. 20, 1876, *BP*, v1, 476; Law, "Round Top," 320.

41. Ibid.

42. *OR*, v27, pt2, 404, 414.

43. *CMH*, v7, 391; Evans, *Cyclopedia*, v1, 59.

44. *OR*, v27, pt2, 396.

45. Ibid., 428; Coles, "Gettysburg Campaign," 8; Ward, "Incidents," 347.

46. Alexander, "Artillery at Gettysburg," 359; James Jackson to his wife, July 7, 1863, ADAH.

47. Coles, "Gettysburg Campaign," 8; *OR*, v27, pt2, 428.

48. CSR, HMR; HMR, ADAH; Oates, *The War*, Appendix A. Estimates of brigade strength at New Guilford are based on analyses of the muster rolls prepared immediately before the battle. There is no way to accurately determine the number engaged from the data available. Sheffield stated the number engaged was 275, *OR*, v27, pt2, 395. The battlefield plaque for

the 4th Alabama gives the number engaged; the remainder are estimated from the scanty information available.

49. Oates, "Gettysburg," 174.

50. Bulger to Law, BSF.

51. Coles, "Gettysburg Campaign," 14.

52. CSR, 48th AL Inf, NA, HMR, 48th AL Inf, ADAH, Thomas J. Lumpkin and Randolph Graves were the captains commanding companies A and H respectively. Compiled service records indicate both were present at New Guilford, however, from the scanty information available it is impossible to determine if either or both were present on the field after the grueling 25-mile march of July 2, 1863. If both were, Thomas Lumpkin would have been the ranking captain and commanded the battalion.

53. *OR*, v27, pt2, 395; CSR, 48th AL Inf, NA; A. O. Dixon to Thomas M. Owens, Oct. 8, 1913, 48th AL, ADAH.

54. Coles, "Gettysburg Campaign," 13, 14.

55. *OR*, v27, pt2, 391.

56. Roebling to Col. Smith, July 5, 1913, RU.

57. Norton, *ADLRT*, 263. See Pfanz, *Second Day*, 206, for the rank and full name of Warren's staff officers.

58. Purifoy, "Lost Opportunity," 217.

59. Farley, "Bloody Round Top."

60. Norton, *ADLRT*, 263; Purifoy, "Lost Opportunity," 217, 218.

61. Smith, "4th Battery," 1290.

62. Hunt, "Second Day," 304, 305.

63. *Maine at Gettysburg*, 181.

64. *OR*, v27, pt1, 515; Stevens, *Berdan's U.S. Sharpshooters*, 535.

65. *New York at Gettysburg*, v2, 868.

66. Stevens, *Berdan's Sharpshooters*, 2.

67. Kurtz, "Berdan's Sharpshooters," 15.

68. White, *Civil War Diary*, 136.

69. *OR*, v27, pt1, 518, 519; *Maine at Gettysburg*, 349, 350.

70. Ibid.

71. Bulger to Law, BSF.

72. Law, "Round Top," 321.

73. Ibid., 321, 322.

74. Hood, *Advance and Retreat*, 58.

75. Ibid., said he sent his adjutant general, Col. Henry Sellers. Law, "Round Top," 322,

identified the officer as Hamilton, who was an aide-de-camp; Crute, *Confederate Staff Officers*, 91, Sellers was the assistant adjutant general.

76. Law, "Round Top," 322; McLaws, "Gettysburg," 72.

77. Ward, "Incidents," 346.

78. Law, "Round Top," 322. Law never knew if his protest was passed on to Lee but from the brief time that elapsed between Hamilton's departure and return, Law suspected it was not.

Chapter 4—Plum Run Valley

1. Polley, *Hood's Texas Brigade*, 167; Bradfield, "At Gettysburg," 236.

2. Bulger to Law, BSF.

3. Oates, *The War*, 207.

4. Scott, "Texans at Gettysburg"; Martin, "Accurate Records," 114.

5. Ward, "Incidents," 347.

6. CSR, 44th AL, Inf, NA. Schaad was exchanged in late August 1863, went home on furlough, and never returned. He was afterwards listed as a deserter.

7. James Jackson to his wife, July 7, 1863, ADAH.

8. Bulger to Law, BSF; "General Bulger, An Alabama Hero," *Montgomery Advertiser*, Oct. 2, 1898.

9. Ward, "Incidents," 348.

10. Law, "Round Top," 323, remembered years later that the time was 5 p.m., but other accounts agree it was about 4 p.m. *OR*, v27, pt2, 407–408, 412; Sorrel, *Recollections*, 159; Sheffield, *OR*, v27, pt2, 395, does not give the time, but reported the 48th was in position about one-half hour before advancing, which is consistent with the brigade being in line between 3 and 3:30 p.m. Oates, *The War*, 207; Col. Jackson, 47th AL wrote his wife on July 7, 1863 that the 47th arrived in front of Round Top about 3:00 p.m., James Jackson to his wife, ADAH.

11. Ward, "Incidents," 348.

12. Mrs. James Jackson to Thomas Owen, July 16, 1902, ADAH; CSR, 7th AL Inf. NA.

13. Hood, *Advance and Retreat*, 59.

14. Robertson to Bachelder, May 11, 1882, *BP*, v2, 860.

15. Texas Troops Folder, GNMP, indicates Hood was with the 1st Texas and wounded after a few paces; Hood, *Advance and Retreat*, 59, said he was wounded 20 minutes after reaching the Peach Orchard. What is important is that he was wounded a short time after the charge began.

16. Scott, "Texans at Gettysburg."

17. Ibid.

18. *Texas Handbook*, v6, 1075.

19. James Jackson to his wife, July 7, 1863, ADAH.

20. Mrs. James Jackson to Thomas Owen, July 16, 1902, 47th AL Inf, ADAH.

21. White, *Civil War Diary*, 164.

22. Ward, "Incidents," 347; *OR*, v27, pt2, 391; Robertson to Bachelder, Apr. 20, 1876, *BP*, v1, 476–477.

23. Ward, "Incidents," 347; Bulger to Law, BSF.

24. *OR*, v27, pt2, 411; Rufus Felder to his mother, July 9, 1863, CRC also reported the brigade moved at quick step.

25. Robertson to Bachelder, May 11, 1882, *BP*, v2, 860.

26. *New Handbook of Texas*, v5, 617, 618; *CMH*, v4, 253, 254.

27. Ward, "Incidents," 347.

28. *OR*, v27, pt2, 404; Robertson to Bachelder, Apr. 20, 1876, *BP*, v1, 476–478.

29. *New York at Gettysburg*, v2, 869.

30. Georg, "Principal Loss," 4.

31. Texas Troops Folder, GNMP.

32. Scott, "Texans at Gettysburg."

33. Ward, "Incidents," 347.

34. J. Mark Smither to his mother, July 29, 1863, CRC.

35. Scott, "Texans at Gettysburg."

36. James Jackson to his wife, July 7, 1863, ADAH.

37. CSR, Co. K, 48th AL Inf, NA; Anderson to E. P. Anderson, July 17, 1863, APJSU.

38. Neal, *Record of Confederate Burials*, GNMP. Turnbow was buried near the Slyder house.

39. James Jackson to his wife, July 7, 1863, ADAH.

40. Ibid.

41. Ward, "Incidents," 347.

42. Ibid.; CSR, 4th AL Inf, NA.

43. Oates, *The War*, 584; HMR, 15th AL Inf, ADAH.

44. *OR*, v27, pt2, 392; Oates, *The War*, 622.

45. HMR, 15th AL Inf, ADAH.

46. Coles, "Gettysburg Campaign," 8; Zach Landrum, Texas Troops Folder, GNMP.

47. James Jackson to his wife, July 7, 1863, ADAH.

48. Smith, Texas Troops Folder, GNMP

49. Ward, "Incidents," 347; Coles, "Gettysburg Campaign," 8; Zach Landrum, Texas Troops Folder, GNMP.

50. Norton, *ADLRT*, 256.

51. *OR*, v27 pt2, 391; Coles, "Gettysburg Campaign," 8.

52. Coles, "Company Sketches," 5.

53. CSR, 4th AL Inf, NA. Coleman was mortally wounded at the Battle of Chickamauga.

54. Coles, "Gettysburg Campaign," 9.

55. Ward, "Incidents," 347; Coles, "Gettysburg Campaign," 9. Halsey was a musician, deserted in Feb. 1865, took the oath to the U.S. and moved to Boston, MA., CSR, 4th AL Inf, NA.

56. James Jackson to wife, July 7, 1863, ADAH.

57. *OR*, v27, pt2, 395.

58. Ibid., 392.

59. Ibid., pt1, 518.

60. James Jackson to his wife, July 7, 1863, ADAH.

61. Bulger, BSF.

62. Ibid.

63. Smith, *History and Debates*, 108–109.

64. Bulger, BSF.

65. *CMH*, v8, 503.

66. Bulger, BSF; CSR, 4th AL Inf, NA; HMR, 47th AL Inf, ADAH.

67. Rice, *Civil War Letters*, 15–18.

68. Ibid., 19.

69. *OR*, v27, pt2, 393.

70. Oates, *The War*, 208.

71. *OR*, v27 pt2, 393; Perry, "Devil's Den," 161.

72. *OR*, v27, pt2, 394.

73. *CMH*, v8, 435; 44th AL Inf; *CWTI*, v10, n36; Oates, "Perry and His Career;" 44th AL Inf, ADAH.

74. Lindsay, 47th AL Inf, ADAH. Actually the enemy was two companies of 2nd U.S. Sharpshooters.

75. HMR, 47th AL Inf, ADAH; CSR, 47th AL Inf, NA.

76. *OR*, v27, pt2, 392.

77. Bulger to Law, BSF, this conclusion is based on Bulger's description.

78. This conclusion would appear to conflict with the regimental history and other correspondence by Oates after the turn of the century when he stated: "General Law rode up to me as we were advancing, and informed me that I was then on the extreme right of our line and for me to hug the base of Great Round Top and go up the valley between the two mountains, until I found the left of the Union line, to turn it and do all the damage I could," Oates, *The War*, 211. Similar statements were made in correspondence. This implies that when the entire line was in Plum Run Valley Law knew the Federal flank rested on Little Round Top and not as they, at first believed, extended nearly to Big Round Top. Therefore, it does not seem reasonable that Law would, at that time, order a turning movement around Little Round Top. Oates did not address this point in his report of the action written immediately after the battle, *OR*, v27, pt2, 392–393. Lt. Charles F. Sawyer of the 4th Maine reported that Little Round Top was not occupied until the sharpshooters on his front engaged the enemy, *OR*, v27, pt1, 509. Unfortunately Oates, in his last years, all too often contradicted previous statements. This appears to be one of them.

79. Oates, "Gettysburg," 175; Oates to Robbins, Feb. 14, 1903, OC.

80. Bulger, BSF.

81. 47th AL Inf, ADAH. Lindsay commanded the battalion from the 47th AL; A. O. Dixon to Thomas M. Owens, Oct. 8, 1913, 48th AL, ADAH, identifies the 48th AL companies; Oates, *The War*, 207.

Chapter 5—Attack on Devil's Den

1. *OR*, v27, pt1, 588.

2. *Maine at Gettysburg*, 181.

3. Walker to Bachelder, Jan. 5, 1885, *BP*, v2, 1094, 1095.

4. Ibid.

5. *OR*, v27, pt1, 509.

6. Walker, "4th Maine at Gettysburg."

7. *Maine at Gettysburg*, 181.

8. Ibid.

9. *OR*, v27, pt1, 588.

10. Tucker, "Orange Blossoms."

11. *OR*, v27, pt1, 161.

12. Ibid., 509.

13. Ibid., 509, 510.

14. *Maine at Gettysburg*, 350.

15. White, *Civil War Diary*, 165.

16. Walker to Bachelder, Jan. 5, 1885, *BP*, v2, 1094, 1095.

17. Perry, "Devil's Den," 161–162; Purifoy, "Horror of War," 254.

18. *OR*, v27, pt2, 394.

19. Ibid.; *Maine at Gettysburg*, 181.

20. Ibid.

21. *OR*, v2, pt2, 394.

22. Perry, "Devil's Den," 161.

23. Ibid.

24. *OR*, v27, pt2, 395, 396.

25. Ibid., v1, pt1, 510.

26. Ibid.

27. Tucker, "Orange Blossoms."

28. Hanford, "Gettysburg."

29. Weygant, "What They Did Here," 869; Weygant, *124th New York*, 175, 176; Tucker, "Orange Blossoms." See also, Georg, "Principal Loss," 5, 6; Pfanz, *Second Day*, 179–186, for an excellent detailed analysis and discussion of the fighting on this part of the battlefield.

30. Walker to Bachelder, Jan. 5, 1885, *BP*, v2, 1095; *Maine at Gettysburg, 183*.

31. *OR*, v27, pt1, 588.

32. Ibid., pt2, 394.

33. Perry, "Devil's Den," 161; *Selma Daily Register*, Mar. 23, 1864.

34. *Maine at Gettysburg*, 182; Walker, "4th Maine at Gettysburg."

35. Sturgis, *War Record*, ADAH.

36. Walker to Bachelder, Jan. 5, 1885, *BP*, v2, 1094, 1095; *Maine at Gettysburg*, 181.

37. Law, "Round Top," 324.

38. Perry, "Devil's Den," 162; Purifoy, "Longstreet at Gettysburg," 293.

39. *OR*, v27, pt2, 396.

40. Perry, "Devil's Den," 162.
41. Ibid.
42. Owen, *Alabama Dictionary*, v3, 934; Jones, Surname File, ADAH; 8th U.S. Census, 1860, Scottsville, Bibb County, Alabama, 776.
43. *New York at Gettysburg*, 1291.
44. *OR*, v27, pt1, 526.
45. *Maine at Gettysburg*, 182; Walker, "4th Maine at Gettysburg."
46. Walker to Bachelder, Jan. 5, 1885, *BP*, v2, 1094, 1095.
47. Ibid.; *Maine at Gettysburg*, 182.
48. *OR*, v27, pt2, 414, 415.
49. Northern, *Men of Mark*, 259–261; Boatner, *Civil War Dictionary*, 59, 60.
50. *OR*, v27, pt2, 396.
51. Ibid., 405.
52. Law, "Round Top," 324.
53. Weygant, "What They Did Here," 870. See also, Georg, "Principal Loss," 6; Pfanz, *Second Day*, 180–190.
54. Weygant, "What They Did Here," 870; Weygant, *124th New York*, 177. See also, Georg, "Principal Loss," 6; Pfanz, *Second Day*, 180–190.
55. *OR*, v27, pt2, 415.
56. Ibid., 426.
57. Ibid., 424.
58. Ibid., 424.
59. Perry, "Devil's Den," 162.
60. *OR*, v27, pt2, 425.
61. Ibid., 394.
62. Journal of Malachi Brown, EU (Copy in 2nd Georgia Folder, RBC, USAMHI).
63. Perry, "Devil's Den," 162.
64. *Maine at Gettysburg*, 182; Walker, "4th Maine at Gettysburg."
65. *Maine at Gettysburg*, 182.
66. *OR*, v27, pt2, 420.
67. Ibid., pt1, 513.
68. Dyer, *Compendium of the War*, 1607; *Pennsylvania at Gettysburg*, v1, 536.
69. *Maine at Gettysburg*, 182.
70. *OR*, v27, pt1, 513; Ayars, "99 Pa."
71. Ayars, "99 Pa."
72. *OR*, v27, pt2, 424.
73. Smith, *Famous Battery*, 104.
74. Bradley, "At Gettysburg."
75. *OR*, v27, pt1, 589.
76. "New York at Gettysburg," 1291.
77. Smith, *A Famous Battery*, 142, 143.
78. "*OR*, v27, pt2, 396; *Daily Huntsville Confederate*, Sept. 11, 1863; J. Mark Smither to his mother, July 29, 1863, CRC.
79. Figures to his parents, July 8, 1863, FC.
80. *OR*, v27, pt2, 396.
81. Ibid., pt1, 577.
82. Ibid.
83. Journal of Malachi Brown, EU (Copy in 2nd Georgia Folder, RBC, USAMHI).
84. *OR*, v27, pt2, 420.
85. Ibid., pt1, 526.
86. *New York at Gettysburg*, v1, 296, 297.
87. Warner, *Generals in Blue*, 139.
88. *OR*, v27, pt1, 526.
89. Ibid., pt2, 420.
90. Ibid., pt1, 589.
91. Ibid., pt1, 526.
92. Floyd, *40th New York*, 202.
93. *OR*, v27, pt2, 395.
94. Ibid., 396.
95. *Maine at Gettysburg*, 182; Walker, "4th Maine at Gettysburg."
96. *Maine at Gettysburg*, 182.
97. Ibid.
98. Ibid.
99. Ibid., 183.
100. Weygant, *124th New York*, 129, 180.
101. Ibid., 180.
102. Smith, *Famous Battery*, 109, 140; Walker, "4th Maine at Gettysburg."
103. Walker to Bachelder, Jan. 5, 1885, *BP*, v2, 1095.
104. HMR, 44th AL Inf, ADAH.
105. *CMH*, v7, 517, 518.
106. *CV*, v17, n5, May 1909, 242; CSR, 44th AL Inf, NA; 44th AL Inf, ADAH.

Chapter 6—Attack on Little Round Top

1. *OR*, v27, pt1, 161, 600.
2. Graham, "On to Gettysburg," 471, 472.
3. *OR*, v27, pt1, 592, 600; Norton, *ADLRT*, 262.
4. *OR*, v27, pt1, 600.

5. Norton, *ADLRT*, 263, 264.

6. Graham, "On to Gettysburg," 475.

7. Norton, *ADLRT*, 264.

8. Johnson, "Heroic Life."

9. Norton, *ADLRT*, 281–285; Warner, *Generals in Blue*, 527–528.

10. Norton, *ADLRT*, 264.

11. Norton, *Army Letters*, 167, 343.

12. Norton, *ADLRT*, 265.

13. Nash, *44th New York*, 146.

14. Chamberlain, *Blood and Fire*, 10; Pullen, *20th Maine*, 110.

15. Each four man file consisted of two men from the front rank and two from the rear rank. The two men from the front rank were on the left. The leading file in the column would go into position on the extreme right of the line of battle.

16. *OR*, v27, pt1, 628. It is not likely that Welch would have thrown skirmishers out to the left if the 20th Maine had been in position at that time. Therefore, it has to be concluded that the 20th Maine was still en route to the intended line of battle.

17. Nash, *44th New York*, 144; Judson, *83rd Pennsylvania*, 21.

18. *OR*, v27, pt1, 630.

19. Nash, *44th New York*, 154.

20. Ibid., 144.

21. Judson, *83rd Pennsylvania*, 66.

22. *OR*, v27, pt1, 628; *Official Army Register*, v5, 289; Graham, "On to Gettysburg," 476.

23. Ibid.; Benjamin F. Partridge to Bachelder, Mar. 31, 1866, *BP*, v1, 243–245.

24. *OR*, v27, pt1, 616.

25. Nesbit, *Through Blood and Fire*, 6.

26. Warner, *Generals in Blue*, 76–77; Boatner, *Civil War Dictionary*, 135; *Maine at Gettysburg*, 273.

27. Ibid., 274, 275.

28. Jacklin, "Famous Old Third Brigade," 46.; Graham, "On to Gettysburg," 475.

29. Norton, *ADLRT*, 265; Nash, *44th New York*, 143; Chamberlain to Nicholson, Aug. 14, 1903, OC, indicated Vincent said "hold at all costs."

30. *OR*, v27, pt1, 623; Chamberlain to Nicholson, Aug. 14, 1903, OC.

31. Chamberlain, *Blood and Fire*, 10. The command and description of the maneuver are given in Hardee, *Hardee's Tactics*, v1, 120–122. Normally to form line of battle the leading four-man file (two men from the front rank and two from the rear) turned right at the intended line and continued in column until they reached the guides. Succeeding files repeated the process until the column was parallel to the line of battle. It then faced left and formed into ranks. The maneuver was precise and avoided chaos, but it did take time to bring the weapons into play. In the command "On the right by file into line" the rear rank of the column marked time just short of the line while the front rank turned right. The leading file stopped at the guides and went into line. Each succeeding two-man file did likewise, going into line on the left of the preceding file. Thus the front rank was ready to commence firing as it formed line of battle. The rear rank began filing into line after the first four men of the front rank were in position. The fire power of the regiment was brought to bear in succession from the right.

32. Chamberlain, *Blood and Fire*, 10.

33. Chamberlain to Nicholson, Aug. 14, 1903, OC.

34. *OR*, v27, pt1, 623; Morrill to Chamberlain, July 8, 1863, *BP*, v2, 1029, 1030.

35. Judson, *83rd Pennsylvania*, 67; *OR*, v27, pt1, 626.

36. Norton, *Army Letters*, 167.

37. *New York at Gettysburg*, v1, 367.

38. Nash, *44th New York*, 144.

39. White, *Civil War Diary*, 165.

40. Judson, *83rd Pennsylvania*, 67.

41. *OR*, v27, pt2, 411.

42. Nash, *44th New York*, 145; *OR*, v27, pt1, 630.

43. Ward, "Incidents," 347.

44. *OR*, v27, pt2, 412.

45. Ibid., v27, pt1, 617.

46. Robbins to Nicholson, Feb. 26, 1903, OC.

47. J. Mark Smither to Mother, July 29, 1863, CRC.

48. Ibid.

49. Barziza, *Adventures of a POW*, 45.

50. J. Mark Smither to his mother, July 29, 1863, CRC.

51. Colonel John C. G. Key, 4th Texas was wounded at the stone wall. Lieutenant

Colonel Benjamin C. Carter became a casualty during the first charge on Little Round Top, *OR*, v27, pt2, 411; Colonel Robert M. Powell and Lieutenant Colonel King Bryan of the 5th Texas were wounded during the first charge on Little Round Top, *OR*, v27, pt2, 412.

52. Ibid., 411, 412; J. Mark Smither to Mother, July 29, 1863, CRC.

53. Ward, "Incidents," 348; *Montgomery Advertiser*, Jan. 6, 1864.

54. Nash, *44th New York*, 153.

55. Scott, "Texans at Gettysburg." Powell was wounded in the first charge and was relaying the events as he understood them.

56. J. Mark Smither to Mother, July 29, 1863, CRC.

57. White, *Civil War Diary*, 166.

58. "Lone Star Over Devil's Den," Texas Folder, GNMP.

59. Rufus K. Felder to his Mother, July 9, 1863, CRC.

60. *OR*, v27, pt1, 617; Nash, *44th New York*, 151; Judson, *83rd Pennsylvania*, 67.

61. Coles, "Gettysburg Campaign," 20.

62. O. W. Damon Diary (copy), 5th U.S. Artillery, Battery D Folder, GNMP. Damon used the terms "sappers" and "miners" to identify the men who cut the road.

63. Rittenhouse, "Little Round Top," 37, 38, 40.

64. Nash, *44th New York*, 145.

65. Rittenhouse, *Battle of Gettysburg*, 38.

66. Rittenhouse, "Little Round Top."

67. *OR*, v27, pt2, 411–412.

68. Norton, *ADLRT*, 258.

69. Coles, "Gettysburg Campaign," 11, indicated the 4th made three charges. Two were made in conjunction with the 4th and 5th Texas; this would have been the third.

70. *OR*, v27, pt2, 391.

71. Coles, "Gettysburg Campaign," 11, 12.

72. Ibid., 12; Norton, *ADLRT*, 259; Judson, *83rd Pennsylvania*, 67.

73. *OR*, v27, pt2, 392.

74. Oates, "Gettysburg," 174; Norton, *ADLRT*, 256–257; *OR*, v27, pt1, 519; Nash, *44th New York*, 144.

75. "General Bulger, an Alabama Hero," *Montgomery Advertiser*, Oct. 2, 1898.

76. *OR*, v27, pt1, 519; Oates, *The War*, 212. It was probably during this conversation with Terrell that Oates learned he was supposed to go between the Round Tops and turn the Federal left; Oates, *The War*, 211. By this time Law would have known that Little Round Top was occupied.

77. Oates, "Gettysburg," 174–176.

78. Bulger to Law, BSF.

79. "General Bulger, an Alabama Hero," *Montgomery Advertiser*, Oct. 2, 1898.

80. Chamberlain to Nicholson, Aug. 14, 1903, OC. In earlier correspondence, Chamberlain said the "Rebels burst upon the 20th Maine with a shout," Chamberlain to Bachelder, n.d., *BP*, v3, 1084, 1086.

81. Bulger, BSF.

82. "General Bulger, an Alabama Hero," *Montgomery Advertiser*, Oct. 2, 1898.

83. Bulger to Law, BSF. This was Bulger's third serious wound in less than a year. Robbins Diary, July 1, 1899, RPSHC, placed Bulger's position about ten yards east of Sykes's Avenue where it descends to the foot of Little Round Top "nearly opposite the southern end of the wing wall of the avenues."

84. "General Bulger, an Alabama Hero," *Montgomery Advertiser*, Oct. 2, 1898.

85. Oates, "Gettysburg," 176; Oates, *The War*, 214, 221.

86. Judson, *83rd Pennsylvania*, 68.

87. Spear to Bachelder, Nov. 15, 1892, NHHS.

88. *OR*, v27, pt1, 623.

89. Judson, *83rd Pennsylvania*, 68.

90. Chamberlain, *Blood and Fire*, 15.

91. Spear to Bachelder, Nov. 15, 1892, NHHS; Chamberlain to Bachelder, n.d., *BP*, v3, 1084, 1086; Chamberlain to Nicholson, Aug. 14, 1903, OC; Nash, *44th New York*, 146; *OR*, v27, pt1, 623.

92. Oates, "Gettysburg," 176.

93. *OR*, v27, pt1, 623.

94. Ibid., pt2, 392.

95. Jordan, *Events*, 43.

96. Oates, "Gettysburg," 176, 177.

97. *OR*, v27, pt1, 623, pt2, 392.

98. Ibid., pt2, 395.

99. CSR, 47 AL Inf, NA; *Montgomery Mail*, July 26, 1863.

100. Ibid., 4th AL Inf, NA.

101. Oates, "Gettysburg," 176; Norton, *ADLRT*, 261.

102. *OR*, v27, pt2, 392; Oates, "Gettysburg," 176.

103. Ibid.

104. *OR*, v27, pt1, 623.

105. Chamberlain to Bachelder, n.d., *BP*, v3, 1084, 1086.

106. Gerrish, "20th Maine."

107. Oates, *The War*, 588.

108. Rittenhouse, *Battle of Gettysburg*, Rittenhouse Papers, LC.

109. Oates, "Gettysburg," 177.

110. Oates to Chamberlain, Mar. 8, 1897, WCL.

111. *OR*, v27, pt1, 624; Chamberlain to Bachelder, n.d., *BP*, v3, 1084, 1086.

112. Chamberlain, *Blood and Fire*, 17.

113. *OR*, v27, pt2, 392; Oates to Chamberlain, Mar. 8, 1897, WCL.

114. Chamberlain, *Blood and Fire*, 21.

115. Oates, *The War*, 137.

116. Ibid., 755.

117. CSR, 15th AL Inf, NA; 15th AL Inf, ADAH.

118. Jordan, *Events*, 44.

119. Chamberlain to Bachelder, n.d., *BP*, v3, 1084, 1086; Chamberlain to Nicholson, Aug. 14, 1903, OC.

120. Judson, *83rd Pennsylvania*, 68. The 83rd PA reported the enemy kept pressing left and got in the rear of the regiment. This was probably Waddell and his men.

121. *OR*, v27, pt2, 411.

122. *Daily Huntsville Confederate*, September 11, 1863.

123. Benjamin Partridge to John Robertson, Aug. 10, 1868, Michigan Archives.

124. *OR*, v27, pt1, 628.

125. *See* Gibney, "A Shadow Passing," for a detailed discussion of the incident.

126. Norton, *ADLRT*, 244; Benjamin F. Partridge to John Robertson, Aug. 10, 1868, Michigan Archives.

127. Chamberlain, *Blood and Fire*, 16.

128. Judson, *83rd Pennsylvania*, 67.

129. Norton, *ADLRT*, 210.

130. Nash, *44th New York*, 223.

131. Norton, *Army Letters*, 165.

132. Judson, *83rd Pennsylvania*, 67.

133. *OR*, v27, pt1, 617.

134. Leeper, "Gettysburg."

135. Ibid.

136. Farley, "Reminiscences."

137. Farley, "Gettysburg."

138. Leeper, "Gettysburg."

139. Farley, "Gettysburg"; Hazen, "140 New York"; Leeper, "Gettysburg"; Leeper, "Statement," *BP*, v2, 894; Farley to Bachelder, May 8, 1878, *BP*, v1, 547; Farley, "Reminiscences."

140. Leeper's Statement, Apr. 28, 1883, *BP*, v2, 897.

141. Farley to Bachelder, May 8, 1878, *BP*, v1, 547.

142. Ibid.

143. Farley, "Reminiscences."

144. *OR*, v27, pt1, 630.

145. Ibid., pt2, 411; Norton, *ADLRT*, 259, 260.

146. Hazen, "140th New York."

147. *Daily Huntsville Confederate*, Sept. 11, 1863.

148. Perry, "Devil's Den," 162.

149. Anderson to E. P. Anderson, July 17, 1863, APJSU.

150. Oates, "Gettysburg," 177; *OR*, v27, pt2, 392; Chamberlain to Nicholson, Aug. 14, 1903, OC.

151. Graham, "On to Gettysburg," 477; Morrill to Chamberlain, July 8, 1863, *BP*, v2, 1029, 1030.

152. Oates, "Gettysburg," 177, 178.

153. Ibid., 178.

154. Chamberlain to Bachelder, n.d., *BP*, v2, 1029, 1030.

155. Melcher, "20th Maine," 315.

156. *OR*, v27, pt1, 624.

157. Ibid., 624, pt2, 395. Oates never elaborated as to how he prepared to withdraw. Chamberlain specifically reported two lines. Since Oates was seriously considering withdrawing it seems reasonable he would throw out a skirmish line to cover his rear. This is the same conclusion drawn by Pfanz, *Second Day*, 235.

158. *OR*, v27, pt1, 624.

159. Spear to Bachelder, Nov. 15, 1892, NHHS; Melcher, *With a Flash of his Sword*, 61.

160. Oates, "Gettysburg," 176.

161. Morrill to Chamberlain, July 8, 1863, *BP*, v2, 1029, 1030; Oates, "Gettysburg," 178.

162. Oates, *The War*, 221, 717.

163. Spear to Bachelder, Nov. 15, 1892, NHHS; Oates, *The War*, 221; CSR, 15th AL NA; HMR, 15th AL, ADAH.

164. *OR*, v27, pt1, 624; Oates, *The War*, 771, 772.

165. Jordan, *Events*, 43, 44.

166. Oates, *The War*, 221.

167. *OR*, v27, pt1, 624.

168. Melcher, *With Flash of His Sword*, 77; Melcher's, "Little Round Top," comments are paraphrased and represent the comments of both. It is impossible to identify the number of prisoners taken during the sweep because the captured tabulated from the CSR, NA and HMR, ADAH include wounded left in field hospitals. Federal accounts greatly overstate the number captured, however. Chamberlain placed the number at 400, Chamberlain to Nicholson, Aug. 14, 1903, OC. Total captured from Law's Brigade was 154 and from Robertson's 120, *OR*, v27, pt2, 339.

169. Bulger, BSF.

170. *OR*, v27, pt1, 625.

171. Morrill to Chamberlain, July 8, 1863, *BP*, v2, 1029, 1030.

172. Judson, *83rd Pennsylvania*, 68. The 83rd Pennsylvania historian described the incident, but was unable to identify the officer. The Confederate officer's identity, therefore, is based on the process of elimination. Four line officers from Law's Brigade were captured. The circumstances under which three were captured are known. Oates and Barnett were severely wounded and left disabled where they fell. Wicker was captured by Chamberlain and identified by Oates, *The War*, 771, 772. Breare is therefore the officer referred to in the account.

173. Jordan, *Events*, 44.

174. *OR*, v27, pt1, 626; CSR, 15th AL Inf, NA; 15th AL Inf, ADAH.

Chapter 7—Night—July 2nd

1. Giles, *Rags and Hope*, 180.

2. Fletcher, *Rebel Private*, 60

3. Giles, *Rags and Hope*, 180.

4. Oates, *The War*, 176, 177; Tyler, *Men of Mark*, 102; *CMH*, v4, 824.

5. Law, "A Night in the Enemy's Lines."

6. Judson, *83rd Pennsylvania*, 68. The Confederate's identity is not known. However, from the description of the incident the wounded man was probably a Texan or Alabamian.

7. *OR*, v27, pt2, 392.

8. Ibid., 395.

9. A. O. Dixon to Thomas M. Owens, Oct. 8, 1913, 48th AL, ADAH; Oates, *The War*, 207.

10. Alleman, *At Gettysburg*, 57, 58; Curran, "Billings at Gettysburg," 24.

11. Alleman, *At Gettysburg*, 57, 58.

12. Ibid.

13. A. O. Dixon to Thomas M. Owens, Oct. 8, 1913, 48th AL, ADAH. Dixon, many years later, told Oates the two companies did not encounter Federal troops, Oates, *The War*, 207. However, from the descriptions of the eyewitness accounts, there probably were a few shots exchanged.

14. *OR*, v27, pt2, 409; Rittenhouse, "Battle of Gettysburg," 42.

15. *OR*, v27, pt1, 618.

16. Nash, *44th New York*, 326.

17. Ibid., 153.

18. *OR*, v27, pt2, 395.

19. "General Bulger, an Alabama Hero," *Montgomery Advertiser*, Oct. 2, 1898.

20. Bulger to Law, BSF.

21. "General Bulger, an Alabama Hero," *Montgomery Advertiser*, Oct. 2, 1898.

22. Judson, *83rd Pennsylvania*, 69.

23. Coco, *Vast Sea*, 99.

24. Bulger to Law, BSF; Barziza, *Adventures of a POW*, 54, reported the Confederate wounded were well treated when they were brought into the lines. The wounded rebels were placed beside the Federal wounded.

25. Chamberlain to Nicholson, Aug. 14, 1903, OC. Oates first mentioned the incident in his article, Oates, "Gettysburg," 181, 182, but Chamberlain did not take issue with Oates at that time.

26. *OR*, v27, pt1, 625.

27. Bulger was obviously one, the second was Col. Robert M. Powell, 4th TX.

28. Norton, *ADLRT*, 113.

29. *Montgomery Advertiser*, Jan. 6, 1864.

30. Nesbit, *Through Blood and Fire*, 82.

31. *OR*, v27, pt1, 625.

32. Nesbit, *Through Blood and Fire*, 86.

33. Coles, "Gettysburg Campaign," 20.

34. Nesbit, *Through Blood and Fire*, 82.

35. CSR, 4th AL Inf, NA; CSR, 48th AL Inf, NA.

36. CSR, 4th AL Inf, NA.

37. 44th AL Inf, ADAH; CSR, 44th AL Inf, NA.

38. Hardin, *12th Pennsylvania*, 154. The Pennsylvanians claimed Chamberlain advanced ahead as a skirmish line, which Chamberlain later vigorously disputed.

39. Jack to Paul, July 21, 1863 (copy), 5th Pennsylvania Reserve Folder, GNMP. Chamberlain was not as kind, implying, rather disdainfully, the Pennsylvanians broke easily and ran.

40. Diary of Private E. D. Benedict, (copy of excerpt) 12th PA Folder, GNMP.

41. Hardin, *12th Pennsylvania*, 155.

42. Judson, *83rd Pennsylvania*, 69; *OR*, v27, pt1, 625, 632.

43. Nesbit, *Through Blood and Fire*, 92, 93.

44. Hardin, *12th Pennsylvania*, 155.

45. *OR*, v27, pt1, 658; Jack to Paul, July 21, 1863 (copy), 5th Pennsylvania Reserves Folder, GNMP.

46. Chamberlain to Bachelder, January 25, 1884, *BP*, v2, 992. Fisher and Hardin maintained that Chamberlain acted as a skirmish line and supported the Pennsylvania brigade.

47. Ward, "Incidents," 348.

48. Nash, *44th New York*, 151.

49. Judson, *83rd Pennsylvania*, 70.

50. Anderson to E. P. Anderson, Aug. 1863, APJSU.

51. Sims, "Recollections," CRC.

52. William Brown to his brother, July 7, 1863 (copy), 83rd Pennsylvania Folder, GNMP.

53. Scott, "On Little Round Top."

54. Rittenhouse, "Little Round Top," 41.

55. Graham, "On to Gettysburg," 478.

56. Scott, "Texans at Gettysburg"; Rittenhouse, "Battle of Gettysburg," 41; "Unknown Diary," (copy) 1st Texas Folder, RBC, USAMHI; James H. Hendrick Letter (copy), 1st Texas Folder, RBC, USAHMI.

57. *OR*, v27, pt2, 411.

58. Davis, *Atlas*, Plate 95.

59. Law, "Round Top," 326; Judson, *83rd Pennsylvania*, 69; *OR*, v27, pt1, 625.

60. "Unknown Diary," (copy) 1st Texas Folder, RBC, USAMHI; James H. Hendrick Letter (copy), 1st Texas Folder, RBC, USAHMI.

Chapter 8—Morning—July 3rd

1. Law, "Round Top," 326.

2. Tyler, *Men of Mark*, 103.

3. *OR*, v27, pt2, 406.

4. Coles, "Gettysburg Campaign," 22.

5. Parsons, "Farnsworth's Charge," map, 394.

6. Law to Bachelder, June 13, 1876, *BP*, v1, 494.

7. Henderson, *Georgia Soldier's Roster*, v1, 833.

8. Lindsay, 47th AL Inf, ADAH, indicated his command was on a prolongation with the main line, but a considerable distance from it. Nine men from Companies D and F were captured July 3; Benedict, *Vermont in the Civil War*, v2, 596, 597 reported the 1st Vermont Cavalry overran a picket position at a house located on a knoll; Black, *Crumbling Defenses*, 40, recalled he assumed command of two companies of Alabama troops when he went into position. Black originally thought these were Georgia troops. He was later corrected by Law. Meyers is also found as Meyers.

9. HMR, 47th AL Inf, ADAH.

10. Ibid.

11. CSR, 47th AL Inf, NA; HMR, 47th AL Inf, ADAH.

12. Scott, "On Little Round Top.

13. *Montgomery Advertiser*, July 26, 1863; CSR, 48th AL Inf, NA; HMR, 48th AL Inf, ADAH.

14. Coles, "Gettysburg Campaign," 21; *Daily Huntsville Confederate*, July 22, 1863.

15. Diary of Private E. D. Benedict, (copy of excerpt, entry for July 3), 12th PA Folder, GNMP.

16. Black, *Crumbling Defenses*, 11–13; *Register of Cadets*, 243; "Col. John Logan Black," 214.

17. Ibid.

18. Black identified Maxwell by his last name. Manarin, *North Carolina Troops*, v2, 28, gives his full name and rank as first lieutenant. He was a member of Company C, 1st Regiment of North Carolina Cavalry.

19. Brooks, *Stories of the Confederacy*, 254; ibid., "The 'horse' battery differed from the 'foot' or 'mounted' field battery in that cannoneers were all mounted, having two extra men to hold the cannoneers' horses when they were dismounted to go into action."

20. Black, *Crumbling Defenses*, 33.

21. Ibid., 19, 31, 32, 36, 37.

22. Ibid., 40.

23. *Dedication*, 86.

24. Law to Bachelder, April 26, 1886, *BP*, v3, 1370.

25. Sims, "Recollections," CRC; Rittenhouse, "Battle of Gettysburg," 42; "Unknown Diary," (copy), 1st Texas Folder, RBC, USAMHI, James H. Hendrick Letter, (copy), 1st Texas Folder, RBC, USAMHI.

26. Law, "Round Top," 326.

27. Law to Bachelder, June 13, 1876, *BP*, v1, 495.

28. *OR*, v27, pt1, 658.

29. Ibid., 658; Jack to Paul, July 21, 1863 (copy), 5th Pennsylvania Reserves Folder, GNMP.

30. *OR*, v27, pt1, 602, 604, 607.

31. Melcher, "Little Round Top."

32. Law to Bachelder, June 13, 1876, *BP*, v1, 434; *OR*, v27, pt2, 396; ibid., 400.

33. Also identified on some maps as the M. Currens house.

34. Alexander, *Fighting for the Confederacy*, 257.

35. Law, "Round Top," 327.

36. Sims, "Recollections," CRC.

37. *OR*, v27, pt1, 376.

38. Pleasonton, "Campaign of Gettysburg," 452.

39. Warner, *Generals in Blue*, 109, 149, 321.

40. *OR*, v27, pt1, 166. The official designation was the Reserve Brigade.

41. Ibid., pt1, 167.

42. Grier to Bachelder, May 14, 1888, *BP*, v3, 1542.

43. Clark, "Farnsworth's Death"; *Pennsylvania at Gettysburg*, v2, 895.

44. Grier to Bachelder, May 14, 1888, *BP*, v3, 1542.

45. Hoffman, "1st Vermont Cav," 16.

46. Ibid., 16.

47. Grier to Bachelder, May 14, 1888, *BP*, v3, 1542.

48. Warner, *Generals in Blue*, 266.

49. Ibid.; Small, "Judson Kilpatrick"; Moore, *Kilpatrick*, 25.

50. *Register of Cadets*, 249.

51. Wittenberg, "Merritt's Regulars," 114.

52. Moore, *Kilpatrick*, 32, 33.

53. Shevchuk, "Farnsworth's Charge," 83.

54. *OR*, v27, pt1, 392.

55. *Pennsylvania at Gettysburg*, 40. Kilpatrick indicates the time was 8:00, but hardly seems likely that four hours were required to travel from Two Taverns to the southern base of Big Round Top.

56. Shevchuk, "Farnsworth's Charge," 85.

57. Clark, "Farnsworth's Death."

58. Benedict, *Vermont in the Civil War*, v2, 533, 538; Waite, *Vermont in the Great Rebellion*, 242.

59. *OR*, v27, pt1, 376.

60. Shevchuk, "Farnsworth's Charge," 84.

61. Hoffman, "1st Vermont Cav," 16.

62. Grier to Bachelder, May 14, 1888, *BP*, v3, 1543.

63. Shevchuk, "Farnsworth's Charge," 84.

64. Parsons, "How Farnsworth was Killed."

65. Grier to Bachelder, May 14, 1888, *BP*, v3, 1543.

66. "General Farnsworth's Death," Participants Accounts, Farnsworth's Folder, GNMP; See also, Shevchuk, "Farnsworth's Charge," 84.

67. Benedict, *Vermont in the Civil War*, 596; Grier to Bachelder, May 14, 1888, *BP*, v3, 1543; Shevchuk, "Farnsworth's Charge," 84; Clark, Farnsworth's Death."

68. Benedict, *Vermont in the Civil War*, 596.

69. *OR*, v27, pt1, 1013; Benedict, *Vermont in the Civil War*, 596, 597; Hoffman, "1st Vermont Cav," 16.

70. Parsons, "How Farnsworth was Killed."

71. Benedict, *Vermont in the Civil War*, 596, 597; Hoffman, "1st Vermont Cav," 16.

72. CSR, 47th AL Inf, NA. Six privates were members of Company D and one was from Company F.

73. Clark, "Farnsworth's Death"; Parsons, "How Farnsworth was Killed."

74. *OR*, v27, pt1, 1013.

75. See primarily *Map of the Battlefield of Gettysburg*, prepared by direction of the Gettysburg Battlefield Commission.

76. Parsons, "How Farnsworth was Killed"; Parsons, "Farnsworth's Charge," 394, Map; Hoffman, "1st Vermont, 16; Benedict, *Vermont in the Civil War*, 596, 597.

77. Clark, "Farnsworth's Death."

78. Hoffman, "1st Vermont Cav," 16.

79. *OR*, v27, pt1, 1013.

80. Parsons, "How Farnsworth was Killed."

81. Grier to Bachelder, May 14, 1888, *BP*, v3, 1542.

82. Ibid.

83. Ibid.

84. *New York at Gettysburg*, v3, 1124.

85. Law to Bachelder, January 13, 1876, *BP*, v1, 494.

86. Phillip A. Work to Tom Langley, May 28, 1908, CRC.

87. Law, "Round Top," 329.

88. *OR*, v27, pt2, 397.

89. Hoffman, "1st Vermont Cav," 16.

90. Wilt to Bachelder, May 17, 1888, *BP*, v3, 1546.

91. Hoffman, "1st Vermont Cav," 16.

92. *CMH*, v5, 709, 710.

93. Manarin, *N.C. Troops*, v1, 40, 42, 74.

94. *CMH*, v5, 709, 710.

95. White, "First Texas."

96. McCarty, "Battle of Gettysburg," UT.

97. Bradfield, "At Gettysburg."

98. McCarty, "Battle of Gettysburg," UT.

99. Shevchuk, "Farnsworth's Charge," 85.

100. Hillyer, *Battle of Gettysburg*, 13.

101. Bradfield, "At Gettysburg," 226. Bradfield incorrectly identified Wilson as being from Company D; he was actually from Company K, Shevchuk, "Farnsworth's Charge," 85.

102. Bradfield, "At Gettysburg," 226.

103. *OR*, v27, pt1, 993.

104. Alexander, *Fighting for the Confederacy*, 257.

105. Law, "Round Top," 327.

Chapter 9—Law Counters Merritt

1. Dunkelberger, "Reminiscences."

2. *OR*, v27, pt1, 393.

3. Crockett Diary Excerpt (copy), 1st U.S. Cavalry Folder, GNMP.

4. Alberts, *Merritt*, 76.

5. Ibid., 12, 15, 24, 25.

6. According to Boatner, a Dragoon was "A soldier who used the horse for transportation to the battlefield, or for mobility on the battlefield, but who dismounted to fight," Boatner, *Civil War Dictionary*, 246.

7. Alberts, *Merritt*, 34.

8. *OR*, v27, pt1, 913.

9. Alberts, *Merritt*, 74.

10. *6th U.S. Survivors*, 3.

11. *OR*, v27, pt2, 752.

12. Ibid.

13. *6th U.S. Survivors*, 3.

14. Marker on South Cavalry Battlefield, Gettysburg, Pennsylvania.

15. *Pennsylvania at Gettysburg*, v2, 849, 850; *OR*, v27, pt1, 155.

16. *OR*, v27, pt1, 155.

17. Ibid., 393.

18. Crockett to Bachelder, Dec. 27, 1882, *BP*, v2, 916.

19. Crockett Diary, entry for July 3, 1863, (copy), 1st U.S. Cavalry Folder, GNMP.

20. Ibid.

21. Not to be confused with the A. Currens and D. Currens houses.

22. *Pennsylvania at Gettysburg*, v2, 853.

23. Crockett to Bachelder, Dec. 27, 1886, *BP*, v2, 916.

24. Gracey, *6th Pennsylvania*, 179.

25. Ibid.

26. *Pennsylvania at Gettysburg*, v2, 853; Gracey, *6th Pennsylvania*, 179.

27. Black, *Crumbling Defenses*, 40.

28. Crockett Diary, entry for July 3, 1863 (copy), 1st U.S. Cavalry Folder, GNMP.

29. Heitman, *Historical Register*, v1, 641; *Register of Cadets*, 245.

30. Crockett Diary, entry for July 3, 1863 (copy), 1st U.S. Cavalry Folder, GNMP; Crockett to Bachelder, Dec. 27, 1886, *BP*, v2, 916.

31. Black, *Crumbling Defenses*, 40, 41.

32. Hart to Bachelder, Mar. 3, 1886, *BP*, v2 1216.

33. Black, *Crumbling Defenses*, 41; Black to Bachelder, Mar. 22, 1886, *BP*, v2, 1241.

34. Crockett to Bachelder, Dec. 27, 1886, *BP*, v2, 916.

35. *Pennsylvania at Gettysburg*, v2, 852.

36. Hart to Bachelder, Mar. 3, 1886, *BP*, v2 1216.

37. Bertrand to Bachelder, Mar. 26, 1864, *BP*, v1, 119.

38. Ibid., 120.

39. Hart to Bachelder, Mar. 3, 1886, *BP*, v2, 1216; Hart to Bachelder, Mar. 5, 1886, *BP*, v2, 1217.

40. Black, *Crumbling Defenses*, 41.

41. Garlington, *Men of the Time*, 192; Sherfesee, "History of Hart's Battery," 500; *CMH*, v 6, 632, 633.

42. Hart to Bachelder, Mar. 5, 1886, *BP*, v2, 1217; Hart to Bachelder, Mar. 3, 1886, *BP*, v2, 1216.

43. Black, *Crumbling Defenses*, 41.

44. Law, "Round Top," 327.

45. Ibid.

46. Hart to Bachelder, Mar 3, 1886, *BP*, v2, 1214.

47. Law to Bachelder, June 13, 1876, *BP*, v1, 493.

48. Ibid.; Law, "Round Top," 328.

49. *OR*, v27, pt2, 402.

50. *Memoirs of Georgia*, v2, 971, 972.

51. McDaniel, "With Unabated Trust," ix.

52. Black, *Crumbling Defenses*, 42.

53. Henderson, *Georgia Troops*, v2, 140.

54. Black, *Crumbling Defenses*, 42. Black's narrative has been paraphrased.

55. Confederate insignia for a colonel and a general officer were similar. Three stars adorned the collar for both. The rank of a general officer was denoted by three stars encircled by braid.

56. Black, *Crumbling Defenses*, 42.

57. Law, "Round Top," 328; Law to Bachelder, June 13, 1876, *BP*, v1, 496.

58. Black, *Crumbling Defenses*, 42. Black, on several occasions, incorrectly referred to the Georgians as Alabamians. Law finally corrected the mistake, Law to Bachelder, Apr. 22, 1886, *BP*, v3, 1370; Law to Bachelder, Apr. 22, 1886, *BP*, v3, 1344.

59. Hart to Bachelder, Mar. 3, 1886, *BP*, v2, 1217.

60. Henderson, *Georgia Troops*, v2, 140.

61. Crockett Diary, entry for July 3, 1863, (copy), 1st U.S. Cavalry Folder, GNMP.

62. Black, *Crumbling Defenses*, 42.

63. Crockett Diary, entry for July 3, 1863, (copy), 1st U.S. Cavalry Folder, GNMP.

64. Law, "Round Top," 328; Law to Bachelder, June 13, 1876, *BP*, v1, 496.

65. *OR*, v27, pt2, 402.

66. Ibid.

67. Hart to Bachelder, Mar. 3, 1886, *BP*, v2, 1217.

68. Law, "Round Top," 328.

69. Merritt reported the Reserves were engaged four hours. It is estimated his fight west of the Emmitsburg Road was about two hours old when Law drove him back on the Emmitsburg Road.

70. Black, *Crumbling Defenses*, 42.

Chapter 10—Farnsworth's Charge

1. Parsons, "How Farnsworth was Killed."

2. *OR*, v27, pt1, 993.

3. This particular feature of the battlefield will be referred to by the terms "D-shaped" hill and "100-foot" hill. See Kross, "Gettysburg Vignettes," 51, for a description of the hill.

4. *Dedication*, 133, 134.

5. Ibid., 134.

6. Ibid., 135.

7. Ibid.

8. Ibid.

9. Law to Bachelder, June 13, 1876, *BP*, v1, 498.

10. *Dedication*, 136.

11. Howe, *Anthology of Another Town*, 173; Allen was listed as bugler of Company K, *Adj. and Inspector Gen. Rept., 1864*, 205.

12. Parsons, "Farnsworth's Charge," 394.

13. *Dedication*, 136.

14. Parsons, "Farnsworth's Charge," 394; "General Farnsworth's Death," Participants Accounts, Farnsworth's Folder, GNMP.
15. Warner, *Generals in Blue*, 148, 150; Boatner, *Civil War Dictionary*, 275. Warner does not identify the nature of the "unfortunate affair."
16. Alberts, *Wesley Merritt*, 58.
17. Parsons, "How Farnsworth was Killed,"
18. Grier to Bachelder, May 14, 1888, *BP*, v3, 1543.
19. *OR*, v27, pt1, 1009.
20. Hoffman, "1st Vermont Cav.," 18; Phillips, "18th Pennsylvania Cav.," 896.
21. Grover commanded Company K. It is known that Company D deployed on the skirmish line. Company M probably did also.
22. Hoffman, "1st Vermont Cav.," 13.
23. Boatner, *Civil War Dictionary*, 901; Warner, *Generals in Blue*, 549; Heitman, *Historical Register*, v1, 1018.
24. Hoffman, "1st Vermont Cav.," 13.
25. Parsons, "Farnsworth's Charge,"·396n.
26. Hoffman, "1st Vermont Cav.," 17.
27. Benedict, *Vermont in the Civil War*, v2, 645.
28. *Dedication*, 137.
29. White, "1st Texas," 185.
30. Bradfield, "At Gettysburg," 236.
31. H. W. Berryman to his mother, July 9, 1863, RBC, USAMHI.
32. Botsford, *Memories*, 9. From Botsford's description the location and time can only be determined through the process of deduction. He mentions the road, old field, cornfield, stone fence and the distance involved which fit the description of the landscape near the 1st Texas. The Alabama companies most likely formed the skirmish line between the Texans and Oates's right company which also extended along a line perpendicular to the main line. Botsford also states that some of the cavalry were captured. There is no indication Parsons lost any of his men captured when he rode in the vicinity of the Meyers house. Therefore, from the available evidence the incident described likely occurred during the 1st West Virginia's charge.

33. White, "1st Texas," 185.
34. Ibid.
35. *OR*, v27, pt1, 1018. It seems that every soldier that participated in a charge described his last one as the most desperate of the war to date.
36. H. W. Berryman to his mother, July 9, 1863, RBC, USAMHI.
37. Bradfield, "At Gettysburg," 236.
38. *OR*, v27, pt1, 1019; Todd, "Recollections of Gettysburg," 240.
39. *OR*, v27, pt1, 1019.
40. Ibid.
41. Law, "Round Top," 328; Law to Bachelder, June 13, 1876, *BP*, v1, 496, 497.
42. Marker, Reilly's battery, GNMP. The second section is about 50 yards southeast of the main marker for Reilly's battery.
43. *OR*, v27, pt1, 1011; Phillips, "18th Pennsylvania Cav.," 896. Maj. William B. Darlington reported the time at 5:00 p.m.; but, it was probably a little after when the 18th Pennsylvania charged.
44. *18th Pennsylvania*, 13, 15; *Pennsylvania at Gettysburg*, v2, 895.
45. *OR*, v27, pt1, 1009.
46. *18th Pennsylvania*, 40.
47. Ibid.; Phillips, "18th Pennsylvania Cav.," 896.
48. Grier to Bachelder, May 14, 1888, *BP*, v3, 1543.
49. *18th Pennsylvania*, 40; Grier to Bachelder, May 14, 1888, *BP*, v3, 1543.
50. Grier to Bachelder, May 14, 1888, *BP*, v3, 1543.
51. White, "1st Texas," 185.
52. *18th Pennsylvania*, 40.
53. *OR*, v27, pt1, 1009.
54. *18th Pennsylvania*, 40.
55. Grier to Bachelder, May 14, 1888, *BP*, v3, 1543.
56. *Pennsylvania at Gettysburg*, v2, 896.
57. Grier to Bachelder, May 14, 1888, *BP*, v3, 1543.
58. Ibid.
59. *18th Pennsylvania*, 40; *OR*, v27, pt1, 943.
60. Jack to Paul, July 21, 1863 (copy), 5th Pennsylvania Reserves Folder, GNMP.
61. Howe, *Anthology of Another Town*, 174.

62. Ibid.

63. Law to Bachelder, June 13, 1876, *BP*, v1, 497.

64. *Dedication*, 87.

65. Ibid.; Law to Bachelder, June 13, 1876, *BP*, v1, 497.

66. Parsons, "How Farnsworth was Killed."

67. Parsons, "Farnsworth's Charge," 394.

68. *Dedication*, 88.

69. Law, "Round Top," 329; Law to Bachelder, June 13, 1876, *BP*, v1, 496.

70. Law to Bachelder, June 13, 1876, *BP*, v1, 497.

71. Jane Law Norvell Collection.

72. *OR*, v27, pt1, 1013; Hoffman, "1st Vermont Cav.," letter of William Wells, (dated July 7, 1863), 18; Benedict, *Vermont in the Civil War*, v2, 599.

73. Hoffman, "1st Vermont Cav.," 18, fn 29.

74. Parsons, "How Farnsworth was Killed."

75. Ibid.

76. Ibid.

77. Coles, "Gettysburg Campaign," 23.

78. Parsons, "Farnsworth's Charge," 395.

79. Coles, "Gettysburg Campaign," 23.

80. Ibid.; Parsons, "How Farnsworth was Killed."

81. Parsons, "How Farnsworth was Killed."

82. CSR, 4th AL Inf, NA; Coles, "Gettysburg Campaign," 24, 25.

83. John Malachi Bowden, EU, Copy in 2nd Georgia Folder, RBC.

84. Kross, "Gettysburg Vignettes," 51.

85. CSR, 4th AL Inf, NA.

86. Coles, "Gettysburg Campaign," 24.

87. Ibid., 24, 25.

88. Parsons, "How Farnsworth was Killed."

89. Parsons, "Farnsworth's Charge," 394.

90. Howe, *Anthology of Another Town*, 175.

91. Ibid., 174, 175.

92. Ibid., 175.

93. Benedict, *Vermont in the Civil War*, v2, 600; Hoffman, "1st Vermont Cav.," 17.

94. Parsons, "How Farnsworth was Killed."

95. *New York Times*, July 21, 1863; Parsons, "Farnsworth's Charge," 395; Parsons, "How Farnsworth was Killed." Parsons did not identify where the group entered the Union lines. However, from the probable

location at the time the logical route would be over ground occupied by the left of Law's Brigade and then around the northern end of Big Round Top.

96. Hillyer, *Battle of Gettysburg*, 13, 14.

97. Parsons, "How Farnsworth was Killed."

98. *Dedication*, 124.

99. Coles, "Gettysburg Campaign," 26.

100. Law to Bachelder, June 13, 1876, *BP*, v1, 497, reported the survivors "ran the gauntlet" to the right of the 1st Texas, which would place the cavalry exit through the weak skirmish line between the Texans and Georgians. This is consistent with the account of Parsons, "Farnsworth's Charge," map, 394.

101. Hillyer, *Battle of Gettysburg*, 14.

102. Bradfield, "At Gettysburg," 236.

103. Todd, "Recollections of Gettysburg," 240.

104. Shevchuk, "1st Texas at Gettysburg," 192, 193.

105. McCarty, "Battle of Gettysburg" UT.

106. Bradfield, "At Gettysburg," 236; Todd, "Recollections of Gettysburg," 240.

107. *OR*, v27, pt1, 1019.

108. Parsons, "Farnsworth's Charge," 395.

109. *OR*, v27, pt1, 1013; Parsons, "Farnsworth's Charge," 395.

110. Parsons, "How Farnsworth was Killed."

111. *OR*, v27, pt1, 1013.

112. Ibid.; Clark, "Farnsworth's Death."

113. Clark, "Farnsworth's Death."

114. Based on analysis of CSR, 47th AL Inf, NA; CSR, 15th AL Inf, NA.

115. Parsons, "Farnsworth's Charge," 395; Botsford, *Memories*, 9.

116. Clark, "Farnsworth's Death."

117. Coles, "Gettysburg Campaign," 25.

118. Oates, *The War*, 236.

119. CSR, 44th AL Inf, NA; CSR, 4th AL Inf, NA; HMR, 44th AL Inf, ADAH.

120. Benedict, *Vermont in the Civil War*, v2, 602.

121. Ibid.

122. Ibid.

123. *Dedication*, 125.

124. Oates, "Gettysburg," 182.

125. Ibid.; Oates, *The War*, 237; Parsons, "Farnsworth's Charge," 396n; Coles, "Gettysburg Campaign," 26.

126. Benedict, *Vermont in the Civil War*, v2, 602.
127. Parsons, "How Farnsworth was Killed."
128. Clark, "Farnsworth's Death."
129. Parsons, "Farnsworth's Charge," 396.
130. Parsons, "How Farnsworth was Killed."
131. Coles, "Gettysburg Campaign," 26, 27. Nix transferred to Co. C, 31st AL as second lieutenant, CSR, 4th AL Inf, NA.
132. CSR, 4th AL Inf, NA.
133. *OR*, v27, pt1, 1008.
134. *Dedication*, 93.
135. Ibid., 90.
136. Parsons, "How Farnsworth was Killed."
137. Ibid.
138. *OR*, v27, pt1, 75, 117.
139. Ibid., 916.
140. Ibid., 993.
141. Coles, "Gettysburg Campaign," 27.
142. Oates, *The War*, 597; John's rank was fifth sergeant, CSR, 15 AL Inf, NA.

Chapter 11—Aftermath of Battle

1. McLaws, "Gettysburg," 87–88.
2. Ibid., 88.
3. McLaws to I. R. Pennypacker, July 31, 1888, Philadelphia *Weekly Press*.
4. *OR*, v27, pt2, 416–417. The exact location of the hill, or rise, described by Benning is not known. McLaws's line was north of the Devil's Den, under cover of woods, and extended almost to the intersection of the Emmitsburg Road and the Wheatfield Road, McLaws, "Gettysburg," 79.
5. McLaws to I. R. Pennypacker, July 31, 1888, Philadelphia *Weekly Press*.
6. *OR*, v27, pt2, 423.
7. Law, "Round Top," 330.
8. Oates, *The War*, 238–239.
9. Ibid., 237–239.
10. *OR*, v27, pt2, 392.
11. Ibid., 395.
12. Ibid., 396. There is no record that St. John was appointed major. Apparently Sheffield appointed him acting major prior to the battle.
13. CSR, 15th AL Inf, NA.
14. Oates, *The War*, 709.

15. *OR*, v27, pt2, 482, 483.
16. Alexander, *Fighting for the Confederacy*, 236.
17. Brown to his brother, Brown Papers, BUL.
18. Survivors Association, *History of the 118th Pennsylvania Volunteers*, 261, 262; William Brown to his brother, July 7, 1863, *83rd Pennsylvania* Folder, GNMP.
19. Scott, "On Little Round Top."
20. Definitions used are: Killed includes those killed on the field of battle or mortally wounded; missing is counted as those captured.
21. CSR, 4th, 15th, 44th, 47th, 48th AL Inf, NA; HMR, 4th, 15th, 44th, 47th, 48th AL Inf, ADAH. A total of 124 officers and men died of wounds, 53 of these occurred in field hospitals around Gettysburg, the remainder in Federal prisons, and 26 died in prison from disease and other causes.
22. CSR, NA; HMR, ADAH. At this point in the war very few, if any, losses were replaced. Percent reduction is based on the estimated number engaged.
23. *CV*, v19, n5, May 1911. Thomas had been promoted to sergeant for "gallant and meritorious service" in early 1863. He was on detached service in Alabama seeking clothing for the 4th Alabama when the Confederacy collapsed, CSR, 4th AL Inf, NA.
24. Oates, *The War*, 675.
25. Cody, "Letters of Barnett Cody," 372, 373.
26. CSR, 47th AL Inf; CSR, 15th AL Inf, CSR; 4th AL Inf, NA.
27. Ibid.
28. Figures to his sister, July 18, 1863, FC.
29. CSR, 44th AL Inf, NA.
30. CSR, 47th AL Inf, NA; 47th AL Inf, ADAH; three of the four brothers perished in the war, which could also be said of many Southern families.
31. CSR, 4th, 15th, 44th, 47th, 48th AL Inf, NA.
32. *CV*, v5, n9, Sept. 1897, 470.
33. Ibid., n10, Oct. 1897, 514.
34. The effective date of Christian's promotion was Nov. 17, 1863, CSR, 4th AL, NA.
35. LRCAI, 1861–1865, M474, roll 101.
36. CSR, 4th, AL Inf, NA.
37. *CMH*, v8, 488, 489.
38. *The Medical and Surgical History*, v2, pt2, 81.

39. *CMH*, v8, 488, 489; CSR, 4th AL Inf, NA.

40. CSR, 4th AL Inf, NA.

41. *CMH*, v8, 488, 489.

42. CSR, 48th AL Inf; CSR, 15th AL Inf, NA.

43. Oates, *The War*, 771.

44. The text is an excerpt from Shaaff's letter seeking Hatcher's appointment and confirmation. Hatcher was elected captain of Co. D, June 23, 1863, CSR, 15th AL Inf, NA. Apparently at that time no one had thought to get a written statement of Wicker's waiver. Though he served as captain of Company L, Hatcher was not formerly appointed captain until Dec. 1864 and confirmed in Mar. 1865.

45. CSR, 15th AL Inf, NA.

46. Oates, *The War*, 634; recalled cavalry raised in the conscript department were not considered very effective and were referred to as "Buttermilk Rangers."

47. CSR, 47th AL Inf, NA; *OR*, v27, pt2, 395.

48. Newell to Martha McKee, July 26, 1863, ML.

49. Mrs. Jackson to Thomas Owen, July 16, 1902, 47th AL Inf, ADAH.

50. CSR, 44th AL Inf, NA.

51. Laine, *Law's Alabama Brigade*, 132, 133, for a discussion of this event. Campbell was killed May 14, 1864.

52. Oates, *The War*, 340.

53. Oates claimed Perry sided with Longstreet during his feud with Law; probably because Law arrested Perry during the first day at the Battle of Chickamauga. However, Perry made a concerted effort to secure Oates an acceptable position after his commission was revoked. See Laine, *Law's Alabama Brigade*, 277, 278 for a discussion of this unfortunate episode.

54. Oates to Cooper, July 20, CSR, 15th AL Inf, NA.

55. Boatner, *Civil War Dictionary*, 135; Warner, *General in Blue*, 76, 77.

56. The citation is from *Medal of Honor Recipients*, 55, for action July 2, 1863; see also, Boatner, *Civil War Dictionary*, 135.

57. Boatner, *Civil War Dictionary*, 693, 694; Warner, *General in Blue*, 400, 401; Nash, *44th New York*, 224.

58. Heitman, *Historical Register*, 469, 597, 641.

59. Warner, *General in Blue*, 549, 550; Heitman, *Historical Register*, 1054. John Hammond became colonel of the 5th New York and was later breveted brigadier general.

60. *Medal of Honor Recipients*, 260.

61. Warner, *General in Blue*, 266, 267; Heitman, *Historical Register*, 706.

Chapter 12—Return to Virginia

1. Imboden, "Retreat From Gettysburg," 423–425.

2. *OR*, v27, pt2, 214, 280, 437, 655; Hudson, "Soldier Boys," 64. The 1st New York Cavalry, Downsville, MD was known variously as the "Carbine Rangers," "Sabre Regiment," and 1st Regiment (Lincoln) Cavalry. It was organized in New York City in 1861 and in July 1863 was attached to Colonel Lewis B. Pierce's brigade, Department of the Susquehanna, Dryer, *Compendium*, 828.

3. *OR*, v27, pt3, 580.

4. CSR, 48th AL Inf, NA.

5. Coles, "Gettysburg Campaign," 29; REC, Co. D, CSR, 44th AL Inf; REC, Co. E, CSR, 44th AL Inf, NA.

6. Coco, *A Vast Sea of Misery*, 143.

7. Anderson to E. P. Anderson, July 17, 1863, APJSU.

8. HMR, 44th AL Inf, ADAH; CSR, 44th AL Inf, NA.

9. Vaughan, "Vaughan Diary," 588; Coles, "Gettysburg Campaign," 29; Purifoy, "Battle Array," 372.

10. Vaughan, "Vaughan Diary," 589–590; REC, Co. C and K, CSR, 44th AL Inf, NA.

11. Purifoy, "Battle Array," 372; Vaughan, "Vaughan Diary," 590; REC, 4th AL Inf, NA.

12. *OR*, v27, pt2, 323, 428.

13. Coles, "Gettysburg Campaign," 32; Vaughan, "Vaughan Diary," 590.

14. McClendon, *Recollections*, 179; Jordan, *Events*, 46, 47; Goodson, "Goodson Letters," 144–147.

15. Simpson, *Texas Brigade*, 294.

16. Newell to Martha McKee, July 24, 1863, ML.

17. Ibid.

18. Reuben Kidd to Sue, July 17, 1863, Pierrepont, *Reuben Kidd*, 330.

19. Daniel to M. A. Daniel, July 27, 1863, DCSU.
20. CSR, 44 AL Inf, NA.
21. Oates, *The War*, 573, 574, 580; CSR, 15th AL Inf, NA.
22. *Southern Advertiser*, July 29, 1863, 15th AL Regimental Folder, GNMP.
23. *OR*, v27, pt2, 324, 362.
24. Ibid., pt1, 999, 1000, pt2, 324, 362; Vaughan, "Vaughan Diary," 591.
25. *OR*, v27, pt2, 362.
26. Ibid.
27. Wise, *17th Virginia*, 160–162; *OR*, v27, pt2, 362, pt1, 945.
28. *OR*, v27, pt1, 937.
29. Ibid., pt2, 362; Coles, "From Falling Waters to Fredericksburg," 1.
30. *OR*, v27, pt2, 417.
31. Wise, *17th Virginia*, 160.
32. Vaughan, "Vaughan Diary," 591.
33. *OR*, v27, pt2, 362.
34. Ibid., 417, 418.
35. Ibid., 489, 490.
36. Ibid., 417, 418.
37. Coles, "From Falling Waters to Fredericksburg," 2; Vaughan, "Vaughan Diary," 591.
38. Oates, *The War*, 250, 251.
39. Ibid.
40. Ibid.
41. Ibid., 251; Jordan, *Events*, 48.
42. *OR*, v27, pt2, 419.
43. Newell to Martha McKee, July 24, 1863, ML.
44. *OR*, v27, pt1, 999, 1004, pt2, 418.
45. Ibid., pt2, 419.
46. Ibid., pt1, 1004, pt3, 753, 754, 805.
47. Ibid., pt1, 1004; Richmond *Dispatch*, Aug. 4, 1863.
48. Oates, *The War*, 251; McClendon, *Recollections*, 181.
49. Oates, *The War*, 251.
50. Richmond *Dispatch*, Aug. 4, 1863.
51. Oates, *The War*, 251.
52. *OR*, v27, pt2, 419.
53. Richmond *Dispatch*, Aug. 4, 1863.
54. *OR*, v27, pt1, 1004.
55. Coles, "From Falling Waters to Fredericksburg," 3, 4.
56. Taylor, *48th Alabama*; Vaughan, "Vaughan Diary," 592.
57. Anderson to E. P. Anderson, Aug. 16, 1863, APJSU.

Epilogue

1. Owen, *Alabama Dictionary*, 1293.
2. Oates to Nicholson, Feb. 11, 1903, OC.
3. Oates to Elihu Root, June 2, 1903, OC.
4. Oates to Nicholson, Feb. 11, 1903, OC.
5. Robbins to Nicholson, Feb. 20, 1903, OC.
6. Robbins Diary, Dec. 19, 1903, RPSHC.
7. Ibid.
8. Robbins to Nicholson, Feb. 11, 1903; Oates to Robbins, July 4, 1903, OC.
9. Robbins Diary, Dec. 19, 1903, RPSHC.
10. Robbins to Nicholson, Feb. 11, 1903, Robbins to Nicholson, Feb. 26, 1903, Robbins to Oates, June 20, 1903, OC; Robbins Diary, Dec. 19, 1903, RPSHC.
11. Ibid.
12. Oates to Robbins, Feb. 14, 1903, OC.
13. Root to Oates, Jan. 22, 1904, OC; Robbins Diary, Dec. 19, 1903, RPSHC.
14. Chamberlain to Bachelder, n.d., *BP*, v3, 1084, 1086.
15. Oates to Robbins, July 18, 1904; Chamberlain to Nicholson, Aug. 14, 1903; Oates to Nicholson, Dec. 29, 1904; Oates to Nicholson, Mar. 1, 1905; Chamberlain to Oates, May 18, 1905, OC; Chamberlain to Nicholson, Mar. 16, 1905, OC.
16. Oates to Root, June 2, 1903, OC.
17. Oates to Nicholson, Nov. 3, 1903, OC.
18. Oates, in his last known correspondence to the commission, still maintained the 15th AL drove the 20th ME's right flank back, Oates to Nicholson, Mar. 1, 1905, OC.
19. Harrison, *Monuments, Markets, Tablets*, 38.
20. Oates, Surname File, ADAH.

Appendix A—Opposing Forces

1. Only those brigades and/or regiments directly engaged with Law's Brigade, or in the immediate vicinity of Law's Brigade, are shown.
2. Confederate organization is from *OR*, v27, pt2, 284–285.
3. Lieutenant Colonel Scruggs fell out during the charge. Major Coleman commanded the

regiment during the assault on Little Round Top. Scruggs returned to command the regiment July 3.

4. Oates fell out during the retrograde movement from Little Round Top across Round Top. Hill replaced him in temporary command until Oates recovered and resumed command July 3.

5. Jackson fell from exhaustion early in the charge across Plum Run Valley. Bulger commanded the regiment until wounded on the slopes of Little Round Top.

6. Sheffield moved up to brigade command after leading the 48th in three charges. Command of the regiment was subsequently turned over to Thomas Eubanks, captain, commanding Company D.

7. First Corps artillery, *OR*, v27, pt2, 285; engaged July 2, 3.

8. Engaged on July 3 in supporting Hood's Division and repulse of Kilpatrick's cavalry. Organization is from *OR*, v27, pt2, 290, 291.

9. Black was present on the Confederate right with detachments from the 1st S.C. Cavalry, 1st N.C. Cavalry, and Hart's Washington Light Artillery.

10. Federal organization is from *OR*, v27, pt1, 155, 159–162, 166, 167. Only those brigades and/or regiments directly engaged with Law's Brigade, or in the immediate vicinity of Law's Brigade, are shown.

11. 3rd Maine, 1st U.S. Sharpshooters engaged elsewhere.

12. Federal organization is from *OR*, v27, pt1, 166, 167. Only those brigades directly engaged with Law's Brigade July 3 are shown.

13. The 6th U.S. Cavalry was not present on the field at Gettysburg.

Appendix B—Organization

1. Organization is based on analysis of CSR, NA; HMR, ADAH, for muster roll and historical data for the period in question.

2. Specific detail assigned was not indicated.

3. Also found as aide-de-camp.

4. Data, except as noted, is from CSR, 4th AL Inf, NA and HMR, 4th AL Inf, ADAH.

5. ( ) indicates acting in some capacity, or in the case Bowles, "absent under arrest."

6. Detailed as forage master.

7. [ ] indicates company affiliation, in this case Company D.

8. Assigned commissary department.

9. Promoted from private, Company B, 4th AL, July 1, 1863.

10. Severely wounded Fredericksburg, VA, Dec. 13, 1862, CSR, 4th AL Inf, NA; given position of color bearer June 8, 1863; severely wounded Sept. 20, 1863.

11. Specific detail assigned was not indicated.

12. Assigned to division.

13. Assigned to division.

14. Company names are from Coles, "Company Sketches," 4th AL Inf, ADAH.

15. Also known as the "Alabama Zouaves," ibid.

16. Also known as the "Canebrake Rifle Guards," ibid.

17. Also known as the "Lauderdale Volunteers," ibid.

18. Data, except as noted, is from CSR, 15th AL Inf, NA and HMR, 15th AL Inf, ADAH.

19. Did not take active part in battle.

20. Forage master.

21. Field & Staff.

22. Field & Staff.

23. Specific detail assigned was not indicated.

24. Attached to General Longstreet's staff.

25. Also commanded regiment.

26. Also called "City Light Guards."

27. Also know as "Eufaula Zouaves," 15th AL Inf, ADAH.

28. Elected captain, but not officially appointed nor confirmed. It is believed he commanded the company.

29. Data, except as noted, is from CSR, 44th AL Inf, NA and HMR, 44th AL Inf, ADAH.

30. Held rank of first corporal.

31. Wagon master.

32. Drum major, Company E.

33. Assign to division pioneer corps.

34. Also served as colonel's orderly.

35. Co. names from the Selma *Reporter*, June 18, 1862.

36. Also called "Cedar Creek Guards," 44th AL Inf, ADAH.

37. Company was named in honor of Nathaniel H. R. Dawson, former captain in the 4th AL. Dawson returned the compliment with a $500 donation for the care and relief of company sick, Selma *Reporter*, June 17, 1862.

38. Also called "Sallie Border's Boys," 44th AL Inf, ADAH.

39. Data, except as noted, is from CSR, 47th AL Inf, NA and HMR, 47th AL Inf, ADAH.

40. Wagon master.

41. Also known as "Tallapoosa Light Infantry," REC, 47th AL Inf, NA.

42. Data, except as noted, is from CSR, 48th AL Inf, NA and HMR, 48th AL Inf, ADAH.

43. St. John was appointed acting major by Sheffield just prior to the Battle of Gettysburg. No records have been located to verify an official application of appointment to the War Department.

44. Mortally wounded, gunshot in side and lung, died July 26, 1863 at David's Island, New York.

45. Drummer.

46. Also known as "Sheffield Rifles."

47. Original Co. G was commanded by Capt. Phillip B. Gilbert. This company was consolidated with Co. E on July 17, 1862. New Co. G was commanded by John S. Moragne.

48. Also known as "Cherokee Guards," SG 11125#1, ADAH.

49. Also known as "Lee County Guards," Amann, *Personnel of the Civil War*, 84.

Appendix C—Roster of Officers

1. Biographical data based on analysis of HMR, 4th, 15th, 44th, 47th, 48th AL Inf, ADAH; CSR, 4th, 15th, 44th, 47th, 48th, NA, U.S. Census, 1860. The roster includes only those officers present for duty July 2–3, 1863.

2. Age at the Battle of Gettysburg.

3. CSR, 15th AL Inf, NA; HMR, 15th AL Inf, ADAH, Hatcher was elected captain of Company L, June 23, 1863 after Robert Wicker had been twice refused promotion by examination boards. He served as captain until December 1864, though not officially confirmed in that rank, when he was appointed and confirmed by Congress.

4. Based on genealogical data from Paul Nowlen, Jenkinsville, SC; great-grandson of W. H. Keller.

5. Commanding provost guard.

Appendix D—Operations July 2, 1863— Devil's Den and Little Round Top

1. Events are listed in order of occurrence. The time noted for a given event is based on analysis of the available information. Many of the participants noted differing times for the same event. The current analysis attempts to reconcile those differences. Where the time for an event is not listed, it is believed the occurrence was between the approximate times listed before and after the event.

2. Law, "Round Top," 319, recalled that the brigade joined the division just before noon.

3. James Jackson to his wife, July 7, 1863, ADAH.

4. Norton, *ADLRT*, 240, 263.

5. Law, "Round Top," 323, remembered years later that the time was 5 p.m., but other accounts agree it was about 4 p.m. *OR*, v27, pt2, 407–408, 412; Sorrel, *Recollections*, 159. Sheffield, *OR*, v27, pt2, 395, does not give the time, but reported the 48th was in position about one-half hour before advancing, which is consistent with the brigade being in line between 3 and 3:30 p.m.; Oates, *The War*, 207.

6. Wright, "Time on Little Round Top," 53; *OR*, v27, pt1, 632, Woodward reported that 45 minutes after the brigade was ordered into position its skirmishers were engaged.

7. *OR*, v27, pt2, 394, Perry reported it was past 5:00 p.m. when Benning came up.

8. Law, "Round Top," 318, Law recalled the battery was overrun about one hour after the brigade began its advance. This would place the time about 5:00 p.m.; Sheffield, referring to the Slaughter Pen, reported the 48th Alabama fought one and one-half hours, *OR*, v27, pt2, 395–396; *OR*, v27, pt1, 493, 494.

9. *OR*, v27, pt1, 617, Rice reported the enemy made repeated assaults for one hour against the 44th New York and 83rd Pennsylvania and did not break his line. The fighting then spread north to Vincent's right

flank. This would place the time between 5:45 and 6:00 p.m.

10. *OR*, v27, pt1, 630, Connor reported Vincent was wounded about one hour after the brigade was engaged.

11. *OR*, v27, pt1, 624, Chamberlain reported the fighting continued about one hour after his line was refused when attacked by the 15th Alabama.

12. Wright, "Time on Little Round Top," 53.

13. Rice's report of the action, *OR*, v27, pt1, 618.

14. Nesbit, *Through Blood and Fire*, 82.

15. Significant events in "Pickett's Charge" are noted for a frame of reference for the events during the Federal cavalry demonstration on the extreme Confederate right.

16. Benedict, *Vermont in the Civil War*, v2, 596, placed the cavalry south of Big Round Top shortly after the noon hour. Law to Bachelder, June 13, 1876, *BP*, v1, 494, remembered the cavalry was first observed in the edge of Bushman Woods in the forenoon. This would have been when the three companies of the 47th Alabama were driven in.

17. Time is based on discussion with researcher John Michael Priest.

18. Law, "Round Top," 327, Law stated that the "grand artillery duel was progressing and before the infantry moved to the attack"

the cavalry appeared in the timber, referring to Bushman Woods.

19. Time is based on discussion with researcher John Michael Priest.

20. Time is based on discussion with researcher John Michael Priest.

21. Law, "Round Top," 327, Law recalled the Georgians were "stretched out to a bare line of skirmishers."

22. From the available accounts "Pickett's Charge" must have been over about one hour when the West Virginians rode against the 1st Texas.

23. *OR*, v27, pt1, 1011; Phillips, "18th Pennsylvania Cav.," 896. Maj. William B. Darlington reported the regiment was ordered to form at 5:00 p.m. It was probably a little after that when the 18th Pennsylvania charged.

24. Perley C. J. Cheney, second lieutenant of Company E, 1st Vermont Cavalry, was wounded about the same time that Farnsworth was killed. A bullet stopped his watch at 5:27 p.m., Parsons, "How Farnsworth was Killed."

25. Merritt reported he was engaged four hours. Since it is estimated he drove in Black's skirmishers about 2:00 p.m., the storm would have moved over the battlefield around 6:00 p.m. or a little after.

Bibliography

Books, Articles and Pamphlets

Albaugh, William A., III. *Confederate Faces, A Pictorial Review*. Wilmington, North Carolina: Broad Publishing Company, 1993.

Alberts, Don E. *General Wesley Merritt: Nineteenth Century Cavalryman*. Dissertation Doctor of Philosophy in History, University of New Mexico, 1975.

Alexander, E. Porter. *Military Memoirs of a Confederate*. New York: Charles Scribner's Sons, 1907.

———. *Fighting for the Confederacy*. Chapel Hill, North Carolina: The University of North Carolina Press, 1989.

———. "The Great Charge and Artillery Fighting at Gettysburg," *Battles & Leaders of The Civil War*. Vol. 3. New York: The Century Company, 1888.

Alleman, Tillie P. *At Gettysburg or What a Girl Saw and Heard at the Battle*. New York, New York: W. Lake Borland, 1889.

Amann, William Frayne, editor. *Personnel of the Civil War*. 2 vols. New York: Thomas Yoseloff, 1961.

Ayars, Peter B. "The 99th Pennsylvania" *National Tribune*, Feb. 4, 1886.

The Bachelder Papers. Ladd, David L., and Audrey J., editors. 3 vols. Dayton, Ohio: Morningside House, Inc., 1994.

Barziza, Decimus et Ultimus. Edited by R. Henderson Shuffler. *The Adventures of A Prisoner of War 1863–1864*. Austin, Texas: University of Texas Press, 1964.

Benedict, G. G. *Vermont in the Civil War. A History of the Part Taken by the Vermont Soldiers and Sailors in the War for the Union, 1861–1865*. 2 vols. Burlington, Vermont: The Free Press Association, 1888. Burlington, Vermont: The Free Press Association, 1888.

Black, John L. *Crumbling Defenses or Memoirs and Reminiscences of John Logan Black*. Macon, Georgia: Eleanor D. McSwain, editor and publisher, 1960.

Boatner, Mark M. *The Civil War Dictionary*. New York: David McKay Company, Inc., 1959.

Botsford, Theophilus F. *Memories of the War of Secession*. Montgomery, Alabama: The Paragon Press, 1911.

Bradfield, James O. "At Gettysburg, July 3," *Confederate Veteran*, vol. 30, no. 6 (June 1922).

Bradley, Thomas W. "At Gettysburg: The Splendid Work Done by Smith's Battery." *National Tribune*, Feb. 4, 1886.

Brewer, Willis. *Alabama, Her History, Resources, War Record and Public Men from 1540 to 1872*. 1872. Reprint, Spartanburg, South Carolina: The Reprint Publishers, 1975.

Brooks, Ulysses R., editor. *Stories of the Confederacy*. Columbia, South Carolina: The State Company, 1912.

Brown, W. J. "General Farnsworth: How He Fell in the Furious Charge at Gettysburg." *National Tribune*, August 25, 1887.

Chamberlain, Joshua L. *Through Blood and Fire*. Gettysburg, Pennsylvania: Stan Clark Military Books, 1994.

Clark, Stephen A. "General Farnsworth—and How He Fell in a Cavalry Charge at Gettysburg." *National Tribune*, Feb. 3, 1887.

Coan, Elisha Coan. "Round Top." *National Tribune*, June 4, 1885.

Coco, Gregory A. *A Vast Sea of Misery, A History and Guide to the Union and Confederate Field Hospitals at Gettysburg, July 1–November 2, 1863*. Gettysburg, Pa.: Thomas Publications, 1988.

Coddington, Edwin B. *The Gettysburg Campaign, A Study in Command*. New York: Charles Scribner's Sons, 1968.

Cody, Barnett H. "Letters of Barnett Hardeman Cody and Others, 1861–1864." Edited by Edmund Cody Burnett. *Georgia Historical Quarterly*, vol. 23 (1939).

Collier, Calvin L. *They'll Do to Tie To:3rd Arkansas Infantry Regiment, C. S. A.* Little Rock: Major James D. Warren, publisher, 1959.

"Col. John Logan Black, of South Carolina." *Confederate Veteran*, vol. 35, no. 6 (June 1927).

Confederate Military History Extended Edition. Vol. 4. "Virginia," 1899. Reprint, with new material. Wilmington, North Carolina: Broadfoot Publishing Company, 1987.

Confederate Military History Extended Edition. Vol. 5. "North Carolina," 1899. Reprint, with new material. Wilmington, North Carolina: Broadfoot Publishing Company, 1987.

Confederate Military History Extended Edition. Vol. 6. "South Carolina," 1899. Reprint, with new material. Wilmington, North Carolina: Broadfoot Publishing Company, 1987.

Confederate Military History Extended Edition. Vol. 7. "Georgia," 1899. Reprint, with new material. Wilmington, North Carolina: Broadfoot Publishing Company, 1987.

Confederate Military History Extended Edition. Vol. 8. "Alabama-Mississippi," 1899. Reprint, with "Additional Sketches Illustrating the Services of Officers and Patriotic Citizens of Alabama." Wilmington, North Carolina: Broadfoot Publishing Company, 1987.

Confederate Military History Extended Edition. Vol. 14. "Texas," 1899. Reprint, with new material. Wilmington, North Carolina: Broadfoot Publishing Company, 1987.

Crute, Joseph H. *Confederate Staff Officers, 1861–1865.* Powhatten, Virginia: Derwent Books, 1982.

Curran, J. A. "Billings at Gettysburg." *The New England Journal of Medicine*, vol. 269, no. 1, July 4, 1963.

Davis, George B., editor. *The Official Atlas of the Civil War.* New York: Arno Press, 1978.

Davis, Jefferson. *Jefferson Davis, Constitutionalist, His Letters, Papers and Speeches.* Dunbar Rowland, editor. 10 vols. Jackson, Mississippi: 1923.

Davis, Nicholas A. *Chaplain Davis and Hood's Texas Brigade.* Edited and with an introduction by Donald E. Everett. San Antonio, Texas: Principal Press of Trinity University, 1962.

Dedication of the Statue to Brevet Major-General William Wells and the Officers and Men of the First Regiment Vermont Cavalry, July 13, 1913. Privately printed, n.d.

Dickert, D. Augustus. *History of Kershaw's Brigade, With Complete Roll of Companies, Biographical Sketches, Incidents, Anecdotes, Etc.* 1899. Reprint, with an introduction by W. Stanley Hoole. Dayton, Ohio: Press of Morningside Bookshop, 1973.

Dryer, Frederick H. *A Compendium of the War of the Rebellion.* Des Moines, Iowa: 1908. Reprinted, Dayton, Ohio: Morningside Bookshop, 1978.

Dubose, Joel C. *Notable Men of Alabama*—Personal and Genealogical with Portraits. Atlanta, Georgia: Southern Historical Association, 1904. Reprinted, Spartanburg, South Carolina: The Reprint Co., Publishers, 1976.

Duncan, Katherine M., and Larry J. Smith. *The History of Marshall County, Alabama.* "Prehistory to 1939." Vol. 1. Albertville, Alabama: Thompson Printing, 1969.

Evans, Clement T., and Allen D. Chandler, editors. *Cyclopedia of Georgia.* 2 vols. "Comprising Sketches of Counties, Towns, Events, Illustrations and Persons Arranged in Cyclopidia Form." Atlanta, Georgia: State Historical Association, 1906. Reprinted, Spartanburg, South Carolina: The Reprint Co., 1972.

Farinholt, B. L. "Battle of Gettysburg-Johnson's Island." *Confederate Veteran*, vol. 5, no. 10 (October 1897).

———. "Escape From Johnson's Island." *Confederate Veteran*, vol. 5, no. 9 (September 1897).

Farley, Porter. "Bloody Round Top." *National Tribune*, May 3, 1883.

Fisher, J. W. "Round Top Again—A Comrade Who Was There Tells His Story." *National Tribune*, April 6, 1885.

Fletcher, William Andrew. *Rebel Private, Front and Rear*. Beaumont, Tex.: Press of the Greer Print, 1908.

Floyd, Fred C. *History of the Fortieth (Mozart) Regiment, New York Volunteers*. Boston, Massachusetts: F. H. Gilson Co., 1909.

Freeman, Douglas S. *Lee's Lieutenants, A Study In Command*. 3 vols. New York: Charles Scribner's Sons, 1942.

Garlington, J. C. *Men of the Time—Sketches of Living Notables, A Biographical Encyclopedia of Contemporaneous, South Carolina Leaders*. Spartanburg, South Carolina: Garlington Publishing Co., 1902. Reprinted, Spartanburg, South Carolina: The Reprint Co., 1972.

"General M. J. Bulger, An Alabama Hero." *Montgomery Advertiser*, October 2, 1898.

Georg, Kathleen. "Our Principal Loss Was in this Place." *The Morningside Notes*, June 12, 1984. Dayton, Ohio: Press of Morningside Bookshop.

Gettysburg Battlefield Commission, Map of the Battlefield.

Gibney, John M. "A Shadow Passing: The Tragic Story of Norvell Welch and the 16th Michigan at Gettysburg and Beyond." *Gettysburg Magazine*, no. 6 (January 1992). Dayton, Ohio: Morningside House, Inc.

Giles, Val C. *Rags and Hope: The Memoirs of Val C. Giles, Four Years with Hood's Brigade, Fourth Texas Infantry, 1861–1865*. Compiled and edited by Mary Lasswell. New York: Coward-McCann, Inc., 1961.

Goodson, Joab. "The Letters of Captain Joab Goodson, 1862–1864. Edited by W. Stanley Hoole. *The Alabama Review*, vol. 10 (April 1957).

Gracey, Samuel L. *Annals of the Sixth Pennsylvania Cavalry*. E. H. Butler & Co., 1868.

Graham, Ziba B. "On to Gettysburg—Ten Days From My Diary of 1863." MOLLUS, Commandery, of the State of Michigan. Vol. 1. March 2, 1889. Reprinted, Wilmington, North Carolina: Broadfoot Publishing Co., 1993.

Hanford, J. Harvey. "Gettysburg—The Experience of a Private in the 124th New York in the Battle." *National Tribune*, Sept. 21, 1885.

Hardin, Martin D. *History of the Twelfth Regiment Pennsylvania Volunteers Corps (First Regiment of the Line)*. New York, New York, 1890.

Harrison, Kath G. *The Location of the Monuments, Markers, and Tablets on Gettysburg Battlefield.* Gettysburg, Pennsylvania: Thomas Publications, 1993.

Hazen, Samuel R. "The 140th New York and Its Work on Little Round Top." *National Tribune*, Sept. 13, 1894.

Heitman, Francis B. *Historical Register and Dictionary of the U.S. Army.* Washington, D.C.: U.S. Government Printing Office, 1903.

Henderson, Lillian, compiler. *Roster of the Confederate Soldiers of Georgia, 1861–1865.* Vols. 1, 2, 6. Hopeville, Georgia: Longino and Porter, Inc., 1959.

Hillyer, George. *Battle of Gettysburg.* From *Walton Tribune.* Address before the Walton County Georgia Confederate Veterans, August 2, 1904.

History of the Eighteenth Regiment of Cavalry Pennsylvania Volunteers, 1862–1865. Edited by the Publication Committee of the Regimental Association. New York, New York: Wynkoop Hallenbeck Crawford Co., 1909.

Hoffman, Elliott W. "The First Vermont Cavalry in the *Gettysburg Campaign.*" *Gettysburg Magazine*, no. 14, Jan. 1, 1996. Dayton, Ohio: Morningside House, Inc.

Hood, John Bell. *Advance and Retreat: Personal Experiences in the United States and Confederate States Armies.* Edited by Richard Current. Bloomington, Indiana: Indiana University Press, 1959.

———. "Letter From General John B. Hood." *Southern Historical Society Papers*, vol. 4 (1876). Reprint, Millwood, New York: Kraus Reprint Company, 1977.

Houghton, W. R., and M. B. Houghton. *Two Boys in the Civil War and Afterwards.* Montgomery, Alabama: The Paragon Press, 1912.

Howe, Edgar W. *The Anthology of Another Town.* New York, New York: Alfred A. Knopf, 1920.

Hudson, Travis. "Soldier Boys in Gray." *Atlanta Historical Journal*, vol. 23, no. 1 (Spring 1979).

Hunt, Henry J. "The Second Day at Gettysburg." *Battles & Leaders of The Civil War.* Vol. 3. New York: The Century Company, 1888.

Imboden, John D. "The Confederate Retreat From Gettysburg." *Battles & Leaders of The Civil War.* Vol. 3. New York: The Century Company, 1888.

"Incidents of Gettysburg." *Sherman Register*, Sept. 8, 1901.

Jacklin, Rufus W. "The Famous Old Third Brigade." MOLLUS, Commandery, of the State of Michigan. Vol. 2, November 1, 1894. Reprinted, Wilmington, North Carolina: Broadfoot Publishing Co., 1993.

Johnson, Charles F. "The Short, Heroic Life of Strong Vincent." *The Erie Journal of Studies*, vol. 17 (Spring 1988).

Jordan, William C. *Some Events and Incidents During the Civil War.* Montgomery, Alabama: Paragon Press, 1909.

Judson, A. M. *History of the Eighty-third Regiment Pennsylvania Volunteers.* Erie, Pennsylvania: B. F. H. Lynn, Publisher, 1865.

King, George Wayne. "The Civil War Career of Hugh Judson Kilpatrick." Master's thesis, University of South Carolina, 1969.

Kross, Gary. "Gettysburg Vignettes." *Blue & Gray Magazine*, vol. 13, no. 3 (February 1996). Columbus, Ohio.

Kurtz, Henry I. "Berdan's Sharpshooters: Most Effective Union Brigade?" *Civil War Times Illustrated*, vol. 1, no. 10 (February 1963).

Laine, J. Gary, and Morris M. Penny. *Law's Alabama Brigade in the War Between the Union and the Confederacy.* Shippensburg, Pennsylvania: White Mane Publishing Co., Inc., 1996.

Law, E. McIver. "The Struggle for Round Top." *Battles & Leaders of The Civil War.* Vol. 3. New York: The Century Company, 1888.

———. "On the Confederate Right at Gaines's Mill." *Battles & Leaders of The Civil War.* Vol. 2. New York: The Century Company, 1888.

———. "A Night in the Enemy's Lines." Richmond *Dispatch*, May 22, 1894.

Law, John Adger. *Adger-Law Ancestral Notebook.* Spartanburg, South Carolina: Jacob Graphic Arts Company, 1936.

Law, Thomas Hart. *Citadel Cadets: The Journal of Cadet Tom Law.* John Adger Law, editor. Clinton, South Carolina: P. C. Press, 1941.

Leeper, Joseph M. "Gettysburg—The Part Taken in the Battle by the Fifth Corps." *National Tribune*, April 30, 1885.

Longstreet, James. *From Manassas to Appomattox: Memoirs of the Civil War in America.* Secaucus, New Jersey: The Blue and Grey Press, 1985.

———. "Lee's Invasion of Pennsylvania." *Battles & Leaders of The Civil War.* Vol. 3. New York: The Century Company, 1888.

———. "Lee's Right Wing at Gettysburg." *Battles & Leaders of The Civil War.* Vol. 3. New York: The Century Company, 1888.

Maine at Gettysburg: Report of the Maine Commissions, Prepared by the Executive Committee. Maine Gettysburg Commission. Portland, Maine: Lakeside Press, 1898. Reprinted, Gettysburg, Pennsylvania: Stan Clark Military Book, 1994.

Manarin, Louis H., compiler. *North Carolina Troops: 1861–1865, A Roster.* "Artillery." Vol. 1. Raleigh, North Carolina: N.C. State Print Shop, 1966.

———. *North Carolina Troops: 1861–1865, A Roster.* "Cavalry." Vol. 2. Raleigh, North Carolina: N.C. State Print Shop, 1966.

Martin, John H. "Accurate Historical Records." *Confederate Veteran*, vol. 7, no. 3 (March 1904).

McClendon, William A. *Recollections of War Times By an Old Veteran While Under Stonewall Jackson and Lieutenant General James Longstreet: How I Got In and How I Got Out.* Montgomery, Alabama: Paragon Press, 1909.

McDaniel, Major Henry. *With Unabated Trust.* Edited by Anita B. Sams. Monroe, Georgia: The Historical Society of Walton County, Inc., 1977.

McKinney, Francis F. "The Death of Farnsworth." *Michigan Alumnus Quarterly Review—A Journal University Perspectives.* Vol. 66 (1959).

McLaws, Lafayette. "Gettysburg." *Southern Historical Society Papers*, vol. 7 (1879). Reprint, Millwood, New York: Kraus Reprint Company, 1977.

McMurry, Richard M. *John Bell Hood and The War For Southern Independence.* Lexington, Kentucky: University of Kentucky Press, 1982.

Mathis, Ray. *In the Land of the Living: Wartime Letters of Confederates from the Chattahoochee Valley of Alabama and Georgia.* Troy, Alabama: Troy State University Press, 1981.

Medal of Honor Recipients, 1863–1973. Washington, D.C.: U.S. Government Printing Office, 1973.

The Medical and Surgical History of the War of the Rebellion. 3 vols. Washington, D.C.: U.S. Government Printing Office, 1877.

Melcher, Holman S. "The 20th Maine at Little Round Top." *Battles & Leaders of The Civil War.* Vol. 3. New York: The Century Company, 1888.

————. "Little Round Top—The Services of the 20th Maine on the Historic Hill." *National Tribune*, Mar. 5, 1895.

————. *With a Flash of his Sword: The Writings of Major Holman S. Melcher, 20th Maine Infantry.* Kearny, New Jersey: Belle Grove Pub. Co., 1994.

Memoirs of Georgia. Vol. 2. Atlanta, Georgia: The Southern Historical Association, 1895. Reprint, Easley, South Carolina: Southern Historical Press.

Memorial Record of Alabama. 2 vols. 1893. Reprint, Spartanburg, South Carolina: The Reprint Company, Publishers, 1976.

Moore, Albert B. *History of Alabama.* University, Alabama: University Supply Store, 1934.

————. *History of Alabama and Her People.* 3 vols. Chicago and New York: The American Historical Society, Inc., 1927.

Moore, James. *Kilpatrick and Our Cavalry, Comprising a Sketch of the Life of General Kilpatrick.* New York, New York: W. J. Widdleton, Publishers, 1865.

Nash, Eugene A. *A History of the Forty-fourth Regiment New York Volunteer Infantry in the Civil War, 1861–1865.* Chicago: R. R. Donnelly & Sons, 1911.

Nesbitt, Mark. *Through Blood and Fire.* Mechanicsburg, Pennsylvania: Stackpole Books, 1996.

New York Monuments Commission for the Battlefields of Gettysburg and Chattanooga, Final Report for the Battlefield of Gettysburg. 3 vols. "New York at Gettysburg." Albany, New York: J. B. Lyon, 1902.

Northern Alabama, Historical and Biographical. 1888. Reprint, Spartanburg, South Carolina: The Reprint Company, Publishers, 1976.

Northern, William J. *Men of Mark in Georgia*. Vol. 3. Atlanta, Georgia: A. B. Caldwell, ca. 1906–1912. Reprinted, Spartanburg, South Carolina: The Reprint Co., Publishers, 1974.

Norton, Oliver W. *The Attack And Defense Of Little Round Top*. 1913. Reprint, with an introduction by John J. Pullen. Dayton, Ohio: Press of Morningside Bookshop, 1983.

———. *Army Letters, 1861–1865*. Chicago, Illinois: O. L. Deming, 1903.

Oates, William C. *The War Between the Union and Confederacy and Its Lost Opportunities with a History of the 15th Alabama Regiment and the Forty-Eight Battles in Which It was Engaged*. 1905. Reprint, with an introduction by Robert K. Krick. Dayton, Ohio: Press of Morningside Bookshop, 1985.

———. "Gettysburg—The Battle on the Right." *Southern Historical Society Papers*, vol. 6 (1876). Reprint, Millwood, New York: Kraus Reprint Company, 1977.

Owen, Thomas M. *History of Alabama and Dictionary of Alabama Biography*. 4 vols. (1921). Reprint, with an introduction by Milo B. Howard. Spartanburg, South Carolina: The Reprint Publishers, 1978.

Parsons, H. C. "Farnsworth's Charge and Death." *Battles & Leaders of The Civil War*. Vol. 3. New York: The Century Company, 1888.

———. "How General Farnsworth was Killed." *National Tribune*, Aug. 7, 1890.

Pennsylvania at Gettysburg—Ceremonies at the Dedication of the Monuments, John P. Nicholson, compilers. Harrisburg, Pennsylvania: William Stanley Ray, State Printer, 1914.

Perry, William F. "The Devil's Den." *Confederate Veteran*, vol. 9 no. 4 (April 1901).

———. "Reminiscences of the Campaign of 1864 in Virginia." *Southern Historical Society Papers*, vol. 7 (1879). Reprint, Millwood, New York: Kraus Reprint Company, 1977.

Pfanz, Harry W. *Gettysburg, The Second Day*. Chapel Hill, North Carolina: The University of North Carolina Press, 1987.

Piston, William Garrett. "Lee's Tarnished Lieutenant: James Longstreet and His Image in American Society." Ph. D. dissertation. University of South Carolina, 1982.

Pleasonton, Alfred. "The Campaign of Gettysburg." *Annuals of the War—Written by Leading Participants North and South*. Philadelphia, Pennsylvania: The Times Publishing Co., 1879.

Polley, J. B. *Hood's Texas Brigade: Its Marches, Its Battles, Its Achievements*. New York: Neale Publishing Company, 1910.

Powell, Robert M. *Recollections of a Texas Colonel at Gettysburg*. Gregory A. Coco, editor. Gettysburg, Pennsylvania: Thomas Publications, 1990.

————. With Hood at Gettysburg—The Experiences of a Texas Officer in One of the Charges at Little Round Top. *Philadelphia Weekly Times*, Dec. 13, 1884.

Pullen, John J. *The Twentieth Maine: A Volunteer Regiment in the Civil War*. Dayton, Ohio: Press of Morningside Bookshop, 1980.

Purifoy, John. "The Lost Opportunity at Gettysburg." *Confederate Veteran*, vol. 31, no. 6 (June 1923).

————. "The Battle of Gettysburg, July 2." *Confederate Veteran*, vol. 31, no. 7 (July 1923).

————. "Longstreet's Attack at Gettysburg, July 2, 1863." *Confederate Veteran*, vol. 31, no. 8 (August 1923).

————. "The Battle of Gettysburg." *Confederate Veteran*, vol. 31, no. 11 (November 1923).

————. "Farnsworth's Charge and Death at Gettysburg." *Confederate Veteran*, vol. 32, no. 8 (August 1924).

————. "The Horror of War." *Confederate Veteran*, vol. 33, no. 7 (July 1925).

————. "In Battle Array at Williamsport and Hagerstown." *Confederate Veteran*, vol. 33, no. 10 (October 1925).

Register of Cadets and Former Cadets, 1802–1963 of the United States Military Academy. West Point, New York: West Point Alumni Association Foundation, Inc., 1963.

Report of the Adjutant and Inspector General of the State of Vermont, From October 1, 1863 to October 1, 1864. 2 vols. Montpelier, Walton's Steam Press, 1864.

Report of the Adjutant and Inspector General of the State of Vermont, From October 1, 1863 to October 1, 1866. Montpelier, Vermont: Watson's Steam Press, 1866.

Rice, Edmond L. *Civil War Letters of James McDonald Campbell, of the 47th Alabama Infantry, with a Brief Sketch of His Life*. Privately printed, n.d.

Richardson, Jesse M., editor. *Alabama Encyclopedia*. Vol. 1. "Book of Facts." Northport, Alabama: The American Southern Publishing Co., 1965.

Rittenhouse, Benjamin F. *The Battle of Gettysburg as Seen From Little Round Top*. MOLLUS, District of Columbia Commandery, May 4, 1887. Reprinted. Wilmington, North Carolina: Broadfoot Publishing Co., 1993.

Robertson, Jerome B. *Touched with Valor*. Edited by Colonel Harold B. Simpson. Hillsboro, Texas: Hill Junior College Press, 1964.

Robertson, John, editor. *Michigan in the War*. Lansing, Michigan: W. S. George & Co., 1882.

Salley, A. S., Jr. *South Carolina Troops in Confederate Service*. Vol. 1. Columbia, South Carolina: R. L. Bryan Co., 1913.

Saval, Wallace M. "Montage of a City Under Siege: Petersburg, 1864 to 1865." Master's thesis. Virginia State College, 1971.

Schevchuk, Paul M. "The 1st Texas Infantry and the Repulse of Farnsworth's Charge." *Gettysburg Magazine*, no. 2, Jan. 1, 1990. Dayton Ohio, Morningside House, Inc.

Scott, John O. "The Texans at Gettysburg." *Sherman Register*, March 31, 1897.

Sherfesee, Louis. "History of Hart's Battery." *Confederate Veteran*, vol. 9, no. 11, November 1901.

Small, William. "Judson Kilpatrick—A Graphic Sketch of the Renowned Cavalry Leader." *National Tribune*, Oct. 27. 1887.

Smith, James E. "The Fourth Battery at Gettysburg." New York Monuments Commission for the Battlefields of Gettysburg and Chattanooga, Final Report on The Battlefield of Gettysburg. *New York at Gettysburg*. Vol. 3. Albany, New York: J. B. Lyon Company, Printers, 1900.

———. *A Famous Battery and its Campaigns, 1861–64*. Washington, D.C.: W. H. Lowdermilk & Co., 1892.

———. "The Devil's Den—The Defense at Gettysburg by Smith's Battery and Its Supports." *The National Tribune*, March 4, 1886.

Smith, William R. *The History and Debate of the Convention of the People of Alabama*. 1861. Reprint, Spartanburg, South Carolina: The Reprint Company, Publishers, 1975.

Sommers, Richard J. *Richmond Redeemed: The Siege at Petersburg*. Garden City, New York: Doubleday and Company, 1981.

Sorrel, G. Moxley. *Recollections of a Confederate Staff Officer*. Bell Irvin Wiley, editor. Jackson, Tennessee: McCowat-Mercer Press, 1958.

Stevens, C. A. *Berdan's U.S. Sharpshooters in the Army of the Potomac, 1861–1865*. Reprint, Dayton, Ohio: Press of the Morningside Bookshop, 1972.

Survivors Association. *History of the 118th Pennsylvania Volunteers, Corn Exchange Regiment, From Their First Engagement at Antietam to Appomattox*. Philadelphia: J. L. Smith, map publisher, 1905.

Survivors of the Sixth U. S. Cavalry. Fairfield, Pennsylvania: Proceedings at the Fifth Annual Reunion, 1888.

Tancig, W. J. *Confederate Military Land Units*. Cranbury, New Jersey: Thomas Yoseloff, 1967.

Taylor, John Dykes. "History of the 48th Regiment, Alabama Infantry, C.S.A." Montgomery (Alabama) *Advertiser*, March 9, 1902.

The War of the Rebellion: A Compilation of the Official Records of the Union and Confederate Armies. Washington, D.C.: U.S. Government Printing Office, 1880–1901.

Todd, George T. "Recollections of Gettysburg." *Confederate Veteran*, vol. 8, no. 5 (May 1990).

Tucker, A. W. "Orange Blossoms: Services of the 124th New York at Gettysburg." *National Tribune* (Jan. 1886).

Tyler, Lyon G. *Men of Mark in Virginia*. Vol. 3. Washington, D.C.: Men of Mark Publishing Co., 1907.

Tyler, Ron, editor. *The New Handbook of Texas*. Vols. 5, 6. Austin, Texas: The State Historical Association, 1996.

Vaughan, P. Turner. "Diary of Turner Vaughan, Co. 'C' 4th Alabama Regiment, CSA. Commenced March 4th, 1863, and Ending February 12, 1864." *Alabama Historical Quarterly*, vol. 18 (1956).

Waite, Otis F. R. *Vermont in Great Rebellion—Containing Historical and Biographical Sketches, Etc*. Claremont, New Hampshire: Tracy, Chase and Co., 1869.

Walker, Elijah. "The 4th Maine at Gettysburg." *National Tribune*, April 8, 1886.

Ward, William C. "Incidents and Personal Experiences on The Battle Field at Gettysburg." *Confederate Veteran*, vol. 8, no. 8 (August 1900).

Warner, Ezra J. *Generals in Blue, Lives of the Union Commanders*. Baton Rouge: Louisiana State University Press, 1964.

———. *Generals in Gray, Lives of the Confederate Commanders*. Baton Rouge: Louisiana State University Press, 1959.

West Point Alumni Foundation. *Register of Graduates and Former Cadets of the U.S. Military Academy*. Cullum Memorial Edition, 1970.

Weygant, Charles H. *One Hundred and Twenty-fourth Regiment, N.Y.S.V.* Newburg, New York: Journal Printing House, 1877.

———. "What They Did Here." *New York Monuments Commission for the Battlefields of Gettysburg and Chattanooga, Final Report for the Battlefield of Gettysburg*, Vol. 2. Albany, New York: J. B. Lyon, 1902.

White, W. T. "First Texas at Gettysburg." *Confederate Veteran*, vol. 30, no. 5 (May 1922).

White, Wyman S. *The Civil War Diary of Wyman S. White, First Sergeant of Company F of the 2nd U.S. Sharpshooter Regiment, 1861–1865*. Russell C. White, editor. Baltimore: Butternut and Blue, 1993.

Wittenberg, Eric J. "Merritt's Regulars on South Cavalry Field: Oh What Could Have Been." *Gettysburg Magazine*, no. 16. Dayton, Ohio: Morningside House, Inc., January 1997.

Williams Huntsville Directory, City Guide and Business Mirror, vol. 1, 1859–1860. Huntsville, Alabama: Strowe Publishing Co., 1972.

Wise, George. *History of the Seventeenth Virginia Infantry, CSA*. Baltimore, Maryland: Kelly, Pilt & Co., 1870.

Wise, Jennings C. *The Long Arm of Lee, or the History of the Artillery of the Army of Northern Virginia*. 2 vols. Lincoln, Nebraska: University of Nebraska Press, 1991.

Wright, James R. "Time on Little Round Top." *The Gettysburg Magazine*, no. 2. Dayton, Ohio: Morningside Press, January 1990.

Yearns, W. Buck, and John G. Barrett, editors. *North Carolina Civil War Documentary*. Chapel Hill, North Carolina: University of North Carolina Press, 1980.

Yeary, Mamie, compiler. *Reminiscences of the Boys in Gray, 1861–1865.* 1912. Reprint, with an introduction by Robert Krick. Dayton, Ohio: Morningside House, Inc., 1986.

Youngblood, William. "Unwritten History of the Gettysburg Campaign." *Southern Historical Society Papers*, vol. 38. Millwood, New York: Kraus Reprint Company, 1977.

Manuscript Sources

Alabama Department of Archives and History, Montgomery, Alabama
    Confederate Muster Rolls Collection
        4th Alabama Infantry Regiment, Box 2, Folders 13–23
            Robert T. Coles. "History of the 4th Regiment Alabama Volunteer Infantry, C. S. A., Army of Northern Virginia"
            Field and Staff
            Historical Muster Rolls
            Turner Vaughan Diary
        15th Alabama Infantry Regiment, Box 8, Folders 12–23
            Field and Staff
            Historical Muster Rolls
        44th Alabama Infantry Regiment, Box 36, Folders 1–11
            Field and Staff
            Historical Muster Rolls
            H. H. Sturgis, "War Record of H. H. Sturgis"
        47th Alabama Infantry Regiment, Box 39, Folders 1–11
            Field and Staff
            Historical Muster Rolls
            Henry C. Lindsay, "Sketch of Gettysburg"
            Mrs. James W. Jackson to Thomas Owen, July 16, 1902
            James W. Jackson to his wife, dated July 7, 1863
        48th Alabama Infantry Regiment, Box, Folders 1–11
            Field and Staff
            Historical Muster Rolls
            Alvin O. Dixon Letter
    Surname File
Auburn University, Ralph B. Draughn Library, Auburn, Alabama
    Joseph Q. Burton, "Sketch of the 47th Regiment Alabama Volunteers"
Bowdoin College Library, Brunswick, Maine
    Elisha Coan Papers
        Account of Colonel William C. Oates, 15th Alabama
Brown University, John Hay Library, Providence, Rhode Island
    William H. Brown Papers, 1861–1865
        William Brown to his brother, July 7, 1863
Confederate Research Center, Hill College, Hillsboro, Texas
    "Recollections of Private A. C. Sims"

J. Mark Smither to his mother, July 5, 1863
Phillip Work File
    Phillip A. Work to Tom Langley, May 28, 1908.
Emory University, Robert W. Woodruff Library, Special Collections, Atlanta, Georgia
    "Journal of Private John Malachi Bowden"
Gettysburg National Military Park, Gettysburg, Pennsylvania
    4th Maine Folder
    Berdan's Sharpshooters Folder
        Berdan's Sharpshooters (copy)
    5th Pennsylvania Reserve Folder
    12th Pennsylvania Reserve Folder
        Excerpt of Diary of Private E. D. Benedict (copy)
    83rd Pennsylvania Folder
    John W. C. Neal, M.D., *Record of Confederate Burials*
    William C. Oates Correspondence (copy)
    Participants Accounts, Farnsworth's Folder
        General Farnsworth's Death
    Texas Troops
        1st Texas Infantry Regiment Folder
        4th Texas Infantry Regiment Folder
        5th U.S. Artillery, Battery D Folder
            O. W. Damon, "War Diary" (copy)
        1st U.S. Cavalry Folder
        6th U.S. Cavalry Folder
            Excerpt (transcribed) of Samuel James Crockett Diary, entry for July 3,
            1863
Huntsville-Madison County Public Library, Zeitler Room, Huntsville, Alabama
    Figures Collection, 82–1, Box 1
        File 2, Copy of Henry Figures Letters
        File 11, Biography
Jacksonville State University, Houston Cole Library, Jacksonville, Alabama
    William E. and Nelda Simpson (compilers). "The Correspondence of John M.
    Anderson, Private, CSA"
Library of Congress, Manuscript Division, Washington, D.C.
    Joshua L. Chamberlain Papers
    Benjamin F. Rittenhouse Papers
        "The Battle of Gettysburg, as Seen From Little Round Top"
National Archives, Washington, D.C.
    Record Group 94, The Adjutant General's Office
        Compiled Service Records of Former Confederates Who Served in the 1st
            through 6th U.S. Volunteer Infantry Regiments, 1864–1866, M1017, roll 25
    Record Group 109, War Department Collection of Confederate Records
        Compiled Service Records of Confederate Soldiers Who Served in Organi-
            zations From Alabama, M311

4th Alabama Infantry, rolls 118–132
    Record of Event Cards
    Compiled Service Records
15th Alabama Infantry, rolls 241–250
    Record of Event Cards
    Compiled Service Records
44th Alabama Infantry, rolls 407–415
    Record of Event Cards
    Compiled Service Records
47th Alabama Infantry, rolls 423–431
    Record of Event Cards
    Compiled Service Records
48th Alabama Infantry, rolls 432–437
    Record of Event Cards
    Compiled Service Records
New Hampshire Historical Society, Concord, New Hampshire
    John B. Bachelder Papers
        Also published as *The Bachelder Papers*. Ladd, David L., and Audrey J.,
            editors. 3 vols. Dayton, Ohio: Morningside House, Inc., 1994.
Personal Collections
    Gordon T. Carter, Montgomery, Alabama
        James B. Barrett Daniel Letters
    Gwendolyn Gross Hicks, Athens, Alabama
        John V. McKee Letters
Rutgers University Libraries, Special Collections and University Archives, New
    Brunswick, New Jersey
    Roebling Collection
        Roebling Letters Transcript
            Roebling to Col. Smith, July 5, 1913
Samford University Library, Birmingham, Alabama
    Special Collection
        James B. Barrett Daniel Letters
State Archives of Michigan, Lansing, Michigan
    RG. 59-14, Box 108, folder 7
    Benjamin F. Partridge to John Robertson, August 20, 1868
United States Army Military History Institute, Carlisle Barracks, Pennsylvania
Robert L. Brake Collection
    1st Texas Collection
        "Recollections of A. C. Sims at the Battle of Gettysburg" (copy)
        Unknown Diary
        James H. Hendrick to Mother, July 8, 1863
        Letter of H. W. Berryman, July 9, 1863 (transcribed)
    Michael Winey Collection
        Isaac Dunkelberger, 1st U.S. Cavalry (copy)

University of Michigan, William L. Clements Library, Ann Arbor, Michigan
  Schoff Civil War Collection
       William C. Oates to Joshua L. Chamberlain, March 8, 1897
University of North Carolina, Southern Historical Collection, Chapel Hill, North
  Carolina
  William McKendree Robbins Papers, #4070
  Thomas Lewis Ware Papers, #1796
University of Texas, Center for American History, Austin, Texas
  Thomas L. McCarty Diary
  Thomas L. McCarty, "Battle of Gettysburg, July 1, 2, & 3, 1863"

Newspapers

Huntsville (Alabama) *Daily Confederate*
Montgomery *Daily Advertiser*
Montgomery *Daily Mail*
New York *Times*
Philadelphia *Daily Evening Bulletin*
Philadelphia *Weekly Times*
Selma *Daily Register*

Secondary Sources

Boyd, Charles E. *The Devil's Den: A History of the 44th Alabama Volunteer Infantry Regiment Confederate States Army (1862–1865)*. Privately printed, 1987.

Braun, Robert A. "The Fight for Devil's Den." *Military Images*, vol. 5, no. 1 (July–August 1983).

Breadey, William F. "Recollections and Incidents of Medical Science." MOLLUS, Commandery, of the State of Michigan, Volume 2, February 4, 1897. Reprinted. Wilmington, North Carolina: Broadfoot Publishing Co., 1993.

Brown, Kent Masterson. "Lee at Gettysburg, The Man, The Myth, The Recriminations." *Civil War*, vol. 11, no. 1 (January–February 1993).

Commager, Henry S. *The Blue and the Gray*. New York: The Fairfax Press, 1991.

Dalton, Pete and Cindi. *Into the Valley of Death—The Story of the 4th Maine Volunteer Infantry at the Battle of Gettysburg July 2, 1863*. Union, Maine: Union Publishing Co., 1994.

"Farnsworth's Ill-Advised Charge in Battle of Gettysburg is Reviewed." *The Gettysburg Times* (1934).

Gallagher, Gary W., editor. *The Third Day at Gettysburg and Beyond*. Chapel Hill, North Carolina: The University of North Carolina Press, 1994.

Hamilton, D. H. *History of Company M, First Texas Volunteer Infantry, Hood's Brigade, Longstreet's Corps, Army of the Confederate States of America*. Waco, Texas: W. M. Morrison, 1962.

Krick, Robert K. *Lee's Colonels, A Biographical Register of the Field Officers of the Army of Northern Virginia.* Dayton, Ohio: Press of the Morningside Bookshop, 1979.

Laney, Daniel M. "Wasted Gallantry: Hood's Texas Brigade at Gettysburg." *Gettysburg Magazine*, no. 16. Dayton, Ohio: Morningside House, Inc., January 1997.

Norton, Oliver W. "Strong Vincent and His Brigade at Gettysburg, July 2, 1863." *The Gettysburg Papers*, vol. 2. Compiled by Ken Brady and Florence Freeland. Dayton, Ohio: Press of Morningside Bookshop, 1978.

Oates, William C. "General William F. Perry and Something of his Life in War and Peace." Montgomery *Advertiser*, March 2, 1902.

O'Brien, Kevin E. "Stubborn Bravery: The Forgotten 44th New York at Little Round Top." *Gettysburg Magazine*, vol. 15. Dayton, Ohio: Morningside House, Inc., July 1996.

Pfanz, Harry W. "The Gettysburg Campaign after Pickett's Charge." *The Morningside Notes.* Dayton, Ohio: Morningside Bookshop, 1982.

Robertson, John, compiler. *Michigan in the War.* Lansing, Michigan: W. S. George & Co., State Printers and Binders, 1882.

Ryan, James G. "Say It Ain't So." *Blue & Gray Magazine*, vol. 13, no. 3 (June 1996). Columbus, Ohio.

Simpson, Harold B. *Hood's Texas Brigade: Lee's Grenadier Guard.* Waco, Texas: Texan Press, 1970.

"Sketch of the Late Major Robbins." *The Gettysburg News*, September 12, 1905.

Stackpole, Edward J. "The Battle of Gettysburg." Special Gettysburg Edition. *Civil War Times Illustrated*, n.d.

Tucker, Glenn. *High Tide at Gettysburg.* Dayton, Ohio: The Press of Morningside Bookshop, 1973.

Vincent, Boyd. "The Attack and Defense of Little Round Top, Gettysburg, July 2, 1863." *The Gettysburg Papers*, vol. 2. Compiled by Ken Brady and Florence Freeland. Dayton, Ohio: Press of Morningside Bookshop, 1978.

Welch, Richard F. "Gettysburg Finale," *America's Civil War*, vol. 6, no. 3 (July 1993).

Wert, Jeffry D. "Gettysburg: The Full Story of the Struggle." *Civil War Times Illustrated*, vol. 27, no. 4 (Summer 1988).

West, John C. *A Texan in Search of a Fight.* Waco, Texas: Texan Press, 1969.

Whitman, William E. S. *Maine in the War: A History of the Part Borne by Maine Troops in the Suppression of the American Rebellion.* Lewiston, Maine: Nelson Dingley Jr. and Co., Publishers, 1865.

Winkler, Mrs. A. V. *The Confederate Capital and Hood's Texas Brigade.* Austin, Texas: Eugene Von Boeckmann, 1894.

Index